D0935529

A CRITICAL INTRODUCTION TO ETHICS

A CRITICAL INTRODUCTION
TO
ETHICS

By PHILIP WHEELWRIGHT, Ph.D.

Professor of Philosophy, Dartmouth College

THE ODYSSEY PRESS

NEW YORK

WITHDRAWN

COPYRIGHT, 1935, BY THE ODYSSEY
PRESS, INC.   ALL RIGHTS RESERVED.
PRINTED IN THE UNITED STATES

SEVENTH PRINTING

BJ
1025
.W46

43750

To
my former teacher
Louise E. Pollard

PREFACE

This book is intended to orient students toward the methods and problems of philosophy by way of ethics. Implicit in the choice and arrangement of materials is the assumption that ethics is a philosophical discipline, whose subject-matter, while significant for the practical affairs of daily life on the one hand, is dialectically interconnected with the more abstruse problems of metaphysics and epistemology on the other. The nature of the self, the meaning of objectivity, the possibility of free choice, the cosmic or chaotic character of the natural world, and the relevance of trans-natural principles of explanation are questions that become persistent for anyone who inquires very far and with much circumspection into the moral realm. I have tried to indicate the meaning and importance of such questions wherever they seemed to be especially pertinent to the ethical discussion, and their more prominent aspects are further developed in the last chapter.

Considerable emphasis is given to methodology. One of the great difficulties that a teacher of ethics ordinarily encounters is a failure on the part of students to think logically—or a perhaps even more hazardous failure to adapt the rules of formal validity to the matter in hand. The first two chapters of this book are accordingly devoted to the formulation of a methodology suitable to the problems and aims of ethics; and the subsequent chapters may be regarded, from one point of view, as studies in the theoretical and practical applications of these methodological principles.

Two appendages, somewhat novel for textbooks of ethics, will possibly increase the book's usefulness. There is a glossary of unfamiliar philosophical terms, devised principally for students who have had no past acquaintance with technical philosophy, although it may prove serviceable also to more advanced students who desire to review certain logical and metaphysical conceptions previously encountered. There is, secondly, an appendix which contains, besides bibliographies and questions appropriate to each chapter, a number of quotations from ethical literature and from papers by former students, intended to provide material for analysis and discussion.

In the quoting of foreign sources it has several times been desirable or expedient to furnish translations of my own. Jowett's translations of Plato, in spite of their well-known merits, strike a modern ear as deficient in the force and naturalness that characterize Plato's own earlier style. I would have been glad to use the excellent Loeb Library translations of Plato had there not been copyright difficulties; the same is true of Welldon's translation of the *Nicomachean Ethics* and of more than one recent translation of Epictetus. Wherever it has been necessary to retranslate a passage, I have endeavored to do so with regard not only for the sense and spirit of the original but also, except in one or two cases specifically indicated, for the accepted English rendering of important key-words.

My debt to Professor Warner Fite's *Moral Philosophy*, to G. E. Moore's *Principia Ethica*, to Ramon Fernandez' *De la personnalité*, and to Max Scheler's *Der Formalismus in der Ethik und die materiale Wertethik* will doubtless be evident to all who know those works. From Alf Ross' *Kritik der sogenannten praktischen Erkenntnis* I have borrowed several ideas, notably for my discussions of utilitarianism and naturalism. During the summer of 1934, while I was writing the final chapters, I used Professor Wilbur M. Urban's *Fundamentals of Ethics* as textbook in an ethics course at New York University; how much of it I may unconsciously have absorbed I do not know, although my conclusions differ in many respects very widely from those of Professor Urban, and my somewhat similar chapter arrangement is accidental, having been decided upon before I had seen his book. Acknowledgment is due to Professor Laurence Buermeyer of the Barnes Foundation and to Professor James Burnham of New York University for such ideas as I may have borrowed consciously or unconsciously from their conversations and writings; and to Professor Theodore M. Greene of Princeton University and Mr. Vernon Venable of Vassar College for their more particular service of reading the galley-proofs and offering some valuable criticisms and suggestions. In fairness to Professor Greene, however, it should be said that he has expressed disagreement with my interpretation of Kant in Chapter VI, as well as with my general metaphysical position.

Acknowledgment, finally, is due to the following publishers who have granted permission to quote from copyrighted publications: to the Dial Press for quotations from Warner Fite's *Moral Philosophy;* to Faber & Faber (London) for a quotation from Evelyn Underhill's translation of Baron von Hügel; to *Fortune,* for a quotation from *Arms and the Men;* to Harcourt, Brace & Co. for quotations from Morris R. Cohen's *Reason and Nature* and Graham Wallas' *The Great Society;* to Harper &

Brothers for a quotation from Edwin A. Burtt's *The Principles and Problems of Right Thinking;* to *The Harvard Law Review* for a quotation from an essay by Former Justice Oliver W. Holmes; to René Hilsum et Cie. (Paris) for a quotation from Ramon Fernandez' *De la personnalité;* to Henry Holt & Co. for quotations from William James' *The Principles of Psychology,* Wilbur M. Urban's *Fundamentals of Ethics,* and James Burnham and Philip Wheelwright's *Introduction to Philosophical Analysis;* to the Houghton Mifflin Co. for quotations from Willard E. Atkins and others' *Economic Behavior,* Aurelia Henry's translation of Dante's *De Monarchia,* John Fiske's *Outlines of Cosmic Philosophy,* and Horace G. Wyatt's *The Art of Feeling;* to International Publishers for a quotation from Trotsky's *Literature and Revolution;* to Longmans, Green & Co. for quotations from Warner Fite's *An Introductory Study of Ethics* and William James' *The Will to Believe;* to The Macmillan Co. for quotations from Stuart Chase's *Tragedy of Waste,* W. Y. Elliott's *The Pragmatic Revolt in Politics,* Nicolai Hartmann's *Ethics,* G. E. Moore's *Principia Ethica,* Treitschke's *Politics,* John Watson's *The Philosophy of Kant,* and Alfred North Whitehead's *Adventures of Ideas;* to the Modern Library for quotations from Constance Garnett's translations of Dostoyevsky's *The Brothers Karamazov* and of Tolstoy's *Anna Karenina;* to Moffat, Yard & Co. for a quotation from John Bakeless' *The Economic Causes of Modern War;* to the New York University Press for a quotation from Marie C. Swabey's *Logic and Nature;* to the Max Niemeyer Verlag (Halle, Germany) for a quotation from Max Scheler's *Der Formalismus in der Ethik und die materiale Wertethik;* to W. W. Norton & Co. for a quotation from Bertrand Russell's *Mysticism and Logic;* to the Oxford University Press for quotations from Tolstoy's *Essays and Letters*

and E. J. Trechman's translation of Montaigne's *Essays;*
to *The Philosophical Review* for the quotation from
Antonio Llano's essay, "Morality the Last of the Dogmas"; to G. P. Putnam's Sons and to Professor Edward
Capps, Editor of the Loeb Classical Library, for a quotation from John W. Basore's translation of Seneca's
Moral Essays; to the Robert Schalkenbach Foundation
(11 Park Place, New York) for a quotation from Henry
George's *Social Problems;* to Charles Scribner's Sons for
quotations from Reinhold Niebuhr's *Moral Man and
Immoral Society,* Friedrich Paulsen's *A System of Ethics,*
and Prince Maximilien of Baden's *Memoirs;* to Simon &
Schuster for quotations from Trotsky's *The History of
the Russian Revolution;* and to the Symposium Press for
quotations from George Boas' essay, "The Measure of
Progress" and James Rorty's essay, "The Great Wall
Facing America."

P. W.

CONTENTS

PART I
THE MEANING AND METHOD OF ETHICS

CHAPTER I

THE MORAL SITUATION

"For you see, Callicles, our discussion is concerned with a matter in which even a man of slight intelligence must take the profoundest interest—namely, what course of life is best."

Socrates, in Plato's *Gorgias*

A BRILLIANT young district attorney, Anthony Ames, is engaged on his most important case. A prominent political boss has been murdered. Suspicion points at a shady character known as Jerry the Bruiser. Aided by the newspapers, which have reported the murder in such a way as to persuade the public of the Bruiser's guilt, Ames feels certain that he can secure a conviction on the circumstantial evidence in his possession. If he succeeds in sending the man to the chair he will become a strong candidate for governor at the next election.

During the course of the trial, however, he accidentally stumbles on some fresh evidence, known only to himself and capable of being destroyed if he chooses, that appears to establish the Bruiser's innocence. If this new evidence were to be introduced at the trial an acquittal would be practically certain. What ought the District Attorney to do? Surrender the evidence to the defense, in order that, as a matter of fair play, the accused might be given every legitimate chance of establishing his innocence? But to do that will mean the loss of a case that has received enormous publicity; the District Attorney will lose the backing of the press; he will appear to have failed, and his political career may be blocked. In that event not only will he himself suffer disappointment, but the generous plans for bestowing comforts on his wife and parents and for giving his children the benefits of a superior education will have to be curtailed. On the other hand, ought he to be instrumental in sending a man to the chair for a crime that in all probability he did not commit? And yet, the Bruiser is a bad lot; even if innocent of the present crime there have doubtless been other offenses of equal magnitude in which he has been involved and escaped detection. Is a fellow like that worth the sacrifice of one's career? Still, there is no proof that the Bruiser has ever committed a crime punishable by death. Until a man has been proved guilty he must be regarded, by a sound principle of American legal theory, as innocent. To conceal and destroy the new evidence, then, is not that tantamount to railroading an innocent man to the chair? . . . So District Attorney Ames reasons back and forth. He knows that it is a widespread custom for a district attorney to conceal evidence prejudicial to his side of a case. But is the custom, particularly when a human life is at stake, morally right? A district attorney is an agent of the government, and his chief aim in that capacity should be to present his accusations in such a way as to ensure for the accused not condemnation but justice. The question, then, cannot be answered by appealing simply to law or to legal practice. It is a moral one: *What is Anthony Ames' duty? What ought he to do?*

Benjamin Bates has a friend who lies in a hospital dying slowly of a painful and incurable disease. Although there is no hope of recovery, the disease sometimes permits its victim to linger on for many months, in ever greater torment and with gradual loss of sanity. The dying man, apprised of the outcome and knowing that the hospital expenses are a severe drain on his family's limited financial resources, decides that death had better come at once. His physician, he knows, will not run the risk of providing him with the necessary drug. There is only his friend Bates to appeal to.

How shall Bates decide? Dare he be instrumental in hastening another's death? Has he a moral right deliberately to take a human life? Besides, suspicion would point his way, and his honorable motives would not avert a charge of murder. On the other hand, can he morally refuse to alleviate a friend's suffering and the financial distress of a family when the means of doing so are in his hands? And has he not an obligation to respect a friend's declared will in the matter? To acquiesce and to refuse seem both somehow in different ways wrong, yet one course or the other must be chosen. *What ought Bates to do? On which side does his duty lie?*

In the city occupied by Crambury College a strike is declared by the employees of all the public transit lines. They have been wretchedly underpaid, and their grievance is generally admitted by neutral observers. The strike ties up business and causes much general inconvenience; except for the few who have cars of their own or can afford taxi fare, there is no way of getting from one part of the city to another. Labor being at this period scarce, an appeal is made by the mayor to college students to serve the community by acting in their spare time as motormen and drivers. The appeal is backed by a promise of lucrative wages and by the college administration's agreement to coöperate by permitting necessary absences from classes.

What ought the students of Crambury College to do? If they act as strike-breakers the regular employees will be starved into submission and forced back to work on the corporations' own terms. If they turn down the mayor's request the community will continue to suffer grave inconveniences until the fight is somehow settled. *What is the students' duty in the matter?* *What is the right course for them to follow?*

1. THE NATURE OF MORAL DELIBERATION

Each of the three episodes just described raises a *moral question.* A moral question has to do with human conduct, with the standards of right and wrong by which it may be determined, and with the attainable goods towards which it may be directed.[1] Any general theory about moral conduct, its standards and aims, is called sometimes a moral theory, but more generally an *ethical theory,* and the subject-matter comprising all such theories is called moral philosophy or *ethics.*

The meaning of ethics may be clarified by comparing it with psychology. Both ethics and psychology deal largely with human behavior, but they differ in the kind of question they raise about it, and consequently in method of investigation. Psychology, being a science, deals with the *facts* of psycho-physical behavior, seeking to discover the causal laws by which behavior is governed and its predictable effects. Ethics too considers the psycho-physical behavior of human beings, but always with reference to some standard of what behavior *ought to be.* Behavior considered in terms of a moral situation is called *conduct.*

It is axiomatic that one's method in any field must be determined with reference to one's end. An engraver who employed the tools of a riveter would be no credit

---

[1]The negative of 'moral' used in this sense, as defining a type of problem or realm of inquiry, is *non-moral,* or *amoral.*

to his craft. A psychologist who tried to use the technique of the mathematician or physicist would find that his results bore little relation to the qualitative variety of people's minds. Similarly, the methods appropriate to ethics are not identical with the methods that have given effective results in biology, psychology, economics, or law. Ethics stands in important relations to each of these disciplines; but whatever materials the ethical philosopher may draw from cognate fields he draws simply as *materials* to which his own distinctive method is to be applied.

The soundest approach to ethical method is through a reflection on our experience of moral situations that from time to time we have had occasion to face. No two moral situations are exactly alike, of course, nor do our deliberations exactly repeat themselves. Some moral situations require less attention than others; and often there is no opportunity to deliberate as fully as the situation deserves. The three situations described at the beginning of this chapter, although perhaps unusual in the severity of their demands, offer typical examples of problems distinctively moral. If the act of moral deliberation implicit in each of them is fully carried out, certain characteristic phases can be discerned.

(i) *Examination and clarification of the alternatives.* What are the relevant possibilities of action in the situation confronting me? Am I clear about the nature of each? Have I clearly distinguished them from one another? And are they mutually exhaustive, or would a more attentive search reveal others? In the case of District Attorney Ames, for example, a third alternative might have been to make a private deal with the Bruiser by which, in exchange for his acquittal, the District Attorney would receive the profits of some lucrative racket of which the

Bruiser had control. No doubt to a reputable jurist this line of conduct would be more repugnant than either of its alternatives; it exemplifies, nevertheless, the ever-present logical possibility of going 'between the horns'[1] of the original dilemma.

(ii) *Rational elaboration of consequences.* The next step is to think out the probable consequences of each of the alternatives in question. As this step involves predictions about a hypothetical future, the conclusions can have, at most, a high degree of probability, never certainty. The degree of probability is heightened according as there is found some precedent in past experience for each of the proposed choices. Even if the present situation seems wholly new, analysis will always reveal *some* particulars for which analogies in past experience can be found or to which known laws of causal sequence are applicable. Such particulars will be dealt with partly by analogy (an act similar to the one now being deliberated about had on a previous occasion such and such consequences) and partly by the inductive-deductive method: appealing to general laws (deduction) which in turn have been built up as generalizations from observed particulars (induction). Mr. Ames, we may suppose, found the materials for this step in his professional knowledge of law and legal precedent, as well as in his more general knowledge of the policies of the press, the gullibility of its readers, and the high cost of domestic luxuries.

(iii) *Imaginative projection of the self into the predicted situation.* It is not enough to reason out the probable consequences of a choice. In a moral deliberation the chief interests involved are not scientific but human and practical. The only way to judge the comparative desirability of two possible futures is to live through them both

[1]See Glossary.

in imagination. The third step, then, is to project one-self imaginatively into the future; *i.e.*, establish a dramatic identification of the present self with that future self to which the now merely imagined experiences may become real. Few persons, unfortunately, are capable of an imaginative identification forceful enough to give the claims of the future self an even break. Present goods loom larger than future goods, and goods in the immediate future than goods that are remote. The trained ethical thinker must have a sound *temporal perspective*, the acquisition of which is to be sought by a frequent, orderly, and detailed exercise of the imagination with respect to not yet actual situations.

(iv) *Imaginative identification of the self with the points of view of those persons whom the proposed act will most seriously affect.* Whatever decision I make here and now, if of any importance, is likely to have consequences, in varying degrees, for persons other than myself. An important part of a moral inquiry is to envisage the results of a proposed act as they will appear to those other persons affected by them. I must undertake, then, a dramatic identification of my own self with the selves of other persons. The possibility of doing this is evident from a consideration of how anyone's dramatic imagination works in the reading of a novel or the witnessing of a play. If the persons in the novel or play are dramatically convincing it is not because their characters and actions have been established by logical proof, but because they are presented so as to provoke in the reader an impulse to project himself into the world of the novel or play, to identify himself with this and that character in it, to share their feelings and moods, to get their slant on things.

In most persons, even very benevolent ones, the social consciousness works by fits and starts. To examine fairly the needs and claims of other selves is no less hard and is often harder than to perform a similar task with regard to one's own future self. Accordingly the ethical thinker must develop *social perspective*—that balanced appreciation of others' needs and claims which is the basis of justice.

In this fourth, as in the third step, the imaginative projection is to be carried out for each of the alternatives, according as their consequences shall have been predicted by Step ii.

(v) *Estimation and comparison of the values involved.* Implicit in the third and fourth steps is a recognition that certain values both positive and negative are latent in each of the hypothetical situations to which moral choice may lead. The values must be made explicit in order that they may be justly compared, for it is as a result of their comparison that a choice is to be made. To make values explicit is to give them a relatively abstract formulation; they still, however, derive concrete significance from their imagined exemplifications. District Attorney Ames, for example, might have envisaged his dilemma as a choice between family happiness and worldly success as against professional honor. Each of these is undoubtedly good, that is to say a value, but the values cannot be reduced to a common denominator. Family happiness enters as a factor into Benjamin Bates' dilemma no less than into that of Anthony Ames, but it stands to be affected in a different way and therefore, in spite of the identical words by which our linguistic poverty forces us to describe it, it does not mean the same thing. Family happiness may mean any number of things; so may success, and honor—although these different meanings have, of course, an intelligible bond of unity. Anthony Ames' task is to compare not just any family happiness with any professional honor but the particular exemplifications of

each that enter into his problem. The comparison is
not a simple calculation but an imaginative deliberation,
in which the abstract values that serve as the logical
ground of the comparison are continuous with, and inter-
active with, the concrete particulars that serve as its
starting-point.

(vi) *Decision.* Comparison of the alternative future
situations and the values embodied in each must terminate
in a decision. Which of the possible situations do I deem
it better to bring into existence? There are no rules for
the making of this decision. I must simply decide as
wisely and as fairly and as relevantly to the total comparison as I can. Every moral decision is a risk, for the way
in which a person decides is a factor in determining the
kind of self he is going to become.

(vii) *Action.* The probable means of carrying out the
decision have been established by Step ii. The wished-for
object or situation is an end, certain specific means towards
the fulfillment of which lie here and now within my power.
These conditions supply the premises for an ethical
syllogism. When a certain end, x, is recognized as a good,
and when the achievement of it is seen to be possible
through a set of means a, b, c . . . which lie within
my power, then whichever of the means a, b, c . . . is
an action that can here and now be performed becomes at
just this point my duty. If the deliberative process has
been carried out forcefully and wisely it will have supplied
a categorical answer to the question, What ought I to
do?—even though the answer in some cases may be, Do
nothing.

Naturally, not all experiences of moral deliberation and
choice reveal these seven phases in a distinct, clear-cut
way. Nor is the order here given always the actual order.
Sometimes we may begin by deliberating about the relative

merits of two ends, seeking the means simultaneously with this abstract inquiry, or after its completion. The foregoing analysis does, however, throw some light on the nature of a moral problem, and may be tested by applying it to the three cases described at the beginning of the chapter.

2. Logical Analysis of a Moral Situation

The usual sign of a moral question is the auxiliary verb, *ought*. Not every 'ought,' however, is a moral ought. There must be distinguished: (1) the logical 'ought,' as in "The balance ought to be $34 but I make it $29," "From the appearance of the sky I should say we ought to have snow tonight," "The story ought never to have had a happy ending"; (2) the prudential 'ought,' as in "If you want to avoid colds you ought to try Hydrolux Vapo-lite." These two uses of the word 'ought' express, like the moral ought, propriety with respect to a certain end or standard. But unlike the moral ought, the ought in (1) does not refer directly to human conduct, and while the ought in (2) does have this reference the imperative that it expresses is conditional on a wish. The imperative expressed by the moral ought is, on the contrary, unconditional: You ought to be honorable—not *if* you wish men to respect you; men's respect is a desirable adjunct of being honorable, but you ought to be honorable in any case. The moral ought is what Kant has called a categorical imperative. In being categorical it is distinguished from the prudential ought; in being an imperative, *i. e.*, a call to action, it is distinguished also from the logical ought. It is the moral ought that is the subject-matter of ethics, and it is in this ethical sense, therefore, that the word 'ought' will be used in the present volume. We may now consider the principal factors which the moral ought involves.

Value and possibility

The first factor to be noted in a moral situation is the *presence of value*. Whenever an inclination is felt, that towards which the inclination points is felt to have value. What is felt to have value need not on reflection be *judged* to have value. Judgment can correct our immediate feelings of value, just as in an act of sense-perception judgment corrects and interprets the immediate sense-data. Inclination is thus not identical with value; but it is the psycho-physical basis of its presence.

To say that a value is present in an object is to declare that the object is *in some sense* good. We may therefore restate the first requirement of a moral situation by saying that some things must be recognized as good; or, since good is a relative term, that *some things are recognized as better than others*. But if *a* is better than *b*, *b* is worse than *a*. It follows, then, that some things are *worse* than others, and the first requirement may therefore be restated as an ability to distinguish what is comparatively good from what is comparatively evil. What particular things are good, and what evil, is of course another question. The principle here laid down is simply that to a person who did not set a higher value on some things than on others there could be no moral problem. (Indeed, it is a little hard to see how such a person could have any *problems* at all.) A moral situation presupposes, then, as the first condition of its existence, the recognition of some values or other.

This primary characteristic of a moral situation defines ethics as a *normative* science. Ethics is not a science at all in the same way that the empirical sciences are so designated, and its methods are fundamentally distinct.

It shares, nevertheless, the larger meaning of science, for its subject-matter can be arranged systematically and certain guiding principles be found. But while such sciences as physics, psychology, economics, etc. are primarily concerned with the recording, predicting, and structuralizing of facts, ethics is concerned with facts only secondarily, only so far as they are morally evaluated or judged to be in some way relevant to the application of moral values. That skies are sunny in New Mexico is a fact; that many people are without lucrative employment is also a fact. Both are equally facts, but our valuations of them differ. It is such differences in valuation, such *normative* differences, that establish the basis of a moral situation.

A second element in any moral situation is *the presence of possible alternatives*. To evaluate anything as good is equivalent to declaring that it ought to be, or ought to persist. Ethics does not stop with the good, with what merely ought to *be;* it accepts this as but one element in the question, What ought to *be done?* To say that a person ought to do a thing implies a power on his part *to do or refrain from doing it*. We do not say that the President of the United States ought to put an immediate stop to all human suffering, for the President, however much he might desire such a consummation, has not the power of achieving it; the most we can say is that the President ought to take such steps as may lie within his power to move towards the goal. Nor, on the other hand, do we say, speaking accurately, that a man ought to obey the law of gravitation, for this is something that he must do willy-nilly. Neither 'must' nor 'cannot' is in the strict sense compatible with 'ought.'[1]

---

[1]The metaphysical consequences of this statement are discussed in Chapter XII.

These two elements, the presence of value and the presence of possible alternatives in a moral situation, are intimately related, for in order that the alternatives may have moral significance some kind of value must be attached to each of them.   In some cases the value of each alternative is assigned rationally.   In other cases, the most familiar of which are those described as 'battling with temptation,' our rational judgment assigns value to only one of the alternatives; the other is merely *felt* to have value, as a result of our experiencing a strong inclination towards it.   But in either type of situation there must be some value, whether deliberately judged or spontaneously felt, attached to both alternatives, in order that there may be a moral problem.

For example, there exist for me the possible alternatives of plucking a blade of grass or of not doing so, but the situation is not a moral one, for neither alternative has (on any likely occasion) any value.   Or again, it lies in my power to go without my dinner.   In this instance one of the alternatives (eating dinner) has value, the other (going without it) has probably none, so that again there is no moral problem.   If, however, I judged that abstention from dinner would be a stoic discipline good for my character, or if by abstaining I could afford to attend a play that I wanted to see, or could devote the dinner hour to some work that needed to be done, the situation would be to this extent a moral one, for a value would be set on each of the alternatives.   Indeed, the great difficulty of moral problems and the indecisiveness of much moral deliberation are due principally to this fact, that both of the alternatives with which our deliberation is concerned are in some manner valued and their values are often incommensurate.

Moral insight

There is still a third prerequisite of the moral situation, as may be gathered from the following illustration. Suppose I am in a restaurant ordering a dinner, and the menu card gives a choice between carrots and broccoli. If I happen to like both of these vegetables the requirements so far stated of a moral situation are met: there are alternative possibilities and there is a value attached to each. Nevertheless the situation is not a moral one. The alternatives presented are simple ends in themselves, the values involved in my choice terminate in the direct enjoyment of what is chosen, and my choice, therefore, has little or no significance beyond the present enjoyment. The situation is pretty much isolated from the rest of my experience. But suppose I am also faced with a choice between lobster and halibut. The lobster is more pleasing to my palate but is sure to cause indigestion. Here we have an elementary moral situation. The alternatives are not merely lobster vs. halibut, nor the enjoyment of the one vs. the enjoyment of the other. The choice is: present enjoyment of lobster *and* subsequent feelings of dyspeptic languor on the one hand vs. present acceptance of halibut *and* a more comfortable aftermath on the other. The values between which I must choose are here *organic*. Each of them is composed of interrelated factors to which, taken singly, I can ascribe a value of some kind, positive or negative; but it is just because the factors are *not* presented to my consciousness singly that the situation is a moral one. Something more than a direct acquaintance with immediately presented goods is required. There is required also an *insight* into the remoter values involved. The third requirement of a moral situation, then, has a double aspect. The choice must be *consequential*. The alternatives are not mere ends-in-themselves terminating here and now; they involve values over and beyond the values of immediate enjoyment. And the agent by whom the choice is to be made must therefore have an imaginative grasp of the consequences, an imaginative insight into the nature of the values that are only hinted at in the present situation.

What is the character of moral insight, of this insight into the values implicit in a moral situation? Ethical philosophers are sometimes misled by the word 'value' into supposing that the values in a moral situation can be calculated, in much the same way that the money-values of goods for sale can be added up and a total value arrived at by arithmetical computation. But economic values are technical and abstract, moral values personal and concrete. A merchant who sells two articles for the same price considers their 'value' (*i.e.*, their exchange value) to be identical. To their respective purchasers, however, their values will not be merely exchange values but use values and therefore different in kind, for the whole value of each will be determined by a variety of sentiments, interests, and purposes which the purchaser entertains towards the purchased object. Furthermore, in a moral situation there is often no sharp distinction between present and future by which the two can be set side by side in the mind and compared. "The present," as Warner Fite has written, "is a question of the present scope of imagination."[1] We say of some men that they 'live' in the future, and the metaphor has a degree of literal truth. (It is in things of the imagination that metaphors do have literal truth.) The essential question is where one's interests lie (*i.e.*, what they refer *to*, what they aim *at*), and human interests are so manifold that the question

[1] *Moral Philosophy*, Chap. XIII. (Dial Press.)

cannot be answered identically for any two persons, nor
for the same person at different times.

3. THE GOOD AND THE RIGHT

What I want to do is frequently opposed to what I know
I ought to do; *i.e.*, the present good is often incompatible
with what seems to be right.   As previously stated, there
must be some inclination towards both of the alternatives
with which any moral deliberation is concerned.   This is
the same thing as to say that both alternatives are felt
or thought in some way to be good.   But the qualities
of the two goods may be altogether different.   Say that
I am tempted to enter a pastry-shop in order to provide
a pleasant sensation for my palate but that I know I ought
to save my money and keep my digestion good and my
brain clear for this evening's studies.   There is an inclination to enter the shop; there is also an inclination, of
another kind, to pass by without entering.   The inclination to enter is strong, impulsive, irrational; whereas—

Quite other is the prompting of the 'ought.'   It is not so
much a drive as an inner exhortation.   It is not impulsive, but
imperative.   And what we experience is not ourselves impelled,
but ourselves impelling, ourselves impelling ourselves, indeed
ourselves impelling ourselves against impulse.[1]

The situation is a sufficiently familiar one.   The strongest
actual propensity at a given moment is towards a course
of action contrary to the one towards which duty beckons.
An effort is required to break away from the fascination
of the immediate.   The sense that such an effort is required, that it *can* be made, and that it would be better to
make it because the result would be an eventually greater
good, are conditions of a feeling of 'ought.'

The good and the right, though often specifically op-

---

[1] Horace G. Wyatt, *The Art of Feeling*, pp. 169–170.   (Houghton Mifflin.)

posed, are related at bottom. Their actual conflicts are explained by a distinction within the meaning of 'good'—between intrinsic and extrinsic goods. A good is called *intrinsic* when it is judged worthy of being sought for its own sake, *i.e.*, when it is an end in itself; *extrinsic* when it is sought as a means to some other good. The relation is a shifting one, for it is not always possible to distinguish sharply between the end and the means: what is an end from one point of view may be regarded as a means from another. Nevertheless we can say in general that the good of a surgical operation is extrinsic: it must be referred to the greater health that is to come. The enjoyment of a glass of wine is an intrinsic good, a 'good in itself': the wine is not enjoyed for the sake of anything distinct from the enjoyment. Still other goods are at once intrinsic and extrinsic: an enjoyable *and* nourishing dinner, a refreshing *and* cleansing bath, and the like. Often the right course of action will consist in choosing some extrinsic good (say, diligent study) which is the only available means to the attainment of some important intrinsic good (say, a professional career). On such occasions the rightness of the action is founded on the good to which it leads, but to the agent it may not appear to partake of any of the character of that remote good. Thus it happens that if the agent is tempted by some more immediate good (such as the pleasures of a lazy life) the conflict, which would be more rationally conceived as a conflict between two goods (present leisure vs. future career) acquires the appearance of a conflict between the present good (leisure) and the present right course of action (diligent study).

The paradox of volition

Situations in which there is a genuine moral struggle, in which a temptation must be conquered by a putting forth

of moral effort, are crucial for morality. The ultimate
justification of a moral principle (and, indirectly, for any
ethical theory) is the possibility that it can be made an
effective force in moral struggles. William James describes the moral struggle as a situation in which "a rarer
and more ideal impulse is called upon to neutralize others
of a more instinctive and habitual kind"; in which
"strongly explosive tendencies are checked, or strongly
obstructive conditions overcome." He continues:

We *feel*, in all hard cases of volition, as if the line taken, when
the rarer and more ideal motives prevail, were the line of greater
resistance, as if the line of coarser motivation were the more
pervious and easy one, even at the very moment when we refuse
to follow it. He who under the surgeon's knife represses cries
of pain, or he who exposes himself to social obloquy for duty's
sake, feels as if he were following the line of greatest temporary
resistance. . . .
The ideal impulse appears . . . a still small voice which
must be artificially reinforced to prevail. Effort is what rein-
forces it, making things seem as if, while the force of propensity
were essentially a fixed quantity, the ideal force might be of
various amount. But what determines the amount of the effort
when, by its aid, an ideal motive becomes victorious over a
great sensual resistance? The very greatness of the resistance
itself. If the sensual propensity is small, the effort is small.
The latter is *made great* by the presence of a great antagonist
to overcome. And if a brief definition of ideal or moral action
were required, none could be given which would better fit the
appearances than this: *It is action in the line of greatest resistance.*[1]

In order to understand James' profoundly valid paradox
we must avoid the popular tendency to explain a moral
situation wholly by analogies drawn from the physical
world. In those aspects of nature studied by physics and
chemistry it is always the line of least, never of greatest

[1] *The Principles of Psychology*, Vol. II, pp. 548–549. (Holt.)

resistance that is followed. The universality of the physical law of least physical resistance, however, is due to the fact that it is not directly applicable to concrete experience, for in *concrete* experience no laws are applicable with unremitting exactitude.[1] Physicists may be allowed to formulate their own laws by the methodology which their technical interests require. But scientific laws tell us nothing directly about moral experience. In this province everyone must be, to a large extent, his own observer. And what is a more assured fact of introspective observation than that in cases of moral struggle *we often can and sometimes do follow the path of greatest resistance?*

What we ought to do, however unappealing originally, can be made, by a concentration of purpose, what we want to do. Intelligence (or, as it has previously been called, insight) is the mediator. The reason why it may be *right for my present self* to forego the pleasures of the pastry-shop is that the sacrifice promotes *a good for my future self:* namely, bodily health and additional money to spend. What I choose is distinct from the greatest immediate satisfaction but not separate from all satisfaction whatever. I have put myself imaginatively in the place of my future self and am thus able to consider the good or the pleasure or the emotional satisfaction apart from, *abstracted* from (*i.e.*, separated by the imagination from) the present experience. This abstractive ability of man is what marks him as rational, and, so far as it becomes effective in directing his conduct, as moral.

There is another way too in which man's abstractive ability shows itself: in the altruistic 'ought.' A person

---

[1] A brilliant demonstration of this statement may be found in the writings of one who is both a philosopher and a research chemist: Emile Meyerson, *Identity and Reality.*

can recognize duties not only towards his own future self but towards other persons also.

Here again intelligence is the mediator. Man is able to consider the good or the pleasure or the emotional satisfaction apart from the individual to be satisfied, apart not only from [the particular experience] but from the experiencer. If emotional satisfaction is the thing desired, it is so for B, C, D and others as well as for A. The happiness of others is just as much an end as my happiness and just as much to be sought after. The 'ought' is the peculiar emotion which now enters to convert this intellectual achievement into conduct.[1]

By this abstractive process the Golden Rule of Jesus, "Do unto others as you would have them do unto you," and the less positive form of the same command, given half a millennium earlier by Confucius, "Refrain from doing to others what you would not have them do to yourself," can be realized as expressions of a binding obligation.

Right and wrong, then, are not hollow sounds nor is discussion about them an idle game. If we mean what we say in designating an action right or wrong, if we are doing more than mouthing a conventional formula, our judgment will in some manner affect our subsequent conduct. Ethics is not a pastime for the understanding alone. Ethical theory calls for moral practice, and the full meaning of ethics becomes intelligible only as we translate theories into moral principles that can be made effective forces in the struggle towards ideal ends.

4. THE SEARCH FOR A STANDARD

But how, it will be asked, is the particular character of right and wrong on any given occasion to be determined? How can one be sure that the development of moral insight (even if such an accomplishment were not in any case

---

[1]Wyatt, op. cit., p. 168.

formidably difficult) will necessarily lead a man to 'right' courses of action and restrain him from 'wrong'? Are there not intelligent villains? May not a man be capable of the most penetrating insights and still choose a career of evil? Superior intelligence seems often to be used merely to invent or discover new types of wrong-doing. Satan, surely, whatever his delinquencies, was no fool. What clear test, then (so the popular quandary runs), can be applied to human conduct so as to determine on each occasion whether it is right or wrong; or (from a somewhat more mature point of view) so as to distinguish the higher of two contending values from the lower? Various such tests are proposed, the most prominent of which follow.

(i) *Inclinations.* "Follow your impulses; do whatever gives you the most enjoyment": people sometimes talk as if in these trite maxims they had discovered a new moral truth. Actually they have done the contrary: they have denied that moral truth exists. If inclinations are the only standard of conduct, then there is no standard by which to choose between one inclination and another. Whatever inclination is strongest at any moment becomes for that reason right. Temptation becomes honorable by the sheer fact of being tempting. Evidently there is no moral standard offered here; there is merely a negation of moral standard.

(ii) *Religious authority.* Acceptance of religious authority as a standard presupposes (1) a belief in God and (2) a belief that God communicates His will, either directly or indirectly, to men. Even when both of these beliefs are held a question of interpretation frequently arises. How is the divine command to be particularized? The Ten Commandments, for example, order us not to steal. Does this apply to short-selling on the stock-market—a practice by which a few individuals are unfairly enriched

at the expense of many? Does it apply to the practice
of ruining your business competitor by price-cutting?
Does it apply to the practice of oil and mining corporations
in wasting the country's natural resources for private gain?
No clear definition of stealing has ever received general
consent, and the divine command is subject to countless
ambiguities.

(iii) *Statute law.* The law of the land is a standard of
right and wrong from which no individual is wholly
exempt. At the same time it is safe to say that no one
obeys all the laws. In the first place, there are numerous
laws on the statute books that have long ago become
obsolete without ever having been annulled. To obey
all the laws an individual would have to employ legal aid
to find out what laws there are and exactly what they
require in terms of conduct. Secondly, even among the
laws that are known, some are held in higher respect than
others. During the period when the eighteenth amend-
ment to the Constitution was in force there were many
so-called 'law-abiding citizens' who had no scruples about
taking a drink. Besides, it is a recognized right of an
American citizen (by voting and in related ways) to seek
to change the existing laws. There must, therefore, be
some standard by which the goodness or badness of actual
laws, as well as of proposed laws, can be judged.

(iv) *Public opinion* is in the long run more authoritative
than statute law, for a law that lacks public support will
not be obeyed and in the end will either be repealed or, as
in the case of many 'blue laws,' ignored by common consent. Nevertheless, public opinion is often wrong. Its
fallibility in particular cases is recognized even by those
who accept it as a generally reliable guide. The vast
majority of men think emotionally and gregariously.
One of the chief tasks of education is admittedly to raise

the standard of public opinion. There must be some higher standard, then, by which we can judge the state of public opinion at any time to be bad or good.

(v) *Conscience* is a part of everyone's standard. Regardless of how we may explain it the existence of a 'still, small voice' that sometimes on crucial occasions says "Do!" or "Refrain!" is a familiar phenomenon. The voice of conscience often prompts us to overcome our inclinations of the moment, and, more rarely, to defy public opinion or the laws. Still, conscience is far from infallible. It can and ought to be educated, and when a man relies on it uncritically it threatens to become but a veil for his impulses.

(vi) *Reason.* Conscience, then, must be controlled by reason, it is often declared. Very true. But that is not to say that reason is *the* standard. Immanuel Kant is the outstanding example of a philosopher who tried to make it so, and as might have been expected, his *applications* of his rationally established principles are every bit as debatable as those of any other moralist.[1] If generosity is better than selfishness that is not because it is more rational: many philosophers, in fact, have held it to be less so. Rationality is a necessary aspect of ethics but not its sufficient criterion. Ethics, in short, must be logical, but ethics is not logic.

(vii) *Nature.* Appeals to 'nature' are burdened chiefly by the ambiguity of the word. The physicist, the biologist, the anthropologist, the psychologist, and the theologian each give the word a different meaning drawn from the subject-matter of his own science. The objections to the naturalistic criterion will be discussed further in Chapter IV.

Evidently no isolated standard of right and wrong is

[1]See Chapter VI, Section 2.

proof against attack.   The function of ethics is not to provide a simple and sure rule by which moral problems can be 'solved.'   An active intelligence revolts against whatever doctrine claims to utter the last word on any matter. Especially is this true in ethics, where the conclusions sought are of such intimate importance to each serious inquirer.   Immediate decisions will often have to be reached by appealing to some convenient rule of thumb or to some already developed habit or preference.   But it is an advantage of theories that they can be inquired into at leisure.   The task of theoretical ethics is not to lay down static norms by which each new moral problem that arises can be decisively answered.   Its task is rather to develop a method suitable for the evaluation and criticism of existing norms and for the exploration of new value possibilities, in order that when moral decisions have henceforth to be made their grounds may be more adequate and more worthy.

CHAPTER II

THE DEVELOPMENT OF CRITICAL METHOD

"O, then we bring forth weeds
When our quick minds lie still . . ."
Shakespeare, *Antony and Cleopatra*

THE FIRST CHAPTER has defined the nature of a moral situation. The next step is to determine valid methods of reasoning about the values that a moral situation involves. By way of introduction to the problem of validity we may first consider some typical examples of invalid ethical reasoning.

1. POPULAR FALLACIES IN ETHICS

A fallacy is an error in reasoning. Fallacies are given various classifications in textbooks on logic, but these are not essential to the present discussion. Instead, we may examine certain specific fallacies that are widely current in moral deliberation and in popular ethical theorizing: specific ways in which thinking about these matters goes wrong.

(i) Platitudes

A platitude is defined by Webster as "a thought or remark which is flat, dull, trite, or weak; a dull, stale, or insipid truism; a commonplace." In ethics a truism is always partially false. This paradox is inevitable, for a truism is an assertion that has become dead through over-repetition, while the subject-matter with which ethics deals is enormously alive. Ordinary conversation teems with platitudes: "Honesty is the best policy," "A penny saved is a penny earned," "My country right or wrong," "Blood will tell," etc., etc. Each of these trite observations has a certain amount of truth, none is wholly true. Honesty in Nazi Germany (1934) is very bad policy, a penny saved during a period of inflation is half a penny lost, the super-patriots who preach militant Americanism are often the readiest to attack governmental procedures contrary to the interests of their own group, and so on. Of particular interest for ethics are the many current platitudes in denunciation of lying, theft, and murder, or in praise of veracity, honest dealing, and respect for human life. We give such judgments lip-service, but in practice hardly anyone is unwilling to admit exceptions. The inconsistency is explained by the ambiguity of the words 'lying,' 'theft,' and 'murder'—an ambiguity that commonly goes undetected by those who employ the platitudes.

Consider the much platitudinized maxim, "Never tell a lie." Lying, people declare glibly, is wrong. Yet everyone makes exceptions. What of the physician who lies encouragingly to a patient about his chances of recovery? Does he do right or wrong? Before replying we should probably want to know something of the patient's character and of the degree of doubt in the physician's mind. If death is almost a certainty, has not the patient a right to know? There may be affairs that he wishes to put in order; he may wish also to prepare his mind to meet the coming ordeal. Suppose, on the other hand, that death is only moderately probable and that the patient is in such a nervous funk that a threat of death might succeed in producing it. Would the physician in such a case do wrong in expressing more optimism than the facts warranted?

In Elizabeth Gaskell's *North and South*, Margaret Hale tells a lie to save her brother Frederick's life. Frederick is an ex-naval officer, sought by the British government on an old and seemingly unjust charge of mutiny, the penalty for which is death. In spite of the danger he makes a secret trip to England to visit his mother in her last illness. Recognized by an ancient enemy who attempts to seize him and win the advertised reward, he gives the man a push, which accidentally proves fatal. Margaret, identified by a doubtful witness, is visited and questioned by a police officer. Having reason to fear that Frederick is not yet safely out of England she denies that she was present at the altercation. Later she repents of her falsehood, accusing herself bitterly of moral wrongdoing. The reader, however, is more likely to agree with her original judgment, and to feel some irritation at a repentance which, had it been timelier, might have resulted in her brother's being swung from the yard-arm.

Most people would agree that situations like these contain mitigating circumstances, which make lying, if not right, at least excusable on a particular occasion. There are even a few rare cases in which a refusal to lie might properly be considered criminally wrong: the case of a theatre manager, for instance, who, when the theatre caught fire, was called upon to avert a panic by announcing that there was no danger. But if such exceptions are admitted veracity can no longer be taken as a strict moral law. In just what circumstances is it permissible to lie? Not on all occasions, surely, may the physician encourage his patients with a false account of their health. Nor would any and all circumstances justify a falsehood for the saving of a brother's life—not, for instance, if his escape would result in an innocent man's condemnation. On the other hand, there are numerous matters of a more trifling sort in which we scarcely ever bother our heads about the propriety of falsehoods: few persons would hesitate to stretch the truth if asked by a gracious hostess whether they had enjoyed her indifferent dinner.   Are the polite untruths demanded by etiquette to be considered lying or not?   If so, then veracity and mendacity are not in themselves right and wrong.   If, on the other hand, untruths told in extenuating circumstances are to be given some milder designation—'white lies,' 'stretching a point,' 'exaggerations,' etc.—then veracity and lying, though the one is now right and the other wrong without qualification, have no determinable relation to specific acts.   A 'lie' no longer means a misstatement of the truth; it means a *morally unjustifiable* misstatement of the truth.   The statement, "Lying is wrong," makes, on this interpretation, no genuine assertion of anything.   It is a *tautology*, the predicate merely repeating a meaning already contained in the subject.   'Lying,' in this tautologous proposition, is a *question-begging* word: the question of whether the proposition, "Lying is wrong," is true is given an affirmative answer not by an appeal to evidence nor as an affirmation of some specific value, but simply because of the meaning of the word 'lying.'

What of the maxim, "Thou shalt not steal"?   Popular opinion is lenient towards stealing when practised on a grand scale and when its methods are sufficiently indirect to avert a too drastic collision with the law.   Conservative citizens who approve of sending pickpockets to jail are often among the first to denounce senatorial investigations into dubious banking and stock-marketing practices. Such citizens give an artificially narrow interpretation to theft.   Socialists, on the other hand, give the word a broader than usual meaning by declaring any exploitation of the country's natural resources for private gain to be a form of theft.   Theft, it seems, is a word no less ambiguous than 'lying,' and the statement, "Theft is wrong," is (by the argument of the preceding paragraph) either tautologous or acknowledged to have exceptions.

What of the maxim, "Thou shalt not kill"?   Does it apply to the conduct of soldiers in war-time?   Does it require that everyone should be a conscientious objector?   Again, does it apply to judicial killings?   Is a judge immoral for condemning a culprit to death, or an executioner for pulling the switch that electrocutes him?   Or, as a third instance, is it unjustifiable to shoot in self-defence or to save the life of another?   Finally, we may ask with Professor Cohen:

> Furthermore, does the absoluteness of the rule, *Thou shalt not kill*, apply only to direct or short-range killing?   We know perfectly well that unless more safety appliances are introduced into mines, railroads, and factories, tens of thousands of workers will surely be killed.   Are those who have the power to make the changes and do not do so guilty of murder?   If in economic competition I take away somebody's bread (to increase my own comfort or power), and he dies of undernourishment or of a disease to which undernourishment makes him liable, am I not killing him?   If by monopolizing our fertile lands we confine the Chinese to a territory insufficient to keep them above the starvation line, are we or are we not guilty of killing them?[1]

Platitudes expressing disapproval of lying, theft, and murder all give rise to the same dilemma: either they are not universally true and require therefore some qualifying word or phrase such as 'usually' or 'in most cases,' or else their truth has an empty, tautologous, purely formal character, affirming nothing save a logical relation between the two terms of which the proposition is composed.   In the one way or the other, by requiring qualifications or by

---

[1] Morris R. Cohen, *Reason and Nature:* Book III, Chap. V, "The Possibility of Ethical Science," p. 431.   (Harcourt, Brace.)

an emptiness of specific meaning, platitudes are but half-truths. "Yet it's true enough *in theory* that lying and murder are wrong," the platitudinarian retorts; "in practice, however, there are bound to be exceptions." The popular dualism between theory and practice is itself a platitude of the most stupid kind. Ethical theory, to the extent that it does not find expression in moral practice, is false. To be sure, we can never achieve a final union between ethical theory and moral practice, for language cannot be given the same *type of specificity* as actual conduct. But Professor Burtt's distinction and warning should be heeded:

None the less, there is a vast difference, and one of fundamental logical bearing, between the thinker who has made a serious effort to criticize his ethical assumptions and one who has only admitted exceptions to them here and there as forced by concrete situations, without attempting to straighten out intellectually the inconsistency involved. With reference to problems of the determination of ends, the latter is in the position that the scientist would occupy if he noticed exceptions to his accepted laws but made no effort to correct the laws in the light of the new facts and had no clear consciousness of the standards of truth and reality that he was really using. Now is it not clear that any man who supposes himself to believe that "Thou shalt not lie" is an absolute prohibition, while accepting the infractions of it which we daily commit as matters of polite courtesy or to avoid some terrible calamity (for example, the deception by which a crowded theatre which has caught fire is quietly emptied), is in exactly this inconsistent and thoroughly illogical state?[1]

(*ii*) *Ambiguous middle term*

The fallacy of the 'ambiguous middle' is potentially present wherever any deductions are made from a plati-

---

[1]Edwin Arthur Burtt, *Principles and Problems of Right Thinking*, pp. 455–456. (Harper.)

tude.   A deduction from a platitude is made by finding a case to fit it.   (1) "A stitch in time saves nine; to have my teeth examined now will be a stitch in time, and may therefore save me the annoyance of cavities and fillings later on."   (2) "A stitch in time saves nine; to build battleships and military aircraft now, while we are still at peace, will be a stitch in time, and may be recommended, therefore, as a precaution against future wars." Are both of these applications equally valid?   Anyone with an ounce of sanity knows that they are not: the principle is valid in the first case, highly dubious in the second.   But is there anything in the statement of the principle itself to show this?   Instead of being stated as a vague platitude the principle would gain in value if the meaning and potential reference of 'a stitch in time' were made more exact.   There are stitches which tear bigger holes than they mend.   Such stitches do not spare the need of later stitches: quite the reverse.   If we believe that military preparations are stitches of this latter variety, we shall consider the second of the two syllogisms invalidated by the ambiguity of the phrase 'a stitch in time.'   This phrase, which is the connecting link by which the two premises of the argument are joined, is called the *middle term* of the syllogism, and Syllogism 2 is therefore said to contain the 'fallacy of the ambiguous middle.'

Sometimes the ambiguity of a middle term is concealed because the argument in which the ambiguity occurs is stated as an *enthymeme: i.e.*, an argument with one premise missing.   "All's fair in love and war, therefore I may repeat gossip that will tarnish my rival's character."   No, it might be replied; you are not justified in stooping to acts of meanness and treachery.   But why not, if *all* is fair?   Does not 'all' embrace everything, meanness and treachery included?   As a matter of fact, it need not.

"Sell all that you have and give it to the poor" was not intended as a command to strip the body literally naked. Nor in love (however it may be with war) is the fairness of everything true without qualification. 'All,' in this argument, is the ambiguous middle term, as becomes evident when the argument is expanded into full syllogistic form: "All's fair in love and war; treachery and meanness are parts of 'all'; they are therefore justified."

Because ambiguities are unavoidable in ethics it does not follow that ethical discussion cannot and should not be clarified. In every ambiguity there is an element of identity, and it is precisely this identity that a developed moral insight seeks to discover. A banker, an athlete, and a gangster all agree that loyalty is an important moral duty, but each interprets loyalty in a different way: to the bank's officers and stockholders as against depositors, or to one's own team as against rival teams, or to fellow-gangsters as against the police. The banker whose mind is wrapped up in conventions will see no resemblance between the gangster and himself: the one stands outside the law, the other keeps within it. But a banker whose social sympathies are combined with a more developed imagination may see resemblances between the gangster's practices and his own that go deeper than any distinction established by statute law. Such a realization is sometimes a first step towards reform. That we are all sinners is not, for the man with moral imagination, an empty platitude. It expresses his recognition of how distant all of us are from any worthy moral goal.

(iii) Rationalization

'Rationalization' is reasoning that is employed not to analyze a moral situation and redirect the reasoner's impulses according to the results of the analysis, but simply to justify a group of impulses or desires already existing. This type of falsification is common and familiar; we all fall, at times, into the snare. "I'm telling you this for your own good," "I never give money to beggars, it only encourages them to beg," "By cheering at football games I am supporting my Alma Mater," "You ought (said by a parent, usually a mother) to be grateful to me for having brought you into the world"—who can say with certainty how much self-deception lies beneath the moral rectitude of such remarks? One of the first steps towards a healthy moral attitude, and hence towards a sound theory of ethics, is to get rid of all such flattering interpretations of our own motives. Only after recognizing what our motives truly are can we be in a position, should it seem desirable, to change them.

(iv) False analogy

All reasoning makes use of analogy. By perceiving likenesses between one thing, event, or situation and others we are enabled to classify it and thereby to apply to it predictions or evaluations that we have found reason to attach to the whole class of similars. Analogical reasoning goes wrong not because we declare a likeness to exist where there is none—between *any* two things there is a likeness of *some* kind: the moon is like a layer-cake in being round, like love in being a traditional theme for poets, and like a quadratic equation in being of interest to astronomers—but because the likeness that is stressed happens to be irrelevant to the matter in hand.

In moral deliberation it is a not uncommon failing to rationalize an inclination by pleading (perhaps only to ourselves) that similar conduct has been right on many occasions. But there are differences as well as similarities: have they, in this comparison, been given due weight?

And the similarities themselves: are they essential, far-reaching, and fairly exact, or are they accidental, trifling, and loose? The unorthodox conduct that is sometimes excusable in a genius may have hardly the same justification in ordinary men. Most people would accept a dishonest gambling tip or an undeserved promotion if it were offered to them: is it right then for *me* to do it? Are my moral sensibilities the same as theirs? I am like them in being human, I am different in being myself. Which consideration is to me on this occasion the more relevant? Conversely, I would not be justified in setting up my own standards of moral action as standards for others to follow. They too must be, in essential matters, guided by their own lights. Some minimum of agreement on moral values is, to be sure, a necessary condition of social life, but we must learn not to expect a too complete unanimity.

In comparisons also between individual and social ethics there is danger of faulty analogical reasoning. The amoralism that is practised almost universally in the world of business enterprise becomes *im*moral when transferred to intimate personal relations. Conversely, the moral praise or blame that we assign to the conduct of individuals has considerably less relevance to our criticism of the policies of nations, for an individual's behavior is or can be ruled by a personal will, whereas a nation's, for the most part, even under a dictatorship, cannot.

(v) *Special pleading*

The 'special pleader' gives convincing support to one side or one solution of a moral question, but does no justice to the other side or to alternative solutions. A capitalist will often give persuasive arguments for capitalism and a communist for communism, but it is the rare, not the usual, capitalist or communist who can examine his enemy's arguments in a fair and objective spirit. 'Rationalization,' in the sense already explained, is one form of special pleading, but not the only form. More deliberate and open is the one-sided argument of an attorney presenting a case to a jury, or of an advertiser demonstrating the excellence of his product. Moral deliberation, however, is something different from legal debates and advertisers' clap-trap. It is characterized by a balanced examination of whatever alternatives are offered.

(vi) Moral indifferentism

One of the most dangerous half-truths that bob up in ethical discussions is embodied in the remark, "It's all a matter of one's point of view." No one could very well deny that moral judgments and ethical theories arise as expressions of some one's point of view: they would be worthless if they did not. But the slogan, "It all depends on your point of view," obviously connotes more than it says, because as it stands it is a truism not worth uttering. For one thing (and this is its most valid meaning) it issues a reminder that there are points of view other than our own, that our own point of view is but one among many; and this reminder is a useful safeguard against dogmatism and intolerance. It is a mark of an educated man to recognize that the actions of other people, though not congenial to himself, may have a legitimate value and justification in terms of a point of view different from his own.

But those who are fond of declaring that morality is all a matter of one's point of view generally mean more than this. They mean that there is no essential difference in moral worth between one point of view and another because there is no way in which the points of view can be objectively compared. Probably they mean, too, that a

point of view is a determinate thing, which can be characterized and classified in the same way that dead objects
and abstract entities can be.   Both of these assumptions
contradict conclusions reached in the first chapter—conclusions which, according to the thesis of this book, are
essential for any clear-sighted moral deliberation and for
any self-consistent ethical theory whatever.   Some points
of view are better than others, and one condition of a point
of view's superiority is the greater degree to which it depends on a developed moral insight: these are necessary
starting-points of ethical inquiry.

Tolerance, it must not be forgotten, is of two kinds.
Some are called tolerant who are indifferent to values,
and who would as lief see one set of values triumph as
another.   Others are called tolerant who, though cherish-
ing certain values, are prevented by wise modesty from
using belligerent means for their propagation.   Tolerance
of the first sort puts a damper on moral choice, for it may
be applied quite as readily to one's own conduct as to
the conduct of others; and tolerance towards oneself is
the handiest ally of moral evil.   But a tolerance based on
wisdom and humility is a recognition that while we are
not primarily responsible for others' morality we are for
our own.   Be lenient and tolerant towards others, severe
towards yourself: such a maxim, though it could not stand
without qualifications, is helpful in reminding us where our
primary responsibility lies.

(vii) *Argument ad hominem*

Similar to the preceding fallacy in its logic but contrary
in its application is the argument *ad hominem:* attacking
not the logical coherence nor practical value of a theory
but the character and motives of the person who upholds
it.   There are cases, of course, in which the motives of

the theorist are decidedly relevant to the argument. If
the owner of a factory or a mine were to attack the workers' right to organize into labor unions on the ground
that it is un-American to interfere with a free contractual
relation between employer and employee, his arguments
would rightly be suspect, for his defense of what he chooses
to call Americanism can hardly have been uninfluenced
by motives of gain and class domination. On the other
hand, we should not push the analysis of other people's
motives too far: first, because in most cases we are largely
ignorant of what they are; secondly, because the argument
ad hominem is double-edged. Everyone's theories, whatever side of a controversy he may take, express in some
manner his own interests; we cannot refute an opponent,
therefore, by pointing this out of him in particular. He
can retort to us in kind. The apologist for capitalism
sometimes declares that communists are merely motivated
by envy of those who possess more than themselves; while
the capitalists, in their turn, are accused of defending the
status quo merely because it protects and encourages them
in the enjoyment of their spoils. Both accusations would
be true if the word 'merely' were omitted; as they stand
both are partly false. Most individuals are motivated
not by selfish considerations alone, but by a confused
mixture of personal considerations and random sympathies together with more abstract values. While the motives of those who take a moral stand or who affirm an
ethical theory are sometimes relevant to an ethical discussion, they should in every case be balanced by a like attention to the motives behind the opposing view (especially
if it is one's own), and both should be subordinated to a
comparison of the values with which the discussion is
primarily concerned.

These are typical examples of the fallacies that are current in popular reasoning about moral matters. To enumerate popular fallacies exhaustively would be as impossible as to enumerate the breezes that fan one's cheek—and for much the same reason. It is excellent practice for the student of ethics to watch for the appearance of such fallacies in conversations and readings, and in the unguarded workings of his own mind.

2. Two Philosophical Fallacies

Popular morality makes almost no attempt to be systematic. Anyone who thinks in terms of platitudes is bound to do a certain amount of inconsistent thinking. "What's sauce for the goose is sauce for the gander" and "One man's meat is another's poison" are, when used without qualification, roughly contradictory. The assertions that they respectively symbolize could not be embraced within one coherent logical system. Yet this does not prevent people from appealing to both assertions promiscuously, as convenience may dictate. Many other pairs of contradictory platitudes will be suggested by a moment's reflection.

Philosophy, on the other hand, is a search after some form of significant consistency. It postulates as one of its starting-points the law of contradiction: that the affirmation and denial of a proposition cannot simultaneously be true in the same respect. If two propositions are contradictory and both have an appearance of being true, qualifications must be made: in what sense, on what occasions, in what relationships, from what points of view can the truth of each be affirmed? Ethics is a branch of philosophy. It is the philosophy of moral conduct and of the standards by which moral conduct and its effects are to be judged. Ethics therefore is a more or less structuralized account of moral values—the degree of structuralization depending on the type of ethical theory in question.

There are many who insist upon a firmer basis for moral judgments than it is the nature of ethical philosophy to provide. If, in addition, they are not content to appeal to some rule or authority or established custom but require a philosophical justification for their categorical morality, there are two opposite types of philosophy to which they may turn. On the one hand there is *factualism*,[1] which reduces ethics to a purely factual basis and seeks to give answers to ethical problems by the same methods that have produced valuable results in the empirical sciences. On the other hand there is *rationalism*, which bases the fundamental propositions of ethics upon the axioms of pure logic.

(i) *Ethics and the empirical sciences*

The argument by which factualists uphold their position runs in general as follows. Is it not the case, they ask, that the basis of all moral evaluations is to be found in the psycho-physical dispositions of men together with their socio-physical environment? This being so, ought we not first to assemble the relevant data provided by psychology, biology, anthropology, and scientific sociology, and derive moral principles from them? Do not such data provide a foundation, and the only sure foundation, for objective moral principles as distinguished from subjective opinions? Factualists answer affirmatively and conclude that ethics, in order to have objective validity, ought to be based on the verifiable results of the empirical sciences.

---

[1]More frequently, but with less accuracy, called *empiricism*.

Ethics and psychology

Of all the sciences it is psychology that has the most intimate connection with ethics, and it is here that an understanding of the exact relation of ethics to the sciences is most important. Every inclination, every moral evaluation, and every moral decision, besides its outward reference, has also the characteristic that it is a fact in some individual's mental life. All consciousness, indeed, has a similar duality of aspect. The mathematician's knowledge of equations, the physicist's knowledge of electrons, and the historian's knowledge of some past event are all, *quâ* knowledge, phases of the mental life of an individual scientist. But knowledge is more than knowledge only: it is always in every case a knowledge *of something*, whether the something be the properties of irrational numbers, the odd behavior of hydrogen atoms, or the date of Napoleon's retreat from Moscow. Psychology has nothing to do with any of these matters, but it does include within its province the psycho-physical behavior of a person engaged in apprehending them. Similarly in ethics, the moral evaluations that make ethics possible are at once psycho-physical impulses, *i.e.*, *acts* of evaluating, and evaluations *of* something. While the two aspects are in actual fact inseparable, it is by taking the one or the other as the point of departure that psychology and ethics are distinguished. Psychology deals with the psycho-physical activities themselves, ethics with the values that are present when such activities have developed to the stage of self-consciousness.

When an impulse has become conscious it is no longer a simple fact capable of translation into a scientific formula. An element of unpredictability has entered. Let the chemist learn the formula of picric acid, and his knowledge does not change the nature of that chemical.   But let a psychologist, professional or amateur, discover in himself a repressed passion, of the existence of which he had not been heretofore conscious; and his newly acquired knowledge is likely to be an effective element in the situation. By becoming conscious of the repression, his personality, of which the repression has been a part, has to that extent changed.   How will the repression manifest itself from now on?   What is to be predicted of a man who reflects on the grounds of his own behavior?

What a sea-anemone *is*, it seems that we can state clearly enough; since we are careful not to endow the sea-anemone with imagination.   Hence it *is* just what it is, a determinate present fact and nothing more.   But when we ask what a man *is* we discover (if we use moral insight) that he never *is* just what he is as a present determinate fact.   .   .   .
I may put the point differently by saying that, in contrast to the sea-anemone, the man more or less knows what he is; and this knowing ought to be a vital part of the man for any study that calls itself 'psychology.'   Say, then, that A is a liar; and add to this that A knows that he is a liar.   What *is* A now?   What is a liar who knows that he is a liar?   Or (in terms of 'fact') what can you predict of him when he finds out and 'comes to himself'?   This is precisely what no one knows, least of all the scientific psychologist.   And this is precisely the moral fact, an indeterminate sort of fact which does not readily meet the requirements of fact.[1]

The moral fact is 'an indeterminate sort of fact' for the reason that it is at once a fact and an expression of value.   The scientific psychologist, by his own avowal, ignores the value-aspect, and the fact that he describes is therefore merely an *abstraction* from the moral fact as it is experienced.   The remoteness of scientific psychology from actual living experience becomes evident to anyone

[1]Warner Fite, *Moral Philosophy*, p. 21.

who compares a description of personality as given in any scientific treatise or textbook with a description given in a novel, say, by Dostoyevsky or Proust or Conrad. Professor Albert Paul Weiss in *A Theoretical Basis of Behaviorism* gives the following account of happiness: "Neurologically the word happiness indicates the extent to which the innate and acquired components of sensori-motor function approach an optimum relationship between the antagonistic processes of individualization and socialization so that the movements of the individual are contributing directly or indirectly to larger or more complex electron-proton aggregates or larger and more complex social organization."[1] Compare with this any imaginative account of a person's happiness, such as George Eliot's description, in *The Mill on the Floss*, of Maggie Tulliver's joy over the return of her brother Tom from school. The comparison will make clear in what sense a scientific description of a conscious experience is 'logically remote' from the experience described.

When the difference between psychology and ethics has been recognized and accepted the importance of each for the other can be rightly understood. Psychological discoveries give to ethics a technical apparatus for dealing with special phases of moral problems. Psychology can often throw light on man's moral preferences and choices by revealing subconscious or physiological conditions of which the possessor is not aware. The discoveries of Freud and Jung in the field of the subconscious and of such behaviorists as Pavlov and Lashley in the field of neural physiology have furnished contemporary ethics with a realistic basis. The psychological studies of William James have had a still more direct relevance to ethical problems, for James had the wisdom to recognize

[1] *A Theoretical Basis of Behaviorism*, p. vii.

how far *any* theory and any method of analysis must always fall short of the central irreducible fact of human consciousness.[1]

Conversely, ethics is an inevitable supplement to the study of psychology, as in the long run it is to all sciences. What is it that makes psychology such a fascinating and important study? The fact that it gives us knowledge of human nature. If it gives us a knowledge of human nature in the concrete, as much everyday conversation and honest literature tend to do, then the study of psychology carries with it an insight into moral values. If, on the other hand, the psychology is strictly 'scientific,' timing and tabulating men's responses to stimuli, dealing only with what can be verified and measured, then it is not directly connected with ethics; but another type of normative question can then be asked about it, namely: What is the *good* of all such technical, laboratory investigations? One psychologist, of the behavioristic school, replies: "Having solved these problems, we hope to reach such proficiency in our science that we can build any man, starting at birth, into any kind of social or a-social being upon order."[2] Well, maybe. But in any case, granted that the behaviorist's dream of power may some day be realized and that this wonderful ability to transform men will be in his possession, the question arises, What use will he make of it? How *ought* men to be reconditioned? Towards becoming more intelligent individualists or towards becoming more efficient unthinking machines, more complaisant to the interests of those who hold power? The question which thus arises inevitably is a question of value, a moral question.

[1] See James' brilliant two-volume *Principles of Psychology*, which, except for a few exploded theories of trifling consequence, is quite as illuminating and much more readable than most of the psychology textbooks published subsequently.

[2] John B. Watson, *The Ways of Behaviorism*, p. 20.

Ethics and anthropology

Another field with which ethics has important relations is anthropology. A study of the origins of moral ideals and social institutions provides a healthy recognition of their relative and more or less accidental nature. As Westermarck's monumental work, *The Origin and Development of Moral Ideas*, demonstrates in rich detail, the basic principles of contemporary morality, which we can so readily support with rational arguments—property rights, monogamy, the keeping of contracts, and numerous others—have had in a majority of cases non-rational and non-moral origins. Tribal custom in all primitive societies is the sole determinant of right and wrong; it is associated with various crude beliefs in the supernatural, and is enforced by ritual and taboo.

Such facts as these, which are clearly of great importance for ethics, are sometimes employed as an argument that moral laws are not binding. How, it is asked, can laws be binding when there is demonstrably no universal agreement as to what they are? There is hardly any custom so cruel and loathsome that it has not at some time or other been permitted, hardly any so trifling and absurd that it has not at some time or other been regarded as a sacred duty. Cannibalism, polygamy, incest, witch-burning, and countless other practices repugnant to modern sensibilities have had their vogue; lending money at interest, attending theatres, and marrying the member of another family have been in certain societies condemned. Are not all standards of morality, then, simply customs that happen to be accepted at some particular time and place? Are there any sure criteria of right and wrong?

Only in a limited sense can we speak of a universal morality. In so far, namely, as there are certain fundamental similarities in the nature and life-conditions of all human beings, in so far will there be certain universally valid fundamental conditions of healthy life. . . . Morality can advance universal propositions: The preservation of human life demands that some attention be given to the care of offspring and the rearing of the young; and in order that this end may be reached the sexes must live together in some permanent form.   Or: A tribe cannot exist without some regulations tending to hinder hostilities among its members; the infraction of such rules tends to breed ruin; hence, murder, adultery, theft, and perjury are bad; justice, benevolence, and veracity, the inner dispositions of the will which prevents such acts are good.

But . . . the rules of a universal human morality must be adapted to the special historical forms and conditions of life before they can be directly employed in determining and judging conduct. The commandment: Treat your neighbor justly and kindly, observe the rules of family and social life, does not mean the same for an African negro as for a European Christian.[1]

Were the men of the Middle Ages wrong in burning heretics and torturing criminals? We tend to answer affirmatively, for the custom is so sharply at variance with modern penal codes. Their methods seem to us brutal and barbarous, but does that prove that another age than ours did wrong in adopting them? "Perhaps," observes Paulsen, "the entire administration of justice in those days, with its brutal methods, was at least a temporarily necessary precondition of the complicated social life of the mediaeval towns." We are in agreement with the inquisitors of the Middle Ages on the general principle that some assurance of social stability is needful; we disagree on how it is to be promoted and what sacrifices of personal liberty we are willing to make in order to secure it.

As Paulsen here indicates, there are observable in the history of human conduct certain rather abstract simi-

[1] Friedrich Paulsen, *A System of Ethics*, pp. 20–21.   (Scribners.)

larities and continuities together with the widest imaginable variety of details.   Neither the abstract resemblances nor the concrete differences can have more than an indirect relevance for contemporary moral problems.   Primitive behavior was, so far as we can say, more completely uncritical and bound by custom than the behavior we call civilized.   Such valuable results as it produced were mostly not of its own seeking.   Primitive magic was the forerunner of science, primitive wars were potent forces in building up group sentiments of loyalty and mutual aid; but wars were fought and magicians were respected for reasons that had nothing to do with these unforeseen results.   Nothing of ethical significance can be deduced from the functions that warfare or magic or other institutions of primitive peoples happen to have served.

Perhaps anthropology's chief service to ethics has been to remind us that moral standards are not eternal, and by that reminder to promote in us a greater tolerance for standards not our own.   This does not mean that anthropology offers a logical basis for denying that our own standards have moral validity, even in some cases an absolute validity, for us.   To suppose so is to fall into the *genetic fallacy*, which is a failure to distinguish between the origins of an institution or an ideal and its present character.   This double aspect of our ideals, as *causally related* to certain origins but as *logically independent* of them is described in the following passage from Nietzsche:

An inquiry into the origin of our moral evaluations and tables of law has absolutely nothing to do with the criticism of them, though people persist in believing it has; the two matters lie quite apart, notwithstanding the fact that the knowledge of the '*pudenda origo*' of a valuation does diminish its prestige, and prepares the way to a critical attitude and spirit toward it.[1]

---

[1]*The Will to Power*, Vol. I, p. 212.   (Macmillan.)

Science must always seek causes; anthropological science must seek remote origins. But for ethics the important thing is not the causes of an act but the act itself, its consequences, and the ideals which it embodies; not the origins of a custom but its present value for those in whose lives it has a contemporary significance.

General criticism of factualism

All attempts like the foregoing, to supply ethics with answers by appealing solely to facts or alleged facts, spring from the same general type of confusion: a failure to distinguish a *descriptive* from a *normative* proposition. Descriptive propositions are statements about fact, and are theoretically verifiable by any competent observer as either true, false, or having a certain degree of probability. Normative propositions are assertions of value: their truth or falsity may therefore legitimately vary for different individuals. Some of the most serious fallacies in ethical reasoning arise from confusing the two types.

Imagine a debate on the merits of capitalism vs. socialism. "Capitalism is here to stay," says one speaker, "so you may as well learn to accept it." "Socialism is bound to come," says the other, "so you'd better give up your antiquated prejudices." If either the continuance of capitalism or the advent of a socialist society were beyond peradventure of doubt (which no cautious thinker would affirm to be the case) we might conclude that it was advisable to adjust our attitude to it. But there would be no logical or psychological necessity of doing so. It would still be possible to discuss which form of society was ideally preferable, even though the ideal form happened to be unattainable. In a normative situation *facts are never coercive.* Given the factual proposition, *x is the case:* we cannot validly infer the truth of the normative proposition, *x is therefore good*, except by making the dubious assumption that whatever is actually the case is good, which is itself a normative judgment. Normative judgments depend partly but never wholly on judgments of fact. Their partial independence is demonstrated by the consideration that a given fact can be evaluated in as many ways as there are points of view brought to bear on it. Ethics, as a normative science, is *autonomous*. Its principles must be found by a study of moral situations themselves; they cannot be deduced from the principles of some other science.

The already discussed argument *ad hominem* reveals the same type of confusion differently applied. No crime should be punishable by death, says one disputant, and offers to back up his assertion with arguments. But his opponent dismisses the arguments with a shrug. "That's your opinion," he replies. "Probably you were conditioned in childhood to dread the sight of blood, and this dread has now become generalized and rationalized into what you call a moral opposition to capital punishment." "Maybe so," the first speaker might legitimately retort, "but what of it? I am concerned not with the causes of my beliefs but with their justification." The argument involved in this conversation breaks down because the two speakers are not talking about the same thing. The first speaker has expressed a judgment about a value: he has asserted a normative proposition. His critic has twisted the assertion into a closely related but logically distinct statement of fact. The distinction may be symbolized: (1) "*x* (the abolition of capital punishment) is right"—a normative proposition, belonging to ethics; and (2) "There are causes, *k, l, m*, of So-and-so's belief in *x*"—a descriptive proposition, belonging to psychology.

This last illustration may also be considered an example of the genetic fallacy. The cynically disposed critic is making the tacit assumption that an effect must have the same moral quality as its cause; that as a child-hood dread of blood has no great moral significance, there-fore neither has a belief about capital punishment that later grows out of it. All our experience testifies to the falsity of this assumption. There is in nature a familiar phenomenon known in philosophical language as *emergence:* effects (provided we leave the abstractions of physics and appeal to our own experience) have to some degree novel characteristics that were not to be found in their causes. Neither hydrogen nor oxygen has the property of quenching thirst, but combined in a certain proportion they create a new substance that does have this property. A sponge-cake has properties that are missing in any and all of its ingredients; otherwise no housewife would go to the trouble of baking one. Emergence is a characteristic of abstract relations too. The word 'sing' has an acknowledged meaning: to make a vocal noise somewhat musical. But 'Sing Sing' does not mean the making of two such noises. Meanings are continually being created wherever human consciousness is active, and as values are a type of meaning we must not expect to find their natures exhausted in their origins. Neither psycho-analysis nor anthropology is able to answer the questions of ethics. Values and facts are independent *types of meaning*, and their relationship should not be over-simplified.

(ii) *The a priori method*

The second way of escape from the uncertainties of ethics is rationalism, which attempts to derive ethical propositions from the axioms of pure logic. While the factualist may be accused of confusing normative with descriptive propositions, the rationalist seems to have confused normative with *a priori* propositions. An *a priori* proposition may be defined as a proposition whose truth or falsity is deducible from its meaning alone. Examine the meaning of such propositions as "4 + 3 = 7" or "A definite thing cannot both be and not be at the same time," and from their meaning alone you perceive them to be true. Examine the meaning of the propositions, "4 + 3 = 9" and "Nothing can be asserted," and from their meaning alone you perceive them to be false. If anyone were to deny either of the first two propositions or affirm either of the latter it would show, if he were not talking deliberate nonsense, that he was evidently attaching some other meaning to the words than the one commonly intended. An *a priori* proposition cannot be denied without contradiction.[1]

Evidently ethical propositions could be put on a firmer basis—could, in fact, be removed beyond dispute altogether—if they could be shown to follow as logical consequences from true *a priori* propositions. Probably the most resolute of all attempts to accomplish such a deduction has been made by Kant, whose philosophy will be expounded in Chapter VI. At present we shall examine an attempt at ethical apriorism made on a smaller scale by John Locke (1632–1704), whose philosophy in most respects runs positively counter to apriorism.

"I doubt not," Locke wrote, "but from self-evident propositions, by necessary consequences, as incontestable as those in mathematics, the measures of right and wrong might be made out, to any one that will apply himself with the same indifference and attention to the one as he does

---

[1] *A priori* propositions may also be designated *structural*, or *analytic*. Kant, in *The Critique of Pure Reason*, makes a subtle and somewhat hazardous distinction between an *a priori* and an analytic judgment, regarding the former as the more inclusive. The distinction is not, however, relevant to the present argument.

to the other of these sciences."[1]   But when urged by his friend Molyneux to produce a system of *a priori* demonstrated ethics Locke at first hesitated and in the end declined to make the attempt.   In his chief philosophical work, *An Essay Concerning Human Understanding*, Locke offers two illustrations of propositions "as certain as any demonstration in Euclid."   They are: "Wherever there is no property there is no injustice" and "No government allows absolute liberty."   Both propositions may be affirmed *a priori*, for in both there is a necessary connection between the meaning of the subject and the meaning of the predicate.   Property, in its broadest sense, signifies a 'right' to anything, and injustice signifies the invasion or violation of that right: injustice presupposes, therefore, the existence of property.   Again, government signifies the establishment of society upon certain laws to which men are required to conform, while absolute liberty would mean that no one need conform to anything: the two ideas are thus incompatible.

But can the moral problem be solved by establishing a body of analytic propositions of this kind? Evidently not, for a genuinely ethical proposition is normative—an assertion of value—and therefore 'synthetic.'[2]   Neither of the examples given by Locke is a synthetic proposition, and hence neither is strictly an assertion of value.   Government and absolute liberty, the second proposition asserts, are incompatible.   Choose which you will have, for you cannot have them both.   But on what grounds can we choose?   If the choice is made wisely it will be based on a thorough scrutiny of what each alternative offers. The results of the double scrutiny will be compared, and our conclusion will take the form of a normative proposi-

---

[1]*An Essay Concerning Human Understanding*, IV. iii. 18.
[2]See Glossary.

tion: one of the alternatives is, all things considered, better than the other. *Which* is better cannot be deductively inferred from the analytic proposition that the two are incompatible. The answer must be found in a comparison of the values that we attach to each. Since governments are of many kinds, our answer will, likely as not, distinguish between those kinds which are preferable to no government at all and those kinds to which no government at all would be preferable. We shall then have reached a conclusion that bears some relevance to moral action. Such a conclusion could not have been reached by demonstration alone. The use of demonstration in ethics is to establish and classify the structural relations among the ideas that enter into moral deliberation. Within these limits demonstration has importance.

Examine now the other of Locke's two propositions: "Wherever there is no property there is no injustice." Can any ethical conclusion be inferred from this? Injustice entails property, the proposition asserts; whence, by the logical process known as 'contraposition,'[1] we may infer that absence of property entails an absence of any way in which the idea of injustice could be applied. Can we infer, then, that since injustice is an evil, property is also an evil? Locke's own political philosophy would certainly not have admitted any such radical inference. Property, he would have said, is evil *to the extent that* it involves injustice, but it does not necessarily do so,[2] and hence is not necessarily evil. Property is the *necessary condition* of injustice, but it is the necessary condition of justice as well (justice and injustice being logically cor-

---

[1] See Glossary.

[2] *I.e.*, the analytic proposition, "Wherever there is injustice there is property," *does not imply* the proposition, "Wherever there is property there is injustice." If we were to *infer* the second from the first we should be committing the fallacy of *illicit conversion.* See Glossary: 'conversion'; also 'imply' and 'infer.'

relative), and accordingly it is not interchangeable with either of them.

To speak more concretely: property creates and constitutes the *possibility* of both justice and injustice. Wherever there is property there is that possibility, and wherever that possibility exists, property also exists. Each implies the other. The relation may be summarized by saying that property is *logically equivalent to* (not injustice, but) the *possibility* of both justice and injustice. From this equivalence the following inference may be validly drawn: *if* a form of society is evil in which there is a possibility of both justice and injustice, *then* property is evil and ought to be abolished. Conservatives, however, would *contrapose* the implication. Instead of presupposing that a society into which justice and injustice can both enter is evil, they would presuppose that property is a desirable institution, one that ought in some form to be preserved. From this presupposition they would infer that a society offering a joint possibility of justice and injustice is likewise essentially good, and ought to be preserved. Injustice they would regard as a deplorable but to some extent inevitable accompaniment of a desirable form of society—a blemish of slight importance as compared with the benefits of privacy, individual initiative, and thrift, which the institution of property is alleged to promote.

In general, the *a priori* method has this difficulty: the only sure principles that it can establish satisfactorily to reasoners of different moral habits and different moral sensibilities are so general that in applying them we readily fall into the fallacy of the ambiguous middle. One method of pinning down the ambiguity is what is known as *casuistry*—an enumeration of all the cases to which a principle or rule applies and all the cases to which it does not. There are strong objections to this method, however.

For one thing, none of the great casuistic enterprises of the world's religious and moral history—neither the Talmudic interpretation of the Old Testament nor the Christian fathers' and later the Jesuits' interpretation of the New—has succeeded in carrying its code of rules into such minute detail as to forestall all moral difficulties. Moral difficulties can never be wholly resolved in advance, for what makes them difficult is mainly their element of novelty. Moral principles are not stone walls. To be applicable without subterfuge or equivocation they must, although retaining a certain normative identity, be adaptable to man's growing needs.

Morals must be a growing science if it is to be a science at all, not merely because all truth has not yet been appropriated by the mind of man, but because life is a moving affair in which old moral truth ceases to apply. . . . But the experimental character of moral judgments does not mean complete uncertainty and fluidity. Principles exist as hypotheses with which to experiment. . . . There is a long record of past experimentation in conduct, and there are cumulative verifications which give many principles a well earned prestige. Lightly to disregard them is the height of foolishness. But social situations alter; and it is also foolish not to observe how old principles actually work under new conditions, and not to modify them so that they will be more effectual instruments in judging new cases.[1]

3. TOWARDS A WORKING METHOD

Both factualists and rationalists make the mistake of expecting from ethics more exact and more certain results than the subject-matter warrants. Normative judgments, when honest expressions of opinion and not unthinking platitudes, are profoundly personal. If they speak true they register something of the way in which a particular individual, as a result of countless instincts,

[1]John Dewey, *Human Nature and Conduct*, p. 239. (Modern Library.)

habits, and past reflections and decisions, has come to look at life. Ethics, consequently, can never have the same degree of precision and finality that is the property of the mathematical and is aimed at by the physical sciences.

To treat the science [of ethics] adequately we ought to be content with that degree of precision which is appropriate to the subject-matter. The same degree of exactitude ought not to be expected in all reasonings alike. . . . Excellence and justice, which are the objects of ethical inquiry, involve much disagreement and uncertainty, so that they come to be looked on as mere conventions, having no natural foundation. The good involves a similar uncertainty, inasmuch as good things often prove detrimental: there are examples of people destroyed by wealth, of others destroyed by courage. In such matters, then, we must be content with a rough approximation to the truth. Let each of the views that are put forward be accepted in this spirit, for it is the mark of an educated mind to seek only so much exactness in each type of inquiry as may be allowed by the nature of the subject-matter.[1]

The Socratic method

It was Aristotle's great predecessor Socrates who offered the first model of ethical theorizing, and still one of the best, in the Western world. Socrates reached no systematic conclusions. As his conversations are reported in Plato's dialogues he appears to have cared mainly about clarifying his own and others' ideas, and ridding himself and them of false ones. His function, he used to say, was like that of a midwife: to assist others in giving birth to their idea-children, and if the ideas proved to be miscarriages, to prick them and toss them away. A typical example of Socrates' method will illustrate the critical or negative process with which sound ethical theorizing must begin.

[1] Aristotle, *The Nicomachean Ethics*, I. iii. 1–4.

In Plato's dialogue entitled *Euthyphro*, Socrates on his way to court (where, as it turns out, he is to stand trial for his life) falls in with Euthyphro, who is traveling from his father's country estate to the same destination. One of the slaves belonging to Euthyphro's father has been killed by a drunken overseer, and the father (incensed chiefly, it may be presumed, by the loss of a valuable chattel) has had the overseer bound hand and foot and thrown into a ditch while awaiting religious advice from Athens on what punishment to mete out. Before the advice could come, however, the overseer has died of exposure, and now Euthyphro sees his duty clear before him: regardless of family ties, to bring his father to trial for the unwitting murder.

Euthyphro.[1]   My father and relatives are all furious with me. They say it is an unholy thing for a son to prosecute his father. As if *they* knew what holiness was!

Socrates.   Do you know what it is, Euthyphro?

Euth.   I'd be a pretty witless fellow if I didn't.

Soc.   What luck then that I've met you! I shall find the knowledge useful at my trial, for I am charged, among other things, with impiety. What is it that you declare holiness and unholiness to be?

Euth.   Why, holiness is just what I am doing now, prosecuting any murderer or despoiler of temples or the like, no matter who he may be, your father or mother or anyone else; and unholiness is the failure to do so.

Soc.   I'm afraid this is not sufficient information, my friend. You would agree, wouldn't you, that there are holy acts other than those you name?

Euth.   Certainly.

Soc.   Must there not be in all holy acts an identical quality whereby they are called holy? If there were not, surely holiness would be without meaning. Explain to me then the *form* (εἶδος) of holiness: the characteristic nature (ἰδέα) by which an

---

[1]This conversation is an abridged paraphrase of Plato's *Euthyphro*.

act that is holy may be distinguished from one that is not.   (1)

Euth.   That's easy enough.   Acts are holy when they are dear to the gods, unholy when not.

Soc.   But don't the gods often disagree about such matters? Your action, for example, might be dear to Zeus while hateful to Hera.   In that case, it would seem to be holy and unholy at once.   (2)

Euth.   I think, at any rate, the gods all agree in condemning a murderer, and in approving one who prosecutes him.

Soc.   Is it this that makes your present action holy?

Euth.   What do you mean?

Soc.   I mean, is it the mere fact that the gods approve of an act that establishes its holiness?   On the contrary, ought we not to suppose that the gods have some reason for bestowing their approval? that they approve of an act only because it *is* holy?   (3)

Euth.   So it would seem.

Soc.   You have told me nothing, then, about the essence (οὐσία) of holiness.   In saying that it is loved by all the gods you have mentioned only an incidental characteristic (πάθος).   (4)

Euth.   That's because you keep moving the argument about and getting me mixed up.   I know what I mean but I can't express it.   (5)

Soc.   Let's try another tack.   You would agree, I suppose, that everything that is holy is right (δίκαιος), but would you say also that everything right is holy?   Would you not declare, rather, that there are examples of right other than holiness, and that holiness is therefore only a part of right?   (6)

Euth.   Yes, that's what I'd declare.

Soc.   What part of right, then, is holiness?   What is its differentiating characteristic?   (7)

Euth.   Holiness, in my opinion, is that part of the right which has to do with our service to the gods.   The remaining part has to do with our service to men.

Soc.   In what does service to the gods consist?   In improving them?

Euth.   Of course not.

Soc.   In what, then?   What result is accomplished by our service to the gods?

Euth.   Many fine results, Socrates.

Soc. No doubt. Farmers, too, accomplish many fine results, but the chief result of their work is the production of food from the land. Tell me, in a similar way, what chief result the gods accomplish by using us as servants.

Euth. Why, I suppose they are gratified, and take pleasure in our serving them.

Soc. See how your arguments have traveled in a circle, Euthyphro, back to a former point. You are again attempting to define holiness in terms of what pleases the gods: a definition that we previously found reason to reject, on the ground that giving pleasure to the gods was an accident of holiness, not its essence. (8)

Socrates in this conversation brings out several points of importance for the methodology of ethics. Referring to the passages indicated by numbers in parentheses: (1) Wherever a word is used generally, there must be a general meaning, or 'form,' to which it refers. Clear thinking in ethics requires that the 'form' should be, so far as possible, defined. To enumerate a few instances to which the word can be applied, as Euthyphro began by doing, is not enough: we are not shown in what respect these instances are alike. (2) Euthyphro attempts a definition of 'holy,' but makes the mistake of trying to define an ethical concept in terms of a fact. Facts, as Socrates illustrates, are double-edged: they can be used to justify any standard, which means that they properly justify none. The facts of the present case might establish the same act as at once holy and unholy. Furthermore, (3) if the fact that the gods love certain kinds of action is *worthy* of being appealed to as a standard of right, this can only be because the gods are good; whence it would follow that they do not take pleasure in any action at all but only in virtuous actions. The nature of virtue is thus (4) something more fundamental than the pleasure that the gods are supposed to take in it. (5) Euthyphro now discovers that he has not, and never did have, any clear idea of what he is talking about: a discovery often concealed under the platitude here ascribed to him. Socrates helps him to make a new attempt: (6) to define holiness it is necessary to discover first of all its *genus*, which is 'right.' The relation of a term to its genus is asymmetrical: if an act is holy it is right, but the converse relation cannot be asserted.[1] Besides the genus, a definition must give (7) the *differentia* of a term. But (8) Euthyphro unguardedly offers as differentia the same consideration (the fact of being acceptable to the gods) that was thrown out earlier in the conversation. His argument is therefore convicted of circularity.

Evidently Euthyphro, for all his early cocksureness, had no clear notion of what he was talking about when he declared his conduct to be morally praiseworthy. Getting rid of cocksure but confused ideas is, as Socrates always insisted, the first step in a philosophical inquiry into any subject. "Are my opinions true?" must be preceded by "Do I know what I mean by them?" for a muddled opinion is neither clearly true nor clearly false.

The procedure of subsequent chapters

Still, it will be retorted, the latter question does remain. When ideas have been clarified, may we not then ask whether or not they are true? And what method of ascertaining their truth does ethics provide? To answer the question adequately would involve an inquiry into the nature of philosophical truth. Such an inquiry will be undertaken in Chapter XII. For the present it is enough to say that in the next five chapters, which ex-

---

[1]When the relation between terms or propositions is asymmetrical, it cannot be directly converted. Consult Glossary for the meaning of 'genus,' 'differentia,' 'symmetrical,' and 'conversion.'

pound certain representative ethical doctrines, the aim will be not to find some one doctrine that can be accepted as true to the exclusion of all others, but, after the Socratic model, to look for the positive truth-values along with the logical and moral limitations of each.

Each of the doctrines about to be examined represents an attempt, or a related group of attempts, to answer the question, *What is the supreme intrinsic good?* The significance of the adjectives should be noted. The distinction between intrinsic and extrinsic goods has already been explained. Independently of this distinction some goods are recognized as taking precedence over others. One good may be called *superior* to another when we would rationally prefer it on such occasions as a choice between the two is necessary. *Inferior* goods are those which we would rationally renounce when by doing so we make a superior good more accessible. The enjoyment of wine, although for those who like it an intrinsic good, is inferior to the good of a kept promise. On most occasions, therefore, where the two are incompatible it becomes a duty to forego wine-drinking.

The ethical philosopher's question, "What good is supreme?" may thus be interpreted to mean: Is there any one good for which, on any occasion whatever, we would willingly renounce *all* other goods? The mystic's love of God is probably for him such a good, but few today are genuine mystics. Aristotle declared the supreme good to be *eudaimonia*, 'an active well-being of the soul,' but his declaration is qualified by the admission that different men interpret well-being in different ways: some as a state of pleasurable feeling, others as success in a political, military, or business career, still others (notably Aristotle himself) as a life devoted to philosophical reflection. No single type of good will be accepted as supreme by all men—

unless (a fallacy several times to be encountered!) the supreme good is stated so broadly (like Aristotle's *eudaimonia*) as to suggest no specific application, or else so ambiguously (like the 'happiness' of the utilitarians) as to be deceptive. An individual may, however, accept some specific type of good as the supreme good for himself, as a directive ideal for his own conduct. Although few of us carry out any ideal with noteworthy consistency our dominant moral tendencies are likely to be in one direction rather than another.

The types of ethical theory that are presented in the next five chapters may be regarded in this light, as theoretical expressions of certain dominant moral tendencies that are active in men. Each of them has some truth; none is *the* truth. Accordingly, the student who cares to approach ethics in a critical spirit will avoid the black-or-white, hero-or-villain type of thinking indulged in by the uneducated. He will neither accept nor reject any ethical theory whole. Rather he will judge each theory by the adequacy with which it interprets human experience and by the worth of its proffered ideal.

PART II
TYPES OF MORAL IDEAL

CHAPTER III

THE PURSUIT OF PLEASURE

*How could
Anything so good
Be bad?*
Old vaudeville song

THE ETHICAL PHILOSOPHY which declares man's *summum bonum*, or supreme intrinsic good, to lie in the enjoyment of the greatest possible amount of pleasure is called *hedonism*.[1]   Because of the excessive ambiguity of the word 'pleasure' the hedonistic philosophy has been espoused by philosophers whose specific moral allegiances were of widely different kinds and the details of whose doctrines have therefore little in common.   But throughout this diversity there is a bond of identical meaning. Pleasure, of whatever kind, is a feeling; all hedonism thus posits *feelings as the locus of moral value*.   Acts, intentions, and motives are morally good so far as they tend to produce a certain kind of feeling or to destroy an opposite kind of feeling, morally bad so far as they tend to destroy that kind of feeling or produce its opposite, and morally indifferent so far as their effect is neither the one nor the other.   Besides agreeing on the locus of moral value most hedonists agree[2] that the value which they are talking about is one to which *the category of quantity can be significantly applied*.   Pleasures and pains, they postulate, stand

---

[1] Derived from the Greek ἡδονή, meaning 'pleasure.'

[2] John Stuart Mill, the most prominent exception to this rule, will be discussed presently.

to each other in relations of more and less. Their test of the moral value of an act is *how much* pleasure and how little pain it produces.[1] Apart from these two modes of agreement theories of hedonism differ, and the principal difference among them lies in the answers given to the question, *by whom* the pleasures and pains which determine moral values are to be felt. The egoistic hedonist cares only for his own pleasures and pains, together perhaps with the pleasures and pains of those so closely and frequently associated with him that their feelings tend spontaneously to be reflected in his own. Universalistic hedonism, or utilitarianism, on the contrary, postulates the equal worth of any two pleasures or pains equal in amount, regardless of by whom they may happen to be felt.

1. Egoistic Hedonism

Egoism is the philosophy which affirms that our own interests are in every case the dominant good, and promotion of them the only worth-while course of action; that other people's interests are none of our affair and to promote them is never our duty except so far as they affect, or seem likely to affect, our own. Sometimes, of course, our own interests happen to be more or less identified with those of another person or social group. But there are plenty of occasions when our interests and theirs are in direct opposition, and while sometimes an adjustment or compromise can be arranged, it is yet often the case, whether because human ingenuity is too weak or human perversity too strong, that no settlement is possible without injury to their interests or to ours. The egoist maintains that in cases of the latter sort one's sole duty is

---

[1] In order to group presence of pleasure and absence of pain under a single concept, hedonists commonly use the words 'happiness' or 'enjoyment.'

always to oneself, at whatever cost to others; and if he is a hedonist he defines this duty in terms of enjoyment.

As human temperaments vary, so the objects or situations or acts that seem to promise most enjoyment also vary. For some men enjoyment is a matter of securing as much pleasure as possible, for others it is primarily a matter of avoiding discomforts and pains; to the former happiness means excitement, to the latter it means tranquillity. This difference has been typified in the history of ethics by two Greek hedonistic philosophers, Aristippus (435–350 B. C.) and Epicurus (341–270 B. C.). Aristippus was the typical pleasure seeker. According to the historian Diogenes Laertius, "he was capable of adapting himself to place, time, and person, and of playing his part most appropriately in any circumstances. . . . He derived pleasure from things that were present and did not toil to procure enjoyment from things not present." Nor was he above resorting to flattery to secure the luxuries he wanted. He was a welcome because sycophantic guest at the court of King Dionysius of Syracuse, and when reproached with having obsequiously knelt before the king in order to beg some favor he retorted coolly, "That is not my fault but Dionysius', who has his ears in his feet." His way of living found a theoretic expression in his hedonistic philosophy, which became known as *Cyrenaicism* after the town of Cyrene where he lived, and which is characterized by three principal doctrines: (1) Our aim should be not a generally happy life but as large a sum of particular pleasures as our wits can procure for us; (2) very intense pleasures are good and to be sought even when they are the occasion of a considerable amount of pain or disgrace, for a life without the excitement of pleasure and pain would be as uninteresting and worthless as a life of continual dreamless slumber; (3) pleasures are attained best if one has the wit and courage to keep control of the situation. This last credo finds pithy expression in Aristippus' remark about his mistress, the lovely courtesan Lais: "I possess her, I am not possessed by her."

A similar doctrine was held by the Athenian man-about-town Callicles, whom Plato quotes as saying that "he who would live rightly must let his desires become as great as possible and not restrain them, and must use courage and practical intelligence to gratify them fully when they are at their height, and must satisfy each new appetite as it arises." For, he adds, a life of pleasure is achieved not by quieting or ordering the desires but by getting "as much of an inflow as possible" of pleasurable sensations.[1]

Epicurus, on the other hand, declared the supreme human good to be *ataraxia*, the tranquil happiness that comes to one who is free from passion, fear, and pain. His philosophy became known as Epicureanism, but the word has subsequently suffered from misuse and is sometimes loosely applied to any hedonistic ideal or way of life whatever. It is true that Epicurus must be classified as a hedonist, for he declares that "every pleasure, because of its natural kinship to us, is good," and denies that a pleasure is ever a bad thing in itself; nevertheless he distinguishes among pleasures: not all are to be sought, for "the means which produce some pleasures bring with them disturbances many times greater than the pleasures themselves." Reckless gratification of the passions and indulgence in every sort of luxury are the source of much ennui and unsatisfied longing, and sometimes of bodily ill-health. Train yourself rather, he bids, to enjoy a simple diet; besides the homely pleasures that you will learn to discover in simple foods you will enjoy the more

---

[1] Plato, *Gorgias*, 491 E–492 A; 494 A–B.

valuable, because more continuous and more lasting, pleasures that come from health, alertness, and absence of pain.

It is not continuous drinkings and revelings, nor the satisfaction of lusts, nor the enjoyment of fish and other luxuries of the wealthy table, which produce a pleasant life, but sober reasoning, searching out motives for all choice and avoidance, and banishing mere opinions, to which are due the greatest disturbance of the spirit.[1]

The banishing of mere opinions and the search for valid motives of choice and avoidance is the aim of Epicurean philosophy, and the good man is necessarily, in Epicurus' opinion, the philosopher. Not that philosophy is good in itself, but rightly pursued it administers to the tranquil life. By such pursuit we may learn to avoid the miseries that come from over-indulgence, and we may banish the disturbance of spirit that comes from groundless fears. One of the fears that most persistently disturb mankind is the fear of death. Philosophy serves the Epicurean ideal by proving that death, if considered rationally, cannot be dreaded:

Become accustomed to the belief that death is nothing to us. For all good and evil consist in sensation, but death is deprivation of sensation. And therefore a right understanding that death is nothing to us makes the mortality of life enjoyable, not because it adds to it an infinite span of time, but because it takes away the craving for immortality.[2]

Since death is nothing painful when it comes, there should be nothing painful in the anticipation of it; that is, it should not be dreaded. Death can be of no concern to the wise man, for "so long as we exist, death is not with us; but when death comes, then we do not exist." But

[1]Letter to Menoecius.
[2]Ibid.

while he will not fear death nor regret its coming, neither will the wise man seek to hasten it by taking his own life. Logically, to be sure, Epicurus' philosophy should justify suicide for those to whom life brings more pains than pleasures. As a matter of fact he probably would have agreed that suicide is justifiable in the rare case where some incurable bodily disease promises a life of unalleviated suffering, or again where some overwhelming and un-pardonable disgrace has ostracized a person from the company and respect of his fellow-beings. In Athens, as later in Rome, suicide for either of these reasons was regarded as a moral act. In most cases, however, the wise man by prudence and self-restraint can secure for himself a surplus of pleasure over pain, especially when he has found, like Epicurus, that the surest and best happiness lies in a state of reflective tranquillity, in the pursuit of philosophy, in ministering as gracefully and enjoyably as possible to the healthful wants of the body, and in living on terms of friendship and mutual respect with others of like purpose.

It is one of the paradoxes of philosophical history that Epicurus, the most widely known and most frequently mentioned of hedonists, is anything but a typical hedonist. Although he uses the terminology of hedonism and accepts the word 'pleasure' (*hedonê*) as descriptive of the highest human good, yet if the manner of putting an ethical doc-trine into practice bears any testimony as to its meaning, Epicurus is closer to the Stoics and to many religious moralists than to the majority of hedonists. The fact that two philosophies as far apart as those of Aristippus and Epicurus should each define the dominant good as 'pleasure' hints at the dangerous ambiguity lurking in the word. The ambiguity will become more evident as we consider the 'proofs' by which hedonism is supported.

The 'proof' of hedonism

The principal argument offered by most hedonists for the truth of their theory is based on the fact, as they declare, that the only motive that ever does or can govern human actions is the desire for one's own happiness—that is, for a maximum of pleasure and a minimum of pain to oneself. This doctrine, that a desire for happiness is the actual and inevitable spring of all human actions, is called *psychological hedonism*, as distinguished from *ethical hedonism*, which sets up happiness as a moral ideal that *ought* to be followed. The two aspects of hedonism are expressed jointly in the opening words of Bentham's *Introduction to the Principles of Morals and Legislation:*

Nature has placed mankind under the guidance of two sovereign masters, pain and pleasure. It is for them alone to point out what we ought to do, as well as to determine what we shall do. On the one hand the standard of right and wrong, on the other the chain of causes and effects, are fastened to their throne.

Psychological hedonism is a doctrine that to many persons seems at first sight highly plausible. There is no question that pleasures and pains exert a powerful pull on everyone. Furthermore, the types of pleasure and pain and the ways of receiving them are so many and varied that when anyone voluntarily renounces a pleasure or voluntarily undergoes a pain it is often possible to show (and always possible to believe) that his action was undertaken for the purpose of pursuing some greater but less obvious or less immediate pleasure, or for avoiding some further pain. The justice of this interpretation is clear in such actions as voluntarily submitting to the surgeon's knife or the dentist's drill, or abstaining from late revelries. Hedonistic motives can be imputed also where the proof of them is less certain: persons who offer elaborate justifications of their conduct frequently seem to be covering up the selfish and secretly pleasurable nature of their true motives. Disgust with such hypocrisy, which is certainly wide-spread, moved Bernard Mandeville (1670–1733) to a more sweeping cynicism:

There is no merit in saving an innocent babe ready to drop into the fire: the action is neither good nor bad, and what benefit soever the infant received, we only obliged ourselves; for to have seen it fall, and not strove to hinder it, would have caused a pain, which self-preservation compelled us to prevent.[1]

If psychological hedonism is universally true, it is argued by the hedonists that ethical hedonism must follow. If men are *in fact* always motivated by pleasure and pain it is quixotic to set up anything else as a moral aim. As John Stuart Mill, a generation later than Bentham, summed up the argument: "The only proof capable of being given that an object is visible is that people actually see it. In like manner the sole proof it is possible to produce that anything is desirable is that people do actually desire it." Happiness, therefore, Mill concludes, since everyone does desire it, must be objectively desirable —that is to say, objectively good. And since everyone not only desires happiness but always prefers a greater happiness to a less, it follows that the greater happiness is always the greater good, and that the endeavor to secure the greatest happiness that lies within our power should be made our highest moral aim.

2. Utilitarianism

Utilitarianism, considered with respect to the fundamental concepts it employs,[2] is a form of hedonism, with

---

[1] From Mandeville's essay, "An Enquiry into the Origin of Moral Virtue," reprinted in Vol. II of *The Fable of the Bees* (Oxford: The Clarendon Press).

[2] In its character as a philosophy of social reform utilitarianism will be considered in Chapter IX.

the specific difference that the actions it commends are not such as necessarily bring most happiness[1] to the individual but to the greatest possible number of people. It has therefore been called universalistic hedonism. From the standpoint of practice the two forms of hedonism, egoistic and universalistic or collectivistic, are far apart. The leaders of the utilitarian school, Jeremy Bentham (1748–1842) and John Stuart Mill (1806–1873), were noted social reformers of their day, while to Epicurus the idea of devoting oneself to the reform of social institutions would have been abhorrent. Nevertheless there is a double sense in which the hedonistic aspect of utilitarian ethics is important. Hedonistic psychology is accepted by Bentham and Mill as a true account of how human motives work, and as a necessary basis, therefore, of any valid theory of social duties. In the second place, although their ethical standard is humanitarian, pointing as it does to the welfare of the greatest number, it stands opposed to religious and ascetic forms of humanitarianism and offers in their place a social ideal formulated in hedonistic terms.

Bentham sets the principles of his utilitarian ethics upon an extreme form of psychological hedonism, which he calls the *principle of self-preference*. Among the many ways in which he states the principle:

On the occasion of every act he exercises, every human being is led to pursue that line of conduct which, according to his view of the case, taken by him at the moment, will be in the highest degree contributory to his own greatest happiness, whatsoever be the effect of it, in relation to the happiness of other similar beings, any or all of them taken together.[2]

---

[1] 'Happiness' for utilitarians as for other hedonists has a strict meaning: presence of pleasure together with absence of pain.

[2] Bentham, *Works*, Vol. IX, p. 5.

David Hume (1711–1776), in his *Inquiry Concerning the Principles of Morals*, had warned against so great a degree of over-simplification as the hedonistic theory of human motives involves. There are, he declared, social or sympathetic as well as egoistic impulses in the human make-up, and no contradiction between them. Just as a man can at one and the same time be acting from the combined motives of egoism and ambition, or equally well from egoism and vindictiveness, so he can from egoism and benevolence. But Bentham's psychology admitted of no such compromise. To him man appeared to be by nature a complete egoist: "Whatsoever evil it is possible for man to do for the advancement of his own private and personal interest, (or what comes to the same thing, what to him appears such), at the expense of the public interest,—that evil, sooner or later, he will do, unless by some means or other, intentional or otherwise, he be prevented from doing it."[1] Holding so inflexible a theory about the nature of man, Bentham was suspicious of theories like those of Hume and Adam Smith which made use of the 'principle of sympathy.' Rely on sympathy and you make individual taste the criterion! How can you get a principle of morality out of that! "What one expects to find in a principle is something that points out some external consideration, as a means of warranting and guiding the internal sentiments of approbation and disapprobation: this expectation is but ill fulfilled by a proposition which does neither more nor less than hold up each of those sentiments as a ground and standard for itself."[2] Bentham as a student of jurisprudence wanted a fast rule, a criterion with an objective meaning and a universal

[1] *Op. cit.*, IX, 192.
[2] *Ibid.*, I, 9.

applicability, and in the principle of self-preference he thought he had discovered the basis of one.

The quantitative principle

A second important aspect of Bentham's theory is his insistence that the only relevant differences between one pleasure or pain and another are differences in amount.

Differences of quality may be disregarded except so far as they can be restated as differences of quantity. The significance of this reduction of qualitative differences among pleasures and pains to purely quantitative differences becomes apparent on examining the logical technique of the sciences. In physics and celestial mechanics, which of all the empirical sciences appear to have become established on the surest, most objective footing, the ultimate differences to which all observable differences of color, warmth, sound, weight, etc. are referred, are differences that can be measured—that is, expressed as quantitative relations. Since Bentham's time, similar though less complete progress has been made in chemistry and, in a less exact way, in biology and physiological psychology. This shift of emphasis has rendered science capable of more exact formulation and, on the practical side, has enabled experiments to be performed and their results to be recorded with a precision that mathematics alone could give and by which alone the wonders of modern invention have become possible. Five centuries before the Christian era Pythagoras had declared the importance of mathematical relations for a right understanding of natural phenomena. He had observed that vibrating strings whose lengths bore simple fractional relations to one another would make pleasant harmonies, but when the lengths bore no such numerical relations the resulting

sounds were discordant. From this and similar observations in other fields Pythagoras drew the conclusion that
"all is number"—all phenomena, that is to say, can be
rationally understood by expressing their differences
numerically, or, in the case of pure qualities such as sound,
color, and moral goodness, by referring them to differences
between one number and another. Because science at
that time, however, was ratiocinative rather than experimental Pythagoras' application of number to qualities
was arbitrary and based principally on religious considerations, so that few important consequences of his theory
were worked out. But after the Renaissance, the importance of measurement in scientific experimentation
came to be generally recognized and to an ever greater
degree the typical problems of science came to be formulated in such a way as to permit of a mathematical solution. When Galileo dropped objects of different weights
from the leaning tower of Pisa in order to discover whether
there was any connection between weight and the speed of
falling, both of which terms can be given mathematical
expression, he ignored the purely qualitative differences
of color, smoothness, etc. as irrelevant to his problem.
Even in chemistry, although in Bentham's day, before
Mendelyeyev had discovered the Periodic Law, the differences among the chemical elements were accepted as
irreducibly qualitative, yet in combining the elements with
one another the methods of quantitative analysis had
already made headway. Could a similar method be employed in ethics? Could a standard of measurement be
found for pleasures and pains?

Bentham decided that it could, and devised a 'hedonistic calculus' by which pleasures and pains might be
evaluated without reference to any but quantitative differences. According to this calculus the moral worth of any

action is to be judged by reference to: (1) the *intensity* of the pleasures and pains it produces, (2) their *duration*, (3) the degree of *probability* that they will occur as predicted, (4) the *promptitude* of their fulfillment, (5) their *fecundity*—i.e., the tendency of a pleasure to be followed by other pleasures or of a pain by other pains, (6) their *purity*—i.e., the freedom of a pleasure from attendant or subsequent pains, and of a pain from attendant or subsequent pleasures, (7) their *social extent*, or the number of persons affected by them. Bentham summed the matter up in the following ditty:

> Intense, long, certain, speedy, fruitful, pure—
> Such marks in pleasure and in pain endure.
> Such pleasures seek if private be thy end;
> If it be public, let them wide extend.
> Such pains avoid whatever be thy view;
> If pains must come, let them extend to few.[1]

The calculus makes possible an objective determination of the morality of any conduct. Make a list of all the pleasures that are likely to result from a proposed action; determine the value of each as measured by each of the seven criteria; add the resultant values together, and put your sum on the credit side of the ledger. Do the same for pains: these are the debit items. Now subtract the total debit from the total credit. Is the result positive? Then the act is morally good and ought to be performed. Is the result negative? Then the act is morally bad and ought to be shunned.

The sanctions of social morality

There remains a third aspect of Bentham's doctrine to be examined: its collectivism. In spite of man's natural

---

[1] *Principles of Morals and Legislation*, Chap. IV.

tendency to seek only his own individual happiness the moral ideal must be stated as the greatest happiness of the greatest number. My own happiness is the motive from which I always do act; promotion of the general happiness is the standard by which the moral worth of my action is to be judged. The apparent contradiction is resolved by an important corollary of utilitarian theory: namely, that the morality of an act consists not in the motive from which the act is done but in the effects, actual or intended, of the act upon society as a whole. This would appear to follow from the principles already laid down, for if the only possible motive of an action is desire for the agent's own greatest happiness there would be no way of differentiating one motive from another. The desire for one's own happiness takes various forms, however, and from repeated experiences we can discern a general tendency on the part of some motives to lead to pleasurable, others to painful consequences. Love of reputation, craving for friendship, desire to help others, and devotion to religion are among the forms of self-interest that on the whole are conducive to socially pleasurable effects, and may derivatively, therefore, be called good. Anger, jealousy, vindictiveness more frequently produce socially painful effects, and may in the same way be called bad. Many other motives, such as self-preservation, love of power, physical desire, and desire for pecuniary gain, show a more or less even balance of good and bad effects, and are for that reason to be regarded as neutral or indifferent. In any of these cases the motive is neither good nor bad in itself, but may be called one or the other depending upon the pleasurable or painful consequences it normally tends to produce. And inasmuch as such consequences are to be calculated in the mathematical manner explained in the last section, it follows that "Vice may be defined to be a miscalculation of chances, a mistake in estimating the value of pleasures and pains. It is false moral arithmetic." Virtue is correct moral arithmetic. In an illustration given by Mill, somewhat differently oriented from those of Bentham:

He who saves a fellow creature from drowning does what is morally right, whether his motive be duty, or the hope of being paid for his trouble; he who betrays the friend that trusts him is guilty of a crime, even if his object be to serve another friend to whom he is under greater obligations.[1]

As Bentham would have interpreted this situation, the betrayer added up only the pleasures of the friend whom he served; his moral arithmetic was falsified and his action made vicious by his failing to take into account and subtract the greater amount of pain caused to the other friend whom he betrayed.

It is not, however, in every case by actual but often by intended effects that the morality of an action is to be judged. If one were to dive into the water intending to save a fellow-creature but were prevented by the current or some other hindrance from doing so, his action would still be praiseworthy, for his intention, i.e., his specifically purposed act, was such that, had it succeeded, it would have increased the totality of human happiness more than any alternative action which at that moment lay within the agent's power. Similarly, a man who intends to betray a friend but is prevented by circumstances from doing so is as guilty and as blamable as if he had succeeded. The important distinction for Bentham, therefore, comes to be not motive vs. action so much as motive vs. intention. In lending money to a friend one's intention is, let us suppose, to put the friend financially on his feet so that he can

---

[1] *Utilitarianism*, Chap. II.

pay his debts and lead a happier, more useful life. But
the motive urging the benefactor to act in this way may
be love of the friend or a wish to be praised for generosity
or a hope of future reciprocal favors. An intention, in
short, is the specific group of consequences aimed at. A
motive, on the other hand, is what prompts or determines
the will, and in the last analysis is "nothing more than
pleasure, or pain, operating in a certain manner."

As pursuit of pleasure and avoidance of pain are the only
effective springs of human action, while the specific intentions to which these give rise may differ in moral worth,
it follows that the way to improve human intentions and
hence, on the whole, human conduct is to arrange so far
as possible that each individual shall receive a greater
amount of happiness from good conduct than from bad.
Arrangements of this kind, whether they exist by nature or as artifices contrived by men, Bentham calls
sanctions.

The sanctions, or systems of pains and pleasures that
give a binding force to any law or rule of conduct, are four.
First there is the *physical* sanction, consisting in the pains
and pleasures that come to us in the ordinary course of
nature without human intervention. Temperance in
eating and drinking, for example, by conserving health
produces pleasure, intemperance by bringing on sickness
or disease produces pain. The relation of this to the
social ideal is clear from the consideration that too much
riotous living on the part of individuals is hardly conducive
to the promotion of universal happiness. Secondly, there
is the *political* sanction, issuing from the laws of the land
together with the threatened penalties for breaking them.
Thirdly, the '*moral*' sanction, which is also called more
accurately the popular sanction: pressure of public opinion,
which furnishes pleasures and pains to a man by bestowing

confidence and honors on him or by punishing him with suspicion and ill-will. Finally, there is the *religious* sanction, the pleasures and pains administered by conscience and, for those who believe in them, the rewards and punishments of the hereafter. All these sanctions tend to promote a closer correspondence between the effects of a man's conduct on society and the effects accruing to himself. If the correspondence were complete there would be no moral problem; but it is not, and the purpose of law, as Benthan interprets it, is to put teeth into the political sanction, so that by legally administering pains to wrongdoers the government will produce in them a degree of unhappiness proportionate to that which their conduct has caused to others.

Mill's heresy

John Stuart Mill, who first coined the word 'utilitarianism' for what Bentham had been content to speak of as 'the theory of utility,' also introduced into the theory a radical and logically subversive modification. Bentham's formulation of the theory had aroused vigorous hostility. Some of the hostility was doubtless such as will always be directed against any social reformer by those who have selfish reasons for keeping the existing institutions unchanged. But there were widespread objections of a more disinterested sort also. To suppose that life had no nobler end than the pursuit of pleasure seemed to many persons a doctrine utterly mean and groveling, worthy only of swine. Carlyle referred to the doctrine as a pig-philosophy. Bentham having by this time died, it was Mill who replied to such critics, charging them with misrepresentation of the utilitarian philosophy, "since the accusation supposes human beings to be capable of no pleasures except those of which swine are capable."

But since it is the case that "human beings have faculties *more elevated* than the animal appetites,"[1] they are capable, as a consequence, of enjoying and pursuing nobler *kinds* of pleasure. The pleasures of the intellect, of feelings refined by the play of imagination, of the exercise of moral impulses have "a much higher value as pleasures" than those of mere sensation. And Mill adds that "it is quite compatible with the principle of utility to recognize the fact, that some *kinds* of pleasure are more desirable and more valuable than others."

It is, of course, nothing of the sort. One has only to read the key-passages in Bentham's writings to realize that distinctions of quality are quite irrelevant to his theory except so far as they might turn out to be indications of differences of quantity. The passages already quoted from Bentham make it clear that *amounts* of pleasure and pain afford the sole criterion. Where the quantity of two pleasures is the same their qualitative differences have no moral significance. Mill argues: "It would be absurd that while, in estimating all other things, quality is considered as well as quantity, the estimation of pleasures should be supposed to depend on quantity alone." Well, no doubt it is absurd, but Bentham committed the absurdity. Mill has simply altered the fundamental principle of Bentham's ethics and has failed, owing to his admiration for Bentham, to realize the gravity of what he has done. The significance of the modification is apparent when it is recalled that Bentham had treated all reasoning about morals as 'moral arithmetic,' all estimation of values as simple measurement. Mill is in the paradoxical situation of one who, having stated a distance in miles, remarks as an afterthought that of course not all of the miles are of equal length.

[1]*Utilitarianism*, Chap. II.   Italics added.

The standard of quality

But perhaps it is better to overlook Mill's ill-advised attempt to make his own theory appear consistent with Bentham's and to consider instead a problem to which Mill's version of utilitarianism gives rise. What is to be the test of quality? Quantities can be measured, they have objective relations of less and greater, but a quality is something absolute. A red color is not less or more of anything than a chord in G-minor or than the taste of caviar or the smell of lilacs. Each simply *is*. So of pleasures, once these are admitted to have differences not exhaustively expressed by any quantitative comparisons: how to decide the superior moral value of one to another? "There is but one possible answer," replies Mill; and he gives it:

Of two pleasures, if there be one to which all or almost all who have experience of both give a decided preference, irrespective of any feeling of moral obligation to prefer it, that is the more desirable pleasure. If one of the two is, by those who are competently acquainted with both, placed so far above the other that they prefer it, even though knowing it to be attended with a greater amount of discontent, and would not resign it for any quantity of the other pleasure which their nature is capable of, we are justified in ascribing to the preferred enjoyment a superiority in quality, so far outweighing quantity as to render it, in comparison, of small account.

Now it is an unquestionable fact that those who are equally acquainted with, and equally capable of appreciating and enjoying, both, do give a most marked preference to the manner of existence which employs their higher faculties. Few human creatures would consent to be changed into any of the lower animals, for a promise of the fullest allowance of a beast's pleasures; no intelligent human being would consent to be a fool, no instructed person would be an ignoramus, no person of feeling and conscience would be selfish and base, even though they should be persuaded that the fool, the dunce, or the rascal is better satisfied with his lot than they are with theirs. . . . A being of higher faculties requires more to make him happy, is capable probably of more acute suffering, and certainly accessible to it at more points, than one of an inferior type; but in spite of these liabilities, he can never really wish to sink into what he feels to be a lower grade of existence.[1]

Two questions are suggested by this important declaration of Mill's: Is it consistent with the 'theory of utility' as stated by Bentham, and if not, which of the two theories comes closer to truth? The first question must be answered negatively by any competent reader who compares Mill's words with Bentham's. When Bentham reduces morality to 'arithmetic' and declares that where equal amounts of pleasure are involved "push-pin [a trifling, popular game of the period] is as good as poetry," he leaves no room for doubt that he would reject everything that Mill has to say about 'higher faculties' and 'more elevated pleasures.' This brings us to the second question: Which of the two utilitarian doctrines is the truer? To most reflective persons Mill's doctrine probably seems the more adequate description of their own feelings. Some may hesitate to confess this, however, on either of two grounds. In periods of black depression, or in moments of whimsy, they may have felt that they would gladly exchange their lot for that of a beast. In the case of nearly all persons, however, states of feeling such as these are transitory and irresponsible, and it is only from the more enduring states of feeling that valid theories of ethics can be built. It is possible also to take issue with Mill on a more theoretic level, particularly when he says: "It is better to be a human being dissatisfied than a pig satisfied; better to be Socrates dissatisfied than a fool satisfied. And if the

---

[1]*Op. cit.*, Chap. II.

fool, or the pig, are of a different opinion, it is because they only know their own side of the question. The other party to the comparison knows both sides." It is the last statement of this quotation that critics, even though they were to accept the normative judgment with which the quotation begins, might challenge. Is not the wise man (suppose them to ask), by the very fact of his wisdom, by reason of the special interests which his superiority gives him, incapable of knowing what it is like to be a fool? Can the temperate man fairly estimate the pleasures enjoyed by a libertine, or the courageous man understand cowardice? Can a man have any inkling (if fables are ruled out) of what it is like to be a pig? Or again, will there be any unanimity of opinion as to which of the two pleasures is superior, on the part of persons who have experienced both? The most competent and sensitive critics frequently disagree as to the merits of a painting or a poem. Would not competent judges of pleasure (supposing there to be any such) disagree in a similar fashion?

To these objections the reply must be that while no judges are omniscient and no agreement even among the most competent judges can be complete, there is nevertheless such a thing as *relative* competency of judgment. Man's knowledge of what it is like to be a pig is partial and uncertain; not wholly non-existent, however, for the tendency to eat gluttonously and wallow in dirt is not entirely absent from man's make-up. The pig, on the other hand, has no knowledge at all of the human condition. Similarly, the truly wise man (not the pedant), the truly temperate man (not the ascetic), and the truly courageous man (not the reckless swaggerer) have some understanding of unwisdom, unrestraint, and cowardice, for the germs of these are in their natures, latent but controlled.[1]   And while we would not all agree on the examples to be chosen it seems reasonable to assert that some persons have had wider experience and are therefore more competent than others to choose wisely between alternative pleasures.   This does not mean that all those with wider experience will come to identical conclusions. Quite the contrary: in ethics we must not expect agreement at every point.   Nevertheless, it may well be the case (although not the 'unquestionable fact' that Mill affirms it) that men of wider experience tend *in general* to prefer a "manner of existence which employs their higher faculties."   Mill's qualitative distinction could on that basis be retained and applied, but only at the cost of abandoning Bentham's ideal of a fool-proof ethics based on 'moral arithmetic.'

3.   CRITICAL ANALYSIS OF HEDONISM

If the alleged 'proof' of hedonism were valid, there would be evidently no use in pursuing ethical inquiries further.   If the hedonistic ideal were the only one possible to espouse honestly, if it were the ideal by which everyone's actions were invariably guided, then all other theories could be dismissed as fantasies, worthless for the student of ethics and of interest only to the abnormal psychologist, who might care to inquire how it was that reasonable men ever came to accept theories so palpably false.   In matters pertaining to values, however, 'proofs' are always more or less fallacious and never coercive.   The nature of dialectical reasoning, as expounded in the preceding chapter, guarantees this, for whenever a value is asserted there is the dialectical possibility of challenging it, of proposing some other and perhaps more inclusive value in its stead. With this general principle as a guide we may examine the

[1]For Socrates' discussion on this point, see Chapter VIII, Section 1.

logic by which hedonism is said to be proved. The supposed proof of hedonism may be put in the form of a
hypothetical syllogism: "If psychological hedonism is
true, then ethical hedonism is true; psychological hedonism
is true; therefore so is ethical hedonism." This syllogism
is logically valid. If both premises are true the conclusion
must be true; so that if we wish to challenge the truth of
the conclusion we must be able to challenge the truth of at
least one premise. Actually it will be found that both
premises are open to serious objection. We shall consider, therefore, in turn the logical objections (1) to the
assertion that psychological hedonism is true and (2) to
the inference from psychological to ethical hedonism.

Fallacies of hedonistic logic

(i) *Fallacy of psychological hedonism.* The assertion,
"Everyone aims to act always in such a way as to secure
for himself the most pleasure and least pain" is formally
a descriptive proposition. It asserts no value, it purports
to be a description of fact, a statement of what is actually
the case. Now a genuine statement of fact is always an
empirical generalization, and the truth of an empirical
generalization is never certain but at best probable. The
belief that ice if put on a hot stove will melt is a generalization so well established by our past experience not only
of stoves and of ice but of the general properties of heat
and of solid substances, that to doubt its truth would be a
waste of time. Yet its truth, while of indefinitely great
probability, is not certain. We can form a clear notion of
ice remaining on a hot stove in a frozen state; there is no
logical incompatibility in such a notion. If an occurrence
of that kind were to surprise us by happening we would
be able to recognize it as happening and to report one
exception to the general rule, provided we had distinct

ideas of ice, of a hot stove, and of the process of melting. It is precisely this condition that is lacking in the doctrine of psychological hedonism. The meaning of 'any moti-vated human action' and the meaning of 'motivated by a desire for pleasure' are confused, not distinct. Their confusion can be demonstrated as follows. When the hedonist says that men aim always at their greatest pleas-ure, he does not mean that they will probably do so, but that they certainly must. Show him an exception—a martyr, let's say, who undergoes tortures and death volun-tarily in defense of an ideal—and he is *prevented by his logic* from recognizing it as an exception. He will explain to you that the martyr chose torture and death because of a belief that to live and endure the self-reproach of having been cowardly would be to him a greater torment than being burnt at the stake or boiled in oil. The martyr's acceptance of a horrible death and the cultured agnostic's preference for a life of ease and refinement, a mother's sacrifices and a libertine's lusts are all explained as aspects of the same desire—to get pleasure and escape pain. Every suggested exception to the rule is reinterpreted by the hedonist as an instance of the rule. Since the rule, therefore, admits no distinction between the type of in-stances that would support it and the type of instances that would challenge it, it is evidently not an empirical generalization. Every statement of fact, however, is an empirical generalization; it follows, then, that the formula of psychological hedonism, "Everyone aims always to secure his own greatest happiness," is not a statement of fact. It gives us, therefore, no information about anything, and we are none the wiser for having learned it. The only reason it ever seems to give information is our proneness to interpret it in our own way—allowing it to mean, for instance, that a great many people spend the greater part of their time looking for rather paltry kinds of happiness. But in giving the principle this more specific interpretation we transform its nature: it does now convey a fact but its truth can no longer be asserted universally; we can say only, "Such is generally the case."

(*ii*) *Fallacy of the inference to ethical hedonism.* The foregoing criticism of hedonistic theory has been directed against the hedonist's minor premise which asserts that psychological hedonism is true. The theory can also be attacked in its major premise, by demonstrating that even if psychological hedonism were true, ethical hedonism would not follow from it. The present analysis may be compared with the analysis in Chapter II of the 'factualist' fallacy, of which the 'proof' of hedonism is a prominent example.

The hedonist starts with the premise, as we have seen, that each person *does* seek his own greatest happiness, and draws the conclusion that he *ought* to do so. The validity of this inference depends on the assumption of an unexpressed major premise that "Whatever human motives do exist are human motives that ought to exist." If the hedonist denies this assumption his inference has no coercive validity. If he accepts it he thereby relinquishes the logical right to criticize human motives: motives are just what they ought to be, and the word 'ought' becomes superfluous. Or, to put the difficulty in another way: If the propositions "Desire for happiness is the motivating force for all human actions" and "Desire for happiness is the motivating force for all *good* (worthy, moral) human actions" are both universally and necessarily true, then 'human actions' and 'good human actions' become logically equivalent, and the word 'good' in the second proposition reduces to a logical zero; that is, 'good' as applied to human actions becomes logically meaningless. Yet hedonists continue to use the word 'good'; they build systems of moral philosophy, designating some actions 'good,' or 'better' than other actions; and declaring that certain types of action 'ought,' or 'ought not,' to be performed. How can this declaration be made reasonably, when by the hedonist's own postulate the only actions that ought to be performed are those that are going to be performed inevitably?

(*iii*) *Fallacy of any attempt to prove ethical hedonism.* In more general terms it may be said that any attempt to prove ethical hedonism is based on a logical identification of pleasure with the good; or as Callicles in Plato's *Gorgias* finally declares, the pleasant and the good are unconditionally one and the same.[1] A general disproof of this logical identification might be stated as follows. A pleasure is a transitory event in an individual's career. Its duration may be shorter or longer, continuous or intermittent, but judged purely as a pleasure it can never continue uninterrupted for a very long time. Even the intellectual and aesthetic pleasures cannot last continuously for more than a few hours at most; for the majority of persons their time-span is much shorter. But a moral quality, considered as such, is never a mere transitory event. The moral character that an act possesses consists in the intelligible relations that the act bears: (1) to the organization of qualities that make up the agent's character, and (2) to the chain of events that the act sets in motion. Among these resultant events there will be various pains and pleasures, affecting both the agent and other persons; the number and character and distribution of such pains and pleasures will be important factors in estimating the

---

[1] *Gorgias*, 495 A-B. A part of Socrates' reply is quoted in Question 5 of the Appendix to this chapter.

moral goodness of the act. But the pleasures themselves, being temporally separate units, are not logically identical with the morality of the act.

(*iv*) *Fallacy of the quantification of pleasures.* Another type of objection to the logic of hedonism has already been hinted at in the discussion of Mill's admission of qualitative distinctions among pleasures. Mill did not explicitly take issue with Bentham, but his divergence on this point shows how unworkable he felt a strictly quantitative standard to be. Measurement requires that the thing to be measured should be capable of analysis into undifferentiated units. Space can be measured because we can employ standard lengths marked off on a ruler or other instrument. Time is measurable only in terms of space:[1] a day, however long it may seem, is *defined* as being no longer or shorter than it takes the sun to return to that position (relatively to the earth) from which it started. Whenever things are measured, then, it is always by referring them to some kind of spatial relation. How is such a reference possible in the case of pleasures? Of Bentham's seven criteria for measuring pleasures and pains only two, social extent and duration, fulfill the requirement of spatial translatability. It is logically possible to give a mathematical statement of the number of persons affected by an action, for each person is a unit, separated in space from each other person. Duration also (except for practical difficulties) can be measured, for the spatial position of the hands of a clock can be noted as the pleasure begins and again as it ends. But there is obviously no way to measure, for example, intensity. Physiological psychologists do, to be sure, measure such physical phenomena as neural stimulation and blood-pressure, and take

[1]For a brilliant demonstration of this proposition see Bergson, *Time and Free Will.*

for granted that these are indications of the intensity of the pleasure that is felt. There is undoubtedly *some* relation between measurable phenomena such as neural reactions and blood-pressure on the one hand and feelings of pleasure and pain on the other. But it is logically impossible to state that the relation between them is one of strict mathematical correspondence, for such a correspondence would be possible only if the feelings themselves (as distinct from their bodily manifestations) were measurable; and this is plainly not the case. We may on a particular occasion *prefer* reading a book to taking a walk: the former, then, we say, would give us (on this occasion) the greater pleasure. But is there any conceivable sense in which we could say that the intensity of the pleasure to be got from reading is twice rather than three times or one and a half times, the intensity of the pleasure to be got from walking? Would we not, by trying to make our comparison of intensities mathematically exact, reduce it to meaninglessness?

(*v*) *The contradiction in utilitarianism.* We have already seen that the egoistic hedonist, if he starts from the premise of hedonistic psychology that each person seeks always his own greatest happiness, ought in strict logic to acknowledge that his ethical conclusion, Everyone ought to do so, is superfluous. An analogous but distinct criticism may be made of the utilitarian logic. If the postulate of hedonistic psychology is true, as Bentham declares it to be, then the utilitarian ideal that each person ought to seek the greatest happiness of the greatest number is not superfluous but, on the contrary, inadmissible. If I always *must* seek my own happiness, in what sense do I have a moral obligation to seek the happiness of others? Sometimes my happiness and theirs will not conflict, but there is a constant danger that they will do so, and in such cases

Bentham leaves no doubt as to what is predetermined to happen: "Dream not that men will move their little finger to serve you unless their advantage in so doing be obvious to them." And yet they *ought* to move their little finger and a great deal more, if the criterion of *social extent* in Bentham's 'hedonistic calculus' means anything. From this aspect of Bentham's theory it follows that even though by the performance of an act that lay within my power I would myself be affected painfully, yet if a 'hedonistic calculus' showed that the social benefits of the act (the pleasures, or loss of pains, to all other individuals that it might affect) exceeded the detriment (pain, or loss of pleasure) to myself, the performance of the act would become my duty, a moral obligation. How is this to be reconciled with Bentham's logical reduction of 'moral obligation' to the simple *matter of fact* that "in the event of his failing to conduct himself in that manner, pain, or loss of pleasure, is considered as about to be experienced by him"? It cannot be so, except by dodging the moral issue that arises when the pain and loss of pleasure, such as an unquiet conscience and social blame that come from neglecting an obligation, are considered to be less than the pain and loss of pleasure that would be entailed by fulfilling it. The question (if formulated in hedonistic terms at all), in cases like these, often becomes: more pleasure for them and less for me, or less for them and more for me? By Bentham's ethical principle the choice ought always to be impersonal: which alternative will produce the greatest amount of pleasure and least pain for the greatest number of individuals?—regardless of whether I am among those benefited or not. But an impersonal choice would mean in some cases that I must voluntarily accept for myself a deficiency of pleasure or an excess of pain. How would this be possible if I were so constituted as always to seek pleasure and avoid pain so far as might lie within my power?

Bentham never answers this question as a logician but always as a social reformer. His proposal, as we have seen, is to pass legislation whereby it would be made to a person's advantage to perform beneficent acts. Such legislation, then, he appears to mean, *ought* to be established. But this only pushes the problem a step farther back. Even if such a redirection of social relations were practicable, wherein would lie the obligation on the part of those who make the laws to strive after such an end? How could there be such an obligation, on Bentham's premises, unless the effort of striving after such reforms were compensated by private advantages to the legislator? And, as for the rest of us, since there are not at present laws capable of insuring a correspondence between public and private happiness, is our duty to work for the good of the greatest number thereby abrogated? According to the logic of Bentham's position we should have to say yes, but his own actions, as a vigorously unselfish reformer tirelessly championing the oppressed, furnish perhaps the best rebuttal to this judgment.

The value of the hedonistic ideal

The foregoing analysis has not been intended to destroy the value of hedonism as an ethical theory. Its purpose was to confute the alleged proofs of hedonism by exposing the fallacious logic on which they rest. Neither hedonism nor any other ethical ideal can be proved. If the hedonistic ideal is accepted it must be accepted freely, on the agent's own moral responsibility and as an expression of his voluntary allegiance. When this characteristic of the hedonistic, as of every other moral ideal, has been admitted, we are in a position to evaluate hedonism on its merits. But it must be remembered that an intelligible evaluation is possible only if we know pretty specifically what we mean when we talk of pleasure or enjoyment: that is, only if we mean some one type of human motive as distinguished from other types. Such specificity, as the preceding argument was intended to demonstrate, is absolutely essential if the normative judgment, "We ought to strive to make our lives more enjoyable," is to have any meaning.

Recognizing this logical requirement we may enumerate certain constituents of an enjoyable life which would be generally agreed on. Good physical and mental health, adequate wealth, pleasant physical surroundings, interesting work, a responsible position in society, agreeable and stimulating friends, a lack of malicious enemies, a properly adjusted sex life, nourishing and tasty food, frequent periods for play, ample opportunities for developing a taste for literature, music, painting, and the other aspects of our cultural heritage—these, if not all, are at least the main part of what would usually be recognized as a happy life. Nearly everyone would recognize such a life to be a good, and if it could be attained by everyone, as a dominant good. But alas, as things now are, its attainment is possible only to a fortunate few. That being the case, which way ought we to direct our efforts—each of us towards securing so felicitous a life for himself (egoistic hedonism) or toward correcting the social maladjustments that prevent its attainment by the many (utilitarianism)? Or is it better to strike some compromise between the two ends? Or is the Stoic's solution finally best—to regard pleasures, since they merely *happen* to us, as a matter of indifference to the wise man; and to make self-discipline, since that alone lies within our power, the dominant, or even the sole intrinsic good? The claims of the alternative ideals of conduct will be considered in forthcoming chapters; as to hedonism it may be said that when the ideal is held by someone whose intelligence protects him from too gross and whose kindliness from too mean an interpretation of its significance, it can be a useful guide to one sort of admirable life.

We are but beasts that perish, therefore—shall we, therefore, enjoy the life of the beast? By no means. Therefore, rather, let us rescue from life what possibilities of sweetness and humanity it may have while yet there is time. Epicurean morality, in other words, though confronted with the fact that man is a perishing animal, is based, like every other morality, upon the idea that man is an intelligent animal. Its question then is, What is the best life for an intelligent being? The Stoics replied to this question by an attempt to invest life with dignity and greatness. The Epicurean doubted the possibility. But he still hoped to make life genial and humane. And this was his conception of the enjoyment of life.[1]

Still, the dangers of the hedonistic, even of the cultivated Epicurean ideal must not pass unnoticed. When the Roman emperor Galba was preparing to abdicate in favor of Licinianus Piso (who, however, was murdered before he could receive the throne) Tacitus reports him as having counselled Piso with these words: "Thus far you have known only adversity; prosperity tests the spirit with sharper goads. For we endure misfortune; but we are corrupted by success." Galba had good reason to issue the warning: his predecessor had been the infamous Nero. But one need not be a Nero to be corrupted by an excess of pleasure. Corruption is various, and often undetected by its victim. We shall not necessarily turn profligate; but perhaps we shall become smug, self-satisfied, indifferent to the claims of other persons, in-

---

[1] Warner Fite, *Moral Philosophy*, pp. 207–208.

sensible to the soul's inner voices. In undergoing such alteration we do not necessarily find life more painful than before: it may, indeed, be more pleasant. For that matter it is possible that an idiot's life can show a greater balance of pleasures over pains than our own. And yet, even if that were demonstrably the case, few would voluntarily consent (if it lay within their power) to become idiots.

Are we to deny, then, the importance of pleasure in the ideal life? By no means. The man who 'renounces the pleasures of life' in order to eat locusts in the wilderness or to spend seven years writing a book undoubtedly finds some kind of perverse pleasure in doing so. This logical ambiguity of pleasure has been discussed already. But the ambiguity has also a practical side. The man who 'accepts life' and the man who 'renounces life' both receive some pleasure because both are satisfying a desire. Without some desire there would be no voluntary act. But desires are of different kinds. A desire may be dictated by some original untutored impulse or by a carelessly acquired and unexamined habit; but it may equally well be the case, to quote Professor Dewey, that "this original impulse is transformed into a different desire because of objects which thought holds up to view."[1] The distinction is, incidentally, of great educational importance, for one of the educator's primary aims should be to assist in refashioning the pupil's impulses so that he may come to be less dependent on the pleasures suggested by unexamined inpulses and habits and may find increasing delight in the objects that thought and cultivated sensibilities hold up to view.

As for utilitarianism, there is a sort of rugged honesty about it that even its opponents must admire. Pleasure

---

[1] Dewey and Tufts, *Ethics*, revised edition, p. 201.

may not be the highest goal at which an individual may aim when the pleasure in prospect concerns only himself. But as a test of social justice a more or less equitable distribution of pleasures and pains among all members of a society has somewhat more to be said for it. An individual may voluntarily accept an ascetic way of life for himself: that is his own affair. But to impose avoidable privations on others, even on the alleged ground that it is good for their souls or their character or what not, is in most cases (apart from the restraints imposed by elders on children) downright immoral.

But there remains a defect in utilitarianism even from the social point of view. Its humanitarian ideal is static. Under the Roman Empire one phase of the utilitarian principle was put into execution, though in a more brutally irrational way than any of the utilitarian philosophers intended. The *plebs* were given bread and circuses to keep them alive and amused, but they had no active employment. While a society in which a large number of citizens are supported as passive consumers is undoubtedly more just than a society in which an equal number are allowed to starve, the ideal society would seem to be one in which its citizens not only received food and entertainment but were permitted and encouraged to serve useful functions too; in which they were not only stuffed with pleasures and shielded from pains but were given a chance to exercise and develop their several abilities. An acceptable moral ideal, whether for society or for the individual, must have a to some extent dynamic character. The next chapter will describe certain proposed forms of a more dynamic ideal.

CHAPTER IV

NATURALISM

Men know not how to be splendidly wicked nor wholly good, and shrink in consequence from such crimes as are stamped with an inherent greatness or disclose a nobility of nature.

Machiavelli, *Discourses*

CALLICLES, the cynical aristocrat in Plato's *Gorgias*, whom we have already met in Chapter III in another connection, is again speaking:

By convention it is called unjust and disgraceful to get some advantage over the majority, and this is what they say is sinful; but nature herself, I believe, declares that it is right for the superior man to get an advantage over the inferior, and the more capable man over the less capable. The truth of this is evident in a variety of ways, both among animals and among men taken collectively in cities and by races—that right is judged to be the rule and advantage of the mightier over the feebler. What other form of right did Xerxes appeal to when he marched against Greece, or his father when he marched against Scythia? One could mention thousands of such cases. It is by following the principle of natural justice, I believe, that they act in this way. We might even call it nature's own law that they follow, though they act at variance with the laws established by ourselves. For we take the best and most vigorous of our number, and while still in their infancy, like lion cubs, we set about training them, and we subjugate them by our magical spells, teaching them to be content with an equal share of things, on the ground that this is fair and right. But if some man were to arise with enough natural power in him, I imagine he would shake off all these teachings and burst his bonds and break free, trampling down our ordinances and tricks, our incantations and our laws, all of which are against nature. Our slave revolts, shows himself master, and in that act there shines forth natural justice.[1]

1. THE LOGIC OF NATURALISM

The word 'naturalism' suffers from a great deal of ambiguity in philosophical discussions.   Generally speaking, it is applied to any theory, ethical or metaphysical, in which the facts of the world of nature are appealed to as supporting the theory in question.   But the word 'nature' itself is not univocal.   It is to Nature that Callicles appeals in justifying ruthless domination by the mightier; and for Callicles the final good of such domination lay, as we saw in Chapter III, in enjoying the greatest possible influx of pleasure.   The Stoics too recommend a life according to Nature, but as Nature according to their metaphysic is a rational whole, their precept comes to mean living a life completely rational and impersonal. In the eighteenth century, Alexander Pope's "First follow nature!" was used as an argument in favor of classical verse-forms and a more civilized way of living, while Rousseau's similar appeal a generation later was an argument for renouncing civilization and emulating the condition of primitive man.   In present-day discussions Nature is appealed to with equal readiness in support of such diverse ideals as capitalism and anarchism, militarism and nudist cults.

All appeals to Nature, however the word may be interpreted, are based upon the same implicit syllogism. The major premise is the normative proposition, "Whatever is natural, and only what is natural, is right (or good, or worthy)."   The minor premise has the appearance of

---

[1]Plato, *Gorgias*, 483 C–484 A. I have translated τὸ δίκαιον 'right' and 'justice,' according as the primary emphasis of the word seemed to be adjectival or substantive.

being a statement of fact: "*a, b, c* . . . are natural, and actions or states of affairs having a character contrary to *a, b, c* are not." The conclusion is evident: "*a, b, c* . . . must therefore be the dominant goods, or, if actions, right." The syllogism is formally valid.

But is the minor premise as truly a statement of fact as it seems? If the word 'natural' in that premise has a workably specific meaning then in many of its usual applications the premise must be false. How could the greatest possible influx of pleasure, recommended by Callicles, and the rational control of all impulses, recommended by the Stoics, both be natural *in the sense of* both being the proper goal of man? As specific human goals they are mutual contraries. Yet there is another sense, certainly, in which both the practical hedonist and the ascetic are following nature in pursuing their contrary aims. Each is carrying out some actually existing impulse. No voluntary action—that is, no action that falls within the province of ethics—is ever performed without a genuine impulse behind it, so that in this very general sense and *only in this sense* every human act is indubitably natural. It is presumably, therefore, this latter and more general meaning of the word that is connoted in any categorical and unsupported statement as to the 'naturalness' of luxurious or of simple living, of a utopian society or of a society based on exploitation and greed. Suppose, however, that this undifferentiated meaning of 'nature' and 'natural' is introduced into the major premise—as, of course, it now must be if the syllogism is to have validity. The major premise becomes ethically meaningless. It asserts that whatever situations do at any time exist are good, and whatever actions are at any time performed are right. Whatever is, is good; whatever is done, is right. Such a view has actually been held by certain philosophers and is logically possible as a theory of metaphysics, but it is inadmissible as a premise for any theory of ethics. As Mr. G. E. Moore observes: "If everything natural is equally good, then certainly Ethics, as it is ordinarily understood, disappears: for nothing is more certain, from an ethical point of view, than that some things are bad and others good."[1] The *a priori* proof of ethical naturalism, then, is vitiated by a fallacy of ambiguity.

As brutes act agreeably to their nature, in following that principle or particular instinct which for the present is strongest in them: does not man likewise act agreeably to his nature, or obey the law of creation, by following that principle, be it passion or conscience, which for the present happens to be strongest in him? . . . Let every one then quietly follow his nature; as passion, reflection, appetite, the several parts of it, happen to be strongest: but let not the man of virtue take upon him to blame the ambitious, the covetous, the dissolute; since these equally with him obey and follow their nature. . . .
Now all this licentious talk entirely goes upon a supposition, that men follow their nature in the same sense, in violating the known rules of justice and honesty for the sake of a present gratification, as they do in following those rules when they have no temptation to the contrary. . . . If by following nature were meant only acting as we please, it would indeed be ridiculous to speak of nature as any guide in morals: nay, the very mention of deviating from nature would be absurd; and the mention of following it, when spoken by way of distinction, would absolutely have no meaning. For did ever any one act otherwise than as he pleased?[2]

Theories, however, have always more specificity of meaning than the premises on which they seem or pretend

---

[1] *Principia Ethica*, p. 42. (By permission of The Macmillan Company, publishers.) See Chapter 1, Section 2, above.
[2] Bishop Butler (1692–1752), Sermon II. Important excerpts from this and other of Butler's sermons are available in Selby-Bigge, *British Moralists*, Vol. I.

logically to rest. The full meaning of a theory must be
sought not only in its logic but in its applications. We
may therefore turn our attention to several distinct types
of naturalistic ethics, in which the 'nature' appealed to is
interpreted in specific ways more or less determined by the
particular set of ideals upheld in each case.

2.   "Might Is Right"

To act rightly, said Thrasymachus in Plato's *Republic*,
is to act in the interest of those who are more powerful
than yourself—in other words, to act as you are compelled
to act.   Those who act in this way are fools and wretched
weaklings, he added; the superior man will act as he
pleases, but he will see to it that others, whom he domi-
nates, follow the standards of right action which he and
those like him have established as best serving their own
interests.   Since the nature of right is thus determined by
the interests of those who happen at any time to be in
power it follows that the old adage, "Might is right," may
be regarded as a statement that the only sanction for any
moral principle is its survival-value—*i.e.*, whether or not
its sponsors have sufficient power to enforce it and to
vanquish competing ideals.   As a corollary it would
follow that ideals are 'right' for only so long as their
sponsors have and continue to exercise power, and that
when the sponsors are vanquished the rightness of the
ideals is destroyed and the rightness of other ideals, upheld
by new groups coming into power, is established.

There are many evidences making this view plausible.
It is by now widely accepted that the ideals of the American colonists in seceding from Great Britain were right,
those of the South in later trying to secede from the Union,
wrong.   The difference is indicated by our referring in the
one case to the Revolution, in the other to a rebellion.   Is

there any sure objective reason for this distinction other than the fact that the colonists won their fight while the Southern States lost theirs? If the Soviet government in Russia prevails and succeeds in spreading its principles, are not its ideals likely to become more widely accepted in the future as right; if it fails, as wrong? Already within Germany the Hitler government has silenced nearly all opposition. Suppose that, with still greater ruthlessness, it were to destroy every critic of the Nazi policies, so that no one was left in Germany who was not a Nazi: would not then the Nazi aims and policies, if the opinions of the outside world were disregarded, be right? And if some group of fascist nations were to vanquish the rest of the world and destroy all opposition everywhere, would not their activities be thenceforth judged right by all who survived? And if living persons at any time agree in judging a thing to be right, is there any significant sense in which it could be called wrong? Doubtless it was considerations like these that once led Former Justice Holmes to remark that Absolute Truth is a majority vote of the nation possessing the most battleships.

To the kinds of power that create standards of right and wrong must be added the tremendous though often very subtle power of propaganda. It is not certain that the pen is always mightier than the sword, but nowadays, when a majority of people in the Western nations are literate and can be influenced by the written word, it is generally acknowledged that the power of governments over their subjects and of armies against a foe is in either case made more secure if the citizens or the soldiers are emotionally persuaded of the rightness of obeying the laws or of following commands.

How does propaganda work? Sometimes, but not usually, by inventing lies. An invented lie runs the danger

of detection and so of proving a boomerang. More often
it is sufficient to suppress certain pieces of news that might
produce widespread opinions and actions of an undesired
sort; or, perhaps more often still, to re-emphasize the news
and suggest, without necessarily stating, certain false
implications to be derived from it. Since most of the
situations that we call 'the news' or 'current events' are
important not primarily as events which simply happen
but as indications of social tendencies, such 'coloring' of
the news may stay within the limits of verbal veracity and
yet falsify in essential ways 'the whole picture.' Furthermore, propaganda is not limited to a falsification of facts;
it may also serve to propagate sets of values. Consider
the devices employed by advertisers to broadcast such
ideals as clean teeth, pure breath, and a schoolgirl com-
plexion; of banks to encourage thrift, and of manufacturers
to encourage buying. National politics offer analogous
and more alarming examples. The owner of a newspaper
syndicate can frequently influence legislation and sometimes decide the issue of war or peace through his power
to control public sentiment. Conversely, a political or
economic group that cannot afford to control an important
section of the press or to buy time on the radio must fail
to get a wide hearing; its doctrines, therefore, have a
diminished survival value and little chance of ever becoming generally accepted as true. Do not these and countless similar examples show that standards of right and
wrong are dependent on the power of the groups whose
interests they promote to validate them?

3. Evolutionary Ethics

Naturalistic ethics was given a new impetus in the latter
part of the nineteenth century by the work of Charles
Darwin (1809–1882). His two books, *The Origin of*

Species (1859) and *The Descent of Man* (1861) substantiated and popularized a revolutionary theory about the history of living organisms on this planet. This theory, though not directly concerned with ethics, was destined to bring about a gradual but extraordinary revolution in much of the ethical thought and discussion that followed. Some of the ethical doctrines that grew out of the Darwinian theory, however, were vitiated by a misunderstanding of exactly what that theory was or else of the deductions that could logically be drawn from it.

It is important to distinguish between two aspects of the theory of evolution, for they differ in the degree to which they can be verified by adequate evidence. The more general of Darwin's contributions, supported by an amazing and varied mass of proof, which he had been gathering through twenty laborious years, was the hypothesis that 'species' (that is, distinct forms of organic life) are mutable, and that many species which today seem widely dissimilar have descended from common ancestors. The evidence for this hypothesis is largely empirical, although, as Professor Cohen reminds us, there was also a "general *a priori* bias in favor of change as a universal trait of nature."[1] It is certainly a fact (although how much weight should be given to it remains uncertain) that the age in which Darwin lived was in a way ready for his theory. The steam-engine had arrived, things were beginning to move, and static were giving way to dynamic conceptions. Those individuals, therefore, whose minds were reflecting the more advanced thought-currents of the day were far readier than their ancestors could have been to accept impermanence as a characteristic of biological species. Nevertheless, the evidence for evolution could not have been rejected lightly by any age in which

[1] Morris R. Cohen, *Reason and Nature*, p. 283.

there was a healthy respect for the results of empirical method. The evidence from paleontology and geographical distribution, from comparative anatomy and embryology, and finally from the experiments unconsciously performed by generations of stock-breeders and gardeners converged too decisively towards a single point.

Natural selection

But there is another aspect of Darwin's theory of evolution: his answer to the inevitable question, How are the mutations in species to be explained? Darwin was a scientist, not a theologian or metaphysician; his answer, therefore, could not make use of such concepts as God, cosmic purpose, or life-force, for explanations like these are too remote from possibilities of specific verification. The clue to the mystery had to be sought in the observation and analysis of the mutations themselves. But how to go about it? The mutations that had marked the descent of man were over and done with, millions of years in the past; and even though in some species there might be natural mutations still occurring, their completion would be in any case a matter not of weeks or years but of centuries, so that no one could hope within his lifetime to observe a natural mutation directly. However, in the artificial mutations brought about by the breeders and gardeners of domesticated animals and plants direct observation was possible. "The keystone of man's success in making useful races of animals and plants," Darwin discovered, was *selection*—selection and propagation by the breeder or the gardener of those specimens whose characteristics he wished to perpetuate and develop. But how could this principle of selection, which as carried out by stock-breeders and gardeners is purposeful, be applied to nature, where the postulates of the modern scientist do not allow telic explanations? After some years' pondering on this question Darwin stumbled on a possible solution by reading Malthus' famous doctrine, in his essay on Population, that population tends to increase in geometrical, the food supply only in arithmetical, ratio. The result would be a more or less constant diminution of the potential food supply relatively to the potential number of animals dependent on it. Darwin saw at once the relevance of this doctrine to his own problem:

> Being well prepared to appreciate the struggle for existence which everywhere goes on from long continued observation of the habits of animals and plants, it at once struck me that under these circumstances favorable variations would tend to be preserved, and unfavorable ones to be destroyed. The result of this would be the formation of new species. Here then I had a theory by which to work.[1]

Starting with this hint, Darwin elaborated his theory of how mutations come about. The process whereby "favorable variations would tend to be preserved and unfavorable ones to be destroyed" became known as natural selection, and the factors at work in it Darwin found to be four: (1) *variation* among the individuals of a species, (2) *the struggle for existence* based on intense competition between members of a species, and between allied species, to get food and escape predatory enemies and diseases, (3) *the survival of the fittest*,[2] or the tendency of the more vigorous and better adapted animals to survive in the struggle until they have reached at least the age of reproduction, and (4) *heredity*, or the tendency of the surviving variations to be passed on to the next generation. The continuance of this process from generation to gener-

---

[1] From a letter written in 1877, quoted by W. B. Scott, *The Theory of Evolution*.
[2] This is Herbert Spencer's phrase, not Darwin's.

ation would have a gradual cumulative effect, resulting at length in very extensive changes.

Philosophical interpretations of evolution

What significance has this biological theory for ethics? There were two ways, Professor Urban observes, in which it was expected to revolutionize ethics:

> In the first place, it was believed that evolution would be able to *explain* the origin, development, and meaning of our moral customs, sentiments, and judgments. In the second place, it was believed that ethics, as a theory of value, could for the first time be put upon a purely scientific and naturalistic basis. In other words, man's place in organic nature being determined, it would then be possible to formulate the nature of human good in organic terms, and thus to find standards for judging human behavior which are, so to speak, embedded in the nature of things.[1]

The first of these effects has been discussed in Chapter III, and the danger of overemphasizing the genetic approach to morals was there pointed out. The Darwinian theory seemed to many to provide a justification for the genetic approach. Pre-Darwinian biology from Aristotle to Lyell had been concerned almost wholly with the nature and classification—or, as Aristotle had said, the *essence*—of existing species. Darwin shifted the emphasis in biology from the question, "What is it?" to the question, "How did it originate?" In ethics, particularly in social ethics, an analogous shift of emphasis, from the *essence* of moral values to their *genesis*, seemed, by a not wholly logical analogy, to be justified. The genetic approach to ethics had been made by several important moralists before Darwin's time—notably by Hobbes, Mandeville, and Rousseau—but these earlier versions of how morality

---

[1]Wilbur M. Urban, *Fundamentals of Ethics*, p. 97. (Holt.)

originated had been somewhat fanciful and largely dictated by the ethical conclusions that the writer was striving to reach.   Now, however, it was felt that Darwin's
great discovery had provided a sound basis for the appeal
to origins, since it had for the first time produced adequate
evidence to show what these origins were.   Accordingly
the quasi-sciences of sociology and anthropology began to
be developed and to be accepted as important backgrounds
for ethics, or even, in the hands of less critical evolutionists,
as offering the materials from which the truth of moral
judgments could be objectively ascertained.

But it is the second effect of Darwin's theory, the attempt to use the theory as a basis for a purely naturalistic
science of ethics, that concerns us here.   In order to understand the exact relation between biological evolution and
evolutionary ethics we must distinguish between the
modest form of the biological theory as Darwin established
it and the vaguer, more pretentious and more popular doctrine to which it gave rise and which may be designated
evolutionism.   Darwin's theory, as we have seen, consisted
of two main propositions: the mutability of species and
the explanatory principle of natural selection.   But a
scientific theory, if it touches the popular imagination at
all, is always liable to such interpretations and extensions
of its significance as may be required to fit it into current
metaphysical conceptions.   Two such conceptions were
widespread in Darwin's day: the idea of cosmic unity and
the idea of progress.   The first of these is a particular expression of man's necessary search for an order in things:
he tends to hypostatize the search by supposing that there
must exist a final, complete, and ultimately simple order
somewhere at the heart of things.   It was no doubt to be
expected, therefore, that the theory of evolution as it
passed from the status of a tentative scientific hypothesis

to a popularly acclaimed doctrine should be interpreted in terms of the prevailing monism. Although neither Darwin nor anyone else has presented enough evidence to make such a belief even probable it became accepted by many an eager evolutionist as little short of certain that the evolutionary process is a single whole; that not only are there mutations from certain species to certain other species (a proposition for which the scientific evidence is strong) but that all the countless existing species of animal and plant life have ultimately descended from the same protoplasmic source (a proposition for which there is not at present any scientific evidence worthy of the name).

The other metaphysical conception that became joined with the Darwinian hypothesis was the idea of progress. This idea, which strikes many persons of today as extremely plausible, if not inevitable, is a product of fairly recent times. It is antagonistic to ancient Greek and mediaeval Christian thought alike, and appears to have come into prominence largely as a part of the ideology surrounding the French Revolution. By the middle of the nineteenth century, because of the rapid and concrete developments in science and industry, and because men's imaginations were becoming more and more concerned with these fields, the idea of progress had gained almost universal acceptance. The typical thinker of the period, since he came to Darwin's theory with a mind already predisposed to think in terms of progress, would see in the theory an objective confirmation of his belief in progress. Furthermore, the fact of his viewing evolution in terms of progress strengthened his tendency to regard evolution as a single continuous process, for by tracing man's origin not to his fellow-mammals but to protozoic slime, the human achievement was so much the more glorified. The glorification of the human achievement made in turn man's superiority to other organisms still more evident; hence (completing the circle) there could be no question but that the evolution of man had been a progress from a lower state to a higher—that is, that the biological evolution had also been a moral evolution.

The ethics of Herbert Spencer

The systematic application of biological evolution to the ideas and methods of ethics was principally the work of one man, Herbert Spencer (1820–1903). From one point of view, Spencer's ethics may be looked on as a logical successor to the ethics of the utilitarians, particularly of Bentham. Like Bentham, Spencer wished to discover an objective standard for determining, measuring, and thus accurately comparing, moral values. But happiness, the standard employed by the utilitarians, is a mere feeling; not capable, therefore, of being measured with any degree of objective precision. If an objective standard of moral value is wanted, it must be found not in the amounts of pain and pleasure that individuals feel but in some quantity objectively ascertainable in the external world. Feelings, from the biologist's standpoint, are of secondary significance; his first concern is with the phenomena of physical life. Here, then, Spencer decided must be the locus of moral value: not feelings, to which measurement could not be strictly applied, but life, to which, taken as a physical phenomenon, it could.

How is life to be measured? By the longevity of the greatest number? Length of life is one, but not the only factor in its measurement. There is another factor, which Spencer describes in the following illustrations. An oyster, protected by its shell and well adapted to the diffused food contained in the water which it draws in, may outlive a cuttle-fish; but in the cuttle-fish, which has

definitely superior powers of dealing with various un-
expected contingencies, "the sum of vital activities during
any given interval" is far greater than in the oyster. So
a worm, protected and nourished by the earth through
which it burrows, may have greater longevity than an
insect, but the insect "during its existence as larva and
imago, may experience a greater quantity of the changes
which constitute life." And the same is true of differences
among men: "The difference between the average lengths
of the lives of savage and civilized is no true measure of
their two lives, considered as aggregates of thought, feeling, and action." Spencer concludes that not only the
length of life but also its fullness, or what he generally
calls its *breadth*, must be taken into account in estimating
it; and that an increase of both factors is involved in the
augmentation of life that accompanies evolution of conduct. "Each further evolution of conduct widens the
aggregate of actions while conducing to elongation of it."[1]
These two biological aspects of life—longevity together
with complexity of successful adaptation to environment—
constitute, for Spencer, the Chief Good.

Two corollaries are implied in this doctrine. The first
is that "the performance of every function is, in a sense,
a moral obligation." Morality requires us not only to
refrain from activities that would be injurious to ourselves
or others; it requires us also to carry on our vital activities
so far as this can be done without injury to the vital activities of other individuals and without danger to the
continuance of our own. Restraint, if pushed beyond the
point required for the conservation of bodily resources,
is immoral.

In the second place, it must be noted that Spencer's
doctrine does not, like the doctrines of Callicles and

[1] *Data of Ethics*, Chap. II.

Thrasymachus, justify excessive selfishness. It is not the length and fullness of one's own life alone that right conduct must promote, for according to the Spencerian postulate it is not the life of any one individual that is intrinsically good, but all life. Egoism and altruism, the promotion of one's own life and the promotion of the life of others, are equally necessary, inasmuch as the maximum of life for all individuals composing a society can be achieved only by relatively unselfish coöperation; and they are equally possible, because "self-sacrifice is no less primordial than self-preservation."

All conduct, in short, is regarded as an adaptation in some way or other to the environment of the individual or of the society of which he is a member; the conduct is good or bad, praiseworthy or blameworthy, according as it represents a successful or unsuccessful adaptation; the success of an adaptation is measured by the extent to which the individual achieving it thereby augments life, whether his own or that of others,—the augmentation being measured in terms both of length and fullness.

Spencer's hedonism

Spencer's ideal is a biological one; when applied, however, to animal life in its more developed forms it has a psychological aspect too. Good actions do as a matter of fact tend to produce pleasure and bad actions pain, although it is not, as we have seen, the pleasure and pain that logically determine them as good or bad. Pleasures, generally speaking, are the mental correlatives of those actions that promote the life of the organism, while pains are the correlatives of actions of the opposite sort. This correlation is offered by Spencer not as a generalization from experience but as "an inevitable deduction from the hypothesis of Evolution." Without such a correlation it would have been impossible for the races of sentient creatures to come into existence. Spencer's proof is as follows:

If we substitute for the word Pleasure the equivalent phrase —a feeling which we seek to bring into consciousness and retain there, and if we substitute for the word Pain the equivalent phrase—a feeling which we seek to get out of consciousness and to keep out; we see at once that if the states of consciousness which a creature endeavors to maintain are the correlatives of injurious actions, and if the states of consciousness which it endeavors to expel are the correlatives of beneficial actions, it must quickly disappear through persistence in the injurious, and avoidance of the beneficial. In other words, those races of beings only can have survived in which, on the average, agreeable or desired feelings went along with activities conducive to the maintenance of life, while disagreeable and habitually avoided feelings went along with activities directly or indirectly destructive of life; and there must ever have been, other things equal, the most numerous and long-continued survivals among races in which these adjustments of feelings to actions were the best, tending ever to bring about perfect adjustment.[1]

To a considerable extent experience supports this deduction. The pains accompanying wounds, bruises, and sprains are the mental concomitants of injury to bodily welfare, and the anticipation of such pains serves as a deterrent from careless or dangerous acts. No one can deny "that the tortures of burning or scalding, and the miseries which intense cold, starvation, and thirst produce, are indissolubly connected with permanent or temporary mischiefs, tending to incapacitate one who bears them for doing things that should be done, either for his own welfare or the welfare of others." Conversely, the pleasures that accompany eating a good dinner, getting married and rearing offspring, and (the example is Spencer's)

[1]*Data of Ethics*, Chap. VI.   Reprinted from Spencer's *Principles of Psychology*.

accumulating property leave "a large balance of advantage, private and public, after making all drawbacks."

It will be objected that there are many exceptions to this rule, such as the pain of surgical operations and the pleasure of getting drunk. Spencer's reply is twofold. To the pleasures of intoxication and the unpleasantness of being operated upon must be added their after-effects. Intoxication may bring joy for the moment, but if indulged in so frequently as to impair bodily health it is certain to produce pains and wretchedness later on. In the second place, the artificial conditions under which we all live in modern civilization create some genuine exceptions to the rule. Because of "the greatness of the change from small nomadic groups to vast settled societies, and from predatory habits to peaceful habits," and more particularly because "the old life of enmity between societies has been maintained along with the new life of amity within each society," human impulses and emotions as well as the bodily constitution fail to achieve a proper adaptation. Pleasure and health, therefore, are imperfectly correlative in present-day society; their perfect correlation would be found only in a society perfectly adapted to the fulfillment of vital needs.

Applications

An ethical theory should always be tested not only by the logic on which it is based but by the deductions regarding special moral duties that can be drawn from it. When the theory of Spencer is subjected to this test it appears less radical than in its abstract formulation. Spencer was by temperament conservative. In particularizing his ideal he gave up few if any of the accepted *mores* of his time; he merely offered a novel means of justifying them. Shall I lie and steal if such a course should be necessary to pre-

serve my life or to increase the sum of my vital activities?
No, this would be serving the ideal short-sightedly.
Truth-telling and respect for property rights are conditions
of human coöperation, and without coöperation the life
of the whole community would be poorer.   Shall I indulge
in sexual promiscuity?   Again no.   I ought rather to
marry and beget offspring, for in this way I would be contributing more effectually to the survival and health of
the species.   Shall I read trashy literature?   By so doing
I am in danger of acquiring false notions of my social
environment and consequently of failing to learn the most
effective modes of adaptation to it.

For it is only by successful adaptation to environment
that life is carried on, and the whole process of evolution
can be conceived as an increasingly complex power of
adaptation.   Lower animals react directly to sensations
of sound, color, and smell; mammals, and particularly
men, have more delicately adjusted powers of choice and
avoidance.

The process of evolution is conceived, therefore, as a progress
from a partial to a complete adjustment to environment, from
a choice of the immediately beneficial and an avoidance of the
immediately injurious to a choice of the greatest benefit on the
whole, from simple to highly complex forms of desire and activity.   The highest stage of the process is shown in the development of our moral ideals; these represent the most complete and
complex adjustment between man and environment, and the
most comprehensive and accurate summation of the conditions
of preserving life.[1]

4.   The Ethics of Nietzsche

An altogether different use of the evolutionary standpoint was made by Friedrich Nietzsche (1844–1900).
Nietzsche's ethics can hardly be referred to as naturalistic

---

[1]Warner Fite, *An Introductory Study of Ethics*, p. 69.   (Longmans, Green.)

in the usual sense of the word, for his conceptions of both nature and evolution are very different from the conceptions of them so far introduced into this chapter. Nietzsche was not a scientist conscientiously following the routine of empirical verification; he was a philologist and a poet, capable of sudden dazzling insights but also of gross overstatements.

The central idea in Nietzsche's philosophy, and one that has too often been misinterpreted by hostile critics, is expressed by his phrase, *the will to power.* 'Will to power' is not merely an expression of moral egotism. Primarily it is Nietzsche's interpretation of essential reality, his statement of a fundamental principle in nature. How could any evolutionary process (Nietzsche is interested not so much in the evolution of lower animals as in the transition from savage to civilized man) take place without it? Because of the struggle for existence, say the Darwinians. No doubt; but why do we struggle? When competition gets hot, why not curl up and die? Struggle for existence becomes meaningless unless we postulate a desire for existence, an active *will* to exist, in the first place. This will to exist is at the same time a will to achieve, a will to dominate. For in order to exist man has had to become subtle and daring through long hardships and compulsion. His will to live becomes thus an unconditional will to power. He becomes a warrior, violent and ruthless, and by his warlike qualities he serves the elevation of the species.

> Careless, mocking, forceful—so does wisdom wish us: she is a woman, and never loves anyone but a warrior.[1]

When the will to power is expressed healthily and naturally it is a noble thing, worthy of our allegiance.   It

---

[1] *Thus Spake Zarathustra.*   (Modern Library translation.)

is embodied in men of the "knightly-aristocratic" type,
the leaders, the warriors, the great ones, whose life is
one of "strong, free, and joyous action." Their morality
is "based on a careful cult of the physical, on a flowering,
rich, and even effervescing healthiness that goes far beyond
what is needed for preserving life." It rejects the common
belief that actions are intrinsically right or wrong:

> To talk of intrinsic right and intrinsic wrong is absolutely
> nonsensical; intrinsically, an injury, an oppression, an exploita-
> tion, an annihilation can be nothing wrong, inasmuch as life is
> *essentially* . . . something which functions by injuring,
> oppressing, exploiting, and annihilating, and is absolutely in-
> conceivable without such a character.[1]

In the case of the multitude, however, the will to power
undergoes a distortion: it takes the form of resentment.
The aristocratic man and the resentful man thus become
the two opposing types of human nature. While the
aristocratic man lives in confidence and openness with
himself, the resentful man is incapable of candor. "His
soul squints; his mind loves hidden crannies, tortuous
paths, and back-doors." His morality is a *slave-morality*,
in every way opposed to the *master-morality* of the aristocrat:

> The revolt of the slaves in morals begins in the very principle
> of *resentment* becoming creative and giving birth to values—a
> resentment experienced by creatures who, deprived as they are
> of the proper outlet of action, are forced to find their compensa-
> tion in an imaginary revenge. While every aristocratic moral-
> ity springs from a triumphant affirmation of its own demands,
> the slave morality says 'no' from the very outset to what is
> 'outside itself,' 'different from itself,' and 'not itself': and this
> 'no' is its creative deed.[2]

---

[1]*Beyond Good and Evil.*   (Modern Library translation.)
[2]*Ibid.*

"The great man is a public misfortune," runs a Chinese proverb; and from the standpoint of the slaves, Nietzsche adds, it is true everywhere. The Chinese alone have the honesty to admit it, but other societies tacitly consent to it by arranging their institutions so that the great man "shall arise as seldom as possible and grow up under the most unfavorable conditions." The great man will appear to his inferiors as a kind of monster, for their morality condemns those who defy it—like a jealous god who will have no other gods beside him. Themselves and those who accept their code, therefore, the inferior ones call good; the rebels, those with intelligence and courage enough to trample down their conventions they call wicked (*böse*).

But the aristocratic man has only contempt for their petty morality. Morality for him is a triumphant affir= mation of his own demands. He is a creator of new values. He 'transvaluates' the old values, passing 'beyond the good and the wicked'[1] and substituting his own valuations: 'good' for the aristocratic warrior virtues, 'vile' or 'mean'[2] for the ideals of the slaves. He alone is the perfect moralist, although by the resentful man he will be called immoral. For he opposes their attempt to pull everyone down to their level, to treat every will as equal; he perceives that their ideal is "a principle hostile to life, a destroyer and dissolver of man, an outrage on the future of man, a symptom of fatigue, a short cut to Nothingness." As the attacking, aggressive man, he is nearer to justice than the man who merely reacts, for he has no need to

---

[1]Nietzsche's translators have established the fashion of translating *böse* as 'evil,' and the phrase 'beyond good and evil' has become current. 'Wicked' seems to me a more accurate rendering. Cf. Salter's explanation that *böse* (which he still translates 'evil') is "the hostile, harmful, destructive, or at least threatening, fear-inspiring—this from the standpoint of those who suffer or fear the harm."—*Nietzsche the Thinker*, p. 228.

[2]*Schlecht.* Usually translated 'bad.' The word connotes contempt.

adopt the tactics, necessary in the case of the reacting man, of making false and biased valuations of his object.   He enjoys, therefore, the freer outlook and the better conscience.

Nevertheless it is not certain that the superman will be victor in the struggle for existence.   For in a state of civilization the slaves are given an advantage by force of numbers and cohesion.   Since the coming of Christianity, indeed, their values have been in the ascendant.   But the fight is still being waged, and it is yet possible that the supermen may realize their strength and the stern ruthless duties it imposes on them, and seize the power for themselves, trampling down those institutions, religious or secular, that impede the free exercise of the creative spirit. The pure struggle for existence cannot be trusted.   Modern ways of living tend to favor the weak rather than the strong; the weak become artificially (that is, by artifice) collectively stronger than the strong.   But their subterfuges do not endow them with positive moral values.   It is not to any strength that Nietzsche assigns intrinsic worth, but only to the strength of the unregenerate 'natural' man, who is a warrior in body and soul.

The Nietzschean ideal differs, evidently, from the Spencerian ideal in an important respect: it is not urged as an ideal on all men, but is intended for those *supermen* who are capable of receiving it.   It requires them to live dangerously and creatively, and thereby with a certain ruthlessness to lay the foundations for a more wholesome society in the future.   The superman's path is symbolized by the three metamorphoses through which he is required to pass.   He begins as a camel, becomes next a lion, and lastly a child.   The camel is submissive, the lion realizes its strength and bursting its bonds captures freedom, but it cannot create.   The child, however, is "innocence and forgetfulness, a new beginning, a game, a self-rolling wheel, a first movement, a holy Yea. Aye, for the game of creating, my brethren, there is needed a holy Yea unto life: the spirit now willeth *its own* will, the world's outcast now winneth *his own* world."[1]

5. CRITICAL ESTIMATE OF NATURALISM

Quite evidently no one set of criticisms will be valid against all of the several philosophies that have here been grouped under the head of ethical naturalism. As was stated at the beginning of the chapter, naturalism is bound to be an ambiguous word, simply because 'nature' is so ambiguous. Stoic rationalism and the humanistic ethics of Aristotle are founded on an appeal to the nature of things, but 'naturalism' could not be stretched to cover their doctrines without losing all distinctive meaning. To Nietzsche likewise the word cannot be applied without equivocation; the inclusion of Nietzsche in this chapter has been partly for convenience of arrangement and partly because of the significant ethical analogies between Nietzsche's philosophy and the various forms of the 'Might is Right' doctrine. In criticizing, therefore, we must be clear as to just which forms of ethical naturalism our criticism meets.

Can Might and Right be synonymous?

The expression 'Might is Right' is less definite than it seems. The little word 'is' is deceptive. In any of the arguments offered in support of the doctrine, 'is' has one meaning; in the uncompromising conclusion that Might offers the only standard by which Right can be judged, the meaning is shifted. The ambiguity is a relational one: the premise declares that displays of force ('force' being interpreted in the broad way indicated in Section 2) have

[1]*Thus Spake Zarathustra.*

a considerable influence in causally determining what notions of Right are likely to survive; from this an attempt is made to conclude that the whole *character and meaning* of Right is *deducible* from the character of the circumstances in which it finds expression. The fallacy is an example of what in Chapter II was defined as the *genetic fallacy*, and can always be challenged by the dialectically valid assertion that our ideals may be *causally related* to certain origins and yet be *logically independent* of them. To trace the origins and estimate the chances of survival of certain existing ideals may throw a good deal of light on their nature, but it offers no coercive proof of whether or not the ideals are worthy. Knowing how an ideal came to be held and estimating its survival probabilities, we can thereby critically evaluate and perhaps change our allegiance to it. But the critical evaluation of one's own allegiance is always dialectical: whatever the facts, the mind that recognizes them as facts can, within limits, bestow or withhold its approval. Even though the holding of an ideal should result in its holder's annihilation, still there have been martyrs in the world—even some martyrs who fought willingly for lost causes. To fight for a 'lost cause' is simply to give practical expression to the logical distinction between two questions: (1) whether an ideal is likely to endure for a long time, and (2) whether during its lifetime it has real power and importance for those to whom it is an expression of truth. The first of these questions is factual, the second largely normative. Because a study of history and a knowledge of humankind seem to require a negative answer to the first, extreme naturalists infer that there must be a negative answer given to the second as well. But the inference is as fallacious as to suppose that because we must die we can therefore attribute no value to life while it lasts.

Limits of evolutionary ethics

In evolutionary ethics the argument from Might to Right is extended beyond the sphere of human actions to the biological conditions favoring the evolution of all living species. The major premise of the argument affirms the credo already mentioned as one of the metaphysical accretions of the Darwinian theory—that the evolutionary process has been a *progress;* that whatever species have evolved are intrinsically better than their predecessors. The minor premise states the Darwinian hypothesis of natural selection: that the means whereby the evolutionary process takes place are the four interrelated factors of variation, struggle for existence, survival of the fittest, and heredity. Whence it is supposed to follow that the unimpeded working of these factors, since they are productive of a process that is also a moral progress, is itself a good to be striven for. Both premises, however, can be challenged. As for the major: Is it all results of evolution that are good? Is every step in the process as good as any other step? Have the faulty adaptations, which to sentient beings possessing them must have had the character of supreme tragedies, been really necessary steps in the march towards biological perfection? Very few biologists would answer affirmatively, and if any did there is no way in which they could conclusively verify their belief. But if it is admitted that some results of evolution are better than others—more adequate modes of adaptation, for example—then these specific results and not the process by which they are arrived at are the intrinsic good, and there is no logical hindrance to their being achieved in some other way than by the law of tooth and nail. But, the minor premise has asserted, it is only by the law of tooth and nail that better adapted organisms are evolved.

This, however, is an assertion that cannot be proved. Even for Darwin it was used only as a working hypothesis, in order to provide an answer that would meet the requirements of exact scientific method. But the question is whether scientific method can possibly give the whole story. Our principal acquaintance with the phenomenon of adaptation to environment is not as it can be observed in molluscs and white mice but as we ourselves make the effort toward adaptation. Is it not turning the whole question topsy-turvy to describe human adaptations, the motives and results of which are directly known to us and are often perceived to have a profound moral significance, in terms of animal adaptations, in which the motivating impulses can only be guessed at? But motives and sentient impulses must not be ascribed to animals, it may be replied; for we can know nothing about their inner life, not even whether they have any. Very possibly, but this is the strongest possible argument for *not* using the behavior of animals as a model in drawing normative conclusions about human conduct: whether animal behavior is sentiently motivated we perhaps cannot be sure; but we do know something about the conscious motives, including the complex moral considerations that impel much human behavior, and on this known territory, therefore, all significant moral inquiry should begin.

A further criticism of Spencer's theory can be directed against his distinction between length and breadth of life. The introduction of breadth into his theory creates a difficulty similar to the one created by Mill's introduction of quality into the utilitarian standard. Spencer had substituted life for the utilitarian standard of happiness on the ground that it could be observed and measured objectively. Length of life and the number of individuals possessing life meet this requirement. But how, other than by subjective impressions, can fullness of life be measured? By the degree to which an individual is adapted to his environment, it is said. But as individuals acquire new variations and more complex possibilities of adaptation their environment changes *ipso facto*. Man's universe is not that of an eagle, nor that of a gnat. In acquiring adaptations against primitive enemies men learned to use weapons, and thus by developing the art of warfare they created new complexities in their environment to which still further adaptations became necessary. An individual who was ideally adapted to the age of chivalry or even the age of steam would be badly fitted to cope with the complexities of this electrical age. Conversely, how can we say that we have a greater fullness of life than the men of the Renaissance? Obviously such an assertion can have no thoroughly objective grounds. Fullness of life, as something distinct from longevity, is undoubtedly important both as a criterion of progress and as a guide to moral action. But it is not a standard to which scientific procedures, in anything like the strict sense of the word, can be applied.

Shortcomings of a superman

Nietzsche's ideal is not touched by any of the foregoing criticisms, for it does not pretend to rest on strict logical proof. Nietzsche asserts a value, and as he has said the assertion of a value is a creative act. It is beside the point to comb his writings for fallacies. Even the numerous inconsistencies of which he is guilty are not necessarily to be looked on either as aesthetic flaws or as logical weaknesses, for it is never certain how far his language is intended to be literal and how far it is metaphor and hyperbole. Instead of a logical exposition the doctrine is the poetic expression of a peculiar insight into the nature

of life. Our criticism, therefore, should ask whether
Nietzsche's conception of life is adequate, whether it does
justice to the whole of human nature.

It does not. Its very limitations are what make it so
fascinating. For it paints in lurid colors one side of life
that is usually kept secret. Its limited insight is, to be
sure, of great value. We are reminded of the danger that
our morality may become a concealment and a justification of our petty interests. We are reminded that the
great ones of our generation are perhaps being thwarted
and ruined by our expectation that they shall conform to
the same standards as those that guide the majority. We
are reminded that authentic genius, whatever its other
characteristics, has always an element of ruthlessness,[1]
towards which we who are not geniuses are often inclined
to be resentful. But for all its value in restoring balance
to our one-sided prejudices, the ideal of the superman must
be judged inadequate on the ground that it provides for the
development of only one group of human impulses, dis-
missing the others as worthless, mean, *schlecht*. Men have
not only a will to power but also impulses of benevolence,
an occasional love of justice, and at times a yearning to
submit to a higher will than their own. As a fact of psychology no one can doubt the presence, to some degree,
of these tendencies in men. By what criterion do we
assert them to be less natural or less noble than the 'law
of tooth and nail'? Our next task, at any rate, will be
to examine certain moral ideals that arise out of an emphasis on human impulses of a contrary sort to those praised
by Nietzsche.

[1]Symbolized strikingly in Jean Cocteau's film, *Le sang d'un poète*, where the
poet is playing cards with his Muse, and at the crucial moment in order to
win the stake he cheats by pulling the ace of hearts from the breast of a boy who
lies slain at his feet.

CHAPTER V

THE IDEA OF DUTY

A philosophy of life which involves no sacrifice turns out in the end to be merely an excuse for being the sort of person one is.

T. S. Eliot

IRRESPECTIVE of the theories by which philosophers, psychologists, or theologians may undertake to explain it, the occasional presence in men of a sense of responsibility, of duty, of what in a given situation is the only right, honorable, decent course to pursue, is an irreducible fact. Something of its nature and way of working has been described at the close of Chapter I. The present chapter will pursue this inquiry, and together with the following chapter will expound the principal types of moral philosophy in which the concept of duty is made primary and essential instead of, as in hedonism and naturalism, derivative.

1. The Fact of Duty

For this is the honest truth, O my countrymen: wherever a man stations himself, thinking it best he should be there, or is stationed by his commander, there he must remain, whatever the danger, thinking neither of death nor of anything else save disgrace. How terribly I would have erred if, while obeying the commanders whom you set over me at Potidaea and at Amphipolis and at Delium and remaining where they stationed me, facing death with my fellows, I were now, through fear of death or anything else, to desert the post at which I was convinced the god had stationed me, with orders to devote my life to philosophy and to the examination of myself and others.

. . . So I say to you, men of Athens, you may follow Anytus' advice or not, acquit me or not, as you see fit; but understand that I will never change my conduct even though I had to die many times over.[1]

These words of Socrates to his judges, when on trial for his life, testify as convincingly as any evidence can convince, that duty was for him something great and real. His attitude was not mere bravado. Had he been willing to placate his judges and compromise, he would have been acquitted of the ridiculous charges preferred against him. As it was, he was condemned by a narrow margin of votes to die. After the trial, when his friend Crito, having bribed the jailors, came to him in prison and urged him to escape, he refused: could it be right to break faith with the city in which he had lived and the laws from which he had received such numerous benefits, simply because their verdict was now hurtful to him and seemingly unfair?

It might be said that Socrates, however, believed in gods and an after-life and in the divine nature of the mission he felt imposed upon him. Probably he did so; nevertheless to an unbiased reader it must be clear that the inner voice of which Socrates speaks in the *Apology* had for him a validity that was independent of any mythological or cosmological beliefs. Moreover, there has been many another who while professing agnosticism or downright atheism has still recognized the supreme validity of moral duty. George Eliot, for example, in a conversation with Frederick Myers on God, Immortality, and Duty, "pronounced with terrible earnestness how inconceivable was the first, how unbelievable was the second, how peremptory and absolute was the third."

George Eliot's novels reveal this preoccupation with

[1]Plato, *The Apology of Socrates*, 28 D–30 B.

duty. In *The Mill on the Floss* Stephen and Maggie are by accident alone in a boat and have drifted on down the stream until they realize they will not be able to reach home before morning. Stephen pleads with Maggie to marry him, but although they are mutually in love, Stephen is engaged to Maggie's cousin Lucy, her dearest friend. Maggie sees her duty clearly, but as the boat glides on she feels herself yielding:

All yielding is attended with a less vivid consciousness than resistance; it is the partial sleep of thought . . . Every influence tended to lull her into acquiescence: that dreamy gliding in the boat which had lasted for four hours, and had brought some weariness and exhaustion—the recoil of her fatigued sensations from the impracticable difficulty of getting out of the boat at this unknown distance from home, and walking for long miles—all helped to bring her into more complete subjection to that strong mysterious charm which made a last parting from Stephen seem the death of all joy. . . .

Yet "across that stealing influence came the terrible shadow of past thoughts." Lulled by present influences Maggie thrusts down this memory, but later, when they have reached a town and she is alone in a hotel room, Stephen no longer with her, the memory returns:

The irrevocable wrong that must blot her life had been committed; she had brought sorrow into the life of others—into the lives that were knit up with hers by trust and love. The feeling of a few short weeks had hurried her into the sins her nature had most recoiled from—breach of faith and cruel selfishness; she had rent the ties that had given meaning to duty, and had made herself an outlawed soul, with no guide but the wayward choice of her own passion.

Nevertheless, is it not too late now to draw back? She has spent the night with Stephen in a boat; she will be disgraced at home.   Again comes the temptation to yield to Stephen.

But close upon that decisive act her mind recoiled; and the sense of contradiction with her past self in her moments of strength and clearness came upon her like a pang of conscious degradation.

Her duty to Lucy and her duty to *her past self* face her as unrelenting barriers.   She leaves Stephen and returns home, disgraced but with the sustaining consciousness of having kept faith.

Readers of *The Mill on the Floss* may debate whether Maggie, in behaving thus, displayed a deep sense of honor or merely a foolish prudery.   But the point to be emphasized is that her sense of duty was to her at any rate a stern and aweful fact.   The two preceding chapters of this volume have been devoted to ethical theories which in one way or another treat the sense of duty as a mere product of our inclinations.   The relation of duty to what, for convenience, we may call inclination, is not a simple one, as George Eliot was amply aware:

The great problem of the shifting relation between passion and duty is clear to no man who is capable of apprehending it; the question whether the moment has come in which a man has fallen below the possibility of a renunciation that will carry any efficacy, and must accept the sway of a passion against which he has struggled as a trespass, is one for which we have no master-key that will fit all cases.[1]

But this shifting relation between passion and duty is all the more reason for developing as clear as possible a

---

[1] *The Mill on the Floss*.   These excerpts, together with the report of the conversation with Frederick Myers, are taken from Franklin Gary's article, "In Search of George Eliot," *The Symposium*, April, 1933.

notion of each.   The next task of the present chapter will be a logical analysis of what duty, as a general concept, means.

2.   The Logic of Duty

When in the previous chapters we examined theories of ethics that fail to include duty as a primary factor in the moral situation we found each of them to contain a grave difficulty.   The difficulty in general is this: that without in some way recognizing duty as having a validity independent of inclinations, actually existing preferences, and calculations of enjoyment, the moral problem tends to disappear into a purely factual problem of one sort or another.   The dilemma is inescapable: either we act in every case as we happen, at the moment of choosing, to like (and if this is universally true then all moral deliberations are futile and all ethical theories are false) or else we can in *some* cases guide our choice of action by appealing to some principle (however faulty or obscure) of what *ought* to be done.

Does this mean that duties ought to be accepted blindly and uncritically?   Or again, does it mean that we can deduce by pure reason what our duties are?   Not in the least; although there will be occasion in the next chapter to comment upon certain philosophers who have held this static and *a priori* notion of duty.   The relation of duty to passion, inclination, and free choice is, as George Eliot has observed, a shifting one, and "clear to no man who is capable of apprehending it."   But among the complexities of human experience there is to be found many a notion of fundamental importance whose outlines are obscure.   This is true not only of ethical concepts; it is true also of aesthetic concepts such as beauty, and of metaphysical concepts such as the self.

What is duty?

Duty, according to G. E. Moore, is "that action, which will cause more good to the universe than any possible alternative."[1] This definition presupposes an understanding of what is meant by good. According to Dr. Moore, the good can be recognized (allowing for error in particular cases) and its meaning understood although an exact definition of it is impossible. It will be observed that Dr. Moore speaks of *possible* alternatives: duty can refer only to actions that are possible, that the individual *can* perform if he only *will*. The action of preventing the occurrence of tornadoes would doubtless cause more good to the universe than the alternative action of doing nothing about them, but one of these alternatives is not humanly possible, and it is therefore not anyone's duty to prevent a tornado's occurrence. Secondly, it will be observed that questions of duty are determined by asking not whether an action will have *some* good or bad result but whether it will cause the most possible good to the universe, or "which, among all the actions possible to volition at any moment, will produce the best *total* result." An action becomes our duty, then, when (1) it lies within our power to perform, (2) will cause more good than any alternative action that lies within our power, (3) not only to ourselves or in some particular respect, but with respect to the total result.

A similar analysis is made by Nicolai Hartmann, who distinguishes between the Ought-to-Be (the good) and the Ought-to-Do (duty), and further distinguishes the *positive* Ought-to-Be from the *ideal* Ought-to-Be. The ideal Ought-to-Be is identical with the good, and logically independent of any question either of existence or of action.

[1]*Principia Ethica*, p. 148; cf. pp. 180–181.

It can be predicated indifferently of what does exist or of what does not: "That a man ought to be honest, straightforward, trustworthy, is something which does not cease to be because somebody is so. The man ought to be even as he then is." If it were the case that nobody were honest, straightforward, and trustworthy, the ideal Ought-to-Be would remain unchanged: it would still be true that a man ought to have these qualities, although it would also be true that no one did have them. As distinguished from the ideal Ought-to-Be, the positive Ought-to-Be "occurs where the ideal finds itself in opposition to reality, where the self-existent values are unreal." That this distinction is a necessary logical step in reaching an exact definition of duty will be evident when it is reflected that there could be no duty in a world where everything was for all time just as it ought to be. For duty to have significance, it is necessary that the Ought-to-Be become positive by standing in opposition to an existing state of affairs whose character is in some respect the negative of the Ought. However, even the positive Ought-to-Be is not the same as an Ought-to-Do, for an Ought-to-Do involves striving, and "not everything that is not, but ought to be, comes into the domain of striving." An Ought becomes striven for only as there is a consciousness of the possibility of attaining it, and an Ought becomes a duty, *i.e.*, an Ought-to-Do, only in so far as there *is* this possibility:

Because something is in itself a value, it does not follow that someone ought to do it; it does mean, however, that it Ought to 'Be,' and unconditionally—irrespective of its actuality or even of its possibility. Accordingly, there is a sense in saying that universal peace among nations ought to 'be.' That has a meaning, not in so far as peace is actual or possible, but in so far as it is in itself valuable. Yet it would be senseless to say that a single individual ought to bring peace about. Conversely, it holds true of goods provided by nature that they ought to be just as they are; yet with them there is no place for an Ought-to-Do. A place for that is not possible until someone is in need of the goods and someone can acquire them by effort. Consequently Ought-to-Do is always conditioned by Ought-to-Be, but Ought-to-Do is not attached to every Ought-to-Be. I ought to do [German, 'make'] what ought to be, in so far as it 'is' not, and in so far as to make it actual is in my power. This double 'in so far as' separates these two kinds of Ought.[1]

These quotations make it evident that duty can be given a sufficiently precise philosophical meaning. The objection may be offered, however, that duty can nevertheless be 'explained' as merely a special kind of impulse, or in Nietzschean terms as a perversion of the will to power, or in the language of psychoanalysis as a sublimation of subconscious desire. None of these explanations, probably, is wholly false, and yet their introduction into a discussion of duty may often be irrelevant and misleading. The student of philosophy should learn to avoid the common tendency to confuse essence with explanation. As Bishop Butler has said, "Everything is what it is, and not another thing." Duty can certainly be regarded as a *kind* of impulse, but the acute reasoner will ask *what* kind, and stress the differentiation. Different fields of study stress different distinctions as relevant to their special problems. A psychologist may deem it pertinent to his problems to group all impulses, moral and non-moral, under a single category in order to arrive at generalizations about such psycho-physical characteristics as they may all be found to share. But in the making of moral decisions as well as in the building of an adequate

---

[1] Nicolai Hartmann, *Ethics*, Vol. I, pp. 247-248. (By permission of The Macmillan Company, publishers.)

theory of moral values the important question is not how an impulse is to be classified and explained by psychologists but what its character is to us who feel ourselves moved by it. An impulse to be loyal and an impulse to be treacherous are both impulses, but from a moral standpoint their difference may be absolute.

Dialectical deduction of 'ought'

But can the fact of duty be proved? it may be asked. Can any positive evidence be given that the Ought is essentially different from mere impulse and inclination? Yes, it can. But with two provisos. The essentiality of any difference is relative to the set of problems being considered, and it is only for ethics that the difference between inclination and duty either can or need be proved essential. Secondly, the proof will be dialectical. It is only by dialectical method that the validity of the terms fundamental to a given field of discussion can be established: i.e., that meanings rather than facts can be demonstrated. The general procedure of dialectic is to start with a meaning that is accepted and by an analysis of that meaning or of its usual applications to demonstrate what other meanings are implicit in it.

A dialectical demonstration of duty or Ought—that is, a demonstration of its validity as a concept for the interpretation of experience, not of course a demonstration of the validity of any particular duty such as loyalty or chastity—is latent in the criticisms already offered of hedonistic, utilitarian, and naturalistic theories of ethics. Take hedonism first. If hedonism is formulated consistently it turns out either to be not an ethical theory at all or else to involve an Ought. If its maxim, "Act always so as to secure the most pleasure and the least pain," is interpreted to mean "Act always in whatever manner

gives most pleasure and least pain *at the moment of acting,"*
it follows that hedonism is not a theory of ethics, for it
predicates an Ought of what (by its own theory) necessarily Is, and therefore merely asserts an ideal Ought-to-
Be, not the positive Ought-to-Be which Dr. Hartmann has
shown to be a precondition of the moral situation.   If on
the other hand the hedonist's maxim is interpreted, somewhat after the manner of Epicurus, to mean, "Act always
so as to secure the most pleasure and the least pain *in the
long run,"* it is evident that an ideal is here set up dis-
tinguishable from the inclination of the moment: we are
pulled in one way by the enticement of a present pleasure,
but we *ought* to restrain the present impulse in order to
have greater enjoyment hereafter.   If this maxim carries
any weight it means that the present 'I' recognizes some
obligation to my future self.   The basis of such recognition may be given any name one pleases: hope and dread
are both there no doubt, as is a sympathetic prevision of
the pleasures and pains later to be enjoyed or suffered.
But the dialectical principle still holds, for the original
dilemma can now be reformulated on a new dialectical
level.   Suppose the hedonist to argue that my choice is
dictated by the character of these mental representations
of future pleasures and pains—representations which are
themselves slightly pleasurable or painful at the moment
of making the choice.   There would then be no moral
problem, since I would necessarily have to choose that
course of action the mental representation of whose effects
is the more pleasurable or less painful here and now.
There can be a possibility of choice and consequently a
moral problem only if the determining power of my present feelings—*i.e.*, the *present* pleasure of contemplating
future pleasures and the *present* pain of contemplating
future pains—is not absolute; only if I can oppose to these

feelings the idea of an *achievable but not inevitable* good (for the Epicurean, a future pleasure), which, though a contemplation of it is not at this moment actually pleasanter than a contemplation of its alternative, I nevertheless judge to hold a promise of greater pleasure *for the future*, and therefore by my hedonistic principles recognize that I *ought* to choose.   Even in a purely egoistic morality then, provided it is a morality and not simply a watered-down theory of psychology, there is a duty postulated to my future self.

In utilitarianism the necessity of accepting an independent idea of duty is more immediately evident.   Bentham and Mill both admit that one's actual inclinations are likely to be dominantly selfish, whereas the utilitarian ideal is altruistic.   Let men be educated, then, they tell us, so that each individual will come to receive more pleasure from beneficent than from selfish actions, and let society be reformed so that by rewards and penalties an action that is pleasurable or painful to the greatest number will be artificially made pleasurable or painful to the individual performing it.   But this argument does not settle the matter as Bentham and Mill suppose.   All it says is that in an ideal society, where the proposed reforms in law and education had already been accomplished, there would be an exact correspondence between the pleasure or pain received by the individual performing the act and pleasure or pain received by the majority of those affected by it.   But in existing societies such a correspondence is strikingly absent.   We ought, then, they say, to set about reforming society.   To reform society is thus affirmed to be an individual's duty even though, prior to the achievement of a utopia, there is no guarantee that this altruistic conduct will bring to oneself a greater margin of pleasure than could be got by some alternative course of action.   The utilitarian thus despite himself accepts duty as a concept independent of pleasure.

Spencer, finally, accepts duty as an independent notion, since in no other way would his appeal to the evolution of species have the slightest relevance to moral questions. The evolutionary process, he presupposes, has been good, and therefore it is our duty to carry it on.   In Spencer's philosophy, indeed, it is even more evident that duty is a primary and independent notion, for Spencer, in the stricter aspects of his theory, is not a hedonist, but postulates the biological health of the race as the primary good, and postulates therefore each person's endeavor to promote it as a duty.

Now granted duty both as a psychological fact and as a dialectically necessary concept, there arises a more practical question: by what means can we know in specific cases what our duty is?   Philosophical, as opposed to more definitively religious, theories of how one's duties can be known are of two types: *intuitionism*, which will be discussed in the remainder of this chapter, and *rationalism*, which will be discussed in the next.

3.   ETHICAL INTUITIONISM

'Intuitionism' is derived from the Latin *intueor*, 'to look at,' 'to have direct (visual) acquaintance with.'   The word is used in ethics to denote those theories which hold that man has or can have a direct acquaintance with the nature of right and wrong.   As the eye perceives an apple to be red, and the validity of the perception for normal observers is not refuted by the fact that some persons are color-blind, so in like manner the mind intuits an action as praiseworthy or blamable and a character as noble or vicious, and the general validity of such intuitions is not refuted by the fact that errors in intuiting are frequent. We possess a certain ability to 'size up' a situation; later on we may amend our moral estimate but the amended estimate is simply a new sizing up. Reason need not be entirely absent from this process, but reason can lead to the most absurd paradoxes unless at every step it is guided by a sense of fitness, a sense of 'where to draw the line,' a sense of how the reasoning is to be guided and interpreted, and in moral matters by an ability to recognize right and wrong. Ethical reasoning presupposes some distinction between right and wrong as its starting-point; it cannot, therefore, be the sole ground of the distinction.

Everyday experience testifies that people do have moral intuitions, which reason can only justify or partially amend. One man 'looks' honest, we say, another 'looks' mean; sometimes we 'recognize' very clearly what we ought to do even though it is hard to find logically articulate reasons for the recognition. Often we speak of being guided by a conscience, but this expression sometimes carries theological connotations which would be objectionable to many persons who would nevertheless not wish to declare that a conscience was lacking to them. The etymological meaning of 'conscience,' however, is suggestive: *con-sciens*, knowing something altogether, as a whole. This grasp of a whole situation in such a way as to have a *kind* of knowledge that could not be deduced from the details of the situation alone is what distinguishes the 'man of imagination,' the wit, and the genius from their less fortunate and more literally minded fellows. In the sphere of morals it is a characteristic of 'moral insight,' as distinguished from blind adherence to rules and customs. Everyone has the faculty to some degree, but the difference of degree is one of the principal marks of a man. Aristotle calls the faculty *noûs*, which is best translated 'intuition.' Plato had found its nature such a mystery that he generally spoke of it in allegory. Shaftesbury calls it the 'moral sense,' Newman 'the illative faculty,' and William James 'the apperceiving mass.' The *Gestalt* theory in psychology, usually associated with the name of Wolfgang Köhler, represents an attempt to describe its cognitions in a more or less scientific manner. We must be careful, however, not to hypostatize this faculty: it is not a substance, but a state of awareness, a way of knowing. William James' adjective *apperceptive* and Professor Hoernlé's *synoptic* ('a seeing together') express one characteristic of this way of knowing—the togetherness of what is known; the word *intuitive* expresses the other important characteristic—the directness of the knowing.

Anthony Ashley Cooper, Earl of Shaftesbury (1671– 1713) was the first of a group of eighteenth century British philosophers who accepted the cognitions of this 'moral sense' as the principal criterion of moral value.

The mind, which is spectator or auditor of other minds, cannot be without its eye and ear; so as to discern proportion, distinguish sound, and scan each sentiment or thought which comes before it.[1]

In human nature the mind discerns a foul and a fair, in human affections a soft and a harsh, in human conduct a virtuous and a vicious as directly and authentically as in musical sounds and in the outward forms of things it perceives a harmonious and a discordant. Even in social matters Shaftesbury believed that the mind "readily discerns the good and ill towards the species or public."

---

[1] *An Inquiry Concerning Virtue or Merit*, Bk. I, Part II, Sec. III. The interested student will find this and other representative quotations from Shaftesbury in either of two anthologies: Selby-Bigge, *British Moralists;* Rand, *The Classical Moralists*.

When, as occasionally happens, the mind is mistaken in these intuitions it is because human inclinations, passions, dispositions, and consequent behavior are represented to the mind in various perspectives; yet in spite of this partiality of viewpoint the heart is forever judging—it cannot remain neutral. There is, therefore, in each moral judgment a certain risk, "a new trial or exercise of the heart," which must take full responsibility for the discernment and choice of what is just and right, worthy and good. If it persistently fails in this discernment it is corrupt. By the use of reason its moral discernment can be guided and improved, and it is only of a rational creature indeed that virtue can be predicated; but reason can only cultivate, not create the "just disposition, or proportionable affection of a rational creature towards the moral objects of right and wrong" in which virtue consists.

Virtue delineated

A contemporary of Shaftesbury was William Wollaston (1659–1724), whose one book on ethics was entitled *The Religion of Nature Delineated.* Wollaston's treatment of the question of right and wrong is more objective than Shaftesbury's and based on a more explicit logic. He gives right and wrong an objective meaning by defining them in terms of true and false. In the second, third, and fourth postulates of his theory he furnishes the logical bases of this identification:

I.   That act, which may be denominated morally good or evil, must be the act of a being capable of distinguishing, choosing, and acting for himself: or more briefly, of an intelligent and free agent. . . .

II.   Those propositions are true, which express things as they are: or, truth is the conformity of those words or signs, by which things are expressed, to the things themselves.   Defin.

III. A true proposition may be denied, or things may be denied to be what they are, by deeds, as well as by express words or another proposition. . . .

IV. No act (whether word or deed) of any being, to whom moral good and evil are imputable, that interferes with any true proposition, or denies anything to be as it is, can be right.[1]

The most distinctive aspect of the theory and the basis of Wollaston's definition of right and wrong is found in Postulate III. Wollaston explains:

It is certain there is a meaning in many acts and gestures. Everybody understands weeping, laughing, shrugs, frowns, etc.; these are a sort of universal language. . . . There are many acts, . . . such as constitute the character of a man's conduct in life, which have in nature, and would be taken by any indifferent judge to have, a signification, and to imply some proposition, as plainly to be understood as if it was declared in words: and therefore if what such acts declare to be, is not, they must contradict truth as much as any false proposition or assertion can.

This is a very important contribution to ethical theory: the interpretation of human actions as having a meaning, in the same way that words have a meaning, though ordinarily, perhaps, less precise. To use one of Wollaston's illustrations: "If a body of soldiers, seeing another body approach, should fire upon them, would not this act declare that they were enemies; and if they were not enemies, would not this military language declare what was false?" Even supposing that the shooting had been an accidental mistake, still it would declare what was false, just as a proposition in words may declare what is false regardless of whether it is or is not an intentional lie. In neither case does the truth or falsity depend upon the affirmer's

---

[1] *Op. cit.*, Sec. I. Representative selections from Wollaston, including the present passage, will be found in both Rand and in Selby-Bigge *op. cit.*

knowledge or ignorance.   In both cases there is a meaning which may be understood and communicated and "what has a meaning, may be either true or false."   It follows, therefore, that "a man may by acts as plainly as by words make a declaration of what is morally good or ill," *i.e.,* of what is right or wrong.

But what criterion have we by which to recognize a true moral judgment and distinguish it from a false? Wollaston considers several criteria that different ethical theories have proposed.   Follow nature?   Yes, if this were to signify "acting according to the natures of things (that is, treating them as being what they in nature are, or according to truth)."   But more often the phrase is employed differently: it tells a man to follow *his own* nature, and since his own nature contains a part that he possesses in common with the brutes, "they appoint him a guide which I fear will mislead him, this being commonly more likely to prevail than the rational part."   Shall the criterion be reason?   Right reason is a partial and necessary guide if by it is meant that which is found by the right use of our rational faculties.   But too often reason is interpreted as an inflexible authority by which bigotry may be upheld, and nothing can be settled because everyone pretends that his own reason is right.   Besides, we may discover moral truths not alone by the explicit workings of reason but also through the perception of matters of fact.   "We ought to regard things as being what they are, which way soever we come to the knowledge of them." The rationalist is too prone to fall into the fallacy of rejecting any truths that may have been arrived at in some manner other than the rational.   Shall the criterion, then, be the innate ideas of morality shared by all mankind? They who deduce the difference between good and evil from certain common principles which they suppose to be

born with us "put the matter upon a very infirm foot.
For it is much to be suspected there are no such innate
maxims as they pretend, but that the impressions of education are mistaken for them: and beside that, the sentiments of mankind are not so uniform and constant, as
that we may safely trust such an important distinction
upon them." Nor, finally, can pleasure be the criterion
of good, for not only is pleasure too variable and uncertain
an accompaniment of our actions, but also there is the
danger that men who look to this standard "will be apt to
sink into gross voluptuousness, as in fact the generality
of Epicurus' herd have done (notwithstanding all his talk
of temperance, virtue, tranquillity of mind, etc.); and
the bridle will be usurped by those appetites which it is
a principal part of all religion, natural as well as any
other, to curb and restrain." None of these foundations
of morality proves on examination to be firm. The only
intelligible, practicable, and undeniable distinction between good and evil is based on "a conformity of men's
acts to the truth of the case or the contrary."

The distinguishing mark of Wollaston's standard is
that it requires the degree of right or wrong in an act to
be judged by the character of the act itself, not by some
partial and relatively abstract criterion such as pleasure
or custom. And if it were asked whether right and wrong
are known by non-rational intuition (as Shaftesbury affirmed) or by reason (as Kant, three generations later, was
to affirm), Wollaston's reply would be that the answer
could not be the same for all cases and that the question,
in any event, was of secondary importance. The primary
question for ethics is the quality of the act, not the manner in which that quality is discerned. Some men may
make a more explicit use of their rational faculties: the

moral good, when finally chosen, will appear to them as the logical result of a series of distinct steps. Other men (perhaps this is oftener true of women) are characterized by a more highly developed intuitive faculty—by a more immediate awareness of the implications and consequences of some choice to be made. Whether moral intuitions have a divine or ultimately biological origin is also outside the present inquiry, although Wollaston as a member of the Church believed the former. His emphasis is on the validity of our intuitions, not on their origin.

The correct moral estimation of actions requires that "times, places, ends intended, and effects that naturally follow, must be added to them." That is to say, an action when judged morally must always be considered in its full relevant context. And since the actions are to be judged by whether or not they conform to "the truth of the case," the relevant context includes every aspect "which is capable of being denied by facts or practice." If a man steals a horse his action says falsely that he has a right to the horse, that the horse belongs to him or has been lent him by the owner. Were we to judge the situation by pleasure and pain alone, it might very possibly be the case that the thief received much pleasure while the horse's owner, if he possessed numerous other horses, would suffer little or no pain. On hedonistic grounds a theft in these circumstances could not be condemned except by an elaborate argument designed to show its eventual deleterious effects on society at large. In many a petty theft, however, it seems very doubtful that the final sum of painful effects to society, if any at all, exceeds the pleasure enjoyed by the thief. Anyhow, the evidence for a balance of painful over pleasurable effects could be no better than probable, whereas a moral judgment of right or wrong is often characterized by certitude. Since moral judgment may be categorical and immediate, it is evidently of a different nature, a different 'essence,' from the arguments leading to it. The theft of a horse is judged (by many of us) as wrong, and the reason for this judgment[1] is found in the nature of the situation being judged, not in some set of effects (such as resultant pleasure) or causes (such as motives) more or less distinct from it. The taking of the horse makes (although not in words) an assertion as to the relationship of rider, horse, and owner that is not true. The action is therefore wrong.

Would Wollaston deny, then, that the effects of an act are to be taken into consideration when a moral estimate of it is made? Not wholly. It is never possible, except by an artificial abstraction, to cleave a situation entirely from its effects. The question is one of relevance. The relevant effects of an action are those about which the action makes some assertion. It might be that the horse-thief, as a result of his action, would get started on the road to wealth, and being of a benevolent disposition would thereafter perform many beneficent acts. But if this result were not foreseeable it would be, although an effect of the action, accidental to it. It would not, therefore, be asserted by the action, and so would be irrelevant to a moral judgment of it. Suppose, however, a pauper steals a loaf of bread to keep himself and his family from starving. In such a case the effect would be relevant to, because in an important sense a part of, the action. The action is not merely the movement of the hand seizing the loaf. The action with which a moral judgment must

---

[1] The student is urged to keep in mind the distinction between the *reason for* a judgment and the *cause of* a judgment. The cause of a moral judgment might equally well be worked out in psychological, biological, sociological, or theological terms, or in all of them together without detriment to Wollaston's argument.

be concerned is more complex. It must be described more fully, as the action of a starving pauper driven to despair by hunger, to whom, in this plight, bread is a more highly prized object than property rights or anything else. His action may be said to assert that total situation. Is the theft, then, moral? No, for the taking of the bread asserts also something else. It implies a false assertion as to the ownership of the bread, and in this respect it is morally wrong.

But what, then, is to be our moral judgment of the action as a whole? Is it right or wrong for the starving pauper to steal the bread? The answer is implied in Wollaston's ninth postulate: "Every act [of a being capable of judgment and choice] and all those omissions which interfere with truth (*i.e.*, deny any proposition to be true, which is true; or suppose anything not to be what it is, in any regard) are morally evil, in some degree or other." The phrase, *in some degree or other*, must not be overlooked. The theft of anything, since it makes a false affirmation, is always *in that respect* wrong. If the theft be regarded as a part of some larger course of action, the total action is "evil in some degree." The adage, *Tout comprendre, c'est tout pardonner*, is therefore false. To understand the whole situation is not to dismiss it without moral approval or disapproval, but rather to see more clearly in what measure each may be justified. This is done by estimating rightly the proportion of moral good and moral evil in the action, which in turn depends on our judgment of whether and to what extent the action contradicts any true proposition.

Other eighteenth century theories

Various developments of 'moral sense' intuitionism, although not always called by that name, were contributed

by later British moral philosophers. Francis Hutcheson
(1694–1746) expounded the faculty of moral awareness by
analogy to the appreciation of beauty. Joseph Butler,
Bishop of Durham (1692–1752),[1] called it 'conscience,' and
undertook to demonstrate its existence by the argument
that our use of words like 'right,' 'wrong,' and 'duty'
show the presence of a faculty within us which recognizes
some object or quality or essence which these words denote. Without such a faculty the words would be as
empty of significance as the terms 'black' and 'white'
would be to a man born blind. Conscience has both a
cognitive and an authoritative aspect. On the one hand
it reflects on actions, persons, and motives, judging them
good or bad, right or wrong; it also makes moral judgments of the second order, e.g., that happiness is the fit
accompaniment of doing right, pain of doing wrong. On
the other hand conscience issues commands. It is not
merely a way of knowing, it is one of the springs of human
action. There are three other springs of human action:
"particular passions and affections," reflective self-love,
and reflective benevolence. Self-love, benevolence, and
conscience are distinguished from the particular passions
and affections in that they offer criteria for the judgment and control or restraint of the latter. In the good
man all three authorities rule harmoniously: self-love
condemns stealing as imprudent, benevolence condemns it
as tending to diminish the general happiness, and conscience condemns it categorically as wrong. But so long
as human nature is imperfect there will be occasional dis-
agreements among the three, and on such occasions conscience should be made the supreme arbiter. Following
Bishop Butler, two other contributions to the 'moral

[1]See principally his *Fifteen Sermons*, important selections from which are
contained both in Selby-Bigge and in Rand, *op. cit.*

sense' theory may be noted: *An Enquiry Concerning the Principles of Morals* by David Hume (1711–1776) and *The Theory of Moral Sentiments* by Adam Smith (1723–1790), author of the better known *Wealth of Nations*.

4. CHRISTIAN ETHICS

A new significance is given to duty and to its intuitive recognition in the ethics of the Christian religion.   Religion in general may be described as a faith in the transcendent: a faith that there is a Something (whether singular or plural) in the universe superior to man, to Whom man owes a special, preëmptive allegiance, and in Whose Presence a unique kind of emotion is experienced. This definition, while not restricting the meaning of religion to the more highly civilized or more intellectual types, emphasizes three aspects that are found in every genuine religion, as opposed to mere theologizing or magic or church-going.   A full-bodied religion has some significance for belief, for feeling, and for action.   While it is the last of these aspects that has the most direct concern for ethics, a religion is misrepresented by abstracting its ethical aspect from the whole fullness of meaning that it connotes.   A religious ethic can be understood only when considered as integrally joined with some form of religious experience and religious belief.   This is true with particular force of Christianity.   An unbeliever can be as moral in his conduct as a devout Christian, but without the Christian's devotion to a Being higher than himself he will completely miss what is primarily distinctive about the Christian way of life.   The inner compulsive force of a true Christian's sense of duty is unintelligible in abstraction from the Christian's sense of standing in a certain relation to God.

Christianity, unfortunately, has become a word with

many meanings. If one were to judge from the behavior
of present-day Christians it would seem that few of them
take the trouble to read the Gospels, and that of those
who do read them few pay the founder of Christianity the
compliment of supposing that he meant what he said.
In the name of Christianity clergymen not uncommonly
seek to justify wars and the maraudings of capitalists,
and Mr. Bruce Barton in *The Man Nobody Knows* has
described Jesus as a super-salesman, a red-blooded go-
getter. Christianity today is caught up in such a manifold confusion that its nature can hardly be discerned
unless we look back to its typical expressions in earlier
times—to the words of Jesus himself and of those who
have undertaken seriously to relinquish all for the sake
of following him.

Christian ethics differs fundamentally from all forms
of secular ethics, even from the semi-religious doctrines
of Plato and the Stoics, in this respect, that its morality
is made to spring directly out of the relation in which an
individual stands to God:

For though the soul may seem to rule the body admirably,
and the reason the vices, if the soul and reason do not themselves
obey God, as God has commanded them to serve Him, they have
no proper authority over the body and the vices. For what
kind of mistress of the body and the vices can that mind be
which is ignorant of the true God, and which, instead of being
subject to His authority, is prostituted to the corrupting influences of the most vicious demons? It is for this reason that
the virtues which it seems to itself to possess, and by which it
restrains the body and the vices that it may obtain and keep
what it desires, are rather vices than virtues so long as there is
no reference to God in the matter. For although some suppose
that virtues which have a reference only to themselves, and are
desired only on their own account, are yet true and genuine
virtues, the fact is that even then they are inflated with pride,
and are therefore to be reckoned vices rather than virtues.

For as that which gives life to the flesh is not derived from flesh, but is above it, so that which gives blessed life to man is not derived from man, but is something above him; and what I say of man is true of every celestial power and virtue whatsoever.[1]

Saint Augustine in this passage is but elaborating the teachings of Jesus himself. When one of the Pharisees who was a lawyer asked, "Which is the great commandment in the law?" Jesus replied: "Thou shalt love the Lord thy God with all thy heart and with all thy soul, and with all thy mind. This is the first and great commandment."[2] Love of neighbor, while important, is put second. This order is sometimes forgotten by modernist and agnostical Christians of the present day to whom Christianity has come to mean no more than a call to social service and an exercise of humanitarian virtues. Humanitarianism is, to be sure, an essential part of Christianity and its omission from the Christian teaching leads to fanaticism or hypocrisy. But it is the second not the first command.

The illative faculty

A convenient philosophical approach to the meaning and possible truth of Christian doctrine is found in the writings of John Henry, Cardinal Newman (1801–1890), particularly in his *Grammar of Assent*. Newman had belonged in his earlier years to the Anglican Church but at the time of writing the *Grammar* he had become converted to Catholicism. Earlier British philosophy had influenced the cast of his thought, and on its secular side his philosophy may be regarded as an oblique development of the empiricism of Hume and, in its ethical aspect, of

---

[1]Saint Augustine, *The City of God*, Bk. XIX, Sec. 25. (Translated by the Rev. Marcus Dods.)

[2]Matthew, 22: 37–38.

'moral sense' intuitionism. The moral sense is for Newman an aspect of a more general *illative faculty*,[1] which
may be defined as an apperceptive grasp of any complicated situation that far surpasses "the assignable media
of perceiving." The faculty is regarded by Newman as
providing a knowledge not only of moral but of religious
truths as well.

In all knowledge, Newman's argument runs, there is
present a non-rational element which may be called *assent*. Neither logical nor empirical proof can ever be
exhaustive; they can convince us only if we are willing
to be convinced by them. In theory we may be content
to judge every proposition as no better than probable.
But normally there is what Locke had called a *surplusage*
of belief over proof. Why do I believe, for instance,
Newman asks, that Great Britain is an island? The
question is not whether Great Britain could be proved to
be an island if anyone took the trouble to sail around it or
to soar high enough in a balloon, but what the grounds
actually are on which most persons believe it to be so.
The grounds, if we stop to consider them, turn out to be
such as these: that we were taught in early childhood that
it is an island, that it is always represented so on maps,
that we have never heard its insularity disputed but on
the contrary find it taken for granted in all books and
conversations on the subject as well as in countless ways

---

[1]Those who share the suspicion, based on misunderstanding, which modern
psychologists entertain towards the word 'faculty' may profitably note the
comment of Max Müller (philologist, philosopher of religions, contemporary
of Newman) on his own use of the word. Declaring that 'faculty' signifies
a mode of action; never a substantial something, Müller adds: "If the English
language allowed it I should even propose to replace 'faculty' by the *Not-yet*,
and to speak of the Not-yet of language and religion, instead of their faculties
or potential energies." (*Lectures on the Origin and Growth of Religion*, p. 23.)
Müller's definition is helpful in clearing up some needless confusion but is not,
I think, sufficiently positive. 'Faculty' connotes more than a not-yetness; it
connotes also an *ability or tendency to become*.

more indirect and harder to define, such as what we know of Great Britain's commercial, political, and military history, what we know of contemporary world events, and of the reported activities of visitors. "Numberless facts, or what we consider facts, rest on the truth of [this assumption]; no received fact rests on its being otherwise." Nevertheless, such circumstantial evidence, while it may give high probability, does not give certainty. On the basis of the evidence alone we ought to keep our judgment in suspension, and to hold a reasonable doubt about the matter. But we don't. If anyone told us that there is a northern isthmus connecting Great Britain with Scandinavia, which navigators have universally conspired to keep secret, we would dismiss him as not worth a hearing. It is not that we would give to such a proposal the very small amount of credence it logically deserves; we would simply give it no credence at all. Can anyone, asks Newman, "bring into one focus of proof the reasons which make him so sure?"

Newman's solution is that in all situations where belief can be a matter of importance there is a "supra-logical judgment," which is "but the true healthy action of our ratiocinative powers, an action more subtle and more comprehensive than the mere appreciation of a syllogistic argument." It is "the exercise of a living faculty in the individual intellect" as opposed to "mere skill in argumentative science" yet it works "not indeed to the exclusion, but as the supplement of logic." It functions not as a discursive process but as a simple unified act, as a direct vision of some truth. This 'illative faculty' is present in everyone but shows itself most strikingly in an Isaac Newton perceiving the cosmic relations implied in an apple's falling, a Napoleon with a clear presentiment of the disposition of the enemy's forces, or a saint beholding God. When it is active in moral matters it is properly called conscience, and while often valuably supplemented by reason it is essentially a trans-rational mode of apprehending right and wrong.

Newman's account of the 'illative faculty' describes the general form that a religious experience will take. Its specific content, what differentiates it from other types of apperceptive intuition, is more directly pertinent to our present inquiry. An adequate comprehension of the meaning of religion and of the content of a religious experience is not possible to one who is utterly a stranger to such an experience, any more than colors can be properly explained to one born blind. This fact presents a serious difficulty to a secular exposition of religious ethics. Understanding and belief are less readily divorced in the case of religion than in philosophical and ethical theories. Nevertheless, certain general characteristics of Christian ethics may be distinguished.

Christian virtues

In contrast and opposition to the Greek affirmation of human life and its attendant values, stands the Christian demand for a renunciation of the things of this world. "Come, take up the cross, and follow me," said Jesus to the man of wealth who asked him for the secret of eternal life. The questioner was a 'moral' man, he had observed all the commandments from his youth. But Christianity requires more than an observance of the commandments; it requires nothing less than a complete rebirth of spirit. "Except a man be born again, he cannot see the kingdom of God." Unconditional renunciation must precede this spiritual reawakening: "Whosoever shall seek to save his life shall lose it; and whosoever shall lose his life shall preserve it." Unconditional love of God, humility before

Him, and unquestioning submission to His will, are the cardinal Christian virtues.

One way in which the ethical significance of Christianity can be appreciated is to observe in what respects it has transformed the cardinal virtues of the Greeks. The four cardinal Greek virtues—temperance, courage, wisdom, and justice—were none of them fitted to the stern requirements of the Christian way of life. In place of temperance, which to the Greeks had meant a wise and moderate enjoyment of desires, Christianity substituted self-abnegation, involving a separation of spirit from flesh and a mistrust of natural bodily impulses. "And if thy right eye offend thee," said Jesus, "pluck it out and cast it from thee. . . . And if thy right hand offend thee, cut it off, and cast it from thee." Similar, sometimes even more excessive, commands are found in the epistles of St. Paul. In place of courage (in the ordinary signification of the word) there was the zeal of martyrdom. Wisdom, so far as it is attained by the processes of unregenerate human reason, was looked on with suspicion. "Surely," says Thomas à Kempis, "an humble husbandman that serveth God, is better than a proud philosopher who, neglecting himself, is occupied in studying the course of the heavens."[1]   To the Christian the only sure wisdom could come through faith. Finally, in place of the dominant Greek virtue, justice, Christianity put the emphasis on love, compassion, and forgiveness:

Ye have heard that it hath been said, An eye for an eye, and a tooth for a tooth:

But I say unto you, That ye resist not him that is evil· but whosoever shall smite thee on thy right cheek, turn to him the other also.

---

[1] *Of the Imitation of Christ*, Part I, Chap. II.

And if any man will sue thee at the law, and take away thy
coat, let him have thy cloak also.   .   .   .
Ye have heard that it hath been said, Thou shalt love thy
neighbor, and hate thine enemy.
But I say unto you, Love your enemies, bless them that curse
you, do good to them that hate you, and pray for them which
despitefully use you, and persecute you.   .   .   .[1]

In every case the direction is away from the relative to the
absolute, and from emphasis on outward character to inner motive.   The Sermon on the Mount contains more
than one reminder of the inward character of true virtue:
it is wrong not only to kill but also to bear a silent grudge,
not only to commit adultery but also to lust in one's heart.
The moral quality of an act consists in the motive and
disposition that lie behind it, not in extraneous and accidental circumstances.   In this respect Christian ethics
resembles Stoicism and the ethics of Kant (the subjects
of the next chapter) but while the Stoic and the Kantian
define the right motive as the rational motive, to the Christian a motive can be right only so far as it is born from a
complete surrender to the will of God.

Is Christianity practicable?

The demands made by Christianity are uncompromising.   Can an ethic so absolute be made to work amid the
complexities of the contemporary world?   As manifested
in most contemporary institutions, to be sure, Christianity
is very far from refusing to compromise.   But it can be
argued that just by reason of that very weakness Christianity is failing to solve the spiritual as well as the practical problems of today.   To the cry of the sceptic that
Christianity will not work a believer in Christ might well
retort by asking, Has it really been tried?   Diplomats

[1]Matthew, 5: 38-44.

have shown no ability to prevent mass-slaughter, nor
business leaders to promote the general happiness. A
prominent cause of economic misery is the excessive and
combative demands that we are accustomed to make of
life. Can any suggested program of social reform be
made genuinely effective so long as the dominant interests
of men are worldly and self-seeking? The question is not
meant to suggest that programs for the reform of society
should cease, but simply that effective social reform must
be based upon a re-education of human loyalties. The
strongest human loyalties are felt by most men not towards
abstractions like Society, Progress, Equality, but towards
persons; a fact of human psychology that goes far to explain the popularity of political dictators. In this same
fact lies much of the potential strength of a religious
ethic. The obligations felt by the religious conscience
are obligations towards a Person, and this gives them
(circumstances being equal) a much greater force.

Two serious objections, however, may be raised. First,
it may be objected that the full power of Christian ethics
is present only to one who accepts (not in every detail
literally, perhaps, but in essential outline) the Christian
revelation as true. But can educated men, cognizant of
the results of science, of the historical causes of superstition and of the psychological explanations of religious experience, be expected to acknowledge the truth of the
gigantic assumptions that Christianity makes—in particular, its primary assumption of the existence of a personal
God? Does in fact such a God exist? This question, on
analysis, develops into the question, How can we know
whether a God exists? And out of this there develops a
third question: What kind of knowledge or belief is involved in the question of whether God exists, and how
can such knowledge or belief be made consistent with the

conclusions of experimental science, and how, finally, is it related to the knowledge of right and wrong? These questions, which lead out of the field of ethics into the peripheral fields of epistemology and metaphysics, will be discussed in the final chapter of the book.

The second objection is of a more practical nature. Important as is the Christian emphasis on self-purification and love as the basic factors in genuine morality, these provide no sufficient criterion for our duties in the contemporary social world. Not counting hypocrites (for such are not true Christians) there are many to whom an acceptance of Christianity seems to offer a justification for quietism and withdrawal from the world. St. Augustine, in the *De Civitate Dei*, holds that the 'earthly city' is ruled by the devil, hence is necessarily unjust and its peace securable only by constant warfare; that salvation consists in indifference to the affairs of the world and withdrawal from it to a contemplation and worship of God and an immersion in the things of the 'heavenly city.'[1] One dangerous result of this dualism, as Reinhold Niebuhr has observed, is that "in contrast between the divine and the human all lesser contrasts between good and evil on the human and historic level are obscured." Dr. Niebuhr believes nevertheless that the Christian insistence on love, in promoting an extension and enlargement of moral ideals, represents a permanent contribution to the moral life:

Religion encourages love and benevolence . . . by absolutizing the moral principle of life until it achieves the purity of absolute disinterestedness and by imparting transcendent worth to the life of others. . . . "If ye love them that love you, what reward have ye?" declared Jesus; and in the

---

[1] A particularly bloodthirsty form of this dualism is found in the conversations of Naphta the Jesuit in Thomas Mann's novel, *The Magic Mountain*.

logic of those words the whole social genius of the Christian religion is revealed.   The transcendent perspective of religion makes all men our brothers and nullifies the divisions, by which nature, climate, geography, and the accidents of history divide the human family.   By this insight many religiously inspired idealists have transcended national, racial, and class distinctions.[1]

In this way religion "absolutizes the sentiment of benevolence and makes it the norm and ideal of the moral life." So far, very valuable.   But benevolence is not justice and is even compatible with the grossest forms of injustice. Religious resources, therefore, to be effective, must be subjected to rational control, and this is true also of the sense of duty generally.   We pass on, therefore, in the next two chapters to ethical theories which emphasize the place of reason in the moral life, beginning in Chapter VI with the more extreme views of Kant and the Stoics and proceeding in Chapter VII to the more balanced philosophy of humanism.

_____

[1]*Moral Man and Immoral Society*, Chap. III.   (Scribners.)

CHAPTER VI

RATIONALISM

When one of the company said, "Convince me that logic is necessary": "Do you wish me to demonstrate this to you?" he asked. "Yes." "Then must I use a demonstrative form of argument?" And when this was admitted: "Then how will you know whether I argue fallaciously?" And as the man was silent: "Don't you see," said Epictetus, "how even you yourself acknowledge that logic is necessary, since without its assistance you cannot so much as know whether it is necessary or not?"

The Discourses of Epictetus

THERE IS a sense in which intuitionism says the last word on moral duty; another in which it is far from adequate. Duty which is truly moral and not a mere conventional and perfunctory obedience to rules has to be recognized and grasped with the whole mind; and this apperception of it is the only sound basis for an enduring and developing moral life. But no one would seriously say that all visions of duty are equally good. That would be to fall into the already discussed 'indifferentist' fallacy. Granted that everyone has what the intuitionists rather too provocatively call a 'moral sense,' which is to say a capacity for distinguishing good from bad and better from worse, still these inner voices do not always pipe the same tune. When conscience speaks ambiguously how shall we judge? When inner voices disagree how shall we declare one rather than another authentic? *Rationalism* answers that conscience speaks with authority only when it speaks rationally; that its valid commands are characterized by (1) absolute self-consistency and (2) freedom from empirical elements such as habit, inclination, and considerations of practicality.

163

Two forms of ethical rationalism are expounded in the present chapter: that of the Stoics and that of Kant. Their chief difference, apart from the underlying and less easily definable difference of intellectual temper between representatives of the ancient and modern worlds, is that the Stoics based their rationalism on certain beliefs about the nature of the universe, while Kant's ethics stands independent of cosmological theories.

1. STOICISM

Soon after Socrates' death an Athenian philosopher named Antisthenes set up a school in a gymnasium in Athens known as the Cynosarges, for which reason he and those who accepted his doctrines and way of life were given the name of *Cynics*. As it happened the word 'Cynic' was identical with the Greek adjective meaning dog-like. Because of the unkempt appearance and unconventional behavior of Antisthenes, and more especially of his disciple Diogenes, the inevitable pun was made and the Cynics were frequently referred to as dogs. Antisthenes considered himself a disciple of Socrates, but in spite of certain superficial resemblances the teachings of the two men are far apart in essential aims. Antisthenes was an out-and-out ascetic. The good life, he declared, consists in curbing our desires rather than fulfilling them. His startling declaration, "I would rather go mad than feel pleasure," and his glorification of *ponos* (painful travail, whether mental or physical) as necessary to strengthen our powers of endurance indicated the forbidding character of his teachings. Philosophy had given him, he said, the ability to hold converse with himself, and it was in philosophical contemplation, not in pleasures, that the only satisfaction of a wise man was to be found.

His disciple Diogenes appears to have gone as far as he

could to outdo the master in eccentricity of conduct. "Live according to nature," was his principal maxim, and this slippery phrase meant in his use of it the doing away with all conventions. It is said that by watching a mouse running about, not looking for a place in which to lie down, not fearing the dark, and not seeking any of the luxuries of life, he discovered the means of adapting himself to circumstances. According to the legend that was soon built up, he slept in a tub in the open air, carried his food about in a wallet, and was not ashamed to beg alms when the occasion arose. Even his begging, however, was unconventional: "My friend, it's for food I want it, not funeral expenses," he is said to have exclaimed to a miserly man who was slow to respond; and on another occasion he was found begging alms of a statue "in order," he said, "to get practice in being refused." By the time Alexander had ascended to the throne of Macedon the fame of Diogenes, then some seventy years old, had spread throughout Greece. One day, as the old philosopher lay sunning himself in his tub, Alexander came riding up with a great retinue, and drawing rein in front of the tub: "I," he announced, "am Alexander the great King." "And I," replied the other with composure, "am Diogenes the Dog." "Are you not then afraid of me?" Alexander asked. "Why, what are you, something good or something evil?" "Something good, of course." "Well," retorted Diogenes, "who would be so foolish as to fear anything good?" Struck with admiration of this answer, Alexander exclaimed, "Ask anything you wish of me, and I will grant it." "Then be so kind," said Diogenes, "as to get out of my sunlight."

The independence of spirit and indifference to material luxuries that are indicated by these anecdotes were qualities prized by the Stoic school, founded a few decades later.

But where the Cynics had taken a perverse delight in flaunting their asceticism in useless and unmannerly ways, the Stoics possessed a more soundly reasoned philosophy and were less inclined to exhibitionism in the expression of it. They translated the Cynic protest against convention into a positive law of duty, and declared that this law must be based on a knowledge of the true laws governing the universe, for the universe seemed to them a living rational whole, of which human conduct was but a microcosmic part. Although Marcus Aurelius the Roman emperor and Epictetus the Greek slave are today the best known representatives of Stoicism, the founder of the Stoic school was Zeno, a Phœnician from the island of Cyprus,[1] who came to Athens about 300 B. C. and hired some kind of a portico or colonnade (in Greek, *stoa*) in which to give lectures. He and his disciples became known, consequently, as 'the men of the Stoa,' or 'the Stoics.'

Logical foundations of the doctrine

As a logical basis on which to build a sound theory of ethics the Stoic philosophy includes also a theory of knowledge and a theory of the nature of the world. The first question to be answered in the Stoic theory of knowledge is how truth can be attained by men. The Sophist philosophers of Socrates' day had doubted the possibility of attaining it at all, basing their doubt on the deceptiveness and relativity of sense-perceptions, on which the quest of truth is dependent. Plato, in answering the Sophists, did not deny the unreliability of the impressions of sense. Sense-impressions are always more or less vitiated by error, he acknowledged, but a knowledge of truth is nevertheless possible if we are wise enough to seek it

---

[1] Not to be confused with Zeno of Elea, author of the famous paradox of Achilles and the tortoise.

not in sensory things but in essential forms and relations.
The Stoics, on the contrary, believed that truth can be
known but that knowledge of it is valid only when firmly
grounded on 'impressions.' By an impression (*phantasia*)
they meant any image produced in the mind by an external object, whether a perceptual image or one of the
train of images that follow the immediate act of perception. An impression "grabs us by the hair, and drags us
to assent"; or, as Plutarch has expressed the matter, it is
a state of the soul which bears witness not only to its own
existence but to that of its object. Often, to be sure, it
bears false witness, as in the case of perceptual errors and
illusions. But the wise man can avoid being made a
victim of error by withholding his assent from impressions
whose significance is uncertain. This does not mean that
the wise man makes no mistakes in practice, for often he
is compelled to act with an insufficient knowledge of the
situation, but his action in such cases, provided he does
not yield up his judgment in the matter, is not to be
blamed on himself since it was caused by circumstances.
The point is illustrated by a tale told of a disciple of
Zeno's to whom King Ptolemy at a banquet offered a
pomegranate made of wax. When the philosopher put the
fruit to his mouth and discovered the trick Ptolemy laugh-
ingly accused him of having assented to a false impression. Not at all, replied the other, he had assented not
to the reality of the pomegranate but only to the probability of its being real. True to the Stoic rule of conduct
he had acted as the circumstances required, but without
giving them his full mental assent.

Full assent is to be given only to 'grasped impressions,'
which to the Stoics implied two things. A 'grasped impression' has the character of certainty: the mind perceives that not more than one interpretation of it is pos-

sible.   More than that, it is an impression that directly
seizes hold of the object itself.   Only from 'grasped impressions' can a true knowledge of Nature and of the
Good be constructed.

The telic principle in nature

Opposed to the atomism of Epicurus the Stoics regarded the universe not as a collection of inert particles
but as an organic unity pulsating with life.   If we look
at some isolated part of the universe it is likely to appear
incomplete, fortuitous, and sometimes positively evil.
Such defects, however, are characteristics not of the universe but simply of the impressions that we receive of the
universe.   There is a rational meaning, a comprehensive
plan, revealed in the universe and intelligible to the man
who gives assent only to that whereof he has been rationally convinced.   A few musical notes heard by chance
through an open door may appear to be without significance to one who, if he were to hear the whole composi-
tion of which they are a part, would recognize how excel-
lently they were adapted to the musical idea which the
composer has expressed.   In like manner it is only when
each particular event or circumstance is seen in its relation to the whole universe that its essentially rational
character can be understood.   The Stoic sage will reflect
on every impression in this way, interpreting it as a
particular expression of the Logos, or rational principle
of the world.   His interpretation, that is to say, will always be *teleological* and *monistic*.[1]

From his interpretation of the universe as rational the
Stoic finds the universe to be also good.   For what, to the
rational man, can be more excellent than rationality itself?   From these premises (that whatever is rational is

---

[1] See Glossary for the meaning of these two words.

good, and that the universe is completely rational) it
follows that the universe is completely good, and that evil
is therefore nothing real.   The unreality of evil is for
most persons a baffling paradox and the least acceptable
part of the Stoic doctrine.   How, they ask, can the reality
of evil be doubted when everywhere we see countless individuals suffering from pain, privation, frustrated desires,
disease and death?   Are not these afflictions evil?   No,
replies the Stoic, they appear evil only when we wrongly
give assent to our limited impressions of them.   It is
repugnant to the foot to step into the mud and if the foot
could think it would suppose this to be a great evil, but
to the man "it is sometimes fitting that the foot should
step in the mud and tread on thorns, and perhaps even be
cut off for the good of the whole organism.   Otherwise
it is not truly a foot"—otherwise, that is to say, it lacks
the true nature of a foot, which consists in being subordinate to the organism of which it is a part.   Likewise a
man, if he thinks of himself as a detached individual, will
suppose that long life and riches and health are apporpri-
ate to his nature and therefore good.   But let him recognize that he is but a tiny detail in the rational structure
of universal Nature, and he will therein acquire a 'reasoned impression,' *i.e.*, a clear rational conviction that
riches and poverty and premature death are, if they occur, expressions of the cosmic plan and therefore good.
"Do your worst, pain, do your worst: you will never com-
pel me to acknowledge that you are an evil," cried the
Roman Stoic Posidonius when suffering from a malign
disease.

The moral ideal

The first distinction the Stoic ethics makes is between
things that lie within our power and things that do not.

We have no power over what our impressions will be; we have power only over the use we shall make of them. When a man is condemned by the emperor to die, all manner of impressions form themselves in his mind. There is the sound of the emperor's words and there is the chain of images to which this perception gives rise. Neither the sound of the words nor the consequent mental pictures of the coming tortures and death are within the power of the beholder. They come to him from external causes. To him belongs the power to decide only this: whether he will cringe before the fate that has overtaken him and falsely judge it to be evil, or whether acknowledging it to be part of the universal perfection he will go forth to meet it with courage and tranquillity.

What aid then should we have ready at hand in circumstances such as these? Why, what else but the knowledge of what is mine and what is not mine, of what is permitted me and what is not? I must die: very well, but must I die groaning? Be fettered: shall it be lamenting? Go into exile: does anyone prevent me from going with a smile, cheerful and serene? "Betray the secrets!" No, I will not, for this is something within my own power. "Then I will fetter you." What's that you say? Fetter me? You will fetter my leg, but not even Zeus can overcome my power of choice. "I will throw you into prison; I will behead that paltry body of yours." Well, when did I ever tell you that mine was the only neck that could not be severed?—Let philosophers study such responses as these, let them write them down daily, and practice them.[1]

The power to choose what attitude one will take towards circumstances is what makes the moral ideal both possible and necessary. The moral ideal of Stoicism is derived from the Stoic doctrine of Nature. Nature is rational and, being rational, it is good. Men ought, therefore, to live according to Nature, i.e., in accordance with

[1] *Discourses of Epictetus*, Bk. I, Chap. I.

Reason. What does this mean in terms of concrete duties? It means first, as we have seen, that the Stoic will acknowledge that all circumstances, even disease and death, being parts of universal perfection, are good and therefore to be faced with tranquillity and with a detached, unemotional sort of approval. But the phrase has a more particular reference too. Although there is no part of the universe that is not rational, man is rational in a special sense, for he has, as distinguished from other forms of life, an ability to make active use of reason in his own person. Reason is thus man's 'ruling principle' and the active working of reason is the only healthy condition of the human soul. The emotions, since they hinder the pure activity of reason, are entirely evil and ought to be ruthlessly weeded out. Even pity is an evil; tranquil benevolence must take its place. To preserve his tranquillity the Stoic must perform his duties without desire. Let him make any sacrifice that may be required in order to help and guide his fellow-men, but if his sacrifice should prove futile let him feel no regret. The essential thing is that he should in every case respond to circumstances in the most rational way: this is his duty and if he has performed his duty as well as he is able it is a matter of indifference to him what effects may follow.

Unlike the Epicurean, the Stoic recognized certain political duties. But even when, like the Stoic emperor Marcus Aurelius, his duties required him to take an active part in the political life of his day, he still regarded himself primarily as a citizen of the world, and his chief moral allegiance was given not to his nation but to all mankind without discrimination, and to that universal Reason of which mankind is an embodiment. *Quâ* emperor, Aurelius had special duties to Rome, but this was owing to the circumstances in which he happened to have been born.

His actions would often be directed to the furthering of
Rome's special interests, but never would his judgment
acknowledge the unqualified rightness of those interests.
It was his duty to benefit the city and the empire so far
as lay within his power, but where he failed to achieve this
end he must be wise enough to recognize that, his failure
being due to circumstances and circumstances being
manifestations of universal Reason, the failure too was
necessarily good.   Thus, while conscientiously performing
all the tasks that God (which was only another name for
universal Reason) had imposed on him by assigning him
to a particular station in life, the Stoic will maintain his
independence and self-sufficiency by excluding from his
mind all desire to see his acts turn out in one way rather
than another.   The outcome must be left to God; the
individual is responsible only for the rationality and un-
swerving justice of his motives.

Critical observations

To many persons the ethics of Stoicism will seem too
austere.   Excessive austerity, however, cannot justly be
criticized if an individual employs it only towards himself.
And it is one of the excellences of Stoicism that in his
dealings with other men the Stoic exhibits no intolerance.
When another person acts irrationally the Stoic will withhold his approval, but he will not condemn, for does not
each person act according to the necessity of his particular
nature?   The Stoic will therefore regard the actions of
other men with the same tranquil detachment with which
he observes the occurrences of Nature—indeed, the actions
of men *are* simply occurrences of Nature, being part of a
single rational universe.

But how, if this is so, it may be asked, is there any room
for freedom in the Stoic's universe?   Regardless of how a

man acts, his action is a necessary and inevitable expression of Nature. Does it not follow, then, that the Stoic seeking tranquillity and the libertine seeking carnal excitement are both of them behaving in ways that their respective natures make necessary? The Stoic would answer affirmatively. In that case, the critic might continue, if the Stoic because of the peculiar nature he possesses must seek tranquillity as inevitably as a stone must roll downwards, what meaning is there in saying that it is his duty to behave in this way? How can there be duty except to one who has the power to choose whether he will perform the duty or leave it undone? The Stoics replied by distinguishing between such necessity as is imposed on a man from without and the necessity that is an expression of his own nature. Freedom, they said, is contrary to necessity of the former kind but identical with necessity of the latter. Yet this reply hardly seems to meet the logical objection already stated, that if I have no power *not* to behave as I am going to, it is only in a pickwickian sense that such behavior can be called my duty. An extended examination of this problem must be reserved, however, for Chapter XII.

2. THE FORMALISM OF KANT

Another type of rationalism, freed from the cosmological assumptions of the Stoics and as a consequence freed from the difficulty of reconciling their doctrine of determinism with the ethical postulate of alternative possibilities, was formulated by Immanuel Kant (1724–1804). Kant's theory is expounded in a fairly short but closely reasoned and somewhat difficult treatise, *Fundamental Principles of the Metaphysics of Morals*.

In an earlier work, *The Critique of Pure Reason*, one of the most influential books in the field of modern philosophy, Kant had undertaken to demonstrate *a priori* what must be the abstract characteristics of any object of cognition whatever. The specific content of what is known cannot, of course, be determined by an *a priori* analysis, for the data of knowledge can only be given by sense-perception. But even in what we call sense-perception or perceptual experience there are certain characteristics that are never absent: to know at all is to know in terms of them. Everything that we perceive is perceived as a *substance*, having *qualities*, capable of some kind of *quantitative* determination, and partaking of *causal* relations with other things. General characteristics such as these, which Kant calls 'categories of the understanding,' constitute the form of every possible experience. It follows that we cannot test their validity empirically. We may appeal to experience to discover whether our bath is cold or hot, but it would be senseless to try to determine empirically whether the bath has any qualities at all. No inquiry could have been begun unless it had. A bacteriologist may conduct experiments in order to learn the causes of the decomposition of meat, but independently of what his experiments may reveal he will not cease to believe that the decomposition does have some cause. The basic forms and relations of objects, Kant concludes, are not 'in' the objects themselves but are the immediate product of man's act of knowing the objects. The reasons why the forms are what they are is to be found in man's rational nature.

In moral matters, too, there is an *a priori* element. Just as the categories of the understanding cannot be deduced from the particular content that sensation supplies, so duty cannot be deduced from the mere *fact* that this or that object is desired, or that we feel an impulse to act in this or that way. Duty and impulse are often hostile, and always logically distinct. Furthermore, our inclinations are varied and often urge us simultaneously to contradictory courses of action; but contradictory courses of action cannot both be right, whence it follows that what is right is distinct in essence from what is desirable. Most important of all, the rightness of a course of action imposes on the individual an absolute obligation to perform it, and "the basis of obligation must not be sought in the nature of man, or in the circumstances in the world in which he is placed, but *a priori* simply in the conceptions of pure reason." Lying and knavery, if they are wrong at all, must be wrong in any circumstances whatever. Truth-telling and the keeping of agreements, if right, must always be our duty. If there exist or were ever to exist rational beings other than men—angels, let's say, or creatures on another planet—the duty of truth-telling and the wrongness of lying would be just as true for them as for us. For like the proposition, "$7 + 5 = 12$," the proposition, "Lying is morally wrong" is true *a priori, i.e.,* self-evidently true to anyone who rationally apprehends its meaning. The truth of neither proposition is given by experience; both may be regarded as universal principles to which (in somewhat different ways) experience must conform.

The *a priori* nature of mathematical propositions needs no proof. But that ethical propositions have a similarly necessary and universal character is less evident. Let us examine, then, the argument by which Kant defends his position.

The categorical imperative

Although it is true that some objects affect us pleasurably and others painfully we are under no obligation to choose the former and reject the latter. The Ought of any hedonistic calculus is what was called in Chapter 1 the 'prudential' Ought. The statement, "You ought to see that play," signifies ordinarily, "*If* you wish to be entertained, *then* you ought to see that play." Spencer's maxim, "Promote life!" turns out on examination to be valid only if one accepts the major premise that 'life' (as Spencer interprets it) is a dominant good. The Spencerian maxim thus becomes: *If* you admire life for its own sake and wish that there should be as much of it as possible, *then* you ought to strive to increase it. Circumstances are not morally coercive. Every obligation imposed by circumstances is conditional on the manner in which the circumstances are evaluated by the agent: it is what Kant calls a *hypothetical imperative*. But a moral obligation is unconditional: Kant calls it a *categorical imperative*.

Where can a categorical imperative be found? As there are two factors in the production of a voluntary action—the nature of the agent and the circumstances in which he happens to be—the imperative must be found in the one or the other. But the circumstances surrounding an action do not command, they simply *are*. They serve only as the *occasions* of putting a command into effect: if I accept the command to speak the truth, circumstances offer me from time to time varied opportunities of making my acceptance effective. Considered from the standpoint of logic, the circumstances are what furnish the minor premise to the ethical syllogism implicit in every conscious moral choice: "Love them that hate you" (a general principle, which may or may not be a categorical imperative and which furnishes the major premise); "Here is one who hates me" (a circumstantial fact: the minor premise); "It is for me, then, to repay this one's hatred with love" (a derived imperative: the conclusion).

An examination of the structure of this syllogism will show why circumstances are not morally coercive: why they impose duties only conditionally. A circumstance (minor premise) can logically imply a command to act (conclusion) only if some general principle is accepted (major premise) under which the circumstance in question may be subsumed.

Since the categorical imperative cannot be derived from the circumstances surrounding an action it must be derived from the nature of the agent. The agent, in performing any action, expresses himself as a will, and it is therefore from the character of the agent's will that the moral worth of an act must be determined. An added proof of this is the consideration that talents of the mind like courage and cleverness, and gifts of fortune like power, riches, honor, health, and happiness, may all be turned to evil ends if directed by an evil will; whence it follows that they cannot be good in themselves. Even qualities which are more directly of service to the good will itself such as moderation, self-control, and calm deliberation, are not good intrinsically. Such value as they possess is derived from the good will which motivates them. If not so motivated they are in danger of being turned to evil ends, as in the case of a villain's measured coolness. Nothing, then, except a good will is intrinsically good.

What determines whether or not a will is good? Kant's reply is that a will is good only so far as it is rational. His proof may be summarized as follows. By the preceding argument it has been established that the goodness of the will is intrinsic, or, in Kant's language, that it has not merely value but *worth*. Its goodness, therefore, is not to be judged by its effects, for these are extrinsic to it. Let each inquirer examine his own will at the moment of making a choice. At the first introspective glance his will may seem to be no more than impulse, or rather a conflict of impulses.   But closer analysis will reveal that some degree of rational control is also present, guiding the impulses and subordinating them more or less to a rationally conceived plan.   Which of these two aspects of the will, the impulsive or the rational, is intrinsic to it? Kant replies, the rational.   In so far as the aim of an organism is merely its own conservation, welfare, or happiness, these aims are more surely achieved by natural impulse than by reason.   Nature herself, in carrying out her purposes, selects the means best adapted for such purposes; so that reason, from this practical standpoint, is superfluous.   Reason must therefore have been imparted to us for some purpose other than the utility and satisfaction of the organism.   It follows that since reason is not competent to guide the will with respect to the satisfaction of impulses and desires, its true function must be to guide the will according to the principles of reason itself: *i.e.*, to produce *a rational will*.   And since the intrinsic goodness of anything consists in the fulfillment of its function, the goodness of the will must consist in being rational, *i.e.*, in functioning rationally.   Only a rational will, therefore, is intrinsically good.

Perhaps it will ease the rigors of Kant's argument to break the exposition at this point by inserting a critical comment.   There seem to be in the last step of the argument three weaknesses: an over-sharp distinction between reason and impulse, a second over-sharp distinction between the intrinsic nature of the will and its effects (as if the nature of a thing could ever be conceived wholly apart from any of its effects!), and thirdly, a somewhat crude telic interpretation of reason and impulse, as if each were preordained for a distinct purpose.   Each of these suppositions reflects a half-truth: in moral questions we

ought always to distinguish *as clearly as we can* our rational from our merely impulsive choices and our motives
from the results of our actions.   Also it is true that so
far as we are successful in distinguishing the rational
from the merely impulsive factors which motivate an
action there is a sense in which these two sets of factors,
having different natures, are fitted to serve different ends.
But a critical differentiation of the qualities to be found
in human motives is not enough for Kant's argument.
Its validity at this point depends on the supposition that
the difference between reason and impulse is absolute.

Duty for duty's sake

Summarizing the results of Kant's argument so far:
(1) The will alone has intrinsic worth.   (2) Its worth is
autonomous—i.e., to be judged not by the effects of the
will but by the character of its inner motivating principle.
(3) This inner motivating principle is rational, and the
good will is therefore the rational will.   From the first
two of these propositions there follows a fourth: that the
moral worth of actions is determined wholly by the motives that impel them, not at all by their effects.   An action is morally good so far, and only so far, as it is motivated by a good will.   Inasmuch as duty is the compelling
motive of the pure good will, this fourth proposition is
equivalent to saying that actions are morally good only
when they are done *from* duty, not merely in accordance
with it.   An action that is done from inclination may
happen to be in accordance with duty, but it will not have
moral worth.   Kant offers an illustration.   To maintain
one's life, while in accordance with duty, has generally no
moral import because almost everyone has a direct inclination to do so.   Again, beneficence to others, while in
accordance with duty, has no true moral worth so long

as the agent is moved by sympathy or direct inclination. If, on the other hand, a man hates life yet preserves it because it is his duty to do so, or if when not moved by sympathy he benefits others in distress, then his action does have moral worth.

Startling as this doctrine may seem, it is logically deducible from the earlier steps of Kant's argument. To prove this, suppose the contrary. Suppose that the action of John Brown, who hates life but preserves it from sheer duty, and the action of James Green, who preserves his life because of a natural inclination to do so, were of equal moral worth. The quality of their worth would evidently not be determined by their respective motives, since these differ, but by the results attained or at least aimed at—namely, preservation of life. The moral worth of the actions would thereby be determined by reference to some principle other than the will. But moral worth, as already stated, is intrinsic worth. It has also been stated that nothing has intrinsic worth but the good will. These last three sentences form an antilogism. Our *ex hypothesi* argument thus falls down, and the supposition from which it started must be abandoned. In this way, by the method of *reductio ad absurdum*,[1] it becomes doubly evident that on Kant's principles actions are morally good only so far as they are motivated by, not merely done in accordance with, the rational will; or, in other words, only so far as they are done from, not merely in accordance with, duty.

How in each case is our duty to be discovered? Or, as the question can be restated, how are the moral laws to which we owe absolute allegiance to be derived? Kant answers: "Since moral laws ought to hold good for every rational creature, we must derive them from the general

---

[1]For the technical terms in this paragraph, see Glossary.

concept of a rational being." Now a rational being is a
being characterized by consistency, or, stated obversely,
a being who is not guilty of self-contradiction. Since,
therefore, moral laws must be derived from the *general
concept* of a rational being, they must be derived from the
principle of rational consistency itself, or, as it is more
often called, the Law of Contradiction. The Law of
Contradiction declares that a thing cannot both be and
not be, and that it cannot both have and not have a given
characteristic. "A is not both B and not B." When this
formula is translated into terms of conduct A stands for
some specific type of human action and B stands for
'right.' Thus applied the Law of Contradiction becomes:
The same action cannot be both right and wrong. Trans-
posing this disjunctive proposition to a hypothetical form,
we get: If an action is ever right, it is not ever wrong; or,
If an action is right on any one occasion it is right on any
occasion whatever. It follows that if my motive is rational (*sc.*, moral) I cannot will that an action should be
performed on any one occasion without at the same time
affirming that it ought to be performed universally. Restated as a law of conduct, this principle becomes: "Act
always in such a way that you could will your action to
become a universal law." And since a moral action, as already demonstrated, must always be performed *from* duty,
not merely in accordance with it, the moral law can be more
precisely formulated as follows: "*Act only on that maxim
whereby you can at the same time will that it should become a
universal law.*" This, then, is Kant's statement of the
categorical imperative.

Applications of the principle

How is the categorical imperative to be applied? It
seems, abstractly formulated, to spin round in a curious

circle: the moral law is that our acts should always be motivated by a respect for moral law. Kant, however, gives several illustrations of his meaning, of which two will be outlined here.

Suppose that a man has been reduced to despair by misfortunes and feels wearied of life but is still so far in possession of his reason that he can ask himself whether it would be a violation of duty to take his own life. Well, let him inquire whether the maxim of his action could be made a universal law for everyone. It could not—at least, not without contradiction. For his implicit maxim is this: It may be adopted as a principle that one's life may be terminated whenever its longer duration seems to promise more evil than satisfaction. The motive by which this principle is determined is evidently self-love. And Kant comments:

It is asked then simply whether this principle founded on self-love can become a universal law of nature. Now we see at once that a system of nature of which it should be a law to destroy life by means of the very feeling whose special nature it is to impel to the improvement of life would contradict itself, and therefore could not exist as a system of nature; hence that maxim cannot possibly exist as a universal law of nature, and consequently would be wholly inconsistent with the supreme principle of all duty.[1]

The acute student will detect in the words 'special nature' an illegitimate use of telic explanation.

As a second illustration, suppose that a man finds himself forced by circumstances to borrow money which he sees no prospect of repaying. Unless he promises to repay it within a definite time, however, nothing will be lent to him. May he, consistently with duty, make the promise? Well, again apply the test. Let him ask, "How

---

[1]*Metaphysic of Morals.* Abbott's translation. (Longmans, Green.)

would it be if my maxim were a universal law?" He will
see that the maxim on which he acts could never hold as
a universal law for everyone but would contradict itself.

For supposing it to be a universal law that everyone when he
thinks himself in a difficulty should be able to promise whatever
he pleases, with the purpose of not keeping his promise, the
promise itself would become impossible, as well as the end that
one might have in view of it, since no one would consider that
anything was promised to him, but would ridicule all such
statements as vain pretences.[1]

Criticisms

Several criticisms may be made of Kant's categorical
imperative, in addition to the criticism of his presuppositions, made a few paragraphs back. In the first place,
supposing the truth of the principle to be granted, its
applications need not be at all like those which serve Kant
as illustrations. A practising Nietzchean might be perfectly willing that his own policy of ruthlessness should be
made a universal law, for if confident of his own superior
resources he might be willing, or even wish, to do battle
with all comers. Secondly, it is not always possible to
apply the principle without contradiction. Suppose that
by means of the principle it is reasoned that one's duty is
to be honest in business, also that one's duty is to support
one's family. In our imperfect society both cannot always
be done. Which duty is superior? Kant's principle
offers no solution. Thirdly, an attack can be made on the
truth of the principle itself. *Is* it one's duty always to
act in a way that one would willingly see universalized?
Most persons would answer no, but since Kant's affirmative answer was not merely affirmed but was offered as
the conclusion of a logical argument, it can be validly

[1]*Ibid.*

challenged only if some step in the argument is challenged also.

Probably the argument's most noticeable flaw is the way in which it applies the Law of Contradiction to human actions. The Law of Contradiction is true only in the abstract. Whenever it is applied qualifications must be introduced. "Mankind cannot be both honest and dishonest" is a proposition palpably false, although it is a formally correct application of the Law of Contradiction. Its material falsity comes from the failure to make such qualifications as are essential to the specific subject-matter about which it makes an assertion. Similarly it may be maintained that the proposition, "Stealing cannot be both right and wrong," is also materially false. It is possible to believe (as most people, to judge by their actions, do) that stealing in certain respects and in certain circumstances is justified, in others not. There is no *a priori* logical objection to making this material distinction. Indeed, it can be regarded as more or less an accident of language and of social custom that the word 'stealing' is applied in just the way it is. Taking a two-cent stamp without permission might be called stealing and thereby put in the same category with robbing a bank. Many persons might be willing to see the first species of stealing made universally permissible without the second. Or they might insist that a further distinction was necessary: between stealing a stamp wantonly and stealing one when the need is urgent. But Kant would not countenance such distinctions; they destroy, he would say, the universality of law. Universality, however, is always relative to the manner in which concepts are employed and terms defined. Is the inheritance of property a species of stealing? Socialistic philosophers would affirm that it is, but there is no indication that Kant's principle led him to accept socialism. From a socialist's standpoint, therefore, Kant might be criticized for not having interpreted the maxim, "Thou shalt not steal," with sufficient universality. It appears, then, that Kant has stated the moral law so abstractly that it seems a somewhat arbitrary matter just what content it should be given.

There is an important and valid side of Kant's doctrine, however, which is better revealed in the reformulation that he afterwards makes of the law. Inasmuch as the law of conduct is also a law of the self, the categorical imperative can be reformulated as commanding a universal respect for selfhood. It may then be expressed: "*So act as to treat humanity, whether in your own person or in that of any other, in every case as an end and never as merely a means.*" In other words, treat every human being as an end in himself, as a thing having intrinsic worth; never as merely a means, as a thing with merely extrinsic value. Professor Fite's comment on this reformulation is valuable:

This rule is merely a restatement of the former rule. When I perform an act which I cannot will to be a law for all, I give the preference to my own advantage and make the interests of others subordinate to my own. I then treat myself as an end to which the others are only means, *i.e.*, I 'make use' of other persons, treating them as if they were of no more significance than objects of wood or stone. But when I so order my action that it becomes the expression of universal law, I make the ends of others identical with my own and treat humanity as such as an end absolute in itself.[1]

On this interpretation Kant's law becomes a rational expression of the Christian principle, "Do unto others as you would have them do unto you." It thereby becomes a principle of supreme importance, if applied with proper

[1]Warner Fite, *An Introductory Study of Ethics.*

reservations, in testing the sincerity and fairness of one's conduct.   Unreason may approve the satisfaction of an impulse in the self and disapprove the same impulse in another.   But the reasonable man will judge his actions according to the same law by which he judges the actions of others.   This rule of justice, though it lacks the positive elements of a fully moral way of life, is at any rate one of morality's important requisites.

CHAPTER VII

HUMANISM

For head with foot hath private amitie
And both with moons and tides.
George Herbert, *Man*

WE HAVE now examined in turn several representative theories of ethics. Their differences have arisen mainly from the fact that each theory, in doing justice to some particular capacity of the self and to some particular need either of the self or of society, spends too great a part of its emphasis in that one direction, and fails thereby to give an adequate account of man's infinite variety. For this reason it has often seemed to men of vigorous understanding and cultivated sensibilities that ethics is a shabby and worthless pursuit, a game of words played as a substitute for the hardier but less logically ordered game of living and making effective decisions.

In every serious theory of ethics there is an important element of truth. An ethical writer, if he is not a humbug, is reporting certain genuine insights of his own into the nature of moral truth. All too often, whether because his insights are limited or because he is eager to achieve a logically coherent theory, he attaches importance too exclusively to insights having some single character. Schopenhauer is a case in point. No one doubts Schopenhauer's sincerity when he writes of the intolerable anguish with which life is cursed. His words ring true; the anguish is something that he has perceived and felt in his own life and in the lives of men and animals about him. But there is no departure from that one minor key: Schopenhauer's entire ethical theory becomes an expression of his pessimism. Nevertheless it would be stupid to ignore or reject a philosopher because his vision of the truth was only partial. Whose, unless God's, could be anything more? We may admire the virtues and way of life practised by Stoic philosophers or by Christian saints, yet not be able to accept either the metaphysical beliefs which are the inseparable accompaniments of traditional Stoicism or the central fact of divine revelation on which original Christianity rests.

How far is it possible to accept the valid insights of each of the major systems of ethics and integrate them into a theory which, while preserving a certain unity of outlook, succeeds in reflecting more adequately the many-sidedness of moral problems and moral decisions as they occur or are made in real life? And in the case of religious ethics, how far can the strictly ethical elements be retained as valid guides for moral conduct if they are uprooted from the religious beliefs that have been their traditional soil? These two questions can be summarized in the single question, How far is a humanistic ethics possible? For *humanism* is the name ordinarily given to that ethical philosophy which has these two characteristics. First, it does justice to the entire nature and all the latent possibilities of man. Enjoyment of pleasures and benevolent feelings towards others, on which the hedonists build their theories, are truly good things, often good *in themselves;* but no less so are self-control, fortitude, a love of honor and a sense of justice, which hedonists would accept only as means whereby eventual pleasures could be secured or pains avoided. Secondly, the ethics of humanism, being derived from the nature of man, is logically independent of a belief in God or in any other metaphysical entity except, of course, human persons. Socrates and Aristotle and Montaigne, like many other humanists, did as a matter of fact believe in a God of one kind or another, but they differ from the Stoics and Jesus in that they found their ethics upon an examination of human capacities instead of making a transcendental appeal.

1. PLATO

The ethics of Plato (427-347 B. C.) defies exact classification. Although it is here classified as a species of humanism there are strongly mystical and transcendental tendencies in it as well. Plato regarded philosophy as the moving image of truth, constantly to be developed by many-sided inquiry and discussion. He mistrusted the written word, holding that a truth put into writing is dead and its meaning more or less destroyed:

Writing, you know, Phaedrus, has this strange characteristic, in which it is rather like portraiture. For the creatures of portraiture stand like living beings but if you ask them a question they remain solemnly mute. The same is true of written words: you might suppose them to speak as if they had intelligence, but just ask them anything with a view to learning what they mean and they go on forever repeating what they have said.[1]

Plato's doubts about the efficacy of the written word are probably the reason why he cast his writings into the form of dialogues, as though to display truth in its moving character while at the same time withdrawing himself from a too complete identification with its assertiveness. His more positive teachings were given orally in the Academy which he founded at Athens, and only fragments of them have been preserved at second hand.

[1]*Phaedrus*, 275 D.

Socrates, as described in Chapter II, laid the foundations of dialectical method in ethics. But his scattered discourses, as they have been recorded in Plato's early dialogues[1] and, less satisfactorily, in the *Memorabilia* of Xenophon, offer no evidence that he ever undertook to build his richly suggestive criticisms and inquiries into a coherent system. The development of a more coherent approach seemed to Plato an urgent need, for a wave of scepticism had broken over Greek thought, and the teaching of the Sophists that moral distinctions are a mere matter of convention or caprice was finding a ready audience. Plato had the wit to perceive that the only way in which a coherent philosophy could be made to prevail against such formidable opponents was by the adoption of their own weapons of argument. In his written dialogues, therefore, he employs with suitable liter-ary embellishments the same dialectical methods that Socrates and the Sophists had employed in speech, pitting Socrates with his method of ironical cross-examination against spokesmen for various popular but obscure opinions of the day. There emerges from the various hints scattered through the dialogues a recognizable unity of doctrine, the ethical aspect of which we have now to examine.

The unity of the good

One of Socrates' most frequently repeated doctrines is that the various excellences and virtues of a good man

---

[1]In his earliest dialogues, such as the *Laches, Charmides, Euthyphro, Apology,* and *Crito,* Plato is giving a probably faithful portrayal of both the manner and content of Socrates' teaching. In the great dialogues of Plato's middle period, such as the *Protagoras, Symposium, Republic,* and *Phaedrus* it is a debated question among classical scholars how far the opinions are to be attributed to Plato and how far they represent an earlier phase of Socrates' thought, which after Socrates' death Plato came to learn by hearsay. In the following exposition of 'Plato's' philosophy it should be kept in mind that there is some doubt, though perhaps a slight one, that the doctrines attributed to him were altogether his.

are not separate accomplishments but simply different aspects of emphases of the one form of Good. To suppose that holiness, justice, wisdom, temperance, and courage are separable 'parts' of goodness, as rabbits and monkeys and lizards are separate parts of the genus 'animal,' or as cobblers, cooks, and carpenters are functionally differentiated parts of the genus 'man,' is to build an absurd caricature of the moral situation. Socrates lost no opportunity to trip the arguments of those who, like Euthyphro, thought they could compartmentalize the virtues. His negative criticisms along such lines clarified the ethical problem for his successors: the problem of defining the good of man in an adequate manner.

Is there such a thing as objective goodness and right? The view expressed by Callicles in Plato's *Gorgias* is, as mentioned in Chapters III and IV, that the good is that which happens to please, and right is whatever someone happens to have the power of enforcing. Plato's philosophy, in opposition to this, sets out to prove that the good has a meaning independent of what anyone's opinion of it happens to be, and that this meaning is determined by the nature of what is most real in the universe. But what is it that is most real in the universe? Plato replies, it is not the objects of sense-experience, for these are ever changing their natures, and even at one time each thing has as many natures as it has possible interpretations. To scratch oneself when having the itch (the illustration is from the *Gorgias*) is both painful and pleasurable simultaneously. The same liquid is both warm and cool according to whether or not one is feverish at the time of drinking it. The same line is both double and half depending on what length we take as the unit of measurement. Heraclitus, probably the most profound and also the most cryptic of Plato's predecessors, had declared that "you cannot step twice into the same river, for new and ever newer waters are flowing on." The flowing river was used by Heraclitus as a symbol of the incessant flux that characterizes all life: "Everything flows on; nothing abides." At the hands of the Sophists this doctrine of universal flux became a philosophy of logical and ethical relativism: there is nothing stable, not even among meanings and values; human opinion is the only criterion of truth, and human opinions change. To which Plato answers that all those aspects of experience which change, or which like the simultaneously warm and cool liquid contain an inherent contradiction, are for that very reason mere appearances, inferior forms of being, and a study confined to them can never give truth. For truth must have as its essential property self-consistency. The philosopher, therefore, must not be content with appearances; he must look past the changing aspects of things and consider their essential form, their intrinsic nature. By this method alone he can come to know reality and grasp the nature of the good.

The cardinal virtues

Let us consider, as the most important ethical application of Plato's philosophy, the manner in which the nature of right and wrong is determined. Thrasymachus has asserted, in the first book of the *Republic*, that the righteous (or 'just') man is a poor simpleton who lets himself be exploited by those who are powerful enough to take advantage of him, and that only the unrighteous, unjust, ruthless man is likely to be successful and therefore wise or happy. Socrates retorts: Are you sure that the path of unrighteousness is the path of wisdom? Think how wisdom is determined in other fields. The genuine lyre-

player and the genuine physician, as opposed to bunglers
and quacks, are distinguished in this, that each of them
has a standard by which he is guided and which he aims
with his whole soul to approximate. The false musician,
on the other hand, thinks not of how he can play the lyre
most perfectly but of how he can outshine other musi-
cians; the false physician, not of how he can promote the
patient's health and happiness best in the long run, but
of how by appearing to make a spectacular cure he can
win more prestige than his colleagues. Is not the just
and righteous man more like the true than like the spuri-
ous artist? For he too aims at a standard, while the unjust man behaves without restraint, trying to outdo
everybody.

What is the standard by which the righteous man is
guided? In answering this question Socrates at the same
time refutes Thrasymachus' claim that the unrighteous
man is happier than the righteous. For by righteousness
we mean the excellence that belongs peculiarly to the
human soul, as distinct from those specialized forms of
excellence that pertain to lyre-playing and doctoring.
Now to discover the excellence of anything we must first
discover its nature, for by the excellence of a thing we
mean the most complete fulfillment of its proper nature.
The excellence of an eye consists in clarity of vision, for
the natural function of the eye is to see. The excellence
of a pruning-hook consists in cutting vine-branches satisfactorily, for cutting vine-branches is the natural function
of the pruning-hook. If the pruning-hook by getting
broken or dulled should fail to perform this function, then
no matter how serviceable it might be for propping against
doors it would no longer be called a good pruning-hook.
Analogously, it is by examining the natural function of

the human soul that we can discover its proper excellence.
What is the soul's natural function? At first sight the
soul has not one function but many, and these may be
brought under three heads. First there is the class of
simple desires and aversions. Next there is the class of
feelings and impulses that might be called our active
impulses: *e.g.*, anger, ambition, and one's zest for life.
Finally, there is the faculty or power by which we deliberate and choose, and this is called *reason*. Reason must
rule both other sets of motives, checking them or giving
them free rein as the occasion warrants. Each of these
three functions, being natural to man, has a peculiar
excellence of its own: to the appetites corresponds the
virtue of *temperance* or *self-control;* to the active impulses,
courage; to the power of reasoning, *wisdom*. *Justice* or
righteousness is a more inclusive virtue than these other
three, although inseparable from them. It consists in
the right functioning of the soul in its entirety, not in
any one of its particular aspects. The just soul is the
well-regulated soul, the soul in which the three virtues of
wisdom, courage, and temperance are all present in right
relations to each other. As the soul is simply man's
whole nature, the attainment of a well-regulated state of
the soul is man's chief excellence. His true happiness
must therefore consist in this attainment, for what greater
happiness is there than the attainment of one's chief
good?

The theory of forms

The foregoing analysis of human virtues might, if
taken alone, seem to be a merely subjective account of
them. But Plato considers virtue to be objective in a
double sense. Virtue has, in the first place, social objectivity: a fully righteous man is possible only in a just

society, and in the fourth book of the *Republic* the worth
of the four cardinal virtues is independently demonstrated
by showing that each of them corresponds to an important
set of social needs and social functions, and that the right
discharge of these functions is possible only if there are
individuals in control of affairs who possess the virtues
in question. The social aspect of Plato's theory will be
referred to again in a later chapter.

There is a second way also in which virtue is objective.
By virtue we mean the Good so far as it pertains to human
conduct. The Good is not a mere human conception.
Human conceptions of what is good are but reflections of
the Form or Essence of goodness, which all men strive to
know and towards which all strive to direct their actions
except when they are misled by error and illusion. To
behold clearly the 'form' of Good is to give up all else
and strive only to attain it. Owing, however, to the imperfections of our physical organisms the Form is ordinarily apprehended but dimly. We are like men chained
in a cave, fixed so as to see only shadows on the wall,
which are cast by real objects moving about in the light
that shines behind us. The shadows bear a likeness to
the substances of which they are reflections, but the
awakened soul will not be content with this approximation, it will struggle to turn and face the real objects and
the light. The things we perceive and the desires and
impulses we feel in ordinary experience are the shadows
on the cave wall. Even in the shadows we catch a hint
of some greater reality lying beyond, which it is our task
to seek and find. Is this beyond the power of most men?
No, not if they will cast aside illusion, for the Form of
Good is imprinted in the soul of each of us. If we refuse
to let external interests divert us we may turn our gaze
inward and discover it there.

2. ARISTOTLE

Evidently Plato is not a complete humanist. His ethics fulfills the positive side of the definition of humanism in that it provides adequately for the values implicit in the different sides of man's nature; but it has also, as just indicated, a transcendental side. A typical humanist does not regard the human ideals of good as sanctioned by existing superhuman entities.

Both Socrates (469–399 B. C.) and Aristotle (384–322 B. C.) are in this latter respect more typical humanists than Plato. With the exception of the great Chinese teacher Confucius (551–478 B. C.), who because of his Oriental cast of mind can hardly be taken as typical of Western humanism, Socrates and Aristotle may be considered the first great representatives of an explicit humanistic ethic. They are related to each other not only in the general character of their ethical teachings and in their acceptance of a common Greek ethical heritage but also in their mutual relation to Plato, who was the follower of Socrates and in turn the teacher of Aristotle. But they differed widely in the breadth of their interests and in their manner of purveying instruction. Socrates avoided lecturing and long discourses; he preferred the question-and-answer method, as described in the second chapter. Furthermore, his interests (in his old age, at any rate, when Plato knew him) were withdrawn from science and given almost wholly to questions about human values. He wrote nothing.

Aristotle's teachings, on the other hand, were given mainly in the form of lectures, delivered, it is said, while walking up and down in the Lyceum at Athens, whence his disciples became known as 'peripatetics' (walkers up and down), and Aristotle's teachings themselves are sometimes designated 'the peripatetic philosophy.' There appears to have been no subject in the educational curriculum of his day in which Aristotle did not offer instruction. Logic, metaphysics, 'physics' (including what we should call biology), psychology, ethics, domestic economics, political science, oratory, and the construction of dramatic poetry are each represented in the corpus of Aristotle's works by at least one treatise. For the most part it appears that the treatises were not written by Aristotle himself, but by disciples, from notes taken at his lectures. There have been preserved two, possibly three such groups of notes relating to ethics; the most complete and best of which is the one assembled by Aristotle's son-in-law Nicomachus and subsequently known as the *Nicomachean Ethics*.

Man's supreme good

Aristotle regards ethics as a branch of the larger study of *politikê*, which, without too strict an adherence to modern usage, we might translate 'political science.' Man is a social animal, and when we seek the supreme good of man we must regard him not as an isolated unit but as a citizen, a member of a community. "In the natural order of things the State is prior to the household and the individual, as the whole is prior to the part." Regarding man in this light, what is the supreme good towards which, if he is reasonable, he will constantly strive? That there must be a supreme good is proven by the following argument: "Every art and every investigation, as well as every action and choice, may be said to aim at some particular good: as, for example, health is the end which is aimed at by the science of medicine, a vessel by the art of shipbuilding, victory by military strategy, and wealth by domestic economy." When we examine the ends of each of the many kinds of human pursuits we find that they tend to fall into a hierarchy: "Bridle-making and all other arts concerned with the making of horses' equipment are subordinate to horsemanship, which in turn, together with every other military employment, is subordinate to the science of strategy"; and similarly with other pursuits. The ends of the master-arts are in every case more to be desired than the ends of the arts subordinate to them, for it is on their account that the subordinate ends are sought after. But what of the ends of the master-arts themselves? Are they in turn subordinate to still other ends? In the rightly constituted man they are. A militarist may come to regard strategy in war as an end in itself; so may a miser come to regard money. But it is man *quâ* militarist and man *quâ* miser who make these unbalanced valuations, whereas the humanist principle[1] requires that serious choices and dominant preferences should always be made by man *quâ* man. What is the dominant end proper to man as such? Everyone would agree, says Aristotle, that it is what the Greeks called *eudaimonia*.

A recurring obstacle to an understanding of ancient thought is the difficulty of providing exact translations for certain key-words. *Eudaimonia* is an example. Its meaning must be grasped precisely if Aristotle's ethics is to be rightly understood, yet there is no single word in our language that will convey it. The usual translation is 'happiness,' but *vital well-being* is quite as important a part of the meaning. In the ancient writings of Homer *eudaimonia* commonly signified prosperity and good fortune

---

[1]Aristotle uses no particular word of which 'humanism' or 'humanist' is a literal translation, but this is because the principles which in these pages are called humanist seemed to him too self-evident to require a name. The expression, 'man *quâ* man' or 'man in so far as he is a man,' used both by Socrates and Aristotle, expressed the cardinal emphasis of humanism.

of an external sort. But there was a deeper meaning as
well, for etymologically the word connotes 'possession of
a good genius'—*i.e.*, of a good inner working principle of
choice and avoidance. The meaning of the word in
Aristotle might be approximately described as follows:
the satisfaction enjoyed by a man in his full status as a
living organism and as a member of a society, as this is
experienced by his active and reflective consciousness.
Because the word 'happiness' has been used in such a
very different sense by Bentham and Mill, whose ideas
of happiness have already been dwelt on, the word *eudaimonia* will be translated in these pages as *well-being*.

All agree that well-being is the goal of human activity,
but do they agree on very much more than a word? The
generality of men suppose that well-being consists in
pleasure. Pleasure is indeed a necessary condition of
well-being, but by no means sufficient to ensure it. Those
who make it the be-all and end-all of existence "show
themselves to be utterly slavish, by preferring a life fit only
for cattle"; none the less their view wins a wide hearing
because of the strength of the desire for pleasure in everyone. Another and smaller group of men, in whom the
urge to action predominates, identify well-being with a
life of honor and success, and devote the main part of their
energies to the securing of fame. Such men Aristotle
considers more admirable than the passive slaves to
pleasure, and the presence of a body of such men is
necessary to carry on the business and defence of the
commonwealth, but as an end of life the idea of political
success falls short on two grounds. Its realization depends as much on the compliance of other persons and on
good luck as on one's own efforts. Besides, among men
of a more refined and reflective type the motive by which

they are driven to pursue honor is largely a desire to as-
sure themselves of their own merit; for unless they are
paltry demagogues it is not by anyone at all that they
care to be honored but by men of good judgment, which
signifies that they desire to be honored for those qualities
in themselves which they deem excellent.   Moral excellence, then, or 'virtue,' is a more fundamental good than
honor in the opinion of those men of action who have the
wisdom to reflect on the grounds of what they are doing.
'Virtue,' the nature of which will be discussed presently,
is even more than pleasure a necessary condition of the
good life, but it too falls short of the standard required,
for "it can be possessed during sleep . . . and in
addition a virtuous man may suffer the greatest wretchedness and ill-fortune, although no one would call a wretched
life a life of well-being, unless for the sake of upholding
a paradox."   Another form which the life of action can
take is the life of money-making, but wealth is even more
evidently not the goal we seek, "for it is good only as
being useful, as a means to something else."   The life
of pleasure and the life devoted to success having both
been found wanting, there remains a third kind of life,
theoretikos, which again brings up a difficulty of translation.   The Greek adjective comes from a verb signifying
to look at, to contemplate, and (since disinterested intellectual activity is usually connoted as well) to speculate.
As used by Aristotle, the verb suggests Matthew Arnold's
phrase, 'to see life steadily and see it whole,' and, since
this is as good a definition as any of the function of philosophy, the life which Aristotle describes as *theoretikos*
may best be called a life of philosophical reflection, or of
reflective contemplation, or, for greater brevity, the *reflective life*.   The characteristics of the reflective life will
be discussed further on.

The humanistic ground of inquiry

The negative side of Aristotle's humanism comes out in his criticism of Plato's theory of Eternal Forms. In the theory that goodness is transcendent, that it is an archetype distinct from the things of the everyday world, while these have truth and value only so far as they imitate it or reflect its nature, Aristotle finds several difficulties: (1) the Good is not by any means as simple as Plato's argument implies; (2) the postulation of an eternal Form of Good which is separate from particular goods does not explain the goodness of particular things but on the contrary introduces a new factor which itself stands in need of explanation; (3) the alleged eternity of the Forms has nothing to do with the moral problem, for "just as a white thing that lasts a long time is no whiter than one that lasts only a day, so the Ideal Good will not be any more truly good because it is eternal"; and (4) most important of all in the present connection, the Eternal Form of Good, since it transcends the world of human experience, "is not practicable nor attainable by man, whereas the Good we seek must be a good within human reach." Why busy ourselves seeking the Good among transcendent notions that we cannot adequately grasp or communicate? The good for man is displayed right here before us, in the nature of man himself. As the excellence or otherwise of a pruning-hook (in the illustration already quoted from Socrates) can be estimated only by one who understands what a pruning-hook is fitted by its nature to do, *i.e.*, what it is good *for*, so the goodness proper to man must be derived from a study of man's natural capacities.

What is man's natural capacity? Aristotle's answer to this question is based on his theory of the logical arrangement of objects in nature. Things fall, he observes, into natural classifications, which can be exhibited in language by the logical method known as 'division.' All things with which the science of nature may deal, *i.e.*, all material objects, are either animate or inanimate. This classification Aristotle regards as *the* main division among natural objects, the first natural dichotomy; not merely one possible division, as contemporary logicians with their dissociation of logic and nature would hold. Aristotle's meaning here need not be disputed; there is an obvious sense in which it is permissible to say that animate-vs.-inanimate is a 'natural' dichotomy, one actually found in nature, while to have begun by distinguishing (let us say) green objects from objects that are not green would have been trifling and artificial. Animate things, in the next place, are divided into animals and other living things that are not animals; animals into vertebrates and invertebrates; vertebrates into mammals and non-mammals; and mammals into what are and what are not men. If we were to subdivide further, we should leave the province of natural science and should classify men according to their functions within the commonwealth, for to classify according to races or nations, as might be done nowadays, would have been repugnant to Aristotle's principle of classification by function. Classification by function is of fundamental importance for Aristotle's philosophy: it is the link that joins his philosophy of nature, his logic, and his ethics into a coherent structure. We must examine its applications, therefore, in order to see what deductions it makes possible.

In any classification the relation between a generic class (*genus*) and the sub-classes (*species*) into which it is divided is called 'subsumption.' Taken as classes, man is subsumed under animal, and animal under living object. When the subsumptive relation subsists between two classes, an important secondary relation also subsists between the *meanings* of the classes so related. The more inclusive class, or *genus*, has a less determinate meaning than the class subsumed under it. This is necessarily so, for if animals constitute a sub-class of living things there must be one or more attributes common to all animals, marking them off from the remainder of living things. The additional attribute or group of attributes by which a sub-class is distinguished is called its *differentia*. In defining a class both its genus and its differentia are given: an animal is not merely a living thing but a living thing *with the capacities of sensation and impulse;* a man is not merely an animal but an animal *with the capacity of reasoning.* These particular differentiæ are basic to Aristotle's definition of human good. To demonstrate their relation one more logical principle is required, the so-called *dictum de omni et nullo*, which postulates that whatever is predicated universally of a genus, whether by affirmation or denial, is predicated also of any of its subordinate species. The important application for ethics is the case of man, who *quâ* man possesses the capacity of reasoning, *quâ* animal the capacities of sensation and impulse, and *quâ* animate object the capacities of organic metabolism (his 'vegetative nature'). What importance has all this for ethics?

Aristotle's ethics has a basic reference to his philosophy of nature, as this has in turn to his logic. The step from logic to philosophy of nature is taken when the differentia of each species is observed to be not merely a quality but a capacity, a potentiality, a function—*i.e.*, an ability and tendency to act in a certain general way. The second step, from philosophy of nature to ethics, is marked by the question: How is the excellence of a thing determined? Aristotle replies: Find the natural function of a thing, and the 'virtue,' or 'specific excellence,' of that thing will consist in performing its function *well*. The virtue of an oak-tree, of a spider, and of a man must each be determined separately, according to the special capacities with which each is by nature endowed. Likewise the virtue of man in general must be distinguished from the virtue of a flute-player or sculptor or any other craftsman, for while a given individual is not only a man but has a more specific function too, and may achieve excellence in that speciality, we still do not call him a superior *man* because he is a skillful performer on the flute. The virtue proper to man must consist in the fulfillment of those capacities which differentiate him from other species and which therefore belong to him essentially *quâ* man. Since man is differentiated by an ability to employ reason, his excellence must be judged by the degree to which this ability is developed and realized.

The rational faculty can be exercised in a twofold manner. The human 'soul' (for which we might prefer nowadays to substitute the word 'self') has besides the 'rational part,' which marks it as human, an 'appetitive part,' which it shares with the beasts, and a 'vegetative part,' which it shares with all living things. The vegetative part (all forms of organic metabolism) cannot be controlled by reason, but the appetitive part (impulsive responses to sensations) can be so controlled. Reason thus has a potential ability not merely to engage in reflective contemplation of the universe, but to control the impulses as well. Consequently, by the principle already stated in the last paragraph, its virtue will be of two kinds. The soul has *intellectual virtue* so far as it actual-

izes its capacity for engaging in reasoning for its own sake
(as in the study of science or philosophy); it achieves
moral virtue so far as it actualizes its capacity for controlling the impulses and appetites.   Nor is it enough that
the capacity should be actualized only once, or only now
and then, in order that the individual be considered virtuous.   Virtue is present only where a *habit* of right
action or right thinking has been formed: only, in other
words, where the right action and right thinking are expressions of an enduring *character*.

The doctrine of the mean

Moral virtue being that kind of virtue that is present
when reason habitually controls the impulses in an excellent manner, we may ask what that excellent manner is.
Aristotle replies:

The virtues such as we have been discussing [*i.e.*, moral
virtues as distinguished from intellectual] are destroyed either
by deficiency or by excess.   We may see this illustrated in the
analogous case of bodily strength and health: strength is destroyed by an excess as well as by a deficiency of bodily exercise;
likewise health is destroyed by too much as well as by too little
food, but is produced, developed, and preserved by a moderate
amount.   So with temperance, courage, and the other virtues:
the man who flees and fears everything and never stands his
ground is a coward, while he who fears nothing at all and is ready
to face everything is rash.   Similarly, the man who partakes
of every pleasure and abstains from none is a profligate, while
he who boorishly shuns all pleasures may be called insensible
(*i.e.*, without feeling).   Thus temperance and courage are destroyed by excess and deficiency but preserved by moderation.[1]

What is meant by acting in moderation—or, as it is
often translated, 'observing the mean'?   Aristotle warns
against being misled by the analogy of the mathematical

[1]*Nicomachean Ethics*, Bk. II, Chap. II.

mean, which can be computed simply. The golden mean
of moral action is not to be thought of as midway between
two extremes. Its position in relation to the extremes
will vary according to circumstances. More courage is
required of a soldier than of a shopkeeper: the courage of
the soldier will bear more resemblance to rashness than
that of the shopkeeper. Similarly, the temperance of a
priest or teacher ought to be somewhat closer to insensi-
bility, while that of an artist or actor might permissibly
lean a little more to the side of licentiousness. Nor is
the principle limited to actions; it is concerned with feelings too:

> For example, one can feel fear, courage, desire, anger, and
> pity, as well as pleasure and pain generally, either too much or
> too little, and in either case wrongly; but to have these feelings
> at the right time and on the right occasions and towards the
> right persons and with a right aim in view and in a right manner
> —this is the middle way and the best, and this is the mark of
> virtue.[1]

From this passage it is evident that the 'doctrine of the
mean' is no simple formula. The doctrine must be applied and the mean on any given occasion must be judged
with the greatest possible prudence. The mean is always
"relative to ourselves, and determined by reason—determined, that is to say, as a prudent man would determine
it."

The relation of the mean to pleasures and pains calls
for special remark. Since a man is not made virtuous by
performing a single virtuous act but only by forming
a habit of virtuous conduct, and since when a habit has
been formed it becomes pleasant rather than painful to
act in accordance with it, we may regard pleasure and pain

---

[1] *Op. cit.*, Bk. II, Chap. VI.

as useful tests of morality.   Does he who performs a heroic
act tremble and hesitate during its execution?   Then it is
less likely that the heroism will be repeated: his courage is
not—not yet, at any rate—deeply ingrained.   Does he
who gives away money find the giving agreeable or the
reverse?   Does he who is temperate find delight in the
state of temperance or does he long in his heart for de-
baucheries?   The test is of course not a final one, for
rules about human behavior are never without exceptions;
nevertheless it offers a reminder that morality must be
judged in terms not of single acts but of developed disposi- •
tions.

The ideal life

Having examined the question of moral virtue we may
return to the question of the good life, for it is in the
interests of the good life, *i.e.*, of human well-being, that
moral virtue ought to be promoted.   Moral virtue is not
itself identical with well-being, for a state of well-being
must be defined as one that is self-sufficient, requiring
nothing more to complete its perfection.   Moral virtue
does require something more, for with a total absence of
pleasure or with an excess of pain a life of moral virtue
would not be adjudged ideal.

Is pleasure, then, a sufficient test of well-being?   By no
means.   Pleasure is *a* good, as shown by the fact that
everyone does, in some manner and to some degree, aim
at it, but it is by no means the chief good.   For the state
of well-being, which has been defined as the chief good,
is an activity of the soul, while pleasure is something passive, something merely felt.   If pleasure were all that were
needed a slave could be considered to have attained the
good life, for in lax and generous households it sometimes
happens that slaves, having fewer responsibilities, enjoy

more pleasures than their masters; yet a slave is not in a state of well-being, for his will belongs to another.   Pleasures are not the inner principle of well-being, they are rather the bloom of health that appears on its surface.

The noblest standard for man is neither pleasure nor moral virtue, but *theoria*, or reflective contemplation: *i.e.*, the enjoyment of reason for its own sake, as an end in itself.   It must be understood, however, that by reflective contemplation Aristotle does not mean an isolated spinning out of theories.   The disinterested enjoyment of reason may, in the developed man, become an authentic expression of the entire self.   Moral virtue is still a part of the ideal, for only when the moral virtues have become embedded habits, only when a good character has been formed, can a man devote himself to reflective contemplation without bias.   Pleasure too is not lacking, for when the contemplative life has itself become a habit there will be no pleasure more intense than its earnest pursuit.   Regarded in this way the life of reflective contemplation is seen as an important expression of the humanistic ideal —an ideal that does justice not merely to a part of human nature but to the whole.

3.   WHAT IS A SELF?

Humanism has been defined as that ethical philosophy which does justice to the full nature of the self without appealing for its truth to any principle other than those implied in the nature of the self.   The definition inevitably suggests the question, What is a self?   Each of us uses the words 'I,' 'me,' 'mine,' and 'myself' and would deride the suggestion that he did not know the meaning of them, yet there are all sorts of inconsistencies even in their everyday use.   It is not the same self that is spoken of (1) in the statement, "He has fallen and bruised himself," (2) in the epithet 'a self-made man,' and (3) in Tennyson's lines:

> Self-reverence, self-knowledge, self-control—
> These three alone lead life to sovereign power.

The bruises touch only the physical body, but the physical body can not be created by its possessor and hence cannot be signified in the second example. We should ordinarily distinguish the material self of the first example from the social and economic self evidently intended by the second, and both of these in turn from the spiritual self intended by the third. The humanist criticism of sectarian theories of ethics such as hedonism, utilitarianism, and rationalism is that they implicitly abstract some partial aspect of the self from the remainder and furnish a morality that is adequate only for that abstracted part. An understanding of humanism, then, requires a more serious examination of the nature of the self.

Self-transcendence

The self has no fixed limits. This statement, though it seem paradoxical at first, is but a particular case of a general metaphysical truth. Things have fixed limits only when we regard them as dead, inert, stuck here or there in space. There is a fixed boundary between the United States and Canada, so long as we distinguish them geographically. But when we come to questions of American vs. Canadian 'rights,' or American vs. Canadian 'culture,' we become involved in endless controversy. Again, Tom's body is clearly marked off from Dick's, but when Tom and Dick are conversing it is not so easy to say *whose* ideas they are which come out in the conversation. As soon as we pass beyond purely conventional conceptions of the self (*e.g.*, as *inhabiting* a physical body) and purely technical conceptions (*e.g.*, behavioristic and associationistic theories of psychology) we are forced to acknowledge that a self is not a determinate unit like a physical body. We can never say, "This much and no more constitutes the personality of a man." Selfhood or personhood, in other words, is *self-transcendent*. There are several respects in which this essential characteristic of a self can be shown.

The first respect in which a self transcends any assignable boundaries is in *knowing an object*. The object that each of us is likely to know most intimately is his own body. Is the body to be regarded as an object which the self knows or as a part of the self? The answer necessarily is: Both or either, depending on the interests at stake and the consequent disposal of attention on any given occasion. Moreover, some parts of the body seem more intimately a part of the self than others. Clothes, too, play a part in 'making the man' not only as he appears to others but as he inwardly feels himself to *be:* how often will fresh apparel cause one to feel 'like a new man'! Again, familiar and cherished possessions become intimately a part of the possessor:

There are few men who would not feel personally annihilated if a life-long construction of their hands or brains—say an entomological collection or an extensive work in manuscript—were suddenly swept away. The miser feels similarly towards his gold, and although it is true that a part of our depression at the loss of possessions is due to our feeling that we must now go without certain goods that we expected the possessions to bring in their train, yet in every case there remains, over and above this, a sense of the shrinkage of our personality, a partial conversion of ourselves to nothingness, which is a psychological phenomenon by itself.[1]

---

[1] William James, *Principles of Psychology*, Vol. I, p. 293.   (Holt.)

'Shrinkage of personality' describes the immediate effect
on Silas Marner of the theft of his gold.   It was as if a
part of himself had been stolen, and George Eliot describes how his personality becomes whole once more
(but as a different personality from what it had been)
when the arrival of Effie the foundling offers a new object
of interest with which he can identify himself.

In a more general way, too, the self can be shown to
enter into a partial identity with the object which it
knows.   Tom espies a gooseberry bush and wonders
when the berries will ripen.   He is *aware* of the bush, and
thinks about the berries, but it is not his awareness and
his thoughts that he is wondering about.   He is not asking
when his *thoughts* of the berries will ripen, for his thoughts
may be given to other matters later on when the berries
themselves become mature.   Are we to say, then, that
the bush is one thing, and Tom-thinking-about-the-bush
is another?   How, in that case, are the two related?   The
popular, common-sense answer to this epistemological[1]
question is that Tom possesses a mental image (in his
head) of the bush, resembling but numerically distinct
from the bush 'out there' in the physical world.   An adequate criticism of this explanation would lead us into a
study of epistemology, which is beyond the scope of the
present textbook.   The following difficulties, however,
may be noted briefly: (1) How could Tom know that the
mental image in his head corresponded to the bush 'out
there,' since by hypothesis he could never be acquainted
with the latter and hence could never compare the two?
(2) How could he know even that there *is* a bush out there,
if his sole evidence is the presence of a mental image in
his head?   (3) *Does* the mental image exist in the head?
Would any conceivable scientific examination of the con-

[1]See Glossary.

tents of Tom's head reveal an *eidolon*,[1] or visible image, of the bush hovering somewhere around the cerebral cortex? Obviously not. But if not in the head and if not identical with the object we may legitimately ask (since the perceptual image of the bush has the appearance of spatial extension) *where* does Tom's awareness of the bush exist? The most logical theory seems to be that the bush and Tom's awareness of the bush are both two things and one. As Professor Whitehead, in somewhat difficult but very precise language, has said:

Subject and object are relative terms. An occasion is a subject in respect to its special activity concerning an object; and anything is an object in respect to its provocation of some special activity within a subject. Such a mode of activity is termed a 'prehension.' Thus a prehension involves three factors. There is the occasion of experience within which the prehension is a detail of activity; there is the datum whose relevance provokes the origination of this prehension; this datum is the prehended object; there is the subjective form, which is the affective tone determining the effectiveness of that prehension in that occasion of experience.[2]

In other words, both the bush and Tom's awareness of the bush must be regarded as aspects of the whole 'prehensive' situation. It is only by a conventional, but very inaccurate abstraction, that we think of the gooseberry bush as one unit and of Tom as a wholly distinct unit. Units of any kind are abstractions, hence to some degree they are falsifications of what is real; and particularly is this the case in dealing with an entity so infinitely complex and variable as the self.

A second respect in which the self transcends assignable boundaries is by becoming identified with other selves.

---

[1]See Glossary.

[2]Alfred North Whitehead, *Adventures of Ideas*, pp. 226–227. (By permission of The Macmillan Company, publishers.)

"Properly speaking," says William James, "a man has as many social selves as there are individuals who recognize him and carry an image of him in their minds. To wound any one of these his images is to wound him." Nor do we exist only in the images that others have of us, we exist also in the images and emotional attitudes that we have of or towards *them*. The relation of self to self is, when conditions are favorable, one of spontaneous mutuality, and in this fact is found the basis of genuinely benevolent action. Egoism and benevolence, though often incompatible, need not be so. When one's self has been developed so as to *include* a large measure of other persons' interests, benevolence becomes one phase of self-expression.

Finally, in addition to being conscious of relatively distinct objects and relatively distinct selves, the self is *self-conscious*[1]—that is to say, *re-flective* in the original meaning of the word (Latin, *reflectere*, to turn around and back). All things are in a state of change and 'becoming,' but the self is dynamic in a special sense. It does not merely become; it possesses, within limits, the faculty of self-knowledge and, through self-knowledge, of self-direction. The inscription that stood over the grotto of the Delphian Oracle, "Know thyself!" is one of the profoundest moral teachings that we owe to the Greeks. For to know one's self is the sure prelude to much else. "Know thyself!" means "Govern thyself!" It bids us become lord and ruler over the kingdom that is rightfully ours: over our instincts and sentiments and thoughts and partial purposes; in a word, over our own persons.

---

[1]This ambiguity of 'self'—of the noun as against the prefix and pronoun—while perhaps confusing, is inevitable. It is due to the fact that we can know the nature of a self only by knowing 'ourselves'—*i.e.*, only by the reflexive mental act which, as our language does not (like the Greek) possess a middle voice, we are obliged to call self-consciousness.

The rôle of imagination

The self-transcendent nature of the self might be summarily expressed by saying that man has the gift of imagination. As the first chapter has already made clear, some decree of imagination, of visualizing alternative possibilities of action and thought, is a condition of any morality or moral consciousness whatever. Nevertheless, individuals differ in the degree to which they are imaginative, and consequently in their respective potentialities for moral goodness. Imagination is not all: some, at least, of our imaginings must culminate in action if we are to be moral. But it is a necessary condition for a morality of any real value. The unimaginative man's morality consists in following the customs of the group in which he lives. Conventional morality is certainly better than no morality at all, and since the imaginative resources of the majority of men are small, it is often more desirable that they should be encouraged to follow some existing set of standards rather than be given the illusion of 'thinking for themselves.' But conventions change, sometimes for the worse; and the safe-keeping and improvement as well as the wise alteration of moral standards must always lie in the hands of that comparatively small number who can forcefully imagine and wisely evaluate what *might be* as distinguished from what *is*.

Humanist ethics accepts as a basic self-evident truth man's ability, by the activity of imagination, to identify himself with far-away objects, with other persons, and with attainable ideals. In this way humanism overcomes what may be called the 'atomistic fallacy' of those philosophers such as Bentham and Spencer who regard human consciousness as a self-contained fact. A self-contained fact is what consciousness can never be. This truth is reiterated again and again in that admirably fresh and provocative account of humanistic ethics, Professor Warner Fite's *Moral Philosophy:*

For the deeper experience, life is more than ever an unsatisfied aspiration. The merely physical consumption of goods is a fact, completed when the goods are consumed. If the desire for goods were only a fact parallel to the process of consumption, enjoyment would be similarly a *fait accompli.* Desire, however, involves consciousness—the consciousness of desire; and the conscious satisfaction of desire only reveals the further implications of the desire yet to be satisfied.

To perceive the present clearly, or to be aware of it in any sense whatever, is just so far to view it in the light of what is not present—that is, of imagination. . . . When the present ceases to be illuminated by what is not present there is no *consciousness* even of the present. When in my meditations I become aware only of the fire before me, I am aware of nothing —I am asleep.

The printed page is another illustration. I am reading Doughty's *Arabia Deserta* in the quiet of the midnight hour before going to bed. If I chance to grow dull and sleepy, then what I find before me is just a printed page. But while imagination remains awake I *am* in the Arabian desert even though I am also in my easy chair.[1]

Consciousness, in short, is not a mere congeries of mental states, a mere effect, or a mere reaction. Those who think of it as a congeries of states think of it as something dead, like a picture gallery; those who call it an effect or a reaction are too prone to forget that it at any rate somehow *knows* the system of things constituting its cause and to which it reacts. Knowing makes an incalculable difference. That is why Professor Fite prefers to describe consciousness in a more adequate way, as 'insight'— *imaginative insight.*

---

[1] Warner Fite, *Moral Philosophy*, pp. 2:5, 233, 257. (Dial Press.)

Man, then, is not only an animal, but an imaginative, self-transcending, self-developing animal: "the only animal who knows that he is an animal." This truth, so foolishly forgotten by many who approach the problems of the self equipped with the methodologies of the sciences, is of the greatest importance for ethics. It means that any standard of moral goodness which does justice to *human* nature (as distinguished from the conceptions of 'nature' formed by physicists, biologists, and scientific psychologists) must be *dynamic:* that is, must be subject to continual criticism and development as the critical imagination of men is brought to bear on it in fresh ways.

Self-control and character

A description of the self would be incomplete without a recognition that it has a power of self-control; that it is not only a self-developing personality but also a self-controlling *character.* Character may be defined as *an enduring psycho-physical disposition to control instinctive impulses in accordance with a regulative principle.*[1] Having a character is thus a fourth way in which the self is capable of self-transcendence: certain regulative principles become intimately a part of it. An overruling consideration that prompted Maggie Tulliver to renounce the desire for a union with Stephen was "the sense of contradiction with her past self," which "in her moments of strength and clearness came upon her like a pang of conscious degradation."[2] What was Maggie's pang of conscious degradation but a sense that her self was about to lose possession of a *principle of coherence* by which her former life had

---

[1] Identical with the definition given by A. A. Roback ("Character and Inhibition," in *Problems of Personality*, edited by Morton Prince, p. 118) except that the word 'control' has been substituted for Dr. Roback's more technical and sometimes pejorative word 'inhibit.'

[2] Previously quoted on p. 133.

been consciously and joyously guided, and that such a
loss was actually a diminution of selfhood? To relinquish
that principle, as Maggie began to perceive, was to rend
"the ties that had given a meaning to duty" and to make
herself "an outlawed soul, with no guide but the wayward
choice of her own passion." Every individual who is not
a moral scarecrow, flapping this way and that with
every fresh gust of impulse, must acknowledge or at least
be seeking for some principle of coherence by which his
choices may be given a direction, and his actions be endowed with some kind of moral significance.

On the other hand, it is desirable that one's principle
of moral coherence should not become too hard and stereo-
typed. "To be coherent," in the words of that discerning
Mexican-French humanist, Ramon Fernandez, "does not
mean *feeling* always the same nor *acting* always the same
in all circumstances, but being ready to stand up to every
circumstance, when once a certain inner perspective has
been established; it does not in the least mean that you
never change, but that the changes of the world find you
always ready to take your own point of view towards
them." The humanist ideal, in this as in other respects,
is to maintain a balance, "an equilibrium of diverse impulses."[1]

4. The Standard of the Cultured Man

With the foregoing complexities of the self kept in mind,
we can form a more exact notion of the task with which
humanist ethics is faced in undertaking to satisfy the
moral requirements of the whole self, not only of a part.
With a few exceptions the leading representatives of
humanism have not attempted to thoroughly systematize
their philosophy. In this have they acted plausibly, for

[1]*De la personnalité*, pp. 86, 132.

since 'the whole self' is no static thing whose characteristics can be determined once for all, an adequate ethics of
humanism is in need of continual revision, as one's experiences are broadened and one's personal insight deepens.

Epicurean and Stoic elements

Aristotle, as has already appeared, accepted pleasure as
a necessary part, though not a sufficient guarantee, of
the good life.   Such an attitude is sound humanism, as it
is sound common-sense.   The brilliant humanist and es-
sayist of the late Renaissance, Michel de Montaigne
(1533–1592), shares this balanced attitude towards pleasures.   On the one hand he declares himself to be "but of
the earth earthy" and to "dislike that inhuman sapience
which would have us despise and hate the care of the
body."   Pleasure ought always to be prized, and Montaigne pours out scorn on those who lack a right appreciation of its excellence:

> Is not man a miserable creature?   Scarcely is it in his power,
> constituted as he is by nature, to enjoy a single pure and entire
> pleasure, yet he is at pains, by reasoning about it, to curtail
> it. . . .
> Man in his wisdom very foolishly exercises his ingenuity in
> lessening the number and sweetness of the pleasures that we
> have a right to; as he industriously and successfully employs his
> artifices in tricking out and disguising the ills and alleviating
> the sense of them.[1]

On the other hand, excess and intemperance in pleasure
are to be condemned.   Pleasures should always be kept
under control, enjoyed only within reasonable limits,
however legitimate they may be.   The pleasure of sex,
for example, is sanctified and made legitimate by marriage;
for that very reason, however, since marriage is a religious

---

[1] The *Essays*, Bk. I, Chap. 30.   The quotations are all from Trechmann's
translation.   (Oxford University Press.)

and holy bond, "the pleasure we derive from it must be
a restrained and serious pleasure, mixed with some austerity; it should be a somewhat discreet and conscientious
voluptuousness." Moderation, the golden mean, is the
rule for pleasures as for all other acts of choice. The only
pleasures to be entirely avoided are those "exotic and
bastard pleasures" that give rise to discontent. Philosophy, therefore, while preaching moderation not flight
from pleasure, yet advises against the heightening of bodily
pleasures by allowing the mind to dwell too much on them,
and she "wittily warns us not to try to excite hunger by
surfeiting, not to stuff instead of merely filling the belly;
to avoid all enjoyment that may bring us to want, and
all food and drink that makes us hungry and thirsty."
In his attitude towards pleasure Montaigne comes very
close to the refined hedonism of Epicurus.

The humanistic philosopher accepts both the Epicurean
and the Stoic attitude as giving expression to an important
part of man's nature. William James (1842–1910), who
may be readily classified as a humanist, has chosen another pair of expressions to describe this opposition of
moral attitudes:

The deepest difference, practically, in the moral life of man
is the difference between the easy-going and the strenuous
mood. When in the easy-going mood the shrinking from
present ill is our ruling consideration. The strenuous mood,
on the contrary, makes us quite indifferent to present ill, if
only the greater ideal be attained. The capacity for the strenuous mood probably lies slumbering in every man, but it has
more difficulty in some than in others in waking up. It needs
the wilder passions to arouse it, the big fears, loves, and in-
dignations; or else the deeply penetrating appeal of some one
of the higher fidelities, like justice, truth, or freedom.[1]

[1] "The Moral Philosopher and the Moral Life," from *The Will to Believe and
Other Essays*, p. 211. (Longmans, Green.)

As both the easy-going and the strenuous mood are parts of the life of man, so the moral insights of Epicurean and Stoic must alike be assimilated by a humanistic ethics.

The Stoic 'higher fidelities' include as paramount goods independence and nobility of mind, and nowhere are these qualities better exhibited than in the Stoic attitude towards death. When the Duke of Verona, in Shakespeare's *Measure for Measure*, visits in prison Claudio who has been condemned to die, he admonishes the prisoner:

> Be absolute for death; either death or life
> Shall thereby be the sweeter. Reason thus with life:
> If I do lose thee, I do lose a thing
> That none but fools would keep. A breath thou art,
> Servile to all the skyey influences,
> That dost this habitation where thou keep'st
> Hourly afflict.[1]

Readiness for death is a Stoic rather than Epicurean theme, and is expressed frequently by the humanists of the Renaissance, on whom the influence of the Roman Stoics, especially Seneca, was strong. While the Epicurean faces death not so much with courage as with a reasoned assurance that there is nothing painful about it, the Stoic faces it with stern courage however painful it may be, for he wishes to defy pain itself. The humanist Montaigne gives expression to this Stoic attitude:

> Just as the enemy is made more fierce by our flight, so pain is puffed up with pride to see us tremble under her. She will surrender on much better terms to one who makes head against her. We must brace ourselves and resist. By backing and giving ground, we attract and call down upon ourselves the destruction that threatens us. As the body by stiffening itself resists attack more firmly, so does the soul.[2]

---

[1]Act III, Scene I.
[2]*Essays*, Bk. I, Chap. 14.

The principle of harmony

"The archer who overshoots his mark," says Montaigne, "misses as well as he who falls short of it. And my eyes trouble me equally when I suddenly mount up into a strong light and when I descend into the shadow." This is Montaigne's reply to those who ask, How shall we be guided? What shall be our standard? Montaigne, like Aristotle, answers: "Be in all things moderate." But how shall we know what is a right degree of moderation? "In ourselves," is the reply, "must the laws of well-doing be found." Custom is not to be despised, for custom, however wrong or foolish particular expressions of it may be, sums up much wisdom learnt in past ages. But morality, though never entirely independent of custom, is something superior to it. Its best guarantee is neither custom nor law, political or moral, not the supposed will of God, but character. The humanist finds the regulative principle that character requires in the principle of moderation, or, more positively, in the principle of the harmonious development of all the impulses and needs, including the most subtle and least practical of them, that make up human personality. Moderation and harmony are not two ideals but one. Aristotle's 'doctrine of the mean' requires that we harmonize that excess of zeal which urges us to go too far with the contrary tendency to draw back and not go far enough. Plato formulates the ideal of harmony more explicitly, as a reasoned subordination of particular impulses and special interests to the regulative principle. The regulative principle, as Aristotle's numerous qualifications of it make clear, is no fast rule, nor is it derived by logic alone. It can be grasped and applied only when we establish a right inner perspective, a healthy adjustment of the mind to a situation.

Certainly not all men can be safely trusted to achieve such an adjustment, but were Plato and Aristotle far wrong in declaring that the only remedy for this lack (so far as there is any remedy) was a wiser system and manner of education?

CHAPTER VIII

PROBLEMS OF PERSONAL MORALITY

Be lord and governor of thy deeds, not servant.
Thomas à Kempis

D URING the exposition just completed of the major
types of ethical theory a variety of specific moral
problems have cropped up by way of illustration. The
present chapter is devoted to a more explicit formulation
of some of the more important of these. No exposition,
naturally, can specify beforehand all possible types of
moral problem that might occur in the life of a conscious
agent. The contingencies of living are too various and
unforeseen. This chapter, accordingly, is not to be regarded as containing in any sense a survey of the field of
individual morality but merely a few prominent and crucial illustrations of the way in which its problems are to
be critically met. Three such problems, or groups of
problems, will be introduced: (1) the marks of virtue in
an individual, (2) the meaning of moral responsibility, and
(3) the basis of duties towards oneself.

1. THE MARKS OF VIRTUE

The ambiguity of many of the terms employed in ethical reasoning has received comment in Chapter II and
been further illustrated in subsequent chapters. It is inevitable that language which refers to complex qualities
like honesty, courage, justice, and their opposites should
be to some degree ambiguous, or at least potentially so,

for the extent of its denotative references cannot be prescribed with complete exactitude in advance: new situations, new experiences require a modification of old definitions and distinctions. When ambiguities are clearly perceived they do no harm. Their evil effects arise from their introduction into an argument, whether purposely or by accident, in such a way as to make one of the related meanings do surreptitious service at a crucial point for some other of them. The word 'immoral,' for instance, is often used in colloquial speech to signify unchaste, but it has also the more general philosophical meaning of morally bad—*i.e.*, bad with respect to any important aspect of the moral standard. To affirm that a man because of sexual irregularities is 'immoral' and therefore not to be trusted in business would be to build a fallacious argument around the ambiguity of the word. Even more dangerous are the ambiguities that directly affect conduct. One may accept nominally such ideals as justice and honesty without necessarily modifying one's conduct thereby. The meaning of the words can be juggled to suit the convenience of the occasion.

Virtues and vices are enduring dispositions in moral agents to perform good and evil actions respectively. When a particular action is called virtuous or vicious it is called so by proxy: not because of its particular effects, which may be modified unpredictably for better or worse by circumstances external to the agent's will, but because of the disposition from which it is believed to spring. One swallow, as Aristotle said in this connection, does not make a summer, nor does one blameworthy act show a depraved soul. But a person's disposition, while independent of any particular set of effects, cannot be judged apart from all of its effects whatever. It is the habitual intent to act in a certain way or towards certain ends that constitutes dispositions. Nor is there any way to formulate the requirements of a virtuous disposition satisfactorily without, by implication at least, designating certain kinds of actions to be done or ends to be aimed at.

Casuistry

Failure to understand the organic interrelation between a person's disposition and his acts has produced two opposite but equally one-sided theories of the nature of virtue. The one is Kant's doctrine that the good will (*i.e.*, the disposition taken in abstraction from the actions in which it eventuates) is the sole and sufficient intrinsically good thing. That Kant failed to maintain his position consistently, being forced to supply his principle with a content by a somewhat arbitrary choice of actions to be considered as expressing the rational will, has been shown in Chapter VI. There is a second theory of the nature of virtue now to be examined, like Kant's in its separation of acts from the motivating disposition but different in attaching moral significance to the acts alone. This theory is called *casuistry* (from the Latin *casus*, a case).

By making acts rather than motives the locus of moral value casuistry reduces moral principles to rules of choice and avoidance. Rules, unlike principles, are ready-made and fixed; they are intended to give a direct reply to any and every question of the form: What specific act shall I do on this occasion? But rules nevertheless are couched in general language and an act of interpretation is needed before they can be fitted to particular cases. In the Mosaic Ten Commandments it is written, "Neither shalt thou steal," but before this rule can be made effective there must be some way of knowing what actions 'stealing' is to cover. The extreme casuist attempts to answer

such questions denotatively—by making a list of all foreseeable types of case in which stealing might occur.
Conduct becomes regulated through specific injunctions
and prohibitions. The Biblical Book of Deuteronomy is
an example of the extremely detailed system of petty rules
that this method of establishing right and wrong engen-
ders.

Casuistry may be described as a legalistic view of
morality. Law is necessarily casuistic. A murderer who
appears before the bar of justice must be reduced for convenience of judicial pronouncement to a particular act
in his career together with the specific intent from which
the act directly proceeds. All the innumerable elements
that make up the rest of the murderer's personality and
that would have considerable bearing on a moral evaluation of his crime are from a legal point of view irrelevant.
That he meant to kill at the moment when he pulled the
trigger satisfies the law's demand for premeditation and
murderous intent.[1]

But whatever justification there may be for accepting
casuistry as a basis of judicial procedure it can never be a
satisfactory basis of moral judgments. It magnifies the
letter of morality to such a degree that the spirit of morality is killed. Moreover, it tends to promote sophistry.
While a man who accepts certain moral principles without
giving absolute obedience to rules may recognize that
there are occasions when a lie is justified and so may
frankly tell a lie on some occasion when a greater good
would be endangered by speaking the truth, a casuist
might utter the same false statement calling it by some
other name than lying, such as 'stretching the truth' or

---

[1]This paragraph is paraphrased from Harold Rosenberg's article, "Character
Change and the Drama" (*The Symposium*, July, 1932) in which Mr. Rosenberg
analyzes the relations and differences between dramatic identities, legal identities, and real persons.

'reinterpreting.' King Henry the Seventh of England evidently knew the advantages of casuistry, for Montaigne relates of him that after covenanting with a Spanish prince for the return of the fugitive Duke of Suffolk and promising that he would not take the duke's life, he commanded in his will that his son should murder the duke immediately after his own decease.

Socrates' doctrine of virtue

No admissible theory of morality can be based upon the character of acts alone any more than upon dispositions alone. An essential condition of a moral way of life is an active intelligence capable at once of foreseeing remote effects of particular acts and of reforming the disposition by a developing relation to ideal ends. Perhaps the most important theme running through the early dialogues of Plato is Socrates' insistence that active intelligence is indispensable to real as against sham virtue. In the *Laches*, for example, he is represented as drawn into a dispute that has arisen about the nature of courage. Two eminent generals, Laches and Nicias, are confident they know what courage is, so Socrates proceeds to cross-examine them:

Socrates:[1] Come then, Laches, and try to tell me what I have asked: what is courage?

Laches: Good Lord, Socrates, there's nothing hard about that. If a person voluntarily stays at his post and wards off the enemy you'd surely call him courageous.

Soc. Perhaps I should, Laches; but I fear you have not entirely answered my question. I wanted your view not only as to soldiers but of courage in other pursuits as well. What of those who display courage amid perils at sea, in disease and poverty, and in giving battle to unworthy temptations? Are not they too courageous?

---

[1]Translated and abridged from Plato's *Laches*.

Lach. Oh, decidedly.

Soc. Well now, if I had asked you the meaning of quickness you would not have confined your definition to quickness of running or quickness of playing the harp; for there is a quickness in practically every action worth mentioning, whether of hands or legs or mouth or voice or mind. If anyone were to ask me: "Socrates, what do you mean by this which in all these cases you term quickness?" I would reply: the capacity of accomplishing much in little time I call quickness, whether with respect to a voice or a man or anything else.

Lach. That would be quite correct.

Soc. Try yourself then, Laches, to give me a similar reply in the case of courage: what kind of capacity is it apart from pleasure or pain or any of the other particular circumstances in which it may be found?

Lach. You mean you wish me to state the natural quality present in all instances of courage? Well, it strikes me as being a kind of endurance of the soul.

Soc. Yet I doubt whether every case of endurance without exception can appear to you courageous. You rank courage among the nobler qualities, do you not?

Lach. Yes, among the very noblest.

Soc. And endurance joined with wisdom is noble and good?

Lach. Certainly.

Soc. But suppose it is joined with folly? Does it not then become, on the contrary, injurious and evil?

Lach. Yes.

Soc. And would you call a thing noble that is evil and injurious?

Lach. Hardly.

Soc. Then you cannot say that endurance of this latter kind is courage, since it is not noble, whereas courage is something noble.

Lach. That is true.

Soc. Then you amend your definition and declare that courage is *wise* endurance?

Lach. I guess so.

Soc. Well, let us see in what respect it is wise. In all respects, whether great or small? Suppose a man endures in spending his money wisely, knowing that his expenditures will

yield him greater profits, would you call such a man courageous?

Lach. Good Lord, no.

Soc. And what about a doctor who endures in refusing meat
and drink to a son or patient suffering from a bronchial disorder
who asks for them?

Lach. That is not courage either.

Soc. And in warfare if a man endures in a willingness to
fight because he has wisely calculated that his allies can be
counted on for support and that the enemy's forces are fewer
and feebler than his own and that he holds the more advanta-
geous position—would you call a man who endured because of
such wisdom and foresight courageous?

Lach. Quite the contrary. It is rather the man who endures
without the benefit of such calculations that I should call
courageous.

Soc. Yet his endurance is more foolish than that of the first
man.

Lach. That is true.

Soc. Similarly, would you not say that he who endures in
a cavalry fight without a knowledge of horsemanship displays
more courage than an expert horseman? And that he who dives
into a pool without much knowledge of how to swim is more
courageous than an expert swimmer?

Lach. How could anyone deny it, Socrates?

Soc. But such individuals in exposing themselves to danger
and enduring it with fortitude behave more foolishly than those
who do the same thing with proper skill?

Lach. Apparently.

Soc. Then you have admitted the same individuals to be
courageous and foolish at once. Such illustrations seem to contradict our former assertion that courage is something noble.
For now we find that courage is present more fully in those
whose endurance is foolish and therefore ignoble!

(Here Nicias enters the argument:)

Nic. Laches talks as if doctors who treat their patients have
some knowledge beyond what pertains to health and sickness.
This, on the contrary, is probably all they know: do you suppose, Laches, that it falls within the province of doctors to
understand whether health is more to be dreaded than sickness?

Don't you think it is often better that a person should be sick?
Indeed, is it not often better that he should die?

Lach.   I imagine it is.

Nic.   And do you think the same things are to be dreaded
by those who ought to die as by those who ought to live?

Lach.   No.

Nic.   Well, does judgment about such matters lie within
the province of doctors or any other technician unless he
possesses also a knowledge of what is rightly to be dreaded and
what is not?   It is the man who possesses knowledge of this
kind that is truly courageous.   . . .

Soc.   If you hold this theory of the nature of courage, Nicias,
you seem obliged either to refuse courage to wild beasts or else
to admit that a beast like a lion or a leopard or even a wild
pig is so wise as to know something which only a few men are
able to know.   . . .

Lach.   Good heavens, Socrates, you argue well!   Now answer
us seriously, Nicias: do you declare that those beasts which we
all admit to be courageous are wiser than we?   Or do you dare
to flout the common opinion and call them not courageous?

Nic.   No, Laches, I certainly don't describe as courageous
either beasts or anything else that from sheer thoughtlessness
has no fear of what is dreadful.   Rather I call them fearless and
silly.   Do you suppose I would call children courageous because
they have no fear of dangers which they do not comprehend?
I maintain rather that to be fearless and to be courageous are
not the same thing.   Courage and forethought, I hold, are
possessed by few; while recklessness, boldness, and fearlessness
without forethought are possessed by men, women, children,
and beasts in great numbers.   Thus the acts that you and most
people call courageous I call reckless, and it is the prudent acts
of which I have been speaking that are courageous.

This is just the answer that Socrates wants and has been
leading up to.   True courage is a form of knowledge: it is
knowledge of what is properly to be dreaded and what is
properly to be risked.   Socrates goes even further in the
remainder of the dialogue and challenges the differentia of
the definition.   'To be dreaded' implies future time, but

it is by one and the same act of knowledge that we grasp present, past, and future, and the same act of knowledge must have the same objects. There is thus no sharp distinction between courage and the other virtues: we can say of them only that each is some aspect of knowledge and meaningless apart from knowledge. In the *Protagoras* Socrates repeats, with a still more elaborate argument, his insistence on the unity of all the virtues. It is not until the *Republic*, a dialogue written in Plato's middle period, the doctrines of which probably belong more to Plato than to Socrates, that the virtues are severally distinguished from each other. But even here the distinction is made on political rather than philosophical grounds: it is a minimum condition of political stability that the great majority of common people, who cannot be expected to possess much wisdom, should at least be temperate in their desires and impulses, and that the militia should be brave. These virtues, though second rate, are socially important. It is in the philosophically minded men to whom Plato entrusts the destinies of his ideal State that courage and temperance and the other virtues are found *par excellence*. In the philosopher-kings each virtue is an expression of that 'turning of the soul towards reality' which is the meaning of wisdom.

Is intelligence enough?

The proposition that intelligence is a necessary condition of the highest form of virtue should not be confused with the proposition that intelligence is a sufficient guarantee of virtue. The first proposition, which the preceding discussion has aimed to establish, asserts that virtue implies intelligence; the second, its 'illicit converse,'[1] is

---

[1]See Glossary.

that intelligence implies virtue. The first proposition is essential to any ethic that is not casuistic, for it declares morality to consist not in the character of actions alone (the actions as such being simply physical events, as unmoral as a beneficent shower or a destructive hurricane) but in the whole intelligible purposeful context which the actions express. The second proposition embodies a more special kind of ethical doctrine, which might be characterized as a 'cult of the intelligence.'

The assertion that intelligence is a sufficient guarantee of moral conduct may mean either of two things. It may be a factual proposition asserting that intelligence, while different in nature from morality, is capable of producing it; that an intelligent man will as a matter of *fact* have the good sense to conduct himself in a moral way. This proposition, being factual, can never be universal or certain; it must be qualified by the adverb 'probably' or 'for the most part,' and its degree of probability or degree of generality will be decreased by each observed case of an intelligent man whose conduct is immoral. But the assertion has also a second meaning, which is the more usual one in philosophical discussions though unfortunately sometimes confused with the first. It may be a postulate about the nature of morality. If so it is true *a priori*. For it would then mean: whatever acts an intelligent person may do are moral acts just *because* and just *to the extent that* they are the expressions of an intelligent person. Intelligence, in short, becomes the sole intrinsic good.

The cult of intelligence is a doctrine shared by philosophers of such diverse tempers as Friedrich Nietzsche and Warner Fite.[1] In Nietzsche's philosophy the doctrine

---

[1]For further discussion of Nietzsche's philosophy see Chapter IV; for Professor Fite's, Chapters II and VII.

is upheld as a ruthless expression of 'master morality.' The superman whose superior qualities will have enabled him to survive and to rule in a society no longer hampered by institutional forms, will possess intelligence as his chief and crowning excellence. So high a worth is set on this virtue and on its achievement and development by the rare spirits who are capable of it that the suffering and death of countless 'slaves' is insignificant in comparison. Professor Fite's version is milder, more humane. He holds out some hope of increased stature for all who by taking thought will follow the decree of the ancient Delphic Oracle: Know thyself.

It would appear that Nietzsche's ruthlessness is the more logical outcome of making intelligence the supreme good. If care is taken not to introduce surreptitiously the meaning of morality into the connotations of intelligence there is no *a priori* certainty that the more intelligent man will be more moral in any recognized or even in any determinate sense. Doubtless if his impulses are humanitarian to begin with, the free development of his intelligence will tend to promote in him the humane type of morality espoused by Professor Fite. But intelligence is as consistent with belligerent, cruel, and selfish impulses as with kindly and generous ones. It is a gross oversimplification of psychological data to suppose a necessary connection between intelligence and impulses of an admirable kind. A more careful distinction is needed. That intelligence *per se* is admirable is true, and remains true even though the intelligence is applied to vicious ends, but this is not to say that the man of vicious intelligence is himself admirable. Our ability to proclaim him intelligent and yet condemn is what makes many a tragedy of character so poignant. The distinction is almost as pertinent here as in the case of an actor whose histrionics or whose profile we admire while despising the man. Not quite as pertinent, to be sure. Intelligence does have a more organic connection with morality than play-acting has, or the cut of the face. But an organic connection is not an identity. Our judgment can analyze things that are materially interconnected. Intelligence and morality, though perhaps never wholly apart, are found to be more or less so in varying degrees. For clear thinking, therefore, they must be postulated as two independent foci of reference.

Plato's approach to the matter is more satisfactory. He was enough of a realist to know that intelligence, to avoid tragic or fruitless results, must be reared on a basis of sound training. The impulses and emotions are as important to educate as the conscious intelligence. The early books of the *Republic* are largely concerned with the question of *basic* education: the right kind of tales, of music, and of bodily rhythms with which to 'condition' children from an early age. The particular measures recommended may seem at times arbitrary or questionable in the light of modern psychology. But their underlying principle is sound; it is a recognition that an individual's intelligence, if it is to be directed towards ends at once socially and individually excellent, must be channelized at its early stages by wise agencies external to itself. Intelligence, while supremely essential to the good life, is not its whole substance.

2. MORAL RESPONSIBILITY

The idea of responsibility is essential to any theory of ethics. While normative judgments are possible without it moral judgments are not. This is clear from the analysis given of a moral situation in Chapter I, and is implied by Dr. Hartmann's analysis of the moral Ought explained in Chapter V. A judgment of ought, as distinguished from a bare judgment of good, implies a pair of possible alternatives between which a choice is to be made, and since the choice has to be made by somebody, *i.e.*, by some *person*, it follows that every moral judgment carries with it a subsidiary judgment (not necessarily made explicit) that there exists a person or persons *responsible* for the action or state of affairs about which the judgment is made. It is this responsible person that has been meant whenever in the foregoing pages the 'moral agent' was spoken of.

So far as the logic of a moral judgment goes it is indifferent whether responsibility is attached to the person making the judgment or to someone else. But it is both easier and less admirable to attach responsibility to others. With regard to future acts acceptance of responsibility by oneself involves an expenditure of moral effort (the nature and difficulties of which have been analyzed at the end of Chapter I) while the shelving of responsibility onto others is a passive kind of act requiring no effort except, figuratively, a rather pleasurable washing of the hands. "Those dunces in Washington are driving the country to ruin" is a type of judgment often expressed by citizens who would not themselves dream of entering politics for any disinterested motive. The pleasure enjoyed by sports fans at games consists largely in the completeness with which they may be free to criticize while abandoning to others responsibility for the events that occur on the playing field. In cases of acts already accomplished— or, more accurately, of choices already made—the assignment of responsibility involves judgments of praise and blame; and the normal tendency is to accept responsibility for the praiseworthy elements alone. For these reasons the injunction in the New Testament, "Judge not," embodies an important moral principle. The task of a moral agent is to judge himself before and more severely than others; it is himself for whom he is primarily responsible.

After all the foregoing reservations have been made it must still be admitted that judgments of responsibility do and must to some extent have a social aspect. An attitude of moral indifferentism towards other persons' acts, while less fatal than indifferentism towards one's own, is destructive of social morality when pushed too far. Social praise and blame are an important factor in the moral choices and moral development of individuals. Penal law, which is properly an institutionalized form of social praise and blame, is necessary to any community except possibly an anarchic commonwealth of saints. Both law and public opinion, when just, are based on the implied admission that individuals are ordinarily to be judged responsible for the deeds they do. The burden of proof is on the lawyer who declares that his client was not responsible. For the correct administration of penal justice, therefore, no less than for the individual task of self-scrutiny it becomes important to inquire what determines an individual as responsible or not responsible for his actions.

Aristotle's doctrine of voluntary actions

It was Aristotle who in the third book of the *Nicomachean Ethics* made the first systematic inquiry into the conditions of moral responsibility. Virtue, he begins, is concerned with feelings and actions, and it is only to such feelings and actions as are believed to be voluntary that praise and blame are meted out. Hence it is necessary for the student of ethics to inquire into the nature of the voluntary. Admitting that at least *some* feelings and actions are voluntary,[1] the question is in what cases they are not.   In the cases, it appears, of actions done under compulsion and of actions done through ignorance. These may be considered separately.

Actions done entirely from compulsion have obviously no moral quality, since, in Aristotle's words, "the cause is external"; "the agent, or rather the person compelled, contributes nothing to the act: as, for instance, if he were to be borne off somewhere by a storm or by men too powerful for him."   Compulsion, however, is not unambiguous, and "what about actions done through fear of greater evils or for the attainment of a noble end?"   Is a political prisoner who under torture gives information damaging to his confederates acting under compulsion or voluntarily?   Constancy under such provocation is more than ever to be admired but a man who weakened would not be called a deliberate traitor.   Acts of this class Aristotle describes as "of a mixed nature but closer to voluntary acts."   Obviously no satisfactory rule for all semi-compulsory acts can be laid down.

Actions done through ignorance require a somewhat different analysis.   "What is done through ignorance is always *unintentional* but it is done *unwillingly* only if pain and regret are felt afterwards."[2]   Furthermore, there is always the question whether the ignorance was justifiable or whether it could have been avoided.   If a hunter

---

[1] The admission has been implied throughout the preceding chapters, since without it moral questions would be meaningless.   It is implied more particularly in the second requirement of a moral situation stated in Chapter I.   Its metaphysical consequences are examined in Chapter XII.

[2] *Nic. Eth.*, III. i. 13.   I have translated οὐχ ἑκούσιον as 'unintentional' or 'involuntary' and ἀκούσιον as 'against one's will' or 'done unwillingly.' The adverbial form is necessitated by the lack in the English language of a passive adjective corresponding to the active adjective 'unwilling.'   In spite of the fact that several translators have rendered ἀκούσιον by 'involuntary' I can see no justification for this in English usage.   'Involuntary' means not actually willed; ἀκούσιον means in opposition to one's will.

accidentally shoots someone in a forest, not knowing anyone was near, his act may be pardoned, but were the same
accident to occur close to a settlement we would blame
its perpetrator on the ground that he should have taken
the precaution of learning who was within range before
he pulled the trigger.

There is in Shakespeare's *Antony and Cleopatra* a situation which illustrates the matter. Caesar, Antony, and
Lepidus have come aboard Pompey's galley for a conference, to arrange a truce. Menas, friend and supporter
to Pompey, draws him aside during the banquet and
whispers a reminder that his three great rivals for world
power are now at his mercy:

> *Menas.*   Thou art, if thou dar'st be, the earthly Jove.
> Whate'er the ocean pales, or sky inclips,
> Is thine, if thou wilt ha't.
> *Pompey.*   Show me which way.
> *Men.*   These three world-sharers, these competitors,
> Are in thy vessel: let me cut the cable;
> And, when we are put off, fall to their throats.
> All there is thine.
> *Pom.*   Ah, this thou shouldst have done,
> And not have spoke on't!   In me 't is villainy;
> In thee 't had been good service.   Thou must know,
> 'T is not my profit that does lead mine honor;
> Mine honor, it.   Repent that e'er thy tongue
> Hath so betray'd thine act.   Being done unknown,
> I should have found it afterwards well done;
> But must condemn it now.   Desist, and drink.
> *Men.*   (*Aside.*)   For this,
> I'll never follow thy pall'd fortunes more.
> Who seeks, and will not take when once 't is offer'd,
> Shall never find it more.[1]

Too often then, it appears, ignorance is used as an
excuse illegitimately.   Acquiescence in ignorance makes

[1] Act II, Scene vii.

ignorance blameworthy. To W. K. Clifford such ignorance is the cardinal sin: "It is wrong always, everywhere,
and for anyone, to believe anything upon insufficient
evidence." It is our duty, he adds, "to guard ourselves
from such beliefs as from a pestilence, which may shortly
master our own body and then spread to the rest of the
town."[1] His declaration is perhaps a little extreme:
'sufficient' evidence in vital matters is not always forthcoming. Even if beliefs can be suspended actions cannot
always wait. As nearly sufficient evidence as possible is
a good rule, but other factors enter. Clifford rightly
condemns a shipowner who sends to sea a ship which he
believes on insufficient evidence to be safe. But it is not
merely the insufficiency of his evidence that justifies cen-
sure; it is also the fact that the shipowner's policy is one
that endangers the lives and property of others more
than his own. If when the ship sank it was discovered that
the owner received more than its value in insurance a neutral observer might suspect that his indirect action in taking
the lives of passengers and crew through carelessness was
perhaps 'unintentional' but not wholly 'against his will.'

Aristotle points out also another type of ignorance
which is not excusable: ignorance of the end. To give
someone a dose of poison in the belief that it is medicine
constitutes an accident; to give poison through ignorance
that murder is wrong constitutes a crime. The ignorance
that excuses is "not ignorance of the universal principles
(for we blame a man for this) but ignorance of particulars,
of the circumstances and specific effects of an act."[2]
This distinction is the obverse of the distinction made by
Nicias in his discussion with Socrates and Laches between

---

[1]"On the Scientific Basis of Morals," in *Lectures and Essays*, Vol. II,
pp. 186, 184.

[2]*Nic. Eth.*, III. i. 14–15.

wisdom about the highest values which is inseparable from morality and technical knowledge or skill which is ordinarily irrelevant to it.

3. THE NATURE OF DUTIES TO ONESELF

Our inquiry concerning virtue may now be particularized. What are the specific virtues that a moral man will observe? The broadest distinction among them is between those that concern primarily oneself and those that concern primarily others. While the distinction must not be overstressed, for probably no virtue is wholly one or the other, it is permissible to examine the two types separately. Justice, as the most objective and therefore most readily analyzed of the social virtues, will be the subject of the next chapter. The present inquiry will be directed towards virtues that have primarily a reference to the agent's own good.

But it is first of all necessary to offer evidence that self-regarding virtues exist. There is a kind of loose-thinking humanitarianism abroad today which regards virtue as *per se* a social thing; which holds that the object of one's duties is always the good of another person or other persons or the good of society at large. This view may be refuted briefly. The premises for a refutation are found in Dr. Hartmann's analysis of the meaning of duty.[1] If I acknowledge a duty (an 'Ought-to-Do') to anyone I thereby acknowledge (1) certain values in that person, (2) which are not completely realized, and (3) the realization of which is within my power. Conversely, when I acknowledge the presence of these three conditions in any person I acknowledge a duty to that person. Now therefore if A acknowledges duties to B and B to A, but neither A nor B acknowledges duties to himself, it follows that

---

[1] See Chapter V of this book, pp. 135–137.

A and B acknowledge values in each other but that neither of them acknowledges values in himself. A and B thus regard each other as something intrinsically good but each regards himself as good only extrinsically. This seems a most unsatisfactory arrangement. The good which we strive to promote in other persons is constantly vanishing, unacknowledged by them, and 'social service' becomes the pursuit of an illusion. Kant was wiser than the inordinate altruists whose only goal is 'service' when he expressed the categorical imperative as a command "to treat humanity, *whether in your own person* or in that of any other, in every case as an end and never as merely a means."

What, then, are the self-regarding virtues? An exhaustive list is naturally out of the question. Virtues are not like apples, so many to a tree; they merge into one another, and distinguished too sharply they become empty abstractions. While extended lists and analyses of the particular virtues have been made by a number of ethical writers,[1] the present discussion will be limited to three of the more important and representative of those virtues that consist in promoting the good of the agent: self-control, candor, and dignity.

(i) Self-control

Self-control, while by no means the chief among the virtues, is an indispensable condition of a virtuous life. Other virtues, so far as they do not 'come naturally' to a person but must be acquired with effort, are impossible without it. Each virtue represents a victory over contrary temptations, which is to say a victory over base or

---

[1]Notably by Aristotle (*Nicomachean Ethics*, Bks. III, IV), Spinoza (*Ethics*, Bk. IV), Paulsen (*A System of Ethics*, Bk. III), and Nicolai Hartmann (*Ethics*, Part II, Secs. IV–VII). Plato's analysis (*Republic*, Bk. IV) of the four virtues, temperance, courage, wisdom, and justice, may also be consulted in this connection.

at any rate less valued impulses in oneself. The Greek philosophers, accordingly, recognized 'temperance' as one of the cardinal virtues, and Plato makes it the first (though not the highest) prerequisite of a good life as well as of a stable society.

The opposite of self-control is self-indulgence. The extent to which self-indulgence is morally permissible cannot be answered easily, but too much of it tends to disintegrate (*i.e.*, 'dissipate') the personality. Will and intellect become sluggish through disuse, while the sensibilities become overcharged then blunted until the capacity for enjoyment itself becomes coarsened and diminished. "All passive enjoyments deaden the sensibilities," Paulsen writes; "stronger and more refined excitations are constantly needed to procure feelings of pleasure through the exhausted organ, until at last the chronic state of dullness which is characteristic of the *roué* is reached; the powers of the organism and its irritability are exhausted; nothing is left but the repulsive dregs of life."[1] There is entailed a loss of freedom too. To succumb perpetually to one's desires is to become a slave to them. Desires can be the most tyrannical of masters, and it is related by Plato that Sophocles the dramatic poet when asked in his old age, "How do you feel about love, Sophocles? are you still capable of it?" replied, "Hush! if you please: to my great delight I have escaped from it, and feel as if I had escaped from a frantic and savage monster."

Recognition of the tyranny of desire has from time to time prompted sensitive individuals to renounce worldly pleasures and embrace an ascetic way of life. Asceticism is that moral philosophy and way of life whose fundamental postulate is that *pleasure is intrinsically bad*. Antisthenes the Cynic gave short expression to this philosophy

[1]Paulsen, *op. cit.*, pp. 485–486.

in his declaration previously quoted, that he would rather go mad than feel pleasure. The asceticism of the Greek Cynics may amuse or repel us with its evidences of whimsical exhibitionism, but whatever its drawbacks asceticism answers to a genuine and deep need in certain individuals. Some are by the nature of their impulses more exposed to temptation than others and require more desperate antidotes. This explains why some of the great ascetics of history have been men with unusually strong natural appetites and unusually acute sensibilities.

But it is not necessary to accept asceticism whole in order to receive the benefits of self-discipline. Aristotle proposes a wiser solution: not to spurn all pleasures but by habituating oneself to worthy courses of action to turn these, which may at first be irksome, into something pleasurable. Habits when formed tend on the whole to be pleasurable, and the problem of self-control is thus primarily the problem of forming good habits and strengthening oneself in them. "The great thing," remarks William James, "is to make our nervous system our ally instead of our enemy," and he offers four maxims for the formation and preservation of good habits: (1) "Make automatic and habitual, as early as possible, as many useful actions as [you] can, and guard against the growing into ways that are likely to be disadvantageous to [you]"; (2) "Never suffer an exception to occur till the new habit is securely rooted in your life"; (3) "Seize the very first possible opportunity to act on every resolution you make and on every emotional prompting you may experience in the direction of the habits you aspire to gain"; (4) "Keep the faculty of effort alive in you by a little gratuitous exercise every day."[1] James' advice is particularly

---

[1] *The Principles of Psychology*, Vol. I, pp. 122–127. The whole passage is very much worth reading for those who care about the practical side of ethics.

valuable because of the sound grasp of human psychology on which it is based. The third maxim is an important reminder that it is not resolutions but their *motor effects* that "communicate the new 'set' to the brain," and that "every time a resolve or a fine glow of feeling evaporates without bearing practical fruit is worse than a chance lost; it works so as positively to hinder future resolutions and emotions from taking the normal path of discharge." The fourth maxim indicates the extent to which James accepts a limited and practicable form of the ascetic principle: "Do every day or two something for no other reason than that you would rather not do it, so that when the hour of dire need draws nigh, it may find you not unnerved and untrained to stand the test."

Where, in the practice of self-control, shall we begin? Tolstoy discusses this question in one of his disturbing essays, "The First Step." As self-control is the first condition of a good life, so the first condition of self-control is fasting:

A man's desires are many and various, and in order success-fully to contend with them he must begin with the funda-mental ones—those upon which the more complex ones have grown up—and not with those complex lusts which have grown up upon the fundamental ones. There are complex lusts, like that of the adornment of the body, sports, amuse-ments, idle talk, inquisitiveness, and many others; and there are also fundamental lusts—gluttony, idleness, sexual love. And one must begin to contend with these lusts from the be-ginning: not with the complex, but with the fundamental ones, and that also in a definite order. And this order is deter-mined both by the nature of things and by the tradition of human wisdom.

A man who eats too much cannot strive against laziness, while a gluttonous and idle man will never be able to contend with sexual lust. Therefore, according to all moral teachings, the effort towards self-control commences with a struggle against the lust of gluttony—commences with fasting. In our time, however, every serious relation to the attainment of a good life has been so long and so completely lost, that not only is the very first virtue—self-control—without which the others are unattainable, regarded as superfluous, but the order of succession necessary for the attainment of this first virtue is also disregarded, and fasting is quite forgotten, or is looked upon as a silly superstition, utterly unnecessary.[1]

Tolstoy, it must be noticed, while an ascetic according to popular standards, does not espouse a complete philosophy of asceticism. He does not declare pleasures bad in themselves but in their necessary effects. Asceticism with respect first to food, then to idleness, sex, amusement, display, loquacity, and other such tendencies is recommended not as an end in itself but because such ascetic practices are essential first steps in the attainment of self-control, which is the first step in progress towards the good life. The advice is perhaps not equally much needed by all persons. Each must decide for himself how vigorous are the measures which the achievement of ideal ends in his case requires.

(ii) Candor

No one, of course, either is or wishes to be completely candid with all other people. Perfect candor in all social relations would be like living all one's life in a transparent house. But candor with oneself, while often difficult, is an important part of the moral ideal. It seems, in fact, to be a prerequisite of the other virtues, for without it one's defects and consequent possibilities of self-improvement would pass unperceived. The type of unconscious hypocrite who makes himself a nuisance or a danger to

[1]From "The First Step," in Tolstoy's *Essays and Letters*, pp. 77–78. Translated by Aylmer Maude, in "The World's Classics." (Oxford University Press.)

his fellows while supposing himself to be moved only by noble motives is usually less admirable than the frankly anti-social criminal and often he does quite as much harm. Furthermore, self-consciousness is what constitutes the very being of a self as distinguished from purely material objects; and candor, in the private sense, is simply a frank and full consciousness of oneself. It would seem to follow, then, that if an individual has any duties to himself whatever, the preservation of his own being (that is, his conscious selfhood, not his mere physical organism) is foremost among them.

Candor with others presents a more complex problem. A person too candid is like a leaky sieve, retaining nothing. But some degree of candor is an essential of social intercourse. Communication implies candor, and while much communication is deceptive not all or even most of it can be so, otherwise nobody would believe anyone else and the power of communication would be lost. In Dostoyevsky's *Crime and Punishment* the most bitter of the psychological punishments that come to the murderer Raskolnikov is the realization that as a result of his still undetected crime he has been cut off from all essential communication with his fellow-men:

"Hush, mother," he muttered in confusion, not looking at her, but pressing her hand. "We shall have time to speak freely of everything."

As he said this, he was suddenly overwhelmed with confusion and turned pale. Again that awful sensation he had known of late passed with deadly chill over his soul. Again it became suddenly plain and perceptible to him that he had just told a fearful lie—that he would never now be able to speak freely of everything—that he would never again be able to *speak* of anything to anyone.[1]

---

[1] Bk. III, Chap. III. Constance Garnett's translation. (Reprinted by permission of the Modern Library, New York.)

(iii) Dignity

The various personal virtues, as well as the personal aspects of the social virtues, seem to be primarily justified by the sense one has of one's own worth.   This sense of one's own worth may be called 'dignity' (from the Latin, *dignitas*, worth).   Why should I not perform a base action even though I were perfectly secure from detection? Because, the answer might be, I am I, and I choose to be something worthy of my own admiration rather than something base.   In genuine as opposed to conventional social virtues the same element is essential.   Why should I be just?   The presence of altruistic sentiments and impulses is not enough to account for justice, for altruism is capable of playing favorites.   If the ideal of justice is accepted as a worthy one towards which to direct one's efforts it is because the character of the ideal is more consonant with the kind of self that one admires and chooses to become.   A true sense of justice is thus an outward reflection of a sense of one's own moral worth.

PART III
THE INDIVIDUAL AND SOCIETY

CHAPTER IX

THE PROBLEM OF SOCIAL JUSTICE

Like a pure white color, justice is all too easily soiled.
Dante, *De Monarchia*

SINCE MAN IS to so large an extent a social animal and dependent not only for his livelihood but for his thoughts, valuations, and purposes on the other individuals and social institutions to which he is related, there can evidently be no sharp break between individual and social ethics. A man's individual values are to a very great extent socially conditioned, while social occurrences and social institutions, for their part, possess values only because, in the last analysis, they affect and are judged by individuals. Nevertheless it is possible, and for clarity of exposition often desirable, to distinguish those problems and values which have significance to an individual primarily in his private capacity from those which are meaningless except when referred to a social situation. Energy, prudence, and self-control[1] are virtues whose most immediate and assured value is to the possessor of them. Their value for society is indeterminate until it is known whether their possessor is directing them towards selfish or generous ends. No doubt their value to their possessor will also be modified by the presence or absence in him of

[1] Charles Renouvier (1815–1903) names these (*la force, la prudence,* and *la tempérance*) as the three cardinal virtues of the "elementary sphere of morality," which is characterized by duties towards oneself alone. A duty towards oneself Renouvier defines as "a duty to make and be a certain kind of self, with respect to possible alternatives which are imagined or foreseen, or towards which one is tempted." (*La science de la morale,* Bk. I, Sec. I, Chaps. IV, V.)

benevolence, humility, and a sense of justice; but that they are in some way a positive good to him seems evident, even when their effect on society is doubtful or pernicious. Furthermore, these are virtues which could be practiced by a Robinson Crusoe or a Tarzan, in the absence of all social intercourse.   Benevolence and justice, on the other hand, are virtues which it is clearly impossible to practice in the absence of one's fellows; and in addition, these virtues confer more immediate and more certain benefits upon society than upon the individual who practises them.

1.   The Meaning of Justice

In Chapter I an analysis was made of a typical act of moral deliberation.   True moral deliberation, according to that analysis, involves something more than summarizing the logical arguments for each side of a moral issue.   It is not a matter solely of skilful arguments but of imaginative insight into the situation that is expected to result from the proposed choice.   This imaginative projection of one's present self into a yet unrealized situation is, in effect, a transcending of the 'actual' boundaries of the self; it is an 'ideal' identification of my present self with a self not yet actual but recognized as good and choiceworthy.

Moral insight may be directed not only towards one's own unrealized future self and the situations attendant upon it, but also towards alien selves.   In the latter case, as distinguished from the former, the object of my imagining is not a self which I can hope or choose ever to become; my identification with it is at best partial and ideal, never wholly (or even, as a rule, very) actual.   Nevertheless the two species of imaginative effort are psychologically similar: both transcend, via imagination, the here and now.   In both there is an actual separateness and difference together with an ideal identity.   Renouvier has de-

fined the social aspect of moral deliberation in the following passage:

> The agents will rely on their mutual promises because they
> are similar, or equal, persons, between whom this *divided identity*
> and the substitution of the one person for the other which is
> always rationally possible, establishes what may be called a
> bilateral relation and two rôles that for practical purposes are
> interchangeable. Accordingly, when the one feels morally
> obligated, he is obligated not merely to himself . . . nor
> does the obligation terminate with the wholly personal moral
> situation that has given rise to it; he is obligated to a distinctly
> other self, and the obligation persists so far as that other self,
> whose change alone could release him, has not changed. In this
> reciprocity there is thus a moral community and solidarity
> established by reason. Two persons find that from a moral
> point of view they are as one single person, but with the qualifica-
> tion that this single person takes a double aspect.[1]

The impulsive man is likely to approve impulses in himself which he would condemn in others, or at any rate to
set a higher value upon his own impulses, and to promote
them without giving adequate consideration to the rival
impulses and needs of other persons. Sometimes too,
though perhaps more rarely, we encounter timid, self-
depreciating souls who applaud and promote in others
impulses which may thwart or injure themselves. Neither
of these impulsive attitudes makes for social morality,
since neither gives consideration to the comparative values
involved. To the rational man, on the other hand, an
impulse in himself and the same impulse in another are
held of equal worth, except so far as *some difference other
than the bare difference of selfhood* is present which might
justify a difference in evaluation. Reason, in short, perceives the equal worth of persons *as such;* and any differences in worth must be found not in the simple fact that

---

[1] *Op. cit.*, Vol. I, p. 55.

he is he and I am I (which from a rational point of view is irrelevant) but in specific characteristics by which one person is differentiated from another in a significant way. Significant differences are adjectival, not pronominal.

The disposition to evaluate and decide between competing claims without reference to the mere identity of the claimant is characteristic of the man whom we call just. Whatever else justice may connote, it implies at very least a stern objectivity. Justice is therefore something more than unselfishness, for a person may be unselfish in a quite impulsive and irrational way. The meaning of justice will become more clear by contrasting it with three other and less completely objective social virtues: gratitude, loyalty, and benevolence.

Three imperfect virtues

Some philosophers have found in the sentiment of *gratitude* an explanation of the origin of distributive justice. It has been suggested[1] that justice might have evolved by a gradual acceptance of each of the following principles in turn: (1) "A good deed done by anyone to me ought to be requited by me" (the principle of simple gratitude); (2) "A good deed done by anyone to anyone ought to be requited by the recipient" (this might be called sympathetic gratitude); (3) "A good deed done by anyone ought *somehow* to be requited" (universalized form of the principle of gratitude); (4) "To each according as he has deserved" or "To each according to his deserts" (which is one widely accepted form of the principle of justice). But whatever value this hypothesis (it is no more than that) may have in explaining the origin of justice, it does not diminish the essential difference be-

---

[1] By Henry Sidgwick, for example (*Methods of Ethics*, Bk. III, Chap. V), though in a slightly different form from that given here.

tween what justice in its developed form and gratitude respectively mean.

The difference between the two is made apparent in a question posited by William Godwin, philosophical anarchist and friend and father-in-law of Shelley: If you had to choose whether to rescue Fénelon or your mother from a burning house, what would be your duty? Assuming that one had any time and disposition for reflective choice on such an occasion, gratitude and love would seem to justify choosing to save the mother and let the prelate burn. But justice, declares Godwin, would require rather the rescue of Fénelon if it seemed probable that he was likely to contribute more to the good of mankind. To the question, whether gratitude is not justified towards one's benefactor and whether it is not just to give where one has received, Godwin replies no; that justice requires one to choose rationally, and from a rational point of view the merit of the benefaction was equal, whether the benefit was conferred upon oneself or upon another. "I and another man cannot both be right in preferring our own individual benefactor, for no man can be at the same time both better and worse than his neighbor. My benefactor ought to be esteemed, not because he bestowed a benefit upon me, but because he bestowed it upon a human being."[1] Consequently Godwin condemns gratitude as "a sentiment which would lead me to prefer one man to another from some other consideration than that of his superior usefulness or worth; that is, which would make something true to me (for example this perferableness) which cannot be true to another man and is not true in itself."

This attitude, it will be noted, is akin to that of the Stoics, who denied that a man ought ever to recognize

[1] William Godwin, *An Enquiry Concerning Political Justice*, Bk. II, Chap. II.

special duties to those who stand closest to him. Most persons, however justice might be defined, would probably regard gratitude as having the superior claim in a situation like the above; and Bentham has tried to reconcile the principle of justice with the popular view by arguing that we owe prior consideration to those who stand nearest to us not because they or their relation to us deserve it but because we are in a better position to judge their needs than the needs of strangers, and thus more likely to succeed in our efforts to increase the total amount of happiness in the world. What Bentham's argument shows is that justice ought to be *supplemented* by dispositions of a less austere kind, whose effects are more immediately discerned. But the issue between justice and gratitude is still unresolved in many cases, and Godwin's episode of the burning house appears to be one of them.

Loyalty is more impersonal than gratitude (which is often one of the motives impelling it) and has therefore been more seriously proposed as a virtue to which justice must be made subordinate. Loyalty is easier to admire than justice because it is easier to discern, not requiring like justice a rational examination of competing claims. Furthermore, within a strictly limited sphere loyalty may serve as a basis for a kind of justice. There is loyalty among gangsters, which makes possible a sometimes very stern application of justice within the gang. A gangster's relations with those towards whom he recognizes no claims of loyalty, however, are likely to be guided not by any notion of justice but by expedience, roguery, and violence. Similarly, loyalty to one's nation, or *patriotism*, which Treitschke, like modern defenders of fascism, held to be the supreme virtue, is compatible with a complete absence of morality between nations. Yet notwithstanding its limitations the moral importance of loyalty should not be ignored. Royce, in his *Philosophy of Loyalty*, has plausibly maintained that it is by striving towards more and more socially comprehensive ideals of loyalty that men can be brought to a realization of justice, which Royce conceives as loyalty towards mankind as a whole. This view has been given incidental confirmation by Mr. Lincoln Steffens, who found, during his investigation of civic conditions in Philadelphia a couple of decades ago, that the one effective appeal he could make to an unscrupulous but generous-hearted political boss of that city was to accuse him, not of injustice or dishonesty, but of disloyalty to the million or so voters who counted on him to use his political machine for their good rather than for the good of a few politicians.[1]

Finally, justice must be distinguished from *benevolence*. Benevolence is of course a very valuable disposition for individuals to possess. Without it justice becomes either a bare formula or dangerous fanaticism. Nor are the two virtues necessarily incompatible: a man may work to secure for each individual his proper share of the material conditions of well-being (which is all that the ideal of social justice can very well require) while at the same time giving to some few individuals more than their share of such non-material things as personal interest and encouragement and love, to which the laws of addition and subtraction do not apply. The danger of benevolence lies in the willingness of so many unthinking sentimentalists to accept it not as a desirable supplement to justice but as a sufficient substitute. This produces such anomalies as the spectacle of certain dishonest bankers winning popular approval and support by their affability on the witness stand; or by their contributions to charities which

---

[1] *The Autobiography of Lincoln Steffens:* Part II, Chap. VIII, "The Dying Boss." Similar examples will be found elsewhere in Mr. Steffens' book.

have been perhaps necessitated by the 'rugged individualism' of their business practices.

What, then, is justice as distinguished from such dispositions as benevolence and loyalty, gratitude and love? As a preliminary answer we may say that the just man is "an impartial man, one who seeks with equal care to satisfy all claims which he recognizes as valid and does not let himself be unduly influenced by personal prejudices";[1] that the just society is a society in which the satisfaction of claims and the distribution of goods (and, when necessary, of evils) is settled on some objective principle irrespective of questions of personal identity alone. This definition is still very broad, and is consistent with very dissimilar theories as to the kind of objective principle to be preferred. As a starting-point for a more accurate definition we may examine first a theory which in Chapter III has already been encountered in another connection: *utilitarianism*.

2. The Utilitarian Theory

The objective principle to which the utilitarians appealed in their social ethics was expressed in the phrase, 'the greatest happiness for the greatest number.' The logical difficulties implicit in this formula, the fallacy of the psychological assumption on which it rests, and its limitations as a standard of personal conduct have been discussed in Chapter III. In the present chapter we are to consider utilitarianism rather in its social aspect, as an attempt to derive from its basic principle a theory and program of social legislation that would be at once humanitarian and scientific.

---

[1]Sidgwick, *op. cit.*, p. 268. Sidgwick, too, gives this as merely a preliminary definition, suitable to 'common sense,' and not as one finally satisfactory to himself.

The humanitarian principle

"In the golden rule of Jesus of Nazareth," says Mill, "we read the complete spirit of the ethics of utility. To do as you would be done by, love your neighbor as yourself, constitute the ideal perfection of utilitarian morality." Mill's statement is largely false. Jesus was not a hedonist, nor does 'utility' in any ordinary sense describe his aim. The life of blessedness to which he summons mankind does not have as its primary objective a surplus of pleasures over pains. Nor did morality for Jesus consist, as it did for the utilitarians, in concrete intentions and results, but in purity of heart. But in its humanitarian aspect it is true that utilitarianism shows a superficial likeness to the original Christian teachings. Seeking the happiness of the greatest number, while far from identical with the Christian precept to love one's neighbor, is at any rate closer to the spirit of Jesus' teachings than either the egoistic hedonism of Aristippus or the uncharitable and reactionary social philosophies customarily promulgated by both State and Church.

Jeremy Bentham (1748–1832) was a student of jurisprudence, a reformer of legislation. His moral theory was developed primarily to supply a basis for needed legislative reforms. The plight of British workers in his time was miserable. The Industrial Revolution had herded them by tens of thousands into factories, where the hours were long, the work grueling, and the pay scarcely adequate for bare subsistence. Some idea of these conditions can be got from the materials assembled by Karl Marx half a century later. In 1860 Mr. Broughton Charlton, county magistrate, declared at a Nottingham meeting of which he was chairman, that in the lace trade "children of nine or ten years are dragged from their squalid beds at two, three, or four o'clock in the morning and compelled to work for a bare subsistence until ten, eleven, or twelve at night, their limbs wearing away, their frames dwindling, their faces whitening, and their humanity absolutely sinking into a stonelike torpor, utterly horrible to contemplate." Concerning conditions in the pottery districts the senior physician of the North Staffordshire Infirmary, in a report of the Commissioners, said: "The potters as a class, both men and women, represent a degenerated population, both physically and morally. They are, as a rule, stunted in growth, ill-shaped, and frequently ill-formed in the chest; they become prematurely old, and are certainly short-lived; they are phlegmatic and bloodless, and exhibit their debility of constitution by obstinate attacks of dyspepsia, and disorders of the liver and kidneys, and by chest disease, pneumonia, phthisis, bronchitis, and asthma. . . . That the 'degenerescence' of the population of this district is not even greater than it is, is due to the constant recruiting from the adjacent country, and intermarriages with more healthy races."[1] Such conditions as these led thoughtful and humane people to inquire whether it was not time to challenge the 'right' of the privileged classes to exploit so heartlessly their employees. Some kind of universal principle seemed needed, to which specific problems of adjustment could be referred and by which a program of legislation could be mapped out. To be universal the principle must have primary reference not to members of one class but to all the people whom the legislation would affect, or, failing that, to the greatest possible number of them. And to be a principle of any worth it must be objectively deter-

---

[1] Karl Marx, *Capital*, pp. 109–111 of the Modern Library edition. Marx cites numerous other such examples.

minable and therefore, Bentham argued, formulated in terms of a 'real entity'—the happiness (*i.e.*, pleasure, and absence of pain) of the persons affected. The one ideal that met both of these requirements was the 'principle of utility,' as Bentham called it, which stood for 'the greatest happiness of the greatest number.'

Reasonable as the 'greatest happiness of the greatest number' seemed to Bentham, this was not the ideal by which those in political authority were commonly guided:

Government has, under every form comprehending laws and institutions, had for its object the greatest happiness not of those over whom, but of those by whom, it has been exercised; the interest not of the many, but of the few, or even of the one has been the prevalent interest; and to that interest all others have been, at all times, sacrificed. To these few, or this one, depredation has everywhere been the grand object.[1]

How could this universal abuse of government be corrected? Instead of making any effort to correct it most economists and political and legal theorists, then as now, constructed theories designed to justify the *status quo*. Sir William Blackstone, for example, author of *Commentaries on the Laws of England* and the most widely accepted authority on constitutional law of Bentham's day, went so far as to declare that the system of British jurisprudence was "in the whole and every part of it, the very quintessence of perfection," and that it was an 'indecency' for any individual to set up his private judgment in opposition to the established judgment of the public. Blackstone had been Bentham's tutor at Oxford, but it was Bentham's boast that he had never accepted the other's teachings. "He is infected," Bentham later wrote of him, "with the foul stench of intolerance. No sound principles can be

[1] *The Theory of Legislation*, edited by C. K. Ogden, p. xxviii.

expected from that writer whose first object is to defend a system." The defence of an existing system can always be made plausible if one sticks, as Blackstone did, to an exposition of the traditional rules and precedents of the legal profession. Bentham decided that he must oppose to this technical, legalistic method a 'natural' method, which should have two determining characteristics: it should be derived from the general laws of human nature, and it should be free from principles based on the assumption of 'fictitious entities.'

The 'general laws of human nature' Bentham finds in the over-simplified formula of hedonistic psychology, the 'principle of self-preference' discussed in Chapter III. By referring all interpretations of human behavior as well as all standards of right and wrong, justice and injustice, to this touchstone he believed he could rid ethical theory, more particularly as applied to political ethics and jurisprudence, of the misleading 'fictions' that had plagued it for so long.

The attack on fictions

Bentham had been all his life haunted by ghosts. Certain childhood experiences—tales told by his grandmother and the superstitions of servants—left him subject even in manhood to their visitations. "In no man's judgment," he wrote, "can a stronger persuasion of the non-existence of these sources of terror have place than in mine"; no matter: as soon as he would lie down alone in a dark room the terror would seize him. As he grew up his dread of ghosts became generalized into a dread of anything intangible and elusive. Ghosts and vampires have their counterparts, he discovered, in the numerous 'fictions' of law, philosophy, religion, and everyday thought and discourse. Motion, rest, obligations, rights, goodness, honesty, beauty, and all of the so-called faculties and powers of the mind[1]—what are they but *fictitious entities?* The words represent nothing that can be apprehended by any of the five senses: how, then, can they represent anything at all? The exigencies of language force us to use names as if they referred to real entities when actually they do not. We speak of a body 'in motion,' yet it is not really in anything; of a man 'bound by an obligation,' yet we see no chains; of another who is 'vested with certain rights,' yet rights are not clothes that can be put on as the etymology of 'vested' connotes. Expressions such as these are frequent in political and legal arguments. 'Rights,' 'obligations,' the 'moral sense,' the 'social contract,' and other such expressions, as well as the more general pair of terms 'right' and 'wrong,' are appealed to in arguments more often than not designed to justify the existing institutions and social inequalities. In order, therefore, to establish a utilitarian theory of ethics on a sure foundation Bentham undertook first to devise a logical method by which the true significance of abstract words might be understood. The method was called *paraphrasis*, which he defined as "that sort of exposition which may be afforded by transmuting into a proposition, having for its subject some real entity, a proposition which has not for its subject other than a fictitious entity."[2]

---

[1] What Carl Spitteler, in his epic prose-poem, *Prometheus and Epimetheus*, has called "the -*heits* and -*keits* of things."

[2] Paraphrasis, as Bentham employs and explains it, consists of two steps. First, *archetypation*, which fixes the reference of a word to an observed image—that is, to some *real psychical* (Bentham sometimes says 'pneumatic') entity, whose ulterior source and ulterior reference is some *real physical* entity. By determining the nature of the archetypal image we provide, in the words of Mr. C. K. Ogden, "the foundation and framework for a verbal expression to any degree of explicitness and exhaustiveness that we may need for accurate

Obligations and rights

The most important fictitious entity in the field of moral theory and "the root out of which all these other fictitious entities take their rise" is *obligation*. The real entity to which this word refers must be sought among the concrete feelings of pain and pleasure. "An obligation (*viz.*, the obligation of conducting himself in a certain manner) is incumbent on a man (*i.e.*, spoken of as incumbent on a man) in so far as, in the event of his failing to conduct himself in that manner, pain, or loss of pleasure, is considered as about to be experienced by him." Every obligation thus depends on a hedonistic sanction: *i.e.*, on some pain (or loss of pleasure) that would attend its neglect. Legal and moral obligations differ merely in type of sanction. If the pain in question is some physical or political or economic penalty which those who exercise the powers of government are able and disposed to inflict, the obligation is legal; if the pain is merely the loss of others' approbation and esteem, or a lack of tranquillity caused by a consciousness of having made someone suffer, the obligation is moral.

Correlative with 'obligation' is the name of another fictitious entity, '*rights*.' The same sanction that establishes in one person obligations to someone else, thereby establishes in that second individual certain rights. What is a right? Men are said to have, hold, possess, acquire, lose, or relinquish rights, as if they were something that could be taken up in the hand and let go again. Such

---

translation." This makes possible the second operation, *phraseoplerosis*, which is a 'filling up of the phrase' in such a way as to describe with accurately chosen words the particular 'archetypal image' that has been discovered. Much of the material from which the present exposition of the theory of fictions has been drawn will be found in the selections from Bentham edited by C. K. Ogden in *Bentham's Theory of Fictions*. (Harcourt, Brace.)

language is clearly figurative; Bentham calls it "simple nonsense—nonsense upon stilts." Only by paraphrasis can the true meaning be shown. A "determinate and intelligible meaning" for the word Bentham thinks possible only when the adjunct 'political' is attached. When a man is said to have some political right "the existence of a certain matter of fact is asserted; namely, of a disposition, on the part of those by whom the powers of government are exercised, to cause him to possess, and so far as depends upon them to have the faculty of enjoying, the benefit to which he has a right." But in the case of so-called 'natural rights' no such matter of fact has place. "A man is never the better from having such a natural right; admit that he has it, his condition is not in any respect different from what it would be if he had it not." The most I could mean, were I to say that someone has a natural right to a piece of land, is that "I am of opinion he ought to have a political right to it; that . . . he ought to be protected and secured in the use of it"; in other words, that "the idea of his being so is pleasing to me, and the idea of the opposite result displeasing."

Bentham's reduction of rights and obligations to mere feelings has an important bearing on his theory of social justice. Justice cannot in this theory mean giving to each his due, because a person's 'due' or 'right' has been declared to mean simply what it is pleasing (to the generality of men if it be a moral right, to those in control of government if a political right) that he should have. Units of pain and pleasure rather than persons become the final reference of praiseworthy social conduct. The ideal of the social moralist becomes not fair distribution even of pleasures and pains but the greatest possible total amount of them, regardless of how unfairly they might have to be distributed to achieve this total.

Criticism

It was shown in Chapter III that 'greatest happiness' becomes an almost meaningless phrase when the competing possibilities of happiness are fundamentally different in kind. For our present purpose there is a more significant criticism of the utilitarian theory: *viz.*, that even in cases where measurement is roughly possible Bentham's theory, though it was intended (and largely successful) as a philosophical attack on contemporaneous forms of injustice, yet, if interpreted literally, offers no criterion for justice itself. This failure becomes clear if we apply the utilitarian philosophy to a problem made famous by Charles Lamb. "I remember an hypothesis," he writes in *Essays of Elia*, "argued upon by the young students, when I was at St. Omer's, and maintained with much learning and pleasantry on both sides, 'Whether, supposing that the flavor of a pig who obtained his death by whipping (*per flagellationem extremam*) superadded a pleasure upon the palate of a man more intense than any possible suffering we can conceive in the animal, is man justified in using that method of putting the animal to death?'" Lamb's question is formulated in characteristically utilitarian terms, being concerned with the comparative amounts of pain and pleasure to be got from each of two alternative courses of action, apart from any question of which individuals receive how much of the pain or pleasure, or for what reasons. By a strict application of his principles a utilitarian philosopher could give but one answer to the question. We should be justified in torturing the pig or any other sentient being, he would have to say, provided it were sufficiently probable that a greater total balance of pleasure over pain would result from performing the torture than from leaving it unperformed. By the same logic, if a dozen sadistic inquisitors received so much perverse pleasure from singeing one human victim's flesh that, horrible though the victim's sufferings might be, they were not quite twelve times as great as the average amount of pleasure enjoyed by each of the torturers, then by the hedonistic calculus the torturers would be justified in their pastime. Of course Bentham, being a humane man, would not have accepted any such application of his theory. Probably he would have explained that even though the immediate effects of deliberate cruelty might show a balance of pleasure over pain, such acts ought still to be prohibited because in the long run they are likely to conduce to more pain than pleasure. An explanation like this, however (and it is, difficult to see what other Bentham could have offered) merely plugs the weakness of his theory with a factual assumption for which, by the nature of the case, the evidence can never be adequate. The hypothetical question would still remain: *if* it were the case, or probably the case, that the conditions of the hedonistic calculus would be satisfied by unprovoked cruelty, would that cruelty be justified?

Nor need we appeal to such abnormal instances as the crimes of sadists to show the limits of Bentham's theory. Apologists for the existing order of society with all its brutal injustices sometimes invoke the 'greatest happiness' principle as a support for their views, arguing that the total amount of happiness in society would be diminished by distributing it more equally. Whether or not this is the case is, of course, debatable, but Bentham's principle can still be applied hypothetically: if it *were* the case that a more equal distribution of goods would diminish the total amount of goods to be distributed, which should be chosen, greater equality or greater totality? The question will be examined in the fourth section; but it is at any rate clear that Bentham never answered this question unambiguously. His maxim, 'Everyone to count for one, no one for more than one,' has sometimes been interpreted as a qualification of the 'greatest happiness' principle and a recognition of the principle of equality; but what Bentham seems to have meant by the maxim was simply that in applying the hedonistic calculus to achieve the greatest total happiness the calculation should not be weighted by considerations of the identity, prestige, etc. of the persons affected. In practice, to be sure, Bentham was a zealous proponent of greater equality, particularly of plans for the more even distribution of wealth; but his theoretical justification for this aim was that a more equal distribution of goods was the most likely *means* towards a greater total of happiness.

3. THE MEANING OF RIGHTS

Bentham's doctrine suffers for lack of an adequate theory of rights. In his zeal to demolish false and prejudiced theories of rights he goes so far as to deny the legitimacy of the notion altogether. But unless the rights of individuals are postulated there is no logical way to escape the weird applications of the utilitarian principle just mentioned. Theories aside, we all know that no degree or amount of ecstatic pleasure which a murderer might get from his crime would justify it or go even a little way to justify it, and that the reason it would not is that his victim has certain rights in the matter which the murderer has ignored. In order to arrive at a sound theory of social justice, therefore, we must examine the meaning of rights, together with the correlative notion of obligation.

Rights and obligations

When the conflicting claims of different individuals are rationally adjudged the question arises, which of them is,

in given circumstances, the more justifiable.   A justifiable
claim is called, in the language of social 'ethics, a *right*.[1]
It is an axiom of social ethics that rights possessed by one
person imply duties on the part of others.   This axiom is
self-evident from the meaning of rights and duties.   If one
individual has a right to a piece of land—*i.e.*, he not only
makes a claim to it but his claim is justifiable—it becomes
thereby the duty of other individuals not to take the land
away.   If one has a right to live it is the duty of others
not to kill him.   Duties of this kind, which are implicit
in the rights of other individuals (as distinguished from
duties owed to oneself alone), are called *obligations*.   While
not all duties imply corresponding rights (*e.g.*, one may
recognize 'a duty to the past' or a duty to one's sense of
fitness) it is evident that obligations, as here defined, of
one person do imply possession of rights by another or
others.   In brief: (i) Possession of rights by A implies
obligations on the part of someone other than A, and
(ii) Obligations imposed on A implies the possession of
rights by someone other than A.   As Renouvier has
stated the matter:

In the group constituted by the two agents, the obligation
whose meaning is thus transformed takes the name of *right* or
credit as referring to the one agent, and *duty* or *debit* as referring
to the other, thus forming one single and reciprocal relation.
Both agents, because of the moral association into which they
have entered, are considered as having made a promise, whether
explicitly (*positivement*) or tacitly by reason of their nature as
agents.   To the extent that each of them is the recipient of
a promise, he is a creditor, and has a right, or claim upon his
fellow; to the extent that he is the giver of a promise, he is a

---

[1] *I.e.*, when used as a concrete noun—with the indefinite article or in the
plural.   The adjective 'right,' with which may be connected the abstract noun,
'*the* right,' has already been discussed in previous chapters, notably Chapter
I.   In this latter sense, 'right' would more usually be applied to the fulfillment
of one's obligations than to the assertion of one's 'rights.'

debtor and has a duty to fulfill towards his fellow. The one's credit entails the other's debit, and vice versa. This right and this duty taken together constitute *justice*. For we say it is just that a person should fulfill his duty and just that he should demand his rights, and justice consists of these two mutually related aspects.[1]

Three remarks must be made on the mutually implicative relation between rights and obligations. In the first place, right and duty are correlative only if they refer to the same code or standard. A may have a legal right to gyp B out of some money on the stock market, but when he has succeeded B need not feel any moral obligation to let him keep it.

A second point to be noted is that the implicative relation between rights and obligations does not mean that the two terms so related need be similar in kind. If we postulate that every member of a community has a right to earn an honest living, that assumption entails on other members of the community a variety of obligations for the deduction of which a considerable knowledge of economics is necessary. A naïve observer might suppose that each person was fulfilling his obligations in this respect provided he did not discharge anyone from his employ; but the student of economics is aware that a manufacturer or merchant who over-expands his business, even though the immediate effect is to make more jobs available, may be causing indirectly a great deal of unemployment and misery, either through squeezing out competition or through glutting the market with unwanted goods which will eventually force a curtailment of production.

Finally, the two axiomatic relations between rights and obligations given above should not be confused with two other propositions, which are not axiomatic, since they

[1] *La science de la morale*, Vol. I, p. 55.

can be denied without self-contradiction: *viz.*, (iii) Possession of rights by A implies obligations on the part of A, and (iv) Obligations imposed on A implies possession of rights by A. (iii) and (iv) do not, like (i) and (ii), express logically necessary relations. They are postulated in most but not all systems of social ethics. A theory of absolute monarchy might conceivably assign to the monarch certain rights without any corresponding duties, and to his subjects (or to the lowest of them) duties without corresponding rights. Such a doctrine would doubtless find few supporters today, but it is logically possible, and a denial of it therefore cannot rest on grounds of logic alone.

Legal and moral rights

In examining the meaning of rights it is advisable to take legal rights, because of their greater definiteness, as the point of departure. Ritchie, borrowing from Holland's *Jurisprudence* the definition of a legal right as "a capacity residing in one man of controlling with the assent and assistance of the State, the actions of others," goes on to offer his own analogous definition of a moral right as "a capacity residing in one man of controlling the acts of another with the assent and assistance, or at least without the opposition, of public opinion."[1] More briefly, though perhaps less exactly, Ritchie defines a legal right as "the claim of an individual upon others, recognized by the State," and a moral right as "the claim of an individual upon others recognized by society irrespective of its recognition by the State." These two pairs, especially the former, will serve as working definitions.

It is evident that legal rights are capable of a more exact determination than moral rights. The legal rights

[1] David G. Ritchie, *Natural Rights*, Chap. V, pp. 78–79. (Macmillan.)

272 A CRITICAL INTRODUCTION TO ETHICS

of a given society have been, for the most part, set down in written statutes, and while in particular cases it is often questionable how these statutes are to be interpreted and applied, their interpretation depends for the most part on established and recognized precedents. In a highly homogeneous society a similar measure of agreement is likely to be achieved with respect to moral rights. Indeed, in primitive societies, as well as in more developed societies that are held together by firmly shared religious beliefs, legal and moral rights tend (without ever quite succeeding) to coincide. On the other hand, as Ritchie remarks, "whenever we have a very mixed and heterogeneous society, consisting of persons of different religious beliefs, of different stages of religious disbelief, and at very different grades of intellectual development, questions of moral obligation become more difficult to decide; a greater responsibility is thrown on the individuals immediately affected." Have workmen on strike a moral right to use intimidation towards 'scabs'? Conservative opinion answers negatively; while communists and syndicalists answer affirmatively, on the ground that in a competitive society it is only by 'direct action' that workmen can bring sufficient pressure to bear on their employers to improve permanently their condition. Have a man and woman a moral right to form an extra-marital relation? Has a man in political office a moral right to accept securities at less than the market price from a financial group hoping to secure his support for some legislation favorable to their interests? Has a tramp, homeless and starving through no particular fault of his own, a moral right to keep himself alive by stealing bottles of milk from doorsteps? No unanimity will be found on such questions as these; particular moral rights are conceded by some groups, denied by others; and public opinion, besides being

divided against itself, is undergoing a more or less continual change.

The doctrine of 'natural rights'

Because of the confusion and instability of opinions
about moral rights, many ethical theorists have sought to
establish the existence of 'natural rights'—*i.e.*, rights
which belong to a man by reason of his essential nature,
and the existence of which might therefore be demonstrated on more solid grounds. But this subterfuge,
instead of settling the problem, has merely shifted its
locus from the field of ethics to the field of metaphysics.
What is a man's 'essential' nature? Is a free-born aristocrat, as Aristotle held, different in 'essential' respects
from a slave—which would mean that he possesses natural
rights which a slave lacks? Or is it self-evident that (in
the language of democratic theory) all men are 'created
equal'—with the implication that the same natural rights
are shared by all of them? 'Essential' and 'natural' are
ambiguous words,[1] connoting both (i) what is *original* as
opposed to what is afterwards acquired, and (ii) what is
normal, which in turn "contains both the notion of generally happening, though not necessarily happening, and
the notion of a standard or rule by which things are judged
in respect of quality or merit."[2] There is anthropological
evidence that slavery is not 'natural' in the first sense,
although in this sense of the word it is equally clear that
human equality is not 'natural' either. The appeal to
'natural rights' becomes plausible mainly because the
first meaning of the word is confused with the second.
Consequently Ritchie supplements his previous definitions
of legal and moral rights by defining natural rights as

[1] *Cf.* above, Chapter II, Section 1, and Chapter IV, Section 1.
[2] Ritchie, *op. cit.*, p. 75

"those rights which in [the would-be reformer's] opinion would be recognized by the public opinion of such a society as he admires, and would either be supported or at least would not be interfered with by any of its laws, if it had any laws; they are the rights which he thinks ought to be recognized, *i.e.*, they are the rights sanctioned by his ideal society, whatever that may be."[1]   Still, as Ritchie adds, not all such rights are natural rights, but only the more fundamental of them, from which the others may be deduced or to which they are auxiliary. The right to sue in the courts, for example, and the right when accused to be tried by a jury of one's peers, are not generally classified as natural rights; they are rather means towards securing the fundamental rights of liberty and security.

The principal natural rights of men have been stated variously. In the United States Declaration of Independence it is held to be "self-evident, that all men are created equal, that they are endowed by their Creator with certain inalienable Rights, that among these are Life, Liberty and the pursuit of Happiness." The Virginia Declaration of Rights had previously affirmed "that all men are by nature equally free and independent, and have certain inherent rights, of which, when they enter into a state of society, they cannot by any compact deprive or divest their posterity; namely, the enjoyment of life and liberty, with the means of acquiring and possessing property, and pursuing and obtaining happiness and safety." In the Declaration of the Rights of Man and of Citizens, issued by the National Assembly of France in 1789 and prefixed to the French Constitution of September, 1791, the "natural and imprescriptible rights of man" are listed as "liberty, property, security, and resistance of oppression." In respect of these rights, it is added, "men are born, and

[1] *Op. cit.*, p. 80.

always continue, free and equal"; and later, in the Declaration prefixed to the Constitution of June 24, 1793, equality is explicitly named as one of the natural and imprescriptible rights, the new list comprising "equality, liberty, security, property."[1] Let us examine the more important of these declared rights in turn.

(i) *The right to life.* This is named by the Virginia Bill of Rights and by the Declaration of Independence as the first of the fundamental human rights. That it is a right possessed by all men is a statement requiring, however, important qualifications. In the first place, all but a very few people would agree that there are circumstances, whether created by his own volition or entered into involuntarily, in which a man may be considered to have forfeited this right. Even if one is opposed in principle to capital punishment, there may arise situations in which the taking of one individual's life is necessary in order to safeguard the lives or other fundamental rights of others. In such situations the right to live, if understood in an absolute sense, becomes a paradox. The absolute right to live implies that a man may take any necessary measures to defend his life, and if on a given occasion the necessary measures should involve the killing of an aggressor, who in turn (*ex hypothesi*) has an absolute right to live, there would exist a situation in which the absolute right to live implied its own denial. Again, in war, shipwreck, and other catastrophes it may become the duty of an individual to give up his life if by so doing he can save the lives of a number of others. Again, while a plain citizen, encountering an armed thug, would be acting within his rights if he were to save his life by running away,

---

[1] A convenient text of all four of these declarations is given in the appendix to Ritchie's *Natural Rights*.

we should less readily concede the same right to an officer of the law.

(ii) *The right to liberty* is included in all four of the declarations just quoted, and is frequently appealed to in political speeches and writings of a more or less emotional sort. But the right to liberty cannot, any more than the right to life, be absolute. Aside from being subject to all the same qualifications as those mentioned in the last paragraph, the right to liberty is ambiguous. Life has a meaning about which there can be no serious dispute, but liberty is a relative term. Liberty *from* what, and *for* what? What is called political liberty (*i.e.*, the right to vote) is quite compatible, in the complexities of representative government, with all sorts of real restrictions—as shown by the frequency with which democratic governments legislate unpopular laws; 'religious liberty' has been invoked by the Ku Klux Klan, as in earlier times by the Church of England, to justify suppressive measures against Roman Catholics; while the phrase 'freedom of contract' denotes the policy of open shop, which by weakening the trades unions often amounts in practice to a loss of freedom for workers bargaining for jobs. It is either nonsense or ill-natured irony to say that a man is 'free' to accept an employer's terms or go jobless. 'Freedom of contract' often means that a man may choose between working for wages that doom him and his family to gradual starvation, and starving to death more quickly by not working at all.

(iii) *The right to property*. It will be noticed that the French declarations name property as one of the fundamental rights, that the Virginia Bill substitutes for property the means of acquiring and possessing property, while both it and the Declaration of Independence include the pursuit of happiness in the list. These several variants all spring from a recognition that a right to life and liberty is a meaningless abstraction unless it carries with it a right to the possession of whatever it may be that makes life and liberty possible. Some social philosophers, such as Kropotkin, have therefore maintained that every member of society ought to receive (*i.e.*, has a 'right' to) that bare minimum of goods which would be necessary to keep him alive and to ensure his liberty of thought and action. Opponents of this policy, which they sometimes unflatteringly call the 'vagabond wage theory,' have objected that if put into operation it would destroy initiative and that in particular the more unpleasant sorts of necessary work would not get done. As a counter-reply it has been declared that a bare minimum handout requisite for subsistence is everybody's right, regardless of what one may give or do in return; that luxuries and favored public positions, which could still be distributed by the old competitive method among those who might choose to compete, would provide as much incentive as would be required (particularly as new labor-saving devices were introduced) for getting the necessary work accomplished; and that extremely unpleasant types of work could gradually be more or less eliminated if factories and mines, instead of being instruments of private profit, were turned into self-governing communities.[1] But even if this whole utopian ideal is accepted it does not follow that the right to possess property is unconditional. Logically, such a right must be conditional, at the very least, on there being enough property to go around. If a great drought or devastating war were to leave less than enough food or arable land in the world to support the world's population there would be no point in saying that everyone had an 'imprescripti-

---

[1]*Cf.* Kropotkin, *Anarchist Communism;* also Bertrand Russell, *Proposed Roads to Freedom*, Chap. IV.

ble' right to what, by the nature of the supposed case, not everyone could possess. The question would have to be one not of absolute rights but of just distribution.

4. THEORIES OF JUSTICE

The logical difficulties in any postulate of absolute rights make it evident that rights must be regarded as somehow relative to the organization and possibilities and values of the whole social group against which the rights are asserted. The problem becomes essentially one of fair distribution, of giving to each what is due him when his claims and wants are considered in connection with the claims and wants of his fellows. This problem of fair distribution is the problem of justice in the stricter sense of the word.

Justice, as must already be evident, is a word connoting a variety of meanings. Apart from the confusions introduced by the utilitarian attempt to derive justice from the mechanical and non-moral principle of greatest happiness, and the attempt of certain other ethical groups to formulate some principle of justice that will be consistent with some principle of absolute rights—a logically impossible proceeding, as has just been demonstrated—there are three other potential ambiguities in the word that must be noted.

In the first place, 'justice' like 'rights' can have both legal and moral connotations. Aristotle writes:

Whatever is according to law is just in one sense of the term. . . . Now, the laws prescribe about all manner of things, aiming at the common interest of all, or of the best men, or of those who are supreme in the State; . . . and so in one sense we apply the term 'just' to whatever tends to produce and preserve the happiness of the community and the several elements of that happiness. The law bids us display courage (as not to leave our ranks, or run, or throw away our arms), and temperance (as not to commit adultery or outrage), and gentleness (as not to strike or revile our neighbors), and so on with all the other virtues and vices, enjoining acts and forbidding them, rightly when it is a good law, not so rightly when it is a hastily improvised one. Justice, then, in this sense of the word is complete virtue, with the addition that it is displayed towards others. On this account it is often spoken of as the chief of the virtues; . . . and the saying has become proverbial, "Justice sums up all virtues in itself."[1]

This emphasis on legality as inherent in the notion of justice is typical of the Greek point of view, which regarded ethics and politics as complementary aspects of one problem. Nicolai Hartmann, on the other hand, expresses a widespread contemporary attitude in declaring justice to be "the lowest of the virtues proper" for the very reason that it is so largely political: i.e., permits of being codified and to some extent enforced. In this it is more akin, Hartmann argues, to legality, which looks exclusively to actions, than to morality, which ought to appeal to the agent's disposition. "Such fixation and enforcement go counter to the meaning of morality, the essence of which consists precisely in the freedom of fulfillment from instance to instance and in the spontaneous finding of the right. A commandment authoritative and leaving nothing undetermined is not a moral commandment at all." The claim that justice makes upon a man's conduct is thus purely negative, Dr. Hartmann continues, though it is indeed a necessary condition of the other virtues. Through law with its objective order and equality, justice "makes room in the sphere of actuality for the higher values. The more diversified moral life cannot begin, till the simple conditions are supplied. Justice is the moral tendency to supply these conditions. It is the prerequisite of all further realizations of value. At the same time it is the pioneer among the virtues. Justice is the

[1] *Nicomachean Ethics*, V. i. 12–15.

minimum of morality that paves the way for all the higher forms."[1]

Neither Aristotle nor Dr. Hartmann is limiting justice to mere legality, although both remark a persistent tendency of justice to become embodied in law. Its independence of meaning is never entirely lost so long as it is possible to inquire whether or not existing laws are morally just. The distinction between moral and legal justice, though sufficiently clear in itself, sometimes becomes blunted through confusion with another distinction: justice as a certain kind of disposition in individuals and justice as a relation subsisting among the parts of the social organism. In the former sense we speak of a just man, in the latter of a just government. Aristotle employs both meanings of the word, defining justice as "the sort of *habit* or *character* which makes men apt to do what is just, and which further makes them *act* justly and *wish* what is just";[2] but in completing his definition by giving the differentia of justice (to call it a habit or character is to give merely its genus) Aristotle turns to an examination of the particular way in which the just man will tend and wish to promote the distribution of goods—*i.e.*, to the type of social structure that such a man will endeavor to establish and maintain. The present distinction is not identical with the distinction between moral and legal justice. Law does not and should not, according to most modern conceptions,[3] take account of men's dispositions except so far as they can be objectively shown to impel particular acts. Consequently the purpose of law is thought to be fulfilled if it succeeds in establishing equi-

---

[1]Nicolai Hartmann, *Ethics*, Vol. II, pp. 231–232.

[2]*Nicomachean Ethics*, V. i. 3.   Italics added.

[3]The Greeks, perhaps more wisely, disagreed with this.   See the account of Plato's ideal State in the next chapter.

table relations among the various parts of society. Moral justice, on the other hand, is not correspondingly limited to men's dispositions and motives, for a moral criticism can be made not only of men but of institutions.

A third distinction within the meaning of justice is the distinction between the set of problems connected with the original distribution of goods and the fairly distinct set connected with corrective measures against abuses. These two sets of problems may be designated problems of *distributive* and problems of *corrective* justice. There are three prominent theories of corrective justice, by which its administration by the State is justified: the retributive, reformative, and utilitarian theories. The *retributive* theory is based upon the ancient principle of 'an eye for an eye, a tooth for a tooth'; a man has done wrong, therefore it is just that he should suffer in proportion to the extent of the wrong that he has done. Aristotle upholds this theory when he explains that "when one man is struck and the other strikes, or when one kills and the other is killed, that which is suffered and that which is done constitute an inequality; the judge then tries to restore equality by the penalty or loss which he inflicts upon the offender, subtracting it from his gain."[1] The retributive theory thus represents a primarily backward-looking point of view. The *reformative* theory, on the contrary, looks ahead. It holds that punishment for past offenses is never justified, and that the only legitimate consideration in dealing with social misfits is how to reform and prepare them as individuals to take a constructive place in society. The *utilitarian* theory, finally, agrees with the reformative theory in looking ahead rather than back, but holds that the general happiness is to be considered rather than the supposed rights or well-being of

[1] *Nichomachean Ethics:* V. iv. 4.

the individual malefactor. The function of criminal law as Bentham interprets it is to supply a potential threat of pains subsequent upon wrong-doing so that each member of society, intent on securing only his own happiness, will find it to his advantage not to deprive others of theirs.

We may now attempt a more precise examination of the nature of distributive justice. In making this examination it is permissible to put aside at the outset the theory referred to in Chapter IV, that questions of justice are in the end nothing but questions of physical strength, guile, or propaganda; for this theory gives no answer to the moral question of how justice *ought* to be understood and applied; it undertakes to show that moral questions about justice are meaningless rather than to solve them. We may dismiss also in the present connection the identification of justice with blind obedience to an absolute monarch or a fascist State, for this is merely to change the meaning of the word. An equally perverse but more subtle change in the word's meaning has been shown to be involved in utilitarianism. Questions are not solved by shifting their sense.

The most essential element in the idea of justice seems to be what Professor Urban has called 'the feeling for moral symmetry.'[1] Aristotle in like manner defines the morally just man as the 'fair' or 'equal' man, who takes no more and no less than his share; and moral justice as 'fair distribution.'[2] This recalls the definition attributed to Simonides in the first book of Plato's *Republic*, that justice is 'the restoring to each man his due.' But, as that dialogue goes on to show, the great question to be

---

[1] *Fundamentals of Ethics*, p. 211.

[2] ἰσότης (*Nic. Eth.*, V.1.8). 'Equality' would be a more nearly literal translation, but misleading because the Greek word, as Aristotle's subsequent discussion shows, embraces both 'arithmetical' (absolute) equality and 'geometrical' (proportional) equality. (*Nic. Eth.*, V. iii. 13 and V. iv. 3.)

settled is, on what principle each man's 'due' is to be determined. Sidgwick has suggested that justice involves equality except where a sufficient reason for inequality can be given, but he recognizes that this definition too is not final, for ethics must be critical towards what constitutes a sufficient reason. Nowadays, for example, few persons would see any logical connection between believing in God and being entitled to testify in court, but in Christian Europe a few centuries ago the connection seemed practically self-evident, and atheism was held an amply sufficient reason for the forfeiture of all political rights. At any rate, the recognition that the sense of justice implies a feeling for moral symmetry and that justice is achieved only as goods are distributed according to some principle of fairness towards all the individuals concerned, succeeds at least in focalizing the problem. Fair distribution means that if there is a certain quantity of good to be divided between A and B, half ought to be given to each, so long as all that is known about them is that each is an individual—*i.e.*, so long as no reason is known for preferring one to the other. But A never does differ from B solely in being an individual, and the question therefore occurs, what kind of inequality between A and B supplies reasonable ground for an inequality in the shares assigned to them, and to what degree. Furthermore, it is not always true that there is 'a certain quantity' of good to be divided. A good such as happiness may be increased or diminished by the very process of dividing it, or the means to it, in one way rather than another. If this were thought to be the case the question of justice proper (*i.e.*, of distribution) might have to be supplemented by considerations of how to produce the greatest total amount of good. The question of justice is therefore not a simple one, but the possible answers to it tend to be centered around "two conflicting ideals, each of which on the face of it seems entitled to respect. In the first place the principle that every human being is of equal intrinsic value, and is therefore entitled to equal respect, is one which commends itself to common sense, a principle which may naturally claim to be the exacter expression of the Christian ideal of Brotherhood. On the other hand the principle that the good ought to be preferred to the bad, that men ought to be rewarded according to their goodness or according to their work, is one which no less commends itself to the unsophisticated moral consciousness."[1] What claim to truth has each of these rival ideals, and how far is a satisfactory compromise or reconciliation between them possible?

To each according to merit

Distributive justice, in the opinion of Aristotle, involves the principle of 'proportionate equality': "Just such equality should exist between the things as between the persons [possessing them] . . . For if the persons be not equal, their shares will not be equal."[2] But what is meant by inequality of persons and how is such inequality to be judged in determining the just rewards to be assigned? Three sorts of answer are given.

The first is that the measure of an individual's merit is his success. This view is held quite widely and for obvious reasons by persons who happen to be successful themselves. Tell them that a textile worker is underpaid, and their reply will be that if he were worth more than he is getting he would not have remained a mere textile worker.[3] This sort of reasoning throws no light on the

---

[1] Rashdall, *The Theory of Good and Evil*, Vol. I, p. 223.

[2] *Nic. Eth.*, V. iii. 6.

[3] "They're an unambitious lot," I was told by a business man who during the 1934 textile strike had visited a southern mill-town. And a moment later he added: "They want too much."

moral problem except to make the general declaration that since each person tends to get what he deserves (as proved by the fact that he gets it) no specific moral action is called for. This is the doctrine of *laissez-faire*. It can be criticized both as to logic and as to results. Its logical premise, stated within the preceding parentheses, is clearly question-begging; and its only application is to furnish a ground for self-approval.

The logic of the *laissez-faire* doctrine is usually supplemented in the minds of its sponsors with an assumption about 'natural rights.' A man has a right to earn whatever he can earn honestly, they argue, often referring to this as the 'right to liberty.' Also a man has a right to keep what he has earned, and what is given or willed to him by others (the 'right to property'). That these are a man's legal rights under existing laws is undeniable, but for that reason they are not wholly relevant to the question of moral rights and moral judgment. So far as they are asserted to be moral rights, this assertion invites critical examination of the social goods to whose achievement they are perhaps an obstacle.

A third type of justification for unequal rewards escapes the question-begging fallacy of the first by declaring that some men have greater worth than others, not because they get greater rewards (this is rather conceived as a desirable consequence of their greater worth) but because the kind of work that they do is of greater value to society. A bank director or a corporation president deserves his princely income, it is urged, because his work is vital to the successful running of industry and commerce: a business cannot be run without someone in control, and therefore those in control deserve a lion's share of the profits. But what is meant by calling one man's work more valuable than another's if, as is often the case, both are necessary? The work of riveting or of assembling is every bit as vital to the production of a Ford car as the work of managing the plant or disbursing the capital. To produce the car requires both types of work—certainly the first! But, the argument continues, there are plenty of men who can rivet and assemble, only a few who can direct. Granted that this is at present the case (though the latter half of the assumption might easily be challenged), we may still ask what the causes are that have put some men in a position to perform work for which few are equipped. Is there any evidence that a riveter, if he had been given the same advantages from babyhood as a corporation president, would not have fared as well? By the nature of the case no such evidence is possible. Comparison between the two men is made only after the effects of their respective types of rearing have taken place. It is an open question whether in a society that provided more nearly equal childhood conditions and youthful opportunities for everybody the positions of two such men might not have been reversed.

The most common form of hypocrisy among the privileged classes is to assume that their privileges are the just payments with which society rewards specially useful or meritorious functions. As long as society regards special rewards for important services as ethically just and socially necessary . . . it is always possible for social privilege to justify itself, at least in its own eyes, in terms of the social function which it renders. If the argument is to be plausible, when used by privileged classes who possess hereditary advantages, it must be proved or assumed that the underprivileged classes would not have the capacity of rendering the same service if given the same opportunity. This assumption is invariably made by privileged classes. The educational advantages which privilege buys, and the opportunities for the exercise of authority which come with privileged social position, develop capacities which are easily attributed to innate endowment. The presence of able men among the privileged is allowed to obscure the number of instances in which hereditary privilege is associated with knavery and incompetence. On the other hand it has always been the habit of privileged groups to deny the oppressed classes every opportunity for the cultivation of innate capacities and then to accuse them of lacking what they have been denied the right to acquire.[1]

The special form of the above argument, that the profits accruing from invested capital may be justified as special rewards for "the foresight and thrift of those who sacrificed the immediate pleasures of spending in order that society might have productive capital" had, as Dr. Niebuhr remarks, "a certain validity in the early days of capitalism, when productive enterprise was frequently initiated through capital saved out of modest incomes." But he adds:

The idea, as a moral justification of present inequalities of privilege, has become more and more dishonest, since the increased centralization of privilege and power makes it possible for those who make the largest investments in industry to do so without any diminution of even the most luxurious living standards. Since we are living in a world in which there is too much capital for production and too little for consumption, the argument that economic inequality is necessary for the accumulation of capital resources has lost even its economic validity. Yet it is still used by privileged classes to establish a specious connection between virtue or social function and privilege.[2]

There is another type of argument for social inequality which appeals not to the unequal deserts of individuals (and therefore not to the principle of justice in the strict sense) but to the belief that equal distribution might lower the total amount of good to be distributed and even destroy certain kinds of highly valued good.   Henry James

---
[1]Reinhold Niebuhr, *Moral Man and Immoral Society*, pp. 117–118. (Scribners.)
[2]*Ibid.*, p. 125.

lamented that America had no leisure class, because the valuable traditions of fine manners and fine appreciations tend to wither unless there is a leisure class with time and interest enough to keep them alive. Assuming the truth of this premise, the argument involves the already discussed issue between maximum amount of good and equality in its distribution. Probably no one would insist on equality to the complete exclusion of maximum amount. If twenty explorers were marooned with only enough food to keep five of their number alive until a rescuing party could be expected to arrive, it would hardly be a rational solution to insist on an equal distribution of food with the consequence that everyone would starve, when there stood a chance, by restricting the division of food to a minority, of keeping that minority alive. Similarly, Athenian culture, in the condition of the world as it then existed, was impossible without slavery. Athenian slavery was thus indirectly a necessary condition of the twenty-five hundred years' culture that has stemmed from ancient Athens; a condition, even, of the forces that at length banished slavery from Europe and America. Can we, then, looking back, morally justify Athenian slavery as conducing to a greater total good for mankind than would have been developed without it? And can we on this ground ignore the injustice to the Athenian slaves themselves?

But even if such exceptions to the principle of equal justice are conceded, it becomes dangerous and inhuman to push the concession too far. We should hardly care to be in the position described by Rashdall, of "justifying Egyptian bondage, because without it, in all probability, the modern globe-trotter would have had to eliminate the Pyramids from his program." To the more serious insistence of Henry James that culture requires a leisure class, Dr. Niebuhr has replied:

The fact that culture requires leisure is hardly a sufficient justification for the maintenance of a leisured class. For every artist which the aristocracy has produced, and for every two patrons of art, it has supported a thousand wastrels. An intelligent society will know how to subsidise those who possess peculiar gifts in the arts and the sciences and free them of the necessity of engaging in immediately useful toil.[1]

Equalitarianism

Ever since the ideological shift that accompanied the American and French Revolutions many persons who live under so-called democratic forms of government have accepted the doctrine of equal rights as if it were an axiom of political thought. What the average such person means by the phrase, however, is equality of political rights simply—nor is he very much disturbed by the fact that even political rights are not in fact held equally by all; that in a number of states persons afflicted by poverty are disfranchised, that in others persons with black or brown pigmentation of skin are regularly prevented from exercising their theoretical voting rights, and that factory owners often control the votes of hundreds of employees. Even in the event that political rights were to become equally extended to all sections of the adult population, such extension would not entail greater equality in any real and important sense. From the point of view of a worker it is a pickwickian sort of equality that stops with allowing him to vote for one out of two candidates, when both are committed to policies the net result of which is to perpetuate those economic and social inequalities under which the worker suffers.

When we pass from the ideal of political to the ideal of economic equality several questions arise. If economic equality is interpreted to mean the equal distribution of

[1] *Op. cit.*, p. 128.

goods, regardless of work done, would not this remove the principal incentive to work? Perhaps for most persons it would, although the fancied situation is so distant from anything ever experienced that guesses as to its effects are largely arbitrary and unfounded. At any rate, the objection raised against the 'vagabond wage theory' (p. 277) applies *a fortiori* against the proposal for economic equality. Rashdall has put the objection against complete economic equality on more philosophic grounds, arguing that it would violate a more fundamental sense of the principle of equality:

> To reward the idler as much as the industrious (even if we supposed that the reward would really be for his good) would be to make him count not for one but for several; since his support would impose additional labor on the industrious members of the community.[1]

A second question which the notion of equal distribution suggests: What is it that is to be distributed? Concrete things like food, land, and money? Equal distribution carried out in this way might defeat the ideal of a more genuine equality, for men's needs as well as their capacities to use and enjoy are various, and an equal distribution of concrete things would often produce extremely unequal amounts of well-being.

Often, particularly in the popular American credo, equality is interpreted to mean equality of opportunity. This ideal is a valuable one for the promotion of social reform, but it too suffers from ambiguity. How thoroughly are opportunities to be equalized? As thoroughly as possible? This would involve, as one clear consequence, abolishing the institution of the family, because as long as families exist some individuals will have, at the very least,

---

[1]Rashdall, *op. cit.*, Vol. I, p. 230.

the advantage of more suitable parents than others. It is hard to see, as a matter of fact, how complete equality of opportunity could be ensured except by the enforcement of complete social equality, and this in turn would probably involve a degree of interference in the affairs not only of public but of private life that would be found intolerable. Besides, what would be meant by complete equalization of opportunities? One form in which the problem occurs is known to every classroom teacher. Does equality of opportunity require that the class be conducted at a level of obviousness at which all can understand equally? But such a policy would retard the progress of the brighter students and so deprive them of the opportunity (which the poorer ones would still have) of expressing their particular abilities. Quite as much would the principle of equal opportunity be violated by catering to the brighter students alone. The competent teacher avoids both extremes and seeks some kind of workable compromise, recognizing that in such matters absolute equality is not only unattainable but meaningless.

One of the noblest, and eventually perhaps too one of the most workable expressions of the ideal of equality is embodied in the communist principle, "From each according to his abilities, to each according to his needs." Whatever practical difficulties might be encountered in realizing this ideal, it is free from the logical weaknesses that vitiate the other forms of equalitarianism mentioned above. The equality here primarily demanded is not an equality of external goods, although greater equalization in this respect would of course be recommended as well, but what Rashdall has called 'equality of consideration.' Such paradoxes as that of the twenty marooned explorers become soluble on this basis. Given that fifteen must die and that absolute equality is therefore impossible except by general annihilation, the requirements of 'equality of consideration' would be met by an agreement, for example, to draw lots. Furthermore, consideration of abilities and needs carries justice beyond the search for an abstract equality and tends to identify it with a recognition of the absolute worth of persons, as embodied in Renouvier's maxim: "Recognize the person of your fellow as your equal by nature and in fundamental worth, as being an end in himself; and consequently refrain from making him serve as a mere means towards the attainment of your ends."[1]

[1] *Op. cit.*, Vol. I, p. 58. I do not say that Renouvier's maxim is consistent with the current policies and practices of communism. It is, however, an expression of the anarchistic ideal to which the communist is committed in theory. See Chapter X, Section 3. *Cf.* Kant's second formulation of the moral law, p. 185.

CHAPTER X

THE BASIS OF POLITICAL AUTHORITY

Society is produced by our wants, and government by our wickedness.

Thomas Paine

LOGICALLY INVOLVED in the question of aim is the question of the means by which the aim is to be realized. When the aim is one requiring the coöperation of more individuals than one the question of means will be partly the question of social sanction: that is, of how the requisite conduct is to be enforced on the others. Methods of enforcement are various; for convenience they may be classified under the heads of rational persuasion (*i.e.*, convincing a person), emotional persuasion (by the power of one's personality, or by cajolery, or tears), barter (including all forms of compact, explicit or implied), trickery, and force. It is clear that the division should not be overstressed. Barter is induced by persuasion, invites trickery, and may have finally to be validated by force. Propaganda is a combination of trickery and emotional persuasion, which in turn may be viewed as a kind of force. Nor would it be always easy to draw a line between rational and emotional persuasion. Yet, with all these qualifications, the division is useful as enabling us better to analyze the factors that make social stability more or less possible.

At an early period in mankind's career—so early that we can make only hazardous guesses as to the exact nature of the process—there occurred (simultaneously, no doubt,

with other forms of specialization of function) a centralization of the sanctioning process. How far each of the
five types of sanctioning may have been present in this
development is hardly profitable to discuss: a scientific
answer is not procurable, nor, if it were, would it be altogether relevant to an evaluation of corresponding factors
in present society. The important matter is the result:
the establishment of a centralized authority able by one
method or another to enforce its decisions and decrees,
and recognized as authoritative by all or a considerable
part of the social group over which it rules. This centralized, enforceable authority is *the State*,[1] and its activities
and relations are called *political*. The question of social
justice leads naturally to the question of what form of
State is most apt to realize the ideal, and this in turn leads
to a new question of sanction—the sanction on which the
State itself rests and by which its particular decrees are
conceived to have *authority*. Both of these questions will
be considered in the present chapter, the second one first.

1. The Metaphysics of Sovereignty

The State has been defined by one political philosopher
as "a supreme authority exercising a control over the social
actions of individuals and groups of individuals, and itself
subject to no such regulation."[2] The State, if this definition be accepted, is *sovereign*. From a moral point of
view its sovereignty means that the State has certain
rights (*i.e.*, powers that not only are but ought to be) over

---

[1]The word will be spelled with a capital in order to distinguish its original
political meaning, as here defined, from (i) the non-political meaning, in which
a state is synonymous with a circumstance or set of conditions, and (ii) the
special, derived political meaning applicable to the forty-eight states of the
Union. Under the Articles of Confederation these were States in the original sense, but they lost their essential Statehood in acceding to the Federal
Constitution and in the subsequent course of American constitutional history.

[2]Westel W. Willoughby, *The Nature of the State*, p. 3.

its individual subjects, who in turn have corresponding duties to the State; and that these rights and duties, furthermore, have a validity which gives them precedence over the rights and duties entailed by other social relations into which the individual may enter. How is this State sovereignty sanctioned? The question is an outcome of the distinction between rulers and ruled, which, however qualified or disguised, is present in every society marked by differentiation of function. In democracies there is a tendency to conceal the distinction, because of their sustaining fiction of a government by, as well as for, the people. But at best, a democracy is a government 'by' the people only indirectly and in a general way. The people do not make each law themselves but through chosen (even this choice may be indirect) representatives; whence the question persists, by what principle they are bound to obey the laws when made. Section 3 will introduce certain extreme philosophies which deny any such principle, and thus challenge the very possibility of political sovereignty; for the present we may turn to three outstanding and influential theories by which political sovereignty is upheld, offered respectively by Hobbes, Rousseau, and Hegel.

Political atomism

Thomas Hobbes (1588–1679) was, in a more basic sense than the word generally connotes, an atomist. Not only did he accept the atomic theory as a final and adequate explanation of physical occurrences; he used it as an intellectual model for analogous theories in psychology and politics. His psychological theory is what has subsequently been called associationism, since it postulates the existence of indivisible pieces of awareness, out of which the whole of a man's mental life is supposed to be com-

pounded.[1] The relation of this psychological standpoint
and method to the problems of political philosophy is
seen in Hobbes' theory of reason:

> When a man *reasoneth*, he does nothing else but conceive a
> sum total, from *addition* of parcels; or conceive a remainder,
> from *subtraction* of one sum from another, which, if it be done
> by words, is conceiving of the consequence of the names of all
> the parts, to the name of the whole; or from the names of the
> whole and one part, to the name of the other part. . . .
> These operations are not incident to numbers only, but to all
> manner of things that can be added together, and taken one
> out of another. . . . Writers of politics add together *actions*
> to find men's *duties;* and lawyers, *laws* and *facts*, to find what is
> *right* and *wrong* in the actions of private men. In sum, in what
> matter soever there is place for *addition* and *subtraction*, there
> also is place for *reason;* and where these have no place, there
> *reason* has nothing at all to do.
> . . . Reason in this sense is nothing but *reckoning*, that is
> adding and subtracting, of the consequences of general names
> agreed upon for the *marking* and *signifying* of our thoughts; I
> say *marking* them when we reckon by ourselves, and *signifying*
> when we demonstrate or approve our reckonings to other men.[2]

From this atomistic view of the reasoning process it is a
short step to a similar interpretation of the objects with
which reasoning is concerned. Hobbes' own reasoning
concerned itself largely with political questions, and his
doctrine in that field may be designated, not unfairly, as
'political atomism.' The main steps in his political doctrine might be set down as follows.

(1) *The natural equality of men.* "Such is the nature
of men," Hobbes remarks, "that howsoever they may
acknowledge many others to be more witty, or more elo-
quent, or more learned; yet they will hardly believe there

---

[1] "Concerning the thoughts of man, I will consider them first singly, and
afterwards in train, or dependence upon one another."—*Leviathan*, Chap. I.
[2] *Leviathan*, Chap. V.

be many so wise as themselves; for they see their own wit
at hand, and other men's at a distance.   But this proveth
rather that men are in that point equal, than unequal.
For there is not ordinarily a greater sign of the equal distribution of anything, than that every man is contented
with his share."[1]   The point of the irony is that human
inequalities, judged from a political standpoint, don't
particularly matter: first, because they tend on the whole
to be evened up by divers compensations ("for as to
strength of body, the weakest has strength enough to kill
the strongest, either by secret machinations, or by con-
federacy with others, that are in the same danger with
himself"); secondly, because of an "equality of hope in the
attaining of our ends," whereby one individual, however
deficient in outward respects, becomes the equal of his
fellows in self-esteem, greed, and ambition, and thereby
their potential enemy.

(2) *Egoism.* For Hobbes it is axiomatic that "no man
giveth, but with intention of good to himself; because gift
is voluntary; and of all voluntary acts, the object is to
every man his own good."   It follows that in their natural
condition, where they are not subject to some power strong
enough to overawe them, "men have no pleasure, but on
the contrary a great deal of grief in keeping company."

(3) *The natural state of war.*   Because of men's egoism,
coupled with that vanity which prompts each to think
himself in some way a match for any other, the natural
condition of humankind is war—"such a war, as is of
every man, against every man."   War does not always
consist in actual fighting, but in a general disposition
thereto, the actuality of which is substantiated by countless actions, little as well as big.   When a man goes to
sleep he even in a civilized society locks his doors: "does

---

[1]*Ibid.,* Chap. XIII.

he not there as much accuse mankind by his actions, as I do by my words?"

In man's natural state, *a fortiori*,[1] where "every man is enemy to every man" and where there are no laws and public officers to avenge injuries, but where men live without other security than such as their own strength and invention furnish them—"in such condition, there is no place for industry, because the fruit thereof is uncertain, and consequently no culture of the earth; no navigation, nor use of the commodities that may be imported by sea; no commodious building; no instruments of moving, and . . . no arts; no letters; no society; and, which is worst of all, continual fear, and danger of violent death; and the life of man, solitary, poor, nasty, brutish, and short."

(4) In this natural, warlike state, "the notions of right and wrong, justice and injustice, have no place. Where there is no common power, there is no law; where no law, no injustice." Justice and injustice have meaning only when there exists some common power, capable of setting them up and enforcing them. "*Good*, and *evil*, are names that signify our appetites, and aversions; which in different tempers, customs and doctrines of men, are different."[2]

(5) *Man's natural right* is "the liberty each man hath, to use his own power, as he will himself, for the preservation of his own nature; that is to say, of his own life; and consequently, of doing anything which in his own judgment and reason he shall conceive to be the aptest means thereunto."[3]

(6) But in man's natural state of warfare his natural right to use every means to preserve himself becomes self-defeating; for each other man will have the same right,

---

[1]See Glossary.
[2]*Op. cit.*, Chaps. XIII, XV.
[3]*Ibid.*, Chap. XIV.

and the means of self-defense will often involve taking the property, persons, or lives of his fellows. In this natural warlike state, therefore, "there can be no security to any man, how strong or wise soever he be, of living out the time which Nature ordinarily alloweth men to live." Consequently, to man's natural right to seek and use, when necessary, all helps and advantages of war, there must be counterposed the "precept, or general rule of reason, *that every man ought to endeavor peace, as far as he has hope of obtaining it.*" This precept, *to seek peace, and follow it,* Hobbes calls the first and fundamental law of Nature; as the other, *by all means we can, to defend ourselves,* is "the sum of the right of Nature."

(7) How are the foregoing law and the foregoing right to be made mutually consistent? In their original state they cannot be so; the only solution is to renounce the right to hinder one's fellows, on condition that they make a similar renunciation—on condition, that is to say, that the causes making self-defense necessary are removed. In this mutual relinquishment consists the social *contract.*

(8) But "covenants, without the sword, are but words, and of no strength to secure a man at all." The social contract can be enforced only by the erection (by majority vote, Hobbes later adds) of a central power with sufficient strength to overawe those who might be tempted to break the contract. This power should extend over a large number of men, both for greater political stability within the group and for greater security against external foes; it should be unified in its deliberations and judgments; and it should exist for the longest possible duration.

The only way to erect such a common power, as may be able to defend them from the invasion of foreigners, and the injuries of one another, and thereby to secure them in such sort, as that by their own industry, and by the fruits of the earth, they may nourish themselves, and live contentedly; is, to confer all their power and strength upon one man, or upon one assembly of men, that may reduce all their wills, by plurality of voices, unto one will: which is as much as to say, to appoint one man, or assembly of men, to bear their person; and every one to own, and acknowledge himself to be the author of whatsoever he that so beareth their person, shall act, or cause to be acted, in those things which concern the common peace and safety; and therein to submit their wills, every one to his will, and their judgments, to his judgment. This is more than consent, or concord; it is a real unity of them all, in one and the same person, made by covenant of every man with every man, in such manner, as if every man should say to every man, *I authorize and give up my right of governing myself, to this man, or to this assembly of men, on this condition, that thou give up thy right to him, and authorize all his actions in like manner.* This done, the multitude so united in one person is called a COMMONWEALTH. . . . This is the generation of that great LEVIATHAN. . . . By this authority, given him by every particular man in the Commonwealth, he hath the use of so much power and strength conferred on him, that by terror thereof, he is enabled to [per-]form the wills of them all, to peace at home, and mutual aid against their enemies abroad. And in him consisteth the essence of the Commonwealth; which, to define it, is *one person, of whose acts a great multitude, by mutual covenants one with another, have made themselves every one the author, to the end that he may use the strength and means of them all, as he shall think expedient, for their peace and common defence.*

And he that carrieth this person is called SOVEREIGN, and said to have *sovereign power;* and every one besides, his SUBJECT.[1]

Before proceeding to treat of the flaws in Hobbes' theory it is desirable to notice one objection frequently raised against it which is in the main irrelevant. It is contended that the theory is incorrect historically; that it has been disproved by a mass of anthropological data, which offer no instances of men living in a completely warlike and un-

---

[1] *Op. cit.,* Chap. XVII.

social state where each is pitted against every other. The objection, while factually correct (for it is true that all men, past and present, of whom there are any records, are found living in some kind of social organization, however primitive), is not logically sound. For Hobbes nowhere states that the unsocial state of nature has ever actually existed in a pure form. We do find, however, (what no anthropologist would be likely to deny), societies at stages of greater or less approximation to it. Hobbes may accordingly be interpreted to mean, not that men were once without government and therefore at constant warfare and wholly without a standard of justice; but that *so far as* they lack the advantages of a government that is unified, determined, and strong (in short, so far as, in his view, an existing society recedes from the ideal of monarchy), *to that extent* there are lacking the advantages of peace and a sure standard of justice. The theory interpreted in this way is not a simple statement of historical fact, and so cannot be refuted by a simple appeal to prehistory.

Of the defects more undeniably present in Hobbes' theory, the most prominent is his artificial interpretation of the nature of man. We have met in previous chapters examples of half-truths masquerading as fundamental axioms,[1] and this assumption of Hobbes' appears to be such another. To say that "if any two men desire the same thing, which nevertheless they cannot both enjoy, they become enemies, and . . endeavor to destroy or subdue one another" is perhaps a useful reminder of the shortcomings of human nature, but hardly an adequate description of the infinitely varied and complicated springs of human behavior. It is one further example of running a half-truth to death.

---

[1] Hedonistic psychology, for example, and naturalism, and pure rationalism.

If the half-truth were accepted, and the natural condition of humankind postulated to be one wherein "every man is enemy to every man" and "the notions of right and wrong, justice and injustice, have no place," what possibility would be found of creating morality by means of the social contract? Hobbes declares, to be sure, that the contract must be upheld by force, but he regards it as having a moral sanction too. For in assenting to it each man transfers to the commonwealth his right to govern and defend himself; recognizing, moreover, this transfer as irrevocable, and agreeing thenceforth to authorize all the actions and judgments of the commonwealth as if they were his own, even when they go counter to his personal wishes or interests. To dissent in any respect from what the sovereign may judge fit to be done is to take away from him rights already given, *which is injustice.*[1] But, the critic may urge, if men before making the contract were without any sense of justice or obligation at all, but in a condition of unrestrained warfare, would they not naturally have regarded the contract as no more than a piece of military strategy, to be observed for only so long as the observance of it should be strategically effective? There is no honor in warfare unless brought to it by the personal codes of those engaged, and the independent existence of such codes Hobbes has denied. Obligations, if acknowledged at all, must be acknowledged inwardly; to a man (or creature) to whom duty is meaningless, duties cannot be created by external conditions. Hobbes tries to validate the contract as inwardly binding by postulating that in making it each man submits *his will* to the judgment of the sovereign, thus achieving a 'real unity' of all subjects in one and the same corporate person. But voluntary submission of the will, in such a

[1] *Op. cit.* See, in particular, the first three paragraphs of Chap. XVIII.

way as to make the submission binding upon future conduct, is itself a moral achievement (besides being, as
Hobbes had the wit to perceive, a condition of all other
moral achievements), and would not have been possible
in men to whom the notions of right and wrong were without meaning.

Despite its logical vulnerability, the theory of a social
contract stands out in the history of speculative thought
as one of the most important attempts to discover a
philosophical justification for political authority. Subsequent modifications of the theory have been made largely
with a view to overcoming Hobbes' too sharp cleavage
between the natural and political man. Hugo Grotius
(1583–1645), in his *De Jure Belli et Pacis*, had shown one
way of escape from the difficulty, by distinguishing the
State from Society: man lives naturally in society, for
which reason moral distinctions are not naturally alien
to him; while upon this natural social basis the State is
formed by a deliberate agreement. Spinoza, in his
Tractatus Theologico-Politicus, evaded Hobbes' inconsistency in an opposite fashion: sovereigns, he declared,
possess the right of imposing their wills only so far as they
have the *power* to do so; in all nature, civilized or not, right
is coextensive with power, although in a civil society the
forms which the exercise of power takes tend to be more
indirect and more rational.

Jean-Jacques Rousseau (1712–1778) developed the
contract theory still further. Rousseau appears to recognize two steps in the pre-political development of human
society: a patriarchal form of social organization, in which
life was idyllic and men were free; followed, owing to the
rise of economic activity and private ownership of land,
by the warlike condition described by Hobbes (without,
however, a *complete* absence of moral qualities), whence

the making of a deliberate social contract became necessary. In addition to his more reasonable interpretation
of man's pre-political situation, Rousseau also diverges
from Hobbes in defining the nature of that sovereignty
which the social contract sets up. The Sovereign, he
argues, is the 'general will' itself, not a king or council
of rulers supposed by Hobbes to be capable of representing
it. For no one's will can be represented by another: under
the social contract an individual gives up certain powers,
but his will remains his own. Society is possible, therefore, only so far as the wills of individuals agree: "if the
clashing of particular interests made the establishment
of societies necessary, the agreement of these very interests
made it possible. The common element in these different
interests is what forms the social tie; and, were there no
point of agreement between them at all, no society could
exist."[1] From identifying sovereignty with the exercise
of the general will (which is simply the will of each *so far as*
it is identical with the will of all) Rousseau draws the
corollary that this sovereign general will cannot err; for
"from the very nature of the compact, every act of
Sovereignty, *i.e.*, every authentic act of the general will,
binds or favors all the citizens equally"; to just the extent
that any act or decision fails to do so, it fails to be an expression of the general will.[2] Besides being always in the
right, the sovereign general will has as its object general
rather than particular aims; otherwise it is "acting no
longer as Sovereign but as magistrate." Its proper aim is
to establish and maintain "a form of association which will
defend and protect with the whole common force the person and goods of each associate, and in which each, while
uniting himself with all, may still obey himself alone, and

[1] *The Social Contract*, Bk. II, Chap. I.
[2] *Ibid.*, Bk. II, Chap. IV.

remain as free as before";[1] and this aim is shared by every member of the body politic.   Accordingly, "the Sovereign, being formed wholly of the individuals who compose it, neither has nor can have any interest contrary to theirs"; and therefore need give them no guarantee, for it cannot harm them in any particular.   The converse relation is quite different, however: "each individual, as a man, may have a particular will contrary or dissimilar to the general will which he has as a citizen," and while enjoying the rights of citizenship he may be unwilling to fulfil the duties of a subject.   Were this 'injustice' to become widespread it would prove the undoing of the body politic.

In order then that the social compact may not be an empty formula, it tacitly includes the undertaking, which alone can give force to the rest, that whoever refuses to obey the general will shall be compelled to do so by the whole body.   This means nothing less than that he will be forced to be free; for this is the condition which, by giving each citizen to his country, secures him against all personal dependence.   In this lies the key to the working of the political machine; this alone legitimatizes civil undertakings, which, without it, would be absurd, tyrannical, and liable to the most frightful abuses.[2]

*Idealism**

In the philosophy of Kant, although he was much influenced by Rousseau, the theory of a social contract is abandoned. The allegorical meaning of the social contract theory may be summarized as follows: that outside the political context men have equal rights to life and liberty, but without any concurrent duties to recognize these rights in others; that owing to the self-refuting and warlike situation that would arise if non-political life were ever to become an actuality, men are in fact members of a State;

---

[1] *Ibid.*, Bk. I, Chap. VI.
[2] *Ibid.*, Bk. I, Chap. VII.

that this membership implies a tacit compact by which
one's original rights are transferred to the State in exchange for security and the other blessings that political
life bestows; that because these blessings are more valuable
than the empty unenforceable rights that would have
existed in a state of nature, a man must really will that
the State should exist as sovereign power; for which
reason he is morally obliged, without being any the less
free, to submit to, and indeed to authorize all that the
State does and decrees. (Rousseau would qualify this
last clause: all that the State *in its proper capacity*—*i.e.*, so
far as it functions as a State ought!—does and decrees.)
Kant dispenses with the contract theory, because even in
its allegorical interpretation it implies the possibility of a
society in which men have rights without duties, and this
possibility Kant denies. Such rights as freedom and
equality accrue to an individual from his membership in
the body politic; they have no status outside it ('prior to
its formation,' in the language of the social contract doctrine). Conversely, their status within the body politic
is guaranteed:

The law-giving power can belong only to the united will of
the people. For since this power is the source of all right, it
cannot through its law in any way do wrong to anyone. Now, if
someone should issue a decree respecting *another* person, it is
always possible that he might therein do him wrong, but this
is never possible in what he decided respecting himself (for
volenti non fit iniuria). Thus the concordant and united will of
all individuals can be the universally united legislative will of
the nation only so far as each one makes for all, and all for each,
the very same decision. The members of such a society (*societas
civilis*), *i.e.*, of a State, who are united with respect to law-
making are called citizens (*cives*), and the rightful attributes
inseparable from the existence of each citizen in his proper
capacity are: political *freedom*, by which he obeys no law save

that to which he has given his consent; civil *equality*, by which he recognizes no one in the nation as his superior, unless one whom he may as lawfully hold morally obligated as the other him; thirdly, the attribute of civil *autonomy*, by which he owes his existence and maintenance not to the caprice of anyone else in the nation, but solely to his own rights and powers as a member of the common weal; and as a corollary of this last attribute, civil *personality*, by which he may be represented by no one else in political transactions.[1]

Such a State, guaranteeing to each individual the rights of freedom, equality, autonomy, and personality, is possible only so far as each individual in turn recognizes the duty of observing these rights in others.   Accordingly, the two cardinal maxims of Kant's ethical doctrine, Always so to act that you could will your act to be made a universal law for all rational beings, and To treat every person as an end in himself, never as only a means, are supplemented by a third maxim which Kant propounds as the *political* test of right conduct: "A given action is right if it or the freely chosen maxim on which it rests can be consistent, according to some universal law, with the freedom of everyone else."[2]   The supreme political wrong is to hinder another person in any action that can itself exist consistently with universal law.

The positive relation between political freedom and political submission is affirmed even more strikingly by Hegel (1770–1831).   Hegel's political theories are built upon and in terms of his revolutionary theory of logic. According to this theory, all possible objects of thought are related to one another dialectically.   Nothing is merely what it is.   Try to understand anything adequately: you can do so only by introducing the notion of its opposite.

---

[1]Kant, *Elements of Political Doctrine*, Sec. 46.
[2]*Ibid.*

It is in terms of such a dialectical relation that freedom and obligation must be conceived:

> A duty or obligation appears as a limitation merely of undetermined obligation and abstract freedom, or of the impulse of the natural will, or of the moral will which fixes upon its undetermined good capriciously. But in point of fact the individual finds in duty liberation. He is freed from subjection to mere natural impulse; . . . he is freed also from that indefinite subjectivity, which does not issue in the objective realization implied in action, but remains wrapped up in its own unreality. In duty the individual enters freely upon a liberty that has substance.[1]

The most fundamental duty that the rational individual must recognize is, in Hegel's theory, to the State. Hegel conceives the State as a living organism from which no part can be separated without death to that part. An individual finds full satisfaction of his real self only in fulfilling his civic duties. As he fails in these, and thus moves outside the pale of the State, he loses "the consciousness and self-respect implied in his being a member of the whole"; and to just that extent he loses individuality. An individual without any political relations at all is a mere abstraction of discourse—like a colorless surface, or a span of time without events. "Such also is the mere ideality of all individual occupations, functions, and corporations, great as may be their impulse to subsist and do for themselves. It is as in the organism, where the stomach assumes independence, and yet is at the same time superseded and sacrificed by becoming a member of one whole."[2]

Political absolutism in the extreme form represented by Hegel, and more recently by Bernard Bosanquet in

---

[1]*The Philosophy of Right*, Sec. 149. (The translation, except for a slight alteration, is that of S. W. Dyde.)

[2]*Ibid.*, Secs. 261 and 276.

The Philosophical Theory of the State, may be regarded, for purposes of analysis, as consisting of three principal steps: (1) a definition of freedom not as absence of all restraint but as self-determination—*i.e.*, as freedom *from nature*, which is freedom *according to reason*, which means control by that abiding system of impulses and ideals which is the 'real self'; (2) an identification of the higher self with the tradition of one's social group; (3) an identification of the social group with the State, which entails as a corollary the conception of political obligation as morally binding.[1] The conception of freedom as rational self-determination is one of the most significant contributions of philosophical idealism, and one to which Plato, Spinoza, Leibnitz, Kant, and Hegel would jointly subscribe. In another context it has been discussed in Chapter VI. The second proposition seems to be an important half-truth over-stated: in terms of his higher, rational self a person does become more fully conscious of the tradition of his social group and of social relations and duties, but this fuller consciousness is not necessarily in the direction of identification. The development of one's rational consciousness may do as much to promote an anti-social individualism as its opposite.[2] Most exceptionable of all is the third proposition, which identifies man's higher self with the relations into which he enters by virtue of membership in the existing State, and which thereby provides a philosophical basis for the most reactionary type of fascism. In opposition to this phase of Hegelian doctrine it may be remarked that there are other types of social relation than those centered in the State, through which an individual's rational self may find expression. Probably the rational

---

[1]Adapted from the analysis given by Norman Wilde in *The Ethical Basis of the State*.

[2]For a good discussion of this point, see Warner Fite, *Individualism*.

self finds social expression most satisfactorily when the existing State is one to which it can freely and honestly pronounce allegiance; but all too often existing States are not of this kind, and when a State is seen to be palpably unjust, the most valid expression of one's consciously social self may be to challenge it.

2. THE LOCUS OF POLITICAL AUTHORITY

A more practical question than that of the theoretic justification of political sovereignty in any form is the question in what part of the body politic the sovereign power is to be vested. With respect to the number of individuals among whom the sovereign power is distributed, governments may be grouped under the heads of autocracy (including both monarchy and uncrowned dictatorship), oligarchy (which is rule by some few), and democracy (in which the sovereign power is at least theoretically distributed among the many).

Monarchy

Absolute rule by one individual is practically unknown today. A nominal autocrat, whether emperor, king, cr fascist dictator, has his powers greatly curtailed by some clique—nowadays most often some group of business interests—that stands behind him and, perhaps unknown to the public, pulls the strings. The ruler's best chance of retaining actual power to himself lies in maintaining an even balance of power among the mutually hostile groups trying to control him; and even this expedient, owing to the unceasing fluctuation of political and economic alignments, is but temporary.

The arguments for concentrating the sovereign power in one man are of two kinds. The belief that kings rule by Divine appointment is at present in eclipse, although

there are still those who hold it. When he first ascended
the throne of Germany the Emperor Wilhelm II declared
that the House of Hohenzollern had been "appointed by
God to reign over the peoples whom We have been called
to rule, and to guide them in accordance with their welfare
and the furtherance of their material and spiritual interests." This was comparatively mild. Later, in 1914,
under stress of war the Kaiser's utterances became apoca-
lyptic. "The spirit of the Lord," he declared, "has
descended upon me because I am the Emperor of the
Germans. I am the instrument of the Almighty, I am his
sword, his agent. Woe and death to those who shall
oppose my will. Woe and death to those who do not
believe in my mission." A similar doctrine is now current
in Japan. Prince Itos, commenting on the new Japanese
Constitution, of which he had been one of the framers,
declared: "The Sacred Throne was established at the time
when the heavens and the earth became separated. The
Emperor is Heaven-descended, divine and sacred: He is
preëminent above all His subjects. He must be rever-
enced and is inviolable. He has indeed to pay respect
to the law, but the law has no power to hold Him account-
able to it."[1]

Dante Alighieri (1265–1321), author of *The Divine
Comedy*, put the argument for monarchy on more rational
grounds. In *De Monarchia* he upholds the ideal of one
universal monarch for the whole world, whose function
in secular, political affairs should correspond to that of the
Pope in spiritual affairs. Aristotle's principle of political
hierarchy, expressed in such phrases as "By nature some
beings command and others obey, for the sake of mutual
safety; for a being endowed with discernment and fore-

---

[1] The three quotations in this paragraph are borrowed from Westel W. Willoughby, *The Ethical Basis of Political Authority*, pp. 98, 99, 91.

thought is by nature the superior and the governor" and "Whatever is composed of many parts, which together make up one whole . . . shows the marks of some one thing governing and another governed,"[1] was extended by Dante to mean that all parts of society, both the parts of kingdoms and the kingdoms themselves, should be ordered with reference to one Monarchy (literally, Princedom) and one Monarch (Prince). Besides this general argument Dante argues to a universal monarchy from the ideals of peace, of justice, and of freedom.

The ideal of peace was one which Dante thought necessary in turn to uphold by rational argument, appealing to the classical Christian view of nature. He begins with two premises: (1) that "God and nature make nothing in vain"—which is to say, that no thing exists without a proper function; and (2) that the ultimate end of a created being is not the being itself but its proper function; nor does the function exist for the sake of the being, but contrariwise. Now, just as nature fashions the thumb for one purpose, the whole hand for another, the arm for still another, and the whole body for a purpose differing from all these, so in human society there is one end specific to each individual, another for the family, and others respectively for the village, the city, the kingdom and the human race. "There is, then, some distinct function for which humanity as a whole is ordained, a function which neither an individual nor a household, neither a village nor a city nor a particular kingdom has the power to perform."[2] What is this distinctive capacity of humanity as a whole? Not bare existence, for that is shared with the elements; nor compounded existence, which is shared with the crystalline substances; nor animate existence,

---

[1]Aristotle, *Politics*, I. ii. 2; I. v. 3.
[2]Dante, *De Monarchia*, Bk. I, Chap. III.

shared with plants; nor intelligent existence, shared with animals; but "intelligent existence through the power or capacity of intellect," which is characteristic of man alone. But in times of war or turmoil men have scant opportunity to live the intellectual life. They can realize their intellectual capacities most fully only in a state of universal peace. And universal peace will come only when all the earth is united under one monarch:

It is self-evident that between any two princes, neither of whom owes allegiance to the other, controversy may arise either by their own fault or by the fault of their subjects. For such, judgment is necessary. And inasmuch as one owing no allegiance to the other can recognize no authority in him (for an equal cannot control an equal), there must be a third prince with more ample jurisdiction, who may govern both within the circle of his right. This prince will or will not be a Monarch. If he is, one purpose is fulfilled; if not, he will again have a coequal beyond the circle of his jurisdiction, and again a third prince will be required. And thus either the process will be carried to infinity, which is impossible, or that primal and highest judge will be reached, by whose judgments all disputes are settled mediately or immediately. And this judge will be the Monarch, or Emperor.[1]

Dante's second argument for monarchy runs as follows. The world is best ordered when Justice is preëminent. Justice meets opposition either from cupidity within the judge or from want of power. The monarch is freest from both of these: he has sufficient (because unlimited) power; and cupidity is impossible to him, because as he has everything there is nothing that he can desire. Justice, therefore, is most effective in the world when subsisting in a sole monarch.[2]

---

[1] *Ibid.*, Bk. I, Chap. X.   (Translated by Aurelia Henry.)

[2] Dante's third argument, appealing to Love, because it may seem to the contemporary reader to be based on a sophistry, is omitted from the present exposition.   It will be found in the Appendix.

Plato's city of philosophers

Dante's doctrine and arguments show the influence of the Greek aristocratic ideal. That ideal, without like Dante's entailing either absolute monarchy or world dominion, is most fully expressed in Plato's *Republic*.

"The formation of a State[1] is due," Plato begins, "to this fact, that we are not individually independent, but have many wants." Our wants are, even at the earliest imaginable stage, too many to be supplied by individual efforts, and as political and economic life is developed for the purpose of serving them, the wants themselves become multiplied without apparent limit. Differentiation of function thus goes on apace, and as the growing State becomes at once a menace to its neighbors and a tempting object for conquest, both its safety and its continued growth require the development of a class of military guardians, as 'watch-dogs' of the State. Those of the guardians who in addition to the virtues of self-control and valor, which are requisite for all of them, possess as well a philosophic love of wisdom are to be given a special course of education which will equip them to become rulers of the State. These philosopher-rulers are spoken of in Plato's later discussion as the true guardians; the military are their auxiliaries. Members of both classes are to be selected from the mass on the basis of their capacity for courage, wisdom, and justice, and are to undergo a most rigorous education designed to develop these virtues in them.

What must distinguish the philosopher-rulers above all

---

[1] πόλις, usually translated city. The Greek *polis*, until the time of the Macedonian conquest, was in size like a city but in political structure (which is here more to the purpose) like a State. Except for this alteration the sentence, which is quoted from the second book of the *Republic*, follows the excellent translation of Davies and Vaughan, in Macmillan's Golden Treasury Series.

else is an ability to distinguish truths from half-truths, reality from illusion. The ability cannot be given to a man, but if latent it can be developed in him. Plato's famous allegory of chained men in a cave (in Book VII of the *Republic*) alludes to the half-spontaneous way in which such development comes about. But while in essence spontaneous, the development of a philosophical mind is furthered by right preparation. After an elementary training, consisting of cultural and gymnastic discipline blended in right proportion and shared by all freeborn members of the community, Plato lays out for the potential guardians a higher program of studies in which mathematics in its various branches that were then known, physics, and harmonics lead up to the study that is of cardinal importance—*dialectic*, the study of truth and of the methods of distinguishing the true from the false.

Like Dante's argument for a universal monarchy, Plato's proposal of a State ruled by an aristocracy of philosophers will doubtless to most readers seem admirable as a moral myth but difficult and above all dangerous to try to realize. Plato himself was awake to the principal danger, of a degeneration in the character of those in control, and his chief goal in outlining his educational program was to forestall such a catastrophe. It is, indeed, a pretty generally recognized truth of political science that the greater the centralization of authority the greater the potentialities of a society for both good and evil. When the supreme political power is in the hands of a few, and *a fortiori* when it is in the hands of one man, the State possesses a greater capacity for efficient action than when no concentrated power exists. Whether such increased efficiency is good or evil cannot be determined without knowing to what aim it is harnessed. It was Plato's lofty hope while concentrating the sovereign power, to purify the aim by selecting and watching over the character of future rulers from babyhood. His program is uncompromising, but milder proposals seem slow to achieve notable success.

Democracy

There are two main types of argument in support of democracy. The one is based on the doctrine of equal rights, and from this as a premise it deduces *a priori* the rightness of an equal distribution of political power. Now, the doctrine of equal rights may mean several things. It may mean that certain specific inequalities such as distinctions in wealth, social status, political rank, etc. are artificial products of society. Or it may go further, as do certain radical behaviorists and certain extreme apologists for communism, declaring that men are actually born equal in all (or all important) respects and that differences of ability and achievement are not native but acquired by the individual, perhaps very early in his career. Hobbes seems to waver ambiguously towards this doctrine, although he would probably not accept the extreme form of it propounded by certain modern behaviorists. Indeed, very few people take that extreme form of the doctrine altogether seriously. Finally, there is the normative meaning, discussed in the last chapter, and sometimes but not always based upon a belief in equality of either of the two preceding kinds. The normative meaning is expressed in the declaration of the Connecticut Bill of Rights (1818), "That all men, when they form a social compact, are equal in rights, and that no man or set of men are entitled to exclusive public emoluments or privileges from the community"; and more incisively in John Locke's dictum that children are born not *in* full equality but *to* it. The particular aspect of the normative meaning that is essential to democracy is equality of *political* rights—that is, of the right to vote, to hold certain offices, to sue in the courts, and the like. Optimists sometimes suppose that equality in these respects is a sufficient guarantee against too great an inequality in the distribution of goods.

The other argument for democracy is pragmatic. Democracy should be preserved not because, or not only because, individuals have equal rights, but because (in the language of Professor John Dewey) it offers individuals larger opportunities for the development of more inclusive social interests. Furthermore, the argument runs, it is to the State's interest to act upon the largest interpretation of experience that is open to it. The State therefore cannot afford to ignore any of its members who, even potentially, may have ideas to contribute derived from their own particular way of life and manner of experience.

No democracy, of course, is pure. It is impossible, especially in a State of any size, that the entire body of people should be consulted on every decision that confronts the commonwealth. Democracies are commonly 'representative' rather than direct, and in general the greater the number and diversity of people composing the democracy, the more clearly impossible it is that they should have a direct voice in its affairs. The early Quakers could uphold the ideal of decision by general accord instead of by a counting of votes, but the social conditions of colonial Pennsylvania are not found in a State embracing a hundred and twenty million people, where any considerable degree of accord is usually either the result of propaganda or the expression of mob emotions. "In real life no one," says Mr. Walter Lippmann, "acts on the theory that he can have a public opinion on every public question, though this fact is often concealed where a person thinks there is

no public question because he has no public opinion."[1]
For a democracy to have a stable character its affairs
must be carried on by representation, *i.e.*, by delegation
of governmental powers to a small number of citizens
elected by the rest.

But representation, too, has its dangers. For James
Madison it was a means whereby "to refine and enlarge the
public views, by passing them through the medium of a
chosen body of citizens, whose wisdom may best discern
the true interest of their country, and whose patriotism
and love of justice will be least likely to sacrifice it to
temporary or partial considerations."[2] But there are
two main impediments to the realization of this generous
aim. First, the electorate, besides having its vote restricted to candidates that were probably not of its own
choosing, is readily stampeded into voting on the basis
of campaign propaganda, the candidate's personality,
pique against the opposition, and similar irrelevancies.
Secondly, even when the elected leaders do possess the
patriotism and love of justice that Madison envisaged,
the conditions of public life tend to confine and often to
nullify the effectiveness of these virtues. Rulers have
always found it necessary to placate or circumvent political opponents; but in modern societies the strongest
opposition is likely to take the more subtle and more
impersonal form of economic pressure. The nature,
causes, and moral import of such pressure will be the
theme of the next chapter.

3. POLITICAL RADICALISM

Although the word 'radicalism' has been shamefully
misused by persons seeking to discredit opponents or to

---

[1] *Public Opinion*, p. 398.
[2] *The Federalist*, No. 10.

verbalize vague political antipathies, it is introduced in
the present context for the specific function of grouping
together several different political philosophies which in
one way or another challenge State sovereignty. The
principal types of political radicalism may be classified as
anarchism, which in its most uncompromising form upholds the ideal of a society based on brotherly love and
mutual aid without any government at all; *communism*,
or *Marxism*, which while upholding some form of the anarchistic ideal as an ultimate future goal, regards a trans-
ference of political as well as economic power to the
proletariat as the necessary first step towards such an end;
syndicalism, which accepts and develops the Marxian
doctrine of class warfare but without Marxism's redeeming
faith in an eventually classless society; and *guild socialism*,
which seeks to make the various trades-unions and professional groups into self-governing political units, which
by mutual agreements and compromises are to create a
State whose political structure shall correspond as far as
possible to the economic functions that it includes.

(i) *Anarchism*

The principal affirmation of anarchism is the inviola-
bility of the individual conscience, and consequently the
wrongness of whatever laws are potentially in conflict
with it; which is to say, the wrongness of any and all laws.
William Godwin (1756–1836), the first defender of anarchism whose writings received widespread attention,
argues ingeniously that if it is permissible in *some* cases
for a man to consult his private judgment as to whether
a law is to be obeyed (a premise which most persons would
grant), then he must consult it in *all* cases before he can
determine whether the case in question falls under that
category or no; "so that from this reasoning it ultimately

appears that no man is obliged to conform to any rule of conduct farther than the rule is consistent with justice."[1] Furthermore, as "every man is bound to resist every unjust proceeding on the part of the community" and as there is no infallible judge to whom the moral controversies thus arising can be referred and "no criterion perspicuously designating any one man or set of men to preside over the rest," there can be only the individual's own private judgment to serve as the criterion of what is just. Government, however, implies the negation of this principle. It works by force, and is in fact "nothing more than a scheme for enforcing by brute violence the sense of one man or set of men upon another."[2] Even those "cases of peculiar emergency" in which the government seemingly must step in to prevent acts of violence or unfairness by one man against another are themselves originally created by the activities of government. For government, since it implies the exertion of force in the enforcement of its commands, is in its very essence wrong: because "force can never be regarded as an appeal to the understanding; and therefore obedience, which is an act of the understanding or will, can have no legitimate connection with it."[3] There is a more natural solution to social difficulties:

Vicious conduct is soon discovered to involve injurious consequences. Injustice, therefore, by its own nature is little fitted for a durable existence. But government lays its hand upon the spring there is in society and puts a stop to its motion. It gives substance and permanence to our errors.[4]

---

[1] *An Introduction to the Principles of Political Justice*, Bk. II., Chap. VI.
[2] *Ibid.*, IV. i.
[3] *Ibid.*, III. vi.
[4] *Ibid.*, I. iv.

Genuine correction of evils must come about through an appeal to men's reason; for all men possess reason, and have "some communication with the common preceptor truth." Truth is "single and uniform," and there must therefore be in the nature of things one just settlement to every dispute, "which all intellects sufficiently roused from the slumber of savage ignorance will be irresistibly incited to approve."

Prince Peter Alexeivitch Kropotkin (1842–1920) developed the anarchist doctrine with a somewhat clearer grasp of economic realities. The son of an aristocratic Russian family, Kropotkin was converted at an early age to anarchism, giving up a scientific career of brilliant promise and suffering two years' imprisonment before finally escaping to England, where most of his writing and teaching was done. He was greatly influenced by the anarchist Bakunin, but Bakunin's doctrine of violence as a means of achieving the anarchist ideal appears to have been repugnant to Kropotkin's more pacifistic temperament.

All existing laws, in Kropotkin's view, fall under three categories: protection of property, protection of persons, and protection of government. Property laws serve to rob the producer of a part of what he produces and secure it to certain favored individuals. An owner's right to his house, for example, is simply the government's bestowal on him of property values that were created not by him but by the workmen who built it, and who have no share in their product, nor even a fair equivalent of a share in it. Protection of government comes to much the same thing as protection of property, for if protection of property is the major end of government, the government in protecting itself still serves that same end. The need of protecting persons, finally, will be greatly reduced when property is abolished, for most crimes take root in the institution of private property, which is a fertile source of temptation to possess another's wealth. Even crimes of passion are likely to be decreased rather than increased when the principal source of social maladjustment is removed; and such crimes as still might persist would not in any case be deterred by governmental action, for men who commit crimes of passion do not stop to reason about the consequences.

Kropotkin's positive program contains proposals for the establishment of voluntary coöperative groups, based on the same principle of motivation as that of trades-unions, scientific societies, and athletic clubs; the establishment of an economic organization to guarantee to each person his minimum needs in food, clothing, and shelter; and a reversal of the process of technical specialization that has come in and been developed with the coming of the machine age: let rather each individual return to a more healthy mode of life by combining brain work with manual work, and so far as possible industry with agriculture. The guiding idea of the program is the principle of mutual aid, which is at least as important a factor in the natural evolution of the species as self-preservation and greed, and which may be inferred to possess, therefore, at least as much 'survival-value.'

(ii) Communism and syndicalism

Marxism (communism) and syndicalism are in agreement with anarchism in regarding the State as necessarily unjust because operated by a small dominant class, having control of capital and therefore of political power and social privileges, and able to exist only by ruthless exploitation of the mass of workers. Marxism, moreover, looks towards the eventual establishment of an anarchistic society based on universal justice for all, following the principle, "From each according to his abilities, to each according to his needs." Marxism's ultimate goal is therefore the eventual abolition of the State, and the possibility of realizing such an ideal is defended by a belief in the perfectibility of men's characters through a behavioristic reconditioning process. But in a society dominated by possessors of wealth the achievement of universal justice is contrary to the interest of those in power. The first step towards a just society must therefore be a political dictatorship by the proletariat; which, however, is to be thought of as a transitional stage, necessary in educating the worker to a consciousness of his function in an industrial society and his rights. The classical justification of this view, based on an elaborate analysis of capitalist society, has been offered by Karl Marx and will be outlined in the next chapter.

Syndicalism, though historically an offshoot of Marxism, is different from it in two important respects. Syndicalists have none of the Marxists' religious faith in man's ultimate perfectibility. Where Marxists attribute human failings to the degrading influence of a society motivated by greed and characterized by ruthless economic warfare, and conclude that in a society from which the incentive of private profits was removed there would be no assignable limits to the improvability of the human race,[1] syndicalists are more inclined to accept the Machiavellian dictum that

---

[1] "The shell in which the cultural construction and self-education of Communist man will be enclosed, will develop all the vital elements of contemporary art to the highest point. Man will become immeasurably stronger, wiser and subtler; his body will become more harmonized, his movements more rhythmical, his voice more musical. The forms of life will become dynamically dramatic. The average human type will rise to the heights of an Aristotle, a Goethe or a Marx. And above this ridge new peaks will rise."—Leon Trotsky, *Literature and Revolution*. The quotation is borrowed from James Burnham's essay, "Marxism and Esthetics," in *The Symposium*, January, 1933.

"all men are bad, and will always, when they have free field, give loose to their evil inclinations."[1]

Secondly, the syndicalist attitude towards the State is more radical than the Marxist, for while Marxists purpose to keep the State during the transitional period of society but to transform its character by transferring its control, syndicalists have no use for the State at all. Politics, they declare, has the effect of distracting the energies of revolutionary workers and of splitting their ranks on irrelevant issues.   Revolution must be achieved entirely through the activities of trades unions.   The effort must be to unite all local trades-unions into a national body, which by paralyzing industry will give power into the hands of the proletariat.

(iii) Guild socialism and political pluralism

Guild socialism is not to be confused with 'national socialism.'   National socialism stands for a retention of political structure and a transfer to the central government (whether by a sudden *coup* or gradually, and whether by usurpation or purchase) of the country's national resources and instruments of production.   It may ally itself with the interests of the working class, as American socialism has done, and thus stand as a half-way house to radicalism, but it is also consistent with fascism and capitalist monopoly, as may be seen in the case of Italy and Germany. Guild socialism, on the other hand, may be characterized

---

[1]The passage from Niccolo Machiavelli (1469–1527), while inconsistent with the political nihilism of the syndicalists, has a general bearing on the present chapter and is worth quoting at length: "They who lay the foundations of a State and furnish it with laws must, as is shown by all who have treated of civil government, and by examples of which history is full, assume that all men are bad, and will always, when they have free field, give loose to their evil inclinations; and that if these for a while remain hidden, it is owing to some secret cause, which, from our having no contrary experience, we do not recognize at once, but which is afterwards revealed by Time, of whom we speak as the father of all truth."—*Discourse on the First Ten Books of Livy*, Chap. iii.

as 'political pluralism'; which holds that the State is only one of the forms of social organization by which human activities are to be channelized and promoted, although it does not go the length of syndicalism in denying that the State can serve any useful function whatever. What it does deny is State *sovereignty*, declaring that men's allegiance must be shared by a number of social groups, and that the allegiance owed to the State is determined simply by the degree to which the State actually fulfills its function of arbitrating fairly among the various proletarian, capitalist, professional, and other groups which are to serve as the units of political power.[1]

In the theory of Mr. G. D. H. Cole, one of the most prominent representatives of guild socialism in Great Britain, there are two primary requirements for a healthy society: first, that it organize along functional lines, thus establishing firm social units by grouping individuals according to their (economically) most vital interests; secondly, that each organization be governed on the principle of representative democracy, which becomes a real instrument of effective popular control only when it is set on a functional (instead of, as in the United States, a geographical) basis. When these requirements have been met there will remain the problem of adjusting disputes among the different organizations, and this is to be done by the formation of a 'commune,' a body in every area, regional and national, composed of elected representatives from each of the functional organizations, "brought together for the common determination and discussion of vital problems of policy in which they are all concerned."[2]

---

[1] This characterization of political pluralism is based on the views of two of its leading exponents: Harold J. Laski, *The Problem of Sovereignty* and *A Grammar of Politics*, and Leon Duguit, *Law in the Modern State*.

[2] *The Future of Local Government*, p. 177.

Political radicalism, of whatever type, offers a powerful and serious challenge to the existing social order. To arrive at a balanced estimate of either radical or conservative theories of the State it is not enough to keep the discussion on the level of pure political theory; a part of our material must be furnished by the character and working of existing States in their concrete and observable manifestations. Modern society, as everyone knows, is capitalistic: its chief enterprises are motivated by a competitive struggle for profits. An analysis of capitalism, therefore, and a discussion of its ethical significance will be the theme of the next chapter.

CHAPTER XI

OUR BUSINESS CIVILIZATION

"I like the Walrus best," said Alice: "because he was a little sorry for the poor oysters."

"He ate more than the Carpenter, though," said Tweedledee. "You see he held his handkerchief in front, so that the Carpenter couldn't see how many he took: contrariwise."

"That was mean!" Alice said indignantly. "Then I like the Carpenter best — if he didn't eat so many as the Walrus."

"But he ate as many as he could get," said Tweedledum.

This was a puzzler. After a pause, Alice began, "Well! They were both very unpleasant characters —"

Lewis Carroll, *Through the Looking-Glass*

1. THE NATURE OF CAPITALISM

PROBLEMS of social ethics can be made concretely intelligible only by reference to the actual conditions and manner of operation that prevail in a given society. Even the more personal sorts of moral problem cannot of course be entirely divorced from the contemporary social background. Their dependence on it, however, is less direct and less considerable, for an individual in the furtherance of his private moral ideals may, in favorable circumstances, withdraw himself to some extent from the world. When the emphasis is shifted to problems of social justice and the effective administration thereof, no serious discussion is possible without reference to the structure and functioning of the society for which justice is sought. Our own society is capitalistic, and that fact determines certain important respects in which contemporary social ideals, if they are to stand any chance of becoming effective, must differ from the ideals projected by pre-capital-istic forms of society.   An understanding of the nature of capitalism is therefore requisite to a serious discussion of social ethics today.   While the meaning of capitalism is by no means universally agreed upon by economists and social philosophers of all schools, a good working definition may be suggested in terms of four essential characteristics. Capitalism appears to involve: (1) competition for profits, (2) the mechanization of industry, (3) the purchase and exploitation of human labor-power, and (4) corporate, absentee ownership.

(1) *Competition for profits*

Competition is not in itself peculiar to capitalism, nor to civilization, nor to the human species.   Struggle and rivalry in one form or another are found wherever there is life.   It would be fallacious, however, to argue from this fact to the inevitability of that peculiar type of com-petitive struggle that distinguishes capitalism.   Capitalist competition is a struggle for *profits*, and consequently for whatever conduces to greater profits—*e.g.*, cheap raw materials, cheap labor, financial loans, and large markets. In the course of this competitive process, and indeed as a necessary part of it, *industry* (the general word for produc-tion of goods and services) is carried on; but the compe-tition is waged in terms not of industry but of *business*, which means trade and financial operations so far as carried on for the sake of profits.   Productive competition considered in itself is quite another matter.   Renaissance princes often vied with one another to build as many and as beautiful monuments as possible, without expectation of financial profits; individual artists and an occasional self-sufficient craftsman may even today care more about the quality of what they produce than about the accruing profits. But business enterprises are formed purely and simply for the making of profits: if they happen also to maintain the industrial policy of producing more and better products this policy is incidental to their profit-making aim; when greater profits are promised by a curtailment of production or by a deterioration of the product the industrial policy is, as a usual thing, governed accordingly.

(ii) Mechanization of industry

Capitalism involves not only competition for profits but competition by means of increasingly mechanized industrial processes. Industrial mechanization shows itself principally in two ways: in specialization of functions and in standardization of products. Primitive societies develop little specialization. Men have distinct functions from women, and to a few old or gifted men may be assigned the special functions of ruler, priest, and medicineman; beyond that all share the same work, alternately hunting, fighting, and observing tribal ceremonies. As societies become more civilized, wants are increased and in order to supply them industry becomes gradually specialized. Plato has given one of the earliest analyses and justifications of such a development:

"Now then, let us construct our imaginary city from the beginning. Evidently its construction will be determined by our natural wants."
"Of course." . . .
"Then let us see by what means our city may be enabled to supply so many wants. To begin with, does not one set of wants require a farmer, another a builder, a third a weaver? . . . And ought not the work of each to be put at the disposal of the commonwealth so that the one farmer, for instance, shall provide enough food for four, spending four times as much time and labor upon its preparation and then sharing it with

others? Or ought he rather to ignore his fellows and produce for his own consumption only a quarter of the amount of food, in a quarter of the time, spending the remainder in building his own house, in providing himself with clothes and shoes, and acquiring everything by his own efforts instead of troubling to share with others?"

"I imagine, Socrates," Adeimantus replied, "that the former plan would be the easier."

"Quite likely," I said; "for in addition it occurs to me as an afterthought that, in the first place, no two individuals are born just alike, but each has certain distinctive natural endowments, one being better suited for one occupation, another for another. Don't you agree?"

"Yes."

"Besides, how is a man most likely to succeed? By dividing his energies among a number of trades or by devoting himself entirely to one?"

"By devoting himself to one."   . . .

"It seems to follow, then, that the easiest way to produce things in superior quantity and quality is for each man to work at just that occupation for which he is best fitted by natural endowment, and to leave other affairs in other hands."[1]

In advocating division of labor as a necessary basis for civilized society Plato did not of course foresee the extent to which specialization would be carried out in modern industry. If he had foreseen he would hardly have approved. In the ideal society that he envisaged, a shoemaker, while restricted to the making of shoes, at any rate made the whole shoe, and a weaver the whole coat, with only the assistance of perhaps two or three apprentices, each of whom was expected to be proficient in all branches of the manufacture. A present-day shoe factory, on the other hand, contains probably no one individual who if left to his own devices could make an entire shoe. Specialization is still more striking in the manu-

[1] Plato, *Republic*, Bk. II.

facture of more mechanical products like the automobile, where an individual worker may be restricted to drilling uniform holes in millions of uniform plates as they are passed up the assemblage line.

Specialization of function both requires and makes possible a greater uniformity in the product. It requires it because "under conditions of specialized mass production, the various parts of a machine are separately made. An automatic screw machine contains many thousands of separately machined pieces. That these parts may be finally assembled into a smooth-working mechanism is possible only because of unvarying fidelity to standard specifications. Variation of as much as 1/100,000 of an inch is in some cases fatal to the usefulness of the part when assembled into the machine."[1] At the same time that it requires it, industrial specialization also makes standardization possible. It does so by the principle of the *transfer of skill* from the worker to the machine. Such standardization and precision as are needed in modern industry could not be achieved by human hands: the area of variation of human effort is too wide. Suppose (to use an example offered by an industrial engineer, Mr. D. S. Kimball) it is desired to drill four holes in a number of plates, so that they bear a certain fixed relation to the edges of the plate. If the operator is equipped with only an ordinary hand-drill he must have a high degree of skill to space the holes accurately, and even at best he will not be able to make them correspond with the high degree of accuracy that is required. But suppose a skilled workman makes a 'drilling jig,' in which by means of set-screws all of the plates can be clamped in exactly the same position and the holes therefore drilled with an equivalent

---

[1] Willard E. Atkins and others, *Economic Behavior*, Vol. I, p. 40. (Houghton Mifflin.)

exactitude. Not only is an extremely high degree of accuracy and uniformity of the product now made possible; it is also the case that the plate can now be satisfactorily drilled by a relatively unskilled worker. The accuracy of the work no longer depends on the skill of the operator but on the accuracy of his tools. Furthermore, in using the hand-drill the skilled mechanic must expend thought as well as skill in properly locating the holes. Not so, the unskilled operator of a drilling jig. The mental labor of locating the holes has been done once for all by the tool-maker and embodied in the drilling jig. Metaphorically we can say, therefore, that a transfer not only of skill but of thought or intelligence has been made from a person to the machine.[1]

(iii) Exploitation of human labor-power

A third aspect of capitalism, which according to the theory of Karl Marx (1818–1883) is the most distinctive of all, is summed up in the Marxian word 'exploitation.' As popular spokesmen for radical views sometimes use this word more for its emotional appeal than for any precisely determined meaning, it is important to note that in Marx's own writings its meaning is quite definite. When a capitalist promoter hires some workers he is considered by Marx to have purchased his employees' 'labor-power.' By labor-power Marx means the total amount of physical efforts that an employee is capable of putting forth. In return for their labor-power the capitalist pays his employees wages, and the wages tend to reach the lowest level at which there are workers to be found: in the long run, apart from such amelioration as may be

---

[1]The illustration is paraphrased from a passage in D. S. Kimball, *Principles of Industrial Organization*, quoted by Atkins and others, *op. cit.*

effected by trades-unions and strikes,[1] this level tends to coincide with the level of bare subsistence. The *value* of what the worker produces, on the other hand, is determined not by the amount of labor-power he puts forth, but by the amount of 'socially necessary labor.' The amount of socially necessary labor that a workman, by a given expenditure of labor-power, happens to achieve depends partly on the efficiency of the machine that he operates and on the efficiency with which his factory is managed, partly on the degree to which society has need of his product. The *price*, again, differs from the value of a product. When the product is treated as a commodity, *i.e.*, offered for sale, the price that it happens to command will depend not only on the extent to which there is a social need of it and on the extent to which this need is supplied from other sources, but on a complicated set of market factors, one of the most important of which is the price-pegging done by monopolistic combines. Since the wages of labor are determined by the cost of producing labor, *viz.*, by the subsistence level, and since the price of a commodity normally rises much above the cost of producing labor and of raw materials, a *surplus value* is created. This surplus value becomes the property of the capitalists (*i.e.*, directors, stockholders, bankers, etc.) who have staked the enterprise.

The process by which surplus value is created is considered by Marxists to be an 'exploitation' of the workers because of the Marxian postulate that nothing which the capitalist does produces any value and that therefore the value that remains as a surplus over the cost of materials and the cost of labor must have been created by wage

---

[1] The fact of such amelioration does not invalidate Marx's theory, for when it occurs it represents to some extent a departure from capitalism in its pure state, by the introduction of socialistic elements. Marx is analyzing the *essence* of capitalism—*i.e.*, what it would be like on a strictly *laissez-faire* basis.

earners and should rightfully belong to wage earners.
This aspect of Marx's doctrine offers a clue to the most
serious of his attacks on capitalism, and it is therefore of
some importance that it should be rightly understood.
Unfortunately most of Marx's expositors appear to mis-
understand it. Even so friendly a critic as Mr. A. D.
Lindsay declares the doctrine to be indefensible. "It depends," Mr. Lindsay says, "on Marx's view that exchange
creates no value, and that can be shown from Marx's own
admissions to be unsound."[1]   Marx, it must be admitted,
is not entirely self-consistent on this point and there is
ample documentary justification for Mr. Lindsay's stric-
ture.   Yet Marx appears to know well enough that exchange does create value.   Knowing this and arguing *ex
hypothesi* from the premise of those individualist economists who say that rewards should be in proportion to
labor—*i.e.*, to the socially useful values created—Marx
evidently means that the capitalist *quâ* capitalist is not
a creator of values but merely a profiteer, receiving whatever surplus values are created by whatever means; and
that so far as a particular individual is instrumental in
creating values, even though he may do so by the work
of managing or of merchandising, he ought *ex hypothesi*
to receive *wages* (not profits) commensurate with the
values he creates.   The fact that the same individual can
be, and frequently is, both a capitalist receiving interest
on his investments and also a salaried worker complicates
but does not invalidate the issue.   Of course if everybody
were capitalist and salaried worker at the same time and
to the same extent, the distinction would be of no practical importance, for everyone would then be exploiter
and exploited to an equal degree.   Such, however, is not
the situation that exists.   There is in every highly indus-

[1] A. D. Lindsay, *Karl Marx's Capital*, p. 89.

trialized country today a class of individuals whose incomes are wholly or predominantly dependent on profits from investments and another class whose incomes are in the form of wages—notwithstanding a middle class which shares the attributes of both. The formation of these two classes and the exploitation by the one of the other is in Marx's view essential to the existence of capitalism: hence his corollary that the resultant inequalities can be removed only by bringing capitalist methods to an end.

(iv) Corporate, absentee ownership

Corporate ownership is a fourth essential attribute of capitalism. In the normal form of capitalist enterprise the owner—*i.e.*, the legally rightful receiver of the created surplus values—is not one individual, nor a few acquainted individuals, but a large number of individuals, having as a rule no interest in the enterprise except to demand that it be run in such a way as to yield the largest financial return on their investment. This fact is of great importance as indicating the entirely impersonal nature of capitalism. Where capitalism is fully developed it becomes completely dehumanized; the reason for which is easy to see. When a single employer owns and manages a business his personal character is likely to make some difference as to his mode of handling it and of dealing with his employees. When the ownership and management are in the hands of a small group of active partners the conduct of the business is likely to become more impersonal, although it is still possible for the characters of the several partners to be reflected to some extent in their business practice. But in the typical large-scale business enterprise of today the personal characters of the individuals who own and manage have little or no causal relation to the business

practices of the firm. The manager who comes in con-
tact with the employees is himself a salaried employee:
should he on his own initiative altruistically reduce the
working hours of his subordinates or increase their wages
in such a way as to lessen the profits of the firm he would
probably be removed from his position. The owners,
for their part, are a board of business directors (not industrial directors) and, in a secondary sense, a large
number of scattered stockholders. None of these owners
normally knows anything about the actual manner of
conducting the industry from which his profits are derived. Each requires only that the profits be as large as
possible. Problems of industrial technique are left to
salaried technicians. If largest profits are created best
by industrial practices unfavorable to the worker or
consumer the possibility of effective protest is minimized
by the greatness of the 'economic distance' between those
who receive their income from ownership of shares in the
corporation and those who control the industrial details.

2.   CAPITALISM AND INDUSTRY

The distinction between business and industry has already been explained. Industry means the actual work
of sowing, reaping, manufacturing, and distributing to the
consumer, of giving medical attention or legal advice, of
supplying instruction or entertainment—in short, the
legitimate production of goods and services in any sense
of the word. Business, on the other hand, is the process
of controlling and increasing not the goods and services
themselves but the economic values (*i.e.*, potential exchange values) implicit in them. Robinson Crusoe on his
island carried on various types of industry but no business
whatever. In a primitive society where there is little or
no calculated exchange of goods and services there is little

or no business, although the degree of industry may be very great. Clearly, then, some industry is a necessary condition of any human life whatever, whereas business is a secondary form of operation and its ultimate importance for human life and happiness can be significantly questioned. *A fortiori*, such a query can be significantly directed against capitalism, which, as the foregoing analysis has shown, is a special development that business technique has taken in modern times. A study of social ethics pertinent to modern affairs must therefore inquire how far and in what specific ways capitalism is of benefit or hindrance to industry.

The advantages of capitalism

Among the chief arguments in favor of capitalism are that it encourages initiative and thrift, and that it promotes progress by making vast industrial undertakings possible through the effective channelization of financial credits. Each of these arguments must be examined in the light of the foregoing analysis of the nature of capitalism, for it may well be the case that they are more valid with respect to some of the aspects of capitalism than to others.

Those who sponsor the first of the two arguments seem to have in mind chiefly the competitive, profit-seeking aspect of capitalism. There is a good deal to be said in favor of the view that a great majority of mankind, being essentially selfish, require the bait of private profits and the goad of having to compete for them in order to accomplish anything of social benefit. This, at any rate, was a corollary drawn by the utilitarians in applying their general doctrine to the problems of economics. That each individual seeks only his own greatest happiness is, as we have seen, a premise of utilitarian psychology.

One of the ways in which Bentham bridged the chasm between this supposed psychological truism and the utilitarian ideal of greatest happiness for the greatest number was by an assumption of fact. It had been affirmed by Adam Smith (1723–1790) in his *Enquiry into the Nature and Causes of the Wealth of Nations* that competitive profit-seeking was the surest way to bring about the greatest measure of public weal. Smith's contention was based upon the thesis of the *natural identity of interests*, more strikingly designated by Halévy as the *spontaneous harmony of egoisms*[1]—*i.e.*, the assumption, afterwards incorporated by Bentham into his utilitarian theory, that since men's dominant motives are egoistic and since the human species does nevertheless survive, it must be supposed that the various selfish aims result somehow in bringing about the good of the species. How, indeed, Bentham asks, could the good of the species be secured in any other way? Humanity could not survive if each individual devoted his energies to promoting his neighbor's interests at the expense of his own. In economics the doctrine received added support. At the time when Smith and Bentham lived, before the rise of the great corporations, it was to an appreciable extent actually the case that rival producers or merchants, each seeking to augment his own profits, would increase the output, improve the quality and lower the price of their commodities, thereby automatically creating benefits for the consumer. This situation gave widespread popularity to the doctrine of *laissez-faire*, which is the doctrine that the public welfare is best promoted by allowing the greatest possible amount of freedom to business men pursuing each his own selfish end, and by removing therefore all governmental restrictions upon business except such restrictions as the

---

[1]Elie Halévy, *The Growth of Philosophical Radicalism*, p. 89.

business men themselves might deem necessary for the
suppression of 'corrupt practices.'

A modern critic is likely to regard the utilitarian
laissez-faire doctrine as a partially true and ideologically
influential expression of the economic conditions that
flourished in Bentham's time rather than as a perennial
truth. What the *laissez-faire* economists did not sufficiently realize was that an increase of output is a benefit
only so long as it is accompanied by a correspondingly
rapid increase of buying-power; that it is often more
profitable to camouflage inferior commodities by clever
advertising and marketing than to improve their quality;
and that the competitive lowering of prices can be avoided
by agreements and mergers among the competing firms.
The classical assumption was, in short, that business competition was in itself sufficient to ensure industrial progress; and this assumption, while roughly verifiable at the
early stages of capitalism, becomes more and more doubtful as capitalism reaches its present-day stage of giant
mergers and the threat of diminishing markets.

A second argument in defense of capitalism is that it
offers the only practicable way of financing large-scale
industry and is therefore today a necessary condition of
human progress and of increasing the means of human
happiness. This argument, it will be observed, rests on
two premises: that large-scale industry is impossible without large-scale business (*i.e.*, without the second and
fourth aspects of capitalism particularly), and that human
progress is to be measured in terms of industrial progress.
The former of these premises raises a question of fact,
which there is not enough evidence as yet to settle decisively: namely, whether a completely socialized State
would be able to carry on large-scale industry without the
stimulus of capitalist competition. The Soviet Republic

offers an excellent laboratory for the experimental testing
of this possibility, but results so far have not justified a
categorical answer one way or the other.   The second
premise raises a normative question: whether a continually increasing production of goods and services is *per se*
a mark of human progress.   Many persons would regard
it as an important part of human progress, but it is in
any case not the whole story.   If industrial expansion
does not produce an increase in human happiness as well
as in external goods it can hardly be called progress in
any very important sense of the word.   But is there any
evidence—indeed, by the nature of the case *can* there
be any evidence—that the average member of our modern
business civilization is happier than the average individual was in the Age of Pericles or of Saint Francis or of
Queen Anne?

We turn now to the other side of the picture and consider certain respects in which it has been claimed that
capitalism, particularly in its more recent stages, has
actually become a hindrance to the effective pursuit of
industry.   Two charges especially have been brought
against capitalism by its critics: it is said to involve (i)
sabotage and waste and (ii) an excessive concentration
of wealth and poverty.

(i) Sabotage and waste

Webster's Dictionary defines sabotage as "malicious
waste or destruction of an employer's property by workmen during labor troubles."   From this original definition,
which identifies sabotage with the activities of the *sabots*
during the French Revolution and their lineal descendants
the French syndicalists of today, the word has acquired
in recent years a broader meaning and now signifies deliberate wanton waste or destruction by anyone at all.

Deliberate waste and destruction are a necessary part of modern business, for business (as distinguished from industry) is carried on solely for the sake of profits, and moral conduct, when practised in business, is practised solely as a means to this end. The typical business man asks, as Stuart Chase has expressed it: "Is the undertaking profitable; if profitable is it legal; if illegal where can I find a good lawyer?" Quick profit is got by a quick turnover. The greatest profit is thus secured by a flow of goods with the shortest possible life. Mr. Chase cites F. L. Ackermann, an architect who has made a wide study of housing wastes in New York City, in illustrating some of the results of the quick turnover policy. New York City apartments are now erected as short-term investments to be torn down and rebuilt as land values shift under them. All the plumbing in New York City has to be replaced on an average of once in eight years. As it takes twice as many plumbers to replace plumbing fixtures as to install them originally, it is evident that three times as many plumbers are used to install and reinstall as would be the case if the buildings were made durable in the first place. Again, house owners in the United States spend half a billion dollars a year in the repair of rusted metal work, the greater part of which loss could have been avoided had more durable materials been manufactured and used originally.[1] Housing is only one of the victims of quick turnover policy: clothes, motor cars, razor blades, and countless other items are made less durable than it would be easily possible to make them if social utility were the primary consideration. "Under capitalism," Mr. Chase remarks, "it is impossible to create an interest in production that is not also an interest in decay and destruction."

[1] Stuart Chase, *The Tragedy of Waste*, p. 74. (Macmillan.)

Another form in which capitalism promotes waste is found in the advertising traffic. Mr. Chase estimates that "in America one dollar is spent to educate consumers in what they may or may not buy for every seventy cents that is spent for all other kinds of education—primary, secondary, high-school, university." Advertising has, to be sure, a rightful function but that function tends to be lost under capitalism:

> The function of advertising, as we see it, lies in the dissemination of news about coming events, new inventions, new products. Theatre and concert advertising, new books, a campaign for public hygiene, a safety campaign, six months space for a new synthetic food, for an alcohol engine that was cheaper than gasoline, for a reliable device for controlling births—would be tolerable and welcome. National advertising for the education of the consumer, if conducted by some impartial and scientific body, might conceivably provide a great channel for eliminating wastes in consumption. But nine-tenths and more of advertising is largely competitive wrangling as to the relative merits of two undistinguished and often indistinguishable compounds—soaps, tooth powders, motor cars, tires, snappy suits, breakfast foods, patent medicines, cigarettes.[1]

Advertising, in short, would perform a useful social function if it were directed towards informing consumers of the qualities of goods and educating them to the appreciation and use of better materials. But with a few exceptions this is by no means what it aims to do. Claude C. Hopkins, one of the most successful advertising men of the recent boom era, throws a revealing light on some of the practices of advertisers in his description of how he promoted Pepsodent tooth paste. Having read "book after book by dental authorities on the theory on which Pepsodent was based," he discovered in one book a reference to the mucin plaques on the teeth, which gave

---

[1] *Op. cit.*, p. 113. (By permission of The Macmillan Company, publishers.)

him "an appealing idea." He decided to call the mucin
plaques the film, and "to advertise this tooth paste as
a creator of beauty. To deal with that cloudy film."[1]
It will be noted that Mr. Hopkins displays no interest in
determining the exact nature of the dental 'film,' nor in
whether it is desirable that it should be removed, nor in
whether Pepsodent is compounded in such a way as to be
effective in removing it. Relevant to the last question is
the fact that the formula for Pepsodent was admittedly
established before its advertiser happened to hear about
the dental film. That the methods of promoting this
particular commodity are not unique is shown by ample
documented evidence in such books as Chase and Schlink's
Your Money's Worth, Schlink and Kallet's *A Hundred
Million Guinea Pigs*, Rorty's *Our Master's Voice*, and the
periodic bulletins of Consumers' Research, Inc.

Persons who occasionally give a thought to the future
of human economy will find still more cause for alarm in
a type of waste that threatens to leave permanent and
irremediable results: the despoliation of natural resources.
Three hundred years ago, when the first settlers were establishing themselves in this country, there were some
eight hundred million acres of virgin forest. Today there
are about one hundred and twenty-five million. It is
clear that if this rate of depletion continues the country
will be stripped bare within fifty years. Apart from the
possibilities of reforestation, large projects for which are
now being promoted, it is noteworthy how wastefully the
forests are being used. According to an authoritative
estimate[2] the wood pulp consumed by a single New York
newspaper will account annually for over two thousand
acres of forest land. In procuring the wood, furthermore,

---

[1] *My Life in Advertising*, pp. 151–152.
[2] E. Slosson, *Creative Chemistry*, cited by Chase, *op. cit.*

twenty per cent of the cubic volume of the trees, represented by the branches and stumps, is left on the land to burn or rot; forty per cent is wasted in the mill; all of which if utilized would furnish enormous amounts of charcoal, tar, wood alcohol, acetate of lime, and other valuable by-products. Coal, oil, and other natural resources are similarly wasted by avoidable inefficiencies. When oil is struck there is a race to drill holes in the surrounding property. Whoever drills first, especially if he drills his holes near the boundaries of his property, steals much of his neighbor's oil in a legal manner by drawing it off underground. This situation encourages wasteful competition in drilling, with the result that three barrels of oil out of every four are left unreclaimable underground —by abandoning the fields while much oil is still in the ground, by allowing the gas to escape that forms over the subterranean oil exerting the pressure necessary to force it up, and by letting water run into the oil sands. All such wastage is due not to any lack of scientific means for usefully disposing of the products but to the 'profits first' policy that is inseparable from capitalism.

(ii) Concentration of wealth and poverty

"Everything," Henry George remarked sixty years ago, "tends to awake the sense of natural equality, to arouse the aspirations and ambitions of the masses, to excite a keener and keener perception of the gross injustice of existing inequalities of privilege and wealth. Yet, at the same time, everything tends to the rapid and monstrous increase of these inequalities. Never since great estates were eating out the heart of Rome has the world seen such enormous fortunes as are now arising—and never more utter proletarians."[1] One of George's principal con-

[1] *Social Problems*, p. 34.

tributions to American social philosophy was the insistence
that the multi-millionaire and the pauper are complementary parts of the same picture—correlative effects of the
same set of conditions.   Many economic factors operate
to promote concentration of wealth, and, correlatively,
concentration of poverty.   Rich men stand the best
chance of acquiring more riches, for it is they who have
most power to control banking and industry, the policies
of governments and the decisions of the courts, the fluctua-
tions of the stock market and of foreign exchange.   Matthew Josephson has made a lively and forceful study, in
The Robber Barons, of the way in which certain American
families of great wealth got started.   Mr. Josephson's
conclusions are in general the same as those of everyone
else who has seriously investigated the matter: that in
every case it was by seizing a monopoly of some kind
that the founders of those families laid the foundations
of their wealth.   The early promoters of railroads, such
as the first Commodore Vanderbilt and the first Gould,
became wealthy by buying off or ruining opposition lines;
the Rockefeller oil interests were originally established in
a similar way.   The Astor fortune has stemmed from certain pieces of land once acquired by an early Astor "by
virtue of which his children are now allowed to tax other
people's children—to demand a very large part of their
earnings from many thousands of the present population
of New York.   Its main element is not production or
saving.   No human being can produce land or lay up land.
If the Astors had all remained in Germany, or if there
had never been any Astors, the land of Manhattan Island
would have been here all the same."[1]

---

[1]George, *op. cit.*, p. 54.   The more subtle and complicated methods by which
concentration of capital is carried on today are told in a striking and scholarly
manner in Berle and Means' *The Modern Corporation and Private Property*.

Increased concentration of wealth causes much otherwise avoidable poverty and suffering for millions of less fortunate people. Inadequate wages coupled with the continual threat of unemployment are one set of factors in their plight; the conditions under which their labor must be carried on are another. An illuminating approach to the problem of low wages has been made by G. D. H. Cole.[1] Our economic system, he points out, treats *wages*, *interest*, and *rent* as costs of production, to be kept as low as possible. These three together with *profits* are the exact reflection of the *price* at which goods are sold. Traditional economics thus treats profits as *the* good; as the end and object of the productive process. In opposition Mr. Cole argues that while all income as such, regardless of type, may be accounted a good, money becomes of diminishing utility as a man gets more of it, because while two thousand dollars a year to a poor man may mean the difference between life and death, or at any rate between enjoying the minimum comforts of life and becoming a pauper, an equal amount of money added to the income of a millionaire would be superfluous for procuring the necessaries of life and would have little or no effect upon his enjoyment of luxuries: probably he would simply reinvest it. By Mr. Cole's principle, then, the moral way of regarding the relation of wages to profits would be sharply opposed to the business way.

Unemployment, too, must be considered as one of the evils associated with capitalism. This is not to deny that men were frequently unable to find employment in precapitalistic eras. The problem has become more acute today, however, because of the introduction by capitalism of new types of unemployment. Apart from a minority

---

[1] *A Guide to Modern Chaos*, p. 20.

of citizens who won't work or who are incapable of working, the reasons for unemployment are chiefly three. *Seasonal* unemployment may be dismissed as it is not peculiar to capitalism: in most forms of work, particularly in those more directly connected with the processes of nature, some seasons of the year are more slack than others. *Technological* unemployment is more particularly an outgrowth of capitalism. Pre-capitalistic forms of technological unemployment have not been unknown: Greek farmers of the fifth century B. C. suffered from a dwindling market for their produce owing to the development of maritime commerce and the importation of cheaper substitutes from other Mediterranean shores. But such mishaps were in former times the exception rather than the rule. Under capitalism the building up and destruction of particular industries has become incalculably more rapid, while owing to the severe specialization of function within each industry a great number of employees, when deprived of one type of work, are no longer fitted for anything else. *Cyclical* unemployment is likewise an outgrowth of capitalism. When a commodity has large sales at high prices there is great competition to produce it; whence, owing to the application of large-scale industrial methods, over-production is quickly achieved. To a certain point the 'demand' can be artificially increased by advertising, by new methods of marketing, and by the discovery of new markets. Soon a limit is reached, prices fall, production must be curtailed, and many are thrown out of work. Industrial situations like this are only one of the factors that produce 'business cycles' but they are one of the most important and they illustrate the close relation between capitalism and cyclical unemployment. As a result jointly of unemployment and low wages there results scarcity of buying-power with the attendant phe-

nomenon of poverty in the midst of plenty: essentials like
food and other raw materials dumped into the sea or converted into fertilizer in order to create a 'demand,' thus
raising the price, thus stimulating new productive enterprise, while all the time millions are starving for want of
the destroyed goods.

Conditions of labor under capitalism are likewise open
to criticism.   Let Henry George speak again:

Consider the blacksmith of the industrial era now everywhere
passing—or rather the 'black and white smith,' for the finished
workman worked in steel as well.   The smithy stood by roadside
or street.   Through its open doors were caught glimpses of
nature; all that was passing could be seen.   Wayfarers stopped
to inquire, neighbors to tell or hear the news, children to see the
hot iron glow and watch the red sparks fly.   Now the smith
shoed a horse; now he put on a wagon-tire; now he forged and
tempered a tool; again he welded a broken andiron, or beat out
with graceful art a crane for the deep chimney-place, or, when
there was nothing else to do, he wrought iron into nails.

Go now into one of those enormous establishments covering
acres and acres, in which workmen by the thousands are massed
together, and, by the aid of steam and machinery, iron is converted to its uses at a fraction of the cost of the old system.
You cannot enter without permission from the office, for over
each door you will find the sign, 'Positively no admittance.'
If you are permitted to go in, you must not talk to the workmen;
but that makes little difference, as amid the din and the clatter,
and whir of belts and wheels, you could not if you would.   Here
you find men doing over and over the selfsame thing—passing,
all day long, bars of iron through great rollers; presenting plates
to steel jaws; turning, amid clangor in which you can scarcely
'hear yourself think,' bits of iron over and back again, sixty
times a minute, for hour after hour, for day after day, for year
after year.   In the whole great establishment there will be not
a man, save here and there one who got his training under the
simpler system now passing away, who can do more than some
minute part of what goes to the making of a salable article.
The lad learns in a little while how to attend his particular

machine. Then his progress stops. He may become gray-headed without learning more. As his children grow, the only way he has of augmenting his income is by setting them to work. As for aspiring to become master of such an establishment, with its millions of capital in machinery and stock, he might as well aspire to be King of England or Pope of Rome. He has no more control over the conditions that give him employment than has the passenger in a railroad car over the motion of the train. Causes which he can neither prevent nor foresee may at any time stop his machine and throw him upon the world, an utterly unskilled laborer, unaccustomed even to swing a pick or handle a spade. When times are good, and his employer is coining money, he can only get an advance by a strike or a threatened strike. At the least symptoms of harder times his wages are scaled down, and he can only resist by a strike, which means, for a longer or shorter time, no wages.[1]

George's description refers to conditions sixty years ago. Since his time large-scale industry has increased and its evils are much accentuated. The coming of machinery has resulted not only in a greater monotony but in a speeding up of the individual's labor. Machinery is costly, and to recover the capital cost and interest on it the manufacturer must keep it going—together with the worker who attends it—at the highest possible speed. The capacity of the machine rather than the capacity of the worker tends to become the gauge. In large factories such as those in which automobiles are assembled the worker must either stand the pace set by the machine or quit. Otherwise he would dislocate the work of an entire group of which he is an insignificant unit. One result of this speed-up system is expressed in the slogan 'too old at forty.' Only young workers can stand the pace; and even these are quickly burned out and cast aside.

---

[1] *Social Problems*, pp. 36–37. (Published by the Robert Schalkenbach Foundation, New York.)

3. INTERNATIONAL ASPECTS

A problem of growing importance in regard to capitalism is its relation to war. Capitalism is sometimes supposed, particularly by its socialist and communist critics, to be the sole cause of modern wars: often it is said that wars could not occur if the people were allowed to vote on them. This is probably an overstatement. The conditions leading to a war are complex: economic factors are always to some degree mixed with ideological. Wars could not be waged for long unless they had a basis in popular support. Of course this popular support may be to a considerable extent brought about by propaganda issuing from business interests that stand to profit from a war, but there may also be other powerful business interests whose profits a war threatens to endanger. The indictment most legitimately brought against capitalism in its international aspects is not that it is a force making indiscriminately for war, but rather that whether particular business interests happen to be promoting war or peace they do so not by reason of any concern for the survival and welfare of mankind nor even of their own nation but solely for the sake of quick profits. Such an indictment casts no unfavorable reflection on the individual characters of all business men. We may take for granted that in matters of morality and patriotism the average business man is on a par with the average citizen generally. But the policies of a joint-stock company are independent of the moral ideals that may influence the private lives of the individual stockholders. This principle of the partial independence of social morality in relation to private morality, a principle quite essential to a realistic appraisal of social phenomena, is given a brilliant demonstration in Reinhold Niebuhr's *Moral Man and Immoral Society*.

The amorality of nations

It is Dr. Niebuhr's thesis that although "individual men may be moral in the sense that they are able to consider interests other than their own in determining problems of conduct, and are capable, on occasion, of preferring the advantages of others to their own," this is "more difficult, if not impossible, for human societies and social groups. In every human group there is less reason to guide and to check impulse, less capacity for self-transcendence, less ability to comprehend the needs of others and therefore more unrestrained egoism than the individuals, who compose the group, reveal in their personal relationships." The result is that "the relations between groups must therefore always be predominantly political rather than ethical."[1]

Why is it that the morality of groups is necessarily inferior to that of the individuals that compose them? In part, Dr. Niebuhr thinks, it is "merely the revelation of a collective egoism, compounded of the egoistic impulses of individuals, which achieve a more vivid expression and a more cumulative effect when they are united in a common impulse than when they express themselves separately and discretely." Conversely, it may be stated that man's natural endowment for coöperation—the natural impulse that prompts him to consider the needs of others even when they conflict with his own—becomes, in all but very rare cases, ineffective in relations between social groups.

---

[1] In ascribing an amoral character to group activities Dr. Niebuhr is not himself taking an amoral stand. Quite the contrary: he has set himself the task of finding "political methods which will offer the most promise of achieving an ethical social goal for society." But society itself will never consciously accept a purely moral goal and strive towards it; the formulation of such a goal is the task of the individual reformer who is also enough of a realist both to perceive and utilize man's latent moral capacities and to take account of the limits of human nature, especially in its collective manifestations.

This ineffectiveness cannot be properly accounted for by supposing (with Hobbes and Mandeville) that men are naturally egoists, for this ignores the familiar phenomenon of men who in their relations with other individuals are generous and considerate becoming instruments of an aggressive and unjust national or economic policy.

The phenomenon is clarified somewhat by the following consideration. An individual has a right to sacrifice his own interests in another's behalf, but what statesman is justified in sacrificing the interests of his State to the interests of those outside it? "No State," declares Johannes Haller, whom Dr. Niebuhr quotes, "has ever entered a treaty for any other reason than self-interest. . . . A statesman who has any other motive would deserve to be hung." We can no doubt understand a statesman who is an out-and-out egoist looking only to his own advancement and gain. We can understand and admire a statesman who conscientiously subordinates his own interests to the interests of those he governs. But a third kind of statesman, one who was willing to sacrifice both his own and his fellow-citizens' interests to the interests of outsiders, would be thought mad—if indeed such a prodigy could ever have made his way into statecraft in the first place. Certainly he would find but few followers and would never succeed in putting his projects into effect. Or if by any chance he did, his behavior would be viewed with suspicion and incomprehension even by those whom it was designed to benefit. Such considerations should suffice to convince one that a human collective cannot act disinterestedly. They show why it is that patriotism (like any other form of group loyalty) transforms individual unselfishness into group egoism. This seems a paradox but it is a sufficiently familiar one. Patriotism gives expression both to the individual's self-subordination to the nation and to his self-assertion expressed vicariously through the nation. The combination gives, in Dr. Niebuhr's words, "a tremendous force to national egoism, which neither religious nor rational idealism can ever completely check."

Apologists for war

There are many who will approve of this national egoism, particularly for their own nation, and of the state of war to which sooner or later it always leads. Count Moltke, speaking for that small group of German militarists whose outspokenness caused them to be popularly regarded as the villains of the last war, declared that "war brings out the noblest virtues, courage and self-denial, devotion to duty and readiness for self-sacrifice even to the point of giving up life itself." And his fellow-countryman Treitschke based an approval of war on a philosophy of ruthless political idealism:

When a State recognizes that existing treaties no longer express the actual political conditions, and when it cannot persuade the other Powers to give way by peaceful negotiation, the moment has come when the nations proceed to the ordeal by battle. . . . The righteousness of war depends simply and solely upon the consciousness of a moral necessity. War is justified because the great national personalities can suffer no compelling force superior to themselves, and because history must always be in constant flux; war therefore must be taken as part of the divinely appointed order.[1]

---

[1] *Politics*, Vol. II, pp. 597–598. (Reprinted by permission of The Macmillan Company.) The word 'personality' is not accidental. The State, Treitschke says, is "the most supremely real person, in the literal sense of the word, that exists" (Vol. I, p. 17). It has a real will manifesting itself independently of the individual wills of its members; and it has a real memory, expressed as its "continuity with bygone generations" and in which is found "the continuous legalized intention of the past."

Rhetorical swagger of this kind loses most of its force alongside the plain bare facts of modern warfare:

> Bodies are lying about in the streets and fields often most horribly mutilated, but we must not trouble about the dead; we go on as if they were not there.   All humane feelings vanish. We have only one idea: 'Advance!'[1]

The greatest evil of war is not that men are killed and mutilated—automobile accidents can accomplish as much —but that humane feelings and the sense of fair play are destroyed.   The wars of old romantic tales in which two heroes engage in a hand-to-hand sportsmanlike joust have faded into the oblivion of history.   In the conduct of modern wars sportsmanship and decency have no place. Individuals are insignificant units in a vast machine. Even their opinions and emotions are controlled by officially sanctioned lies which they are powerless until long afterwards to detect.[2]

Not least among the evils of modern wars is their futility and aimlessness.   No nations receive any lasting benefit from a modern war: the cost is too great.   Even America, which as Europe's creditor seemed for a time to have reaped material advantages from the War of 1914–1918, is now, sixteen years after the Armistice, floundering in a depression among the principal causes of which are the economic dislocations that the war brought about.

Nor is the aim of a nation in going to war likely to be single and clearly defined.   Individuals may go to war with idealistic aims: indeed, one function of wartime propaganda is to popularize such aims.   But the causes of war taken as a whole are a baffling complex of factors—eco-

---

[1]Henri Barbusse, quoted in *What Would Be the Character of a New War?*

[2]See Arthur Ponsonby, *Falsehood in War-Time*, for an interesting collection of documents showing some of the diverse ways in which atrocity stories and other lies about the enemy were manufactured in 1914–1918.

.iomic, political, racial, moral.   When a nation seems to itself and perhaps to its allies (never to its enemies!) to be going to war with a moral aim, it is well to question how far this seemingly moral aim is a mere *ideology*—*i.e.,* an ideal or group of ideals fashioned by events which it serves to justify rather than, as it appears to do, originally motivating these events.   For example, a primary reason why France busied herself building a diplomatic network around Germany prior to 1914 and why French nationalism (even before the 1914 German invasion) became so strong, was a feeling widespread among Frenchmen that France had been unjustly robbed of Alsace and Lorraine in 1871 and that revenge and recapture would be morally justified.   But the policy of 'revanche' that guided so much of French policy during the pre-war period was not wholly a matter of national sentiment.   The iron fields of Lorraine were yielding annually about three-quarters of the German consumption of iron.   Furthermore, the Germans had been misled in 1871 by the reports of their geologists into supposing that the boundary lines fixed by the treaty of that year gave all the iron ore on the Briey plateau to Germany; whereas much richer deposits were subsequently discovered on the French side of the border.   This, according to John Bakeless, is one of the chief reasons why the policy of 'revanche' did not die out:

In the minds of the people 'revanche' meant a patriot's desire to see the hereditary foe humbled and the lost provinces again restored to France.   But in the minds of the masters of French industry and the journalists who formed the popular mind, 'revanche'—whatever else it may have meant—implied the restoration within French boundaries of the deposits of coal and iron which industrial growth demanded, and the protection of the fields which were already theirs.[1]

---

[1]*The Economic Causes of Modern War*, p. 153.   (Moffat, Yard.)

The mixture of economic and idealistic motives is a recurring phenomenon throughout American history. The Civil War was fought, at the beginning,[1] over the right of States to secede from the Union. Northern volunteers enlisted with full sincerity to enforce the preservation of their nation. At the same time the war had an economic aspect—it was a battle to the death between the northern manufacturing interests favoring high tariffs and centralized authority and the southern agrarians favoring low tariffs and State individualism. Was the idealistic or the economic factor foremost in provoking the conflict? It would be hard to say.

In the dealings that the United States has had with Latin America a similar mixture of motives is observable. In 1915, for example, a wave of popular indignation swept over the newspaper readers of this country when President Villbrun Guillaume Sam of Haiti had two hundred political prisoners butchered, after which he was in turn seized and beheaded by a mob. To the average newspaper reader it seemed the fulfillment of a manifest moral duty when the United States promptly sent marines to Haiti to restore order. But there was a catch. About a year earlier the United States had tried to impose on Haiti a treaty such as had already been forcibly concluded with Santo Domingo, giving the United States charge of the collection of customs and debts. Haiti had withstood the United States' demands. After the landing of the marines in the summer of 1915, however, Haiti was forced to consent that the United States name a General Receiver and Financial Adviser to control Haitian finances and see that bankers owning Haitian bonds get their due, and to consent further to the United States' armed inter-

---

[1] Later on, in the second year of the war, the slavery question began to take precedence.

vention at any time for the protection of life, liberty, and property. (Property in this connection, be it noted, turns out in practice to mean principally corporate property, including the interest rates claimed by northern banks; liberty, to mean the removal of restrictions on economic penetration.) Possession of financial control facilitated the purchase by northern capitalists of Haitian banks, land, sugar mills, railways, and other property, and enabled them subsequently to manipulate the election of a president favorable to American interests. To a foreign observer this invasion of Haitian rights might have seemed primarily due to economic greed. Whatever truth may lie in such an interpretation the ideological aspect of the invasion is not to be overlooked. "The Americans are in Haiti," the New York *Times* declared editorially, "to raise its people from a state of ignorance and savagery for which their rulers were responsible."[1]

Patriotism traditionally meant a willingness to give one's life blood for one's native home and lands and people. Today there are powerful forces at work trying by propaganda and suppression, through press and radio, textbooks and schools, to translate patriotism into a willingness to fight for American interests abroad: to fight for the Monroe Doctrine, for example, which has come in its modern applications to mean fighting to keep control of the nitrates of Chile or of the silver mines and oil fields of Mexico or of a projected canal in Nicaragua.

"Where freedom is," said Benjamin Franklin, "there is my country." The modern cosmopolitan puts it otherwise. "Where my capital is," he answers, "there is mine."[2]

---

[1]Quoted by Parker Thomas Moon, *Imperialism and World Politics*, on whose authority the present account of the Haitian affair is largely based.

[2]Henry Noel Brailsford, *Property or Peace*, p. 198.

The munitions traffic

An even more direct and intensified causal relation between capitalism and war is found in the case of those businesses whose profits come from the manufacture and sale of munitions. Everyone now knows the story of Sir Basil Zaharoff, munitions magnate and one of the world's wealthiest men, who got his start by helping to inaugurate the Græco-Turkish War of 1897, selling first a submarine to Greece his native country, thereby giving Turks the jitters so that he could sell two submarines to Turkey, which in turn boomed the Grecian market, and so on, finally producing war. Thus it may be said that "the armament industry operates with one curious advantage over any other business in the world; the greater the competition the greater the amount of business for *all* competitors. . . . If a Schneider-Creusot salesman sells 100,000 rifles to Yugoslavia he has already eased the path of the Vickers-Armstrong salesman in selling 200,000 rifles to Italy. . . . The trade in arms is the only one in which an order obtained by a competitor increases that of his rivals."[1]

Nor is it only by stimulating the mutual fears of rival nations that munitions makers promote war. Methods more direct are also used. Often the connection is effected by an interlocking directorate. Thus Skoda, the biggest Czecho-Slovakian armament firm and one of the biggest in Europe, is controlled by a holding company, whose head is a French citizen, M. Eugène Schneider, president of Schneider-Creusot, the leading armament firm of France. M. Schneider is also a director of the Comité des Forges, which through another of its officers owns

---

[1] *Arms and the Men*, by the editors of *Fortune*. (Doubleday, Doran reprint. pp. 47–48.) The last sentence is a quotation from Delaisi, the French economist.

controlling shares in the principal and semi-official newspaper of France, *Le Temps*, an influential organizer of popular opinion. In America, as a second example, the Navy League, which opposed with partial success the disarmament conference between the United States, Great Britain, and Japan in 1930, was not as the name might connote a disinterestedly patriotic organization. Its original founders were eighteen men and one corporation: the corporation was the Midvale Steel Co., seller of armor plate to the government; the individuals included Charles G. Schwab (Bethlehem Steel), J. P. Morgan (U. S. Steel), Col. R. M. Thompson (International Nickel Co., which supplies the government with nickel for making shells), and B. F. Tracy, former Secretary of the Navy and afterwards attorney for the Carnegie Steel Corporation.[1]

4. Capitalism and Human Values

What is to be our final evaluation of capitalism? Are the evils which it contains essential to its nature or merely incidental and capable of elimination without destroying the structure of capitalism itself? This is a major question at issue between the left-wing and right-wing divisions of those who criticize the *status quo*—*i.e.*, between those groups popularly known as radical and those known as liberal. Liberals hope that by applying experimental technique to urgent questions of social and economic life and by developing a program of education that will inculcate a more socialized outlook among members of the coming generations it will be possible to retain the advantages of capitalist enterprise while gradually transforming the forces of reaction and predatory self-interest into forces working for the common weal. Radicals retort

---

[1]These together with many similar facts are substantiated in an interesting book on the munitions traffic: Engelbrecht and Honighan, *Merchants of Death.*

that the liberal attitude is unrealistic, that entrenched
privilege will never voluntarily relinquish any of its
power, and that more socialized programs of education
will be an unrealized dream so long as the schools, the
press, the radio, and other educational media continue to
be, in the last resort, under the domination of capitalist
groups. The issue here at stake may be expressed as
reform vs. revolution: can the faults of capitalism be
corrected within the framework of capitalism itself or
will nothing short of a demolition of capitalism suffice?

The former of these alternatives is illustrated by the
codes formulated by the Rotary International as well as
by many particular business associations for the purpose
of raising the ethical standards of particular types of
business and industry. The Business Methods Program
of Rotary for 1924-1925, as quoted by Professor Taeusch,
proposed that business associations bring pressure upon
their member organizations to discountenance such practices as "(1) Inducing the seller to reduce his prices by
indicating, contrary to fact, that you have received a
lower quotation on the same quality of merchandise;
(2) obtaining an extra discount by leading the seller to
believe that the buyer will order a certain quantity of
goods during the season: (3) arbitrarily taking a discount
after the date for earning the same has expired; (4) mis-
representing market conditions to justify prices charged
or to induce the customer to increase his order."[1] While
the recommendations of Rotary affect mainly the business
practices of wholesale traders and middlemen, governmental agencies such as those embodied in President
Roosevelt's National Recovery Act have undertaken to
carry out similar reforms on a larger scale.

Sceptics may question, however, whether any really sig-

[1] Quoted by Carl F. Taeusch, *Professional and Business Ethics*. (Holt.)

nificant reforms can be brought about in either of these ways. The reforms proposed by Rotary appear, on more careful examination, to be designed principally to benefit in one way or another the small business men of which Rotary is largely composed. Rotary has made no comparable efforts in the interests of the consumer or the employed worker as such. And while it is perhaps too early[1] to predict the outcome of President Roosevelt's N.R.A. policies a cursory reading of the press shows how widely the provisions of the N.R.A. codes are being ignored, often with the connivance of local governmental agencies, as soon as they threaten to curtail the unrestricted profit-taking of the businesses affected. Scepticism as to the possibility of effective partial reforms has led many contemporary thinkers to look askance at the institution of capitalism itself.

Counterfeit moral values

Ruthless business spoliation, whatever its dangers, is a less widely spread result of capitalism than is the passive inclination to accept money values as the final criterion of good. It is a truism that most aspects of contemporary life are tending to become commercialized, even arts and sports. "Today," writes Stuart Chase, "organized recreation is largely in the hands of business interests, and as there is more money to be made from watchers than from players, playing tends to become more and more of a commercial as against a sporting undertaking, and watching becomes a matter of astute publicity and quantity production." As for certain of the arts: "A young virtuoso attempting the entry into a concert tour of America has a strict and time honored path to tread which consists chiefly of bribing the several musical journals by means of

[1]December, 1934.

a sufficient number of paid advertisements to command favorable notices."[1] Granted that there are honorable exceptions and even attempts at organized reform of these tendencies, still their growth under capitalism is a matter for serious reflection. And perhaps even more harmful, because more widespread, is the effect of capitalist society on the character of the average American:

He (your typical American) is out to make money, because in no other way can he acquire equivalent social status. The only way he can make money—or even survive, for the most part, is to exploit or be exploited in the general scheme of mechanized acquisitiveness. His habits, or worse, his lack of sustaining habits, are determined for him by the economic and social compulsion by which he is ruled; these stand over him with the constant threat of failure, starvation, or ostracism. Having no experience, indeed no opportunity for creation—for developing a creative relationship either to materials or to people—he needs 'recreation' and needs it badly. He sings and listens to the singing of jazz songs, and torch songs, the words of which are nonsense, the rhythm of which is perverse and masturbatory rather than normally and vigorously sexual. He dopes himself with similar inhuman nonsense at the movies; he keeps the radio turned on during meals in order to deaden the torture of his unconsciously realized impotence and disintegration; he drives his automobile at seventy miles an hour, killing chickens, cats, and human beings, in order to give himself a momentary feeling of power and significance. He instinctively calls business a 'game' thereby reconciling a conflict: it is appropriate for a game to be silly and even a little cruel. He plays this game at the frantic speed that is appropriate to farce; he hurries to business, hurries through lunch, hurries home again at night, substituting so far as possible motion for emotion. His happiness is never actual, it is always hung in front of him like a feed bag in front of a mule. . . .

The Greeks, as Goethe pointed out, lived creatively in the present. The man in the streets of medieval Paris or London lived emotionally in the promise of an extra-terrestrial heaven.

---

[1] *The Tragedy of Waste*, pp. 97 and 105.

We live in the no-man's land of a disappearing terrestrial future. The dilemma is tragic.   The action is the continuously accelerated action of farce.[1]

Concluding remark

The aim of the present chapter has been to present the case for and against capitalism, not to propose a cure or a solution.   Whether capitalism is capable of being drastically reformed so as more nearly to approximate the moral standards acceptable to humane and enlightened men or whether the establishment of a juster and worthier society must be sought in terms of some different type of social organization is a question which the foregoing discussion has been intended only to formulate, not to answer.   The finding of an adequate answer will doubtless be one of the severest tasks with which students of social ethics during the next few years will be faced.

[1] James Rorty, "The Great Wall Facing America," in *The Symposium*, October, 1932.

PART IV
FROM ETHICS TO PHILOSOPHY

CHAPTER XII

METAPHYSICAL BACKGROUNDS OF ETHICS

Each of us calls those ideas clear that are in the same state of confusion as his own.
Marcel Proust

THERE ARE two types of philosophical problem suggested by a study of ethics. First of all there is the question of what assumptions have to be made if ethics is to exist as a valid field of inquiry. Prerequisite assumptions of this kind are called *postulates*, and their nature has already been hinted at in the analysis of the moral situation given in Chapter I. That there exist available goods which we are free to choose or reject is an ethical postulate, for if it were denied ethical discussion would be meaningless. We may say, therefore, that the *ethical realm of discourse* presupposes this postulate. In addition to the group of postulates, whose truth is presupposed by any ethical theory whatever, there are certain beliefs of another sort—*e.g.*, beliefs in God and in the moral progress of mankind—which, while not presupposed by the ethical realm of discourse as such, have an unusually intimate connection with ethics and are often supposed to afford a necessary basis for a *satisfactory* ethical attitude.

1. ETHICAL DIALECTIC

The problem of the nature and logical presuppositions of ethics is not itself an ethical problem but a philosophical one. It is the task of philosophy to examine the various aspects of experience, or 'realms of discourse,'—

scientific, moral, aesthetic, religious, economic, privately emotional, outwardly everyday aspects, and as many more as these labels fail to cover—determining their natures and their interrelations with one another. Philosophy itself is not so much a realm of discourse as a mode of inquiry. It is a way of dealing with things that is at once profoundly appreciative and profoundly critical. "It sees the familiar as if it were strange," William James has written, "and the strange as if it were familiar. . . . It rouses us from our native dogmatic slumber and breaks up our caked prejudices."[1]

At once the hardest and the most important thing for the incipient student of philosophy to learn is that 'truth' from a philosophical standpoint does not mean quite what it does in any of the more specialized fields of inquiry. The truths of the mathematician have to be stated in terms of numbers and numerical relations, the truths of the physicist in terms of n-dimensional events, the truths of the behaviorist in terms of stimuli and responses and the conditioning of responses, the truths of the psychologist in terms of images, impulses and other phases of awareness, the truths of the economist in terms of exchange-value and its derivatives, the truths of the theologian in terms of the attributes and manifestations of God. But philosophy is the attitude which transcends these compartmentalized views of knowledge. It represents man's striving after some more unified outlook, and consequently involves questions concerning the interrelations of the various realms of inquiry (each containing its own set of presuppositions and its own manner of discourse), and the meanings and values which each of them possesses when viewed with reference to, so far as we can discern it, the Whole. Suppose a man asks, What am I?

[1] *Some Problems of Philosophy*, p. 7.

The physicist answers, an intricate pattern of trillions of electric charges; the chemist, a compound of numerous solids and juices; the biologist, an animal organism struggling to adapt itself to a morally indifferent environment; the behaviorist, a complicated machine responding predictably to stimuli; the psychologist, a congeries of qualitatively diverse mental events; the economist, a social unit with a certain capacity to produce, to earn, to spend, and to consume; the theologian, a living soul bearing the mark of the divine.   Which of these descriptions is true?   To the philosopher the question itself is erroneous: the problem is not one of choice but of integration.   Each of the many fields of knowledge describes some aspect of oneself or of one's world; truth is not confined to any one of them. Philosophy regards truth *dialectically*, recognizing both the positive degree of truth and also the truth-limitations of each of the realms of discourse it investigates.

The nature of dialectic

Dialectic is the technique by which the philosophical attitude is made explicit and effective.   This does not mean that the method of philosophy is essentially different in kind from the thinking that is directed towards normal problems of the everyday world.   For:

All thinking, so far as it is genuinely thinking and not merely a repetition of words, is to an extent dialectical.   Our reasoning is never purely linear, starting with clearly defined presuppositions and moving by a definite number of distinct steps to a strictly implied conclusion.   Once an act of reasoning has been completed it can be represented as consisting of formal relationships. . . .   Such a representation is extremely useful: while it does not describe the way the reasoning took place it does show the implicit relations which determine whether we shall build up formal constructions in one direction rather than another.   But if we think of reasoning in this way it is because we are looking at the results rather than at the actual process.[1]

In scientific reasoning, for example, there is not merely a mustering of separate data from which, when mustered, one conclusion follows with rigorous inevitability.   Data have meaning only by virtue of their interconnections with other known data, with hypotheses regarding data to come, and with intellectual structures into which hypotheses and data are patterned.   A scientific discovery is not a mere addition of a fact to a solid body of preëxistent knowledge.   There is also a newly critical attitude formed towards some aspect of the preëxistent knowledge itself.   Science, in short, like every other field of inquiry, is organic rather than mechanical: scrutinize any one of its aspects thoroughly enough, and there is no foretelling how far you may revolutionize the whole subject-matter.

But while science like all other reasoning is dialectical to some extent, the extent will be in each case limited by the presuppositions and definitions that determine a field of discourse.   Doctors may formulate various hypotheses of the cause of cancer, but no doctor speaking as a scientist would ascribe it to, *e.g.*, a visitation of divine wrath. Animistic interpretations are excluded from a strictly scientific view of the world, for science *by definition* is concerned only with what is (1) publicly and under the same conditions repeatedly verifiable, and (2) expressible in strictly logical, preferably mathematical, terms; and manifestations of God are neither of these.   Even when, as at present, no cause of cancer answering to both requirements has been discovered, scientific inquiry proceeds

---

[1]Burnham and Wheelwright, *Introduction to Philosophical Analysis*, p. 171. (Holt.)

always on the assumption that there is such a cause and that any 'supernatural' explanation is false; as well as on the hope and expectation that future experiments will succeed in discovering such a cause.

Philosophy is characterized on its technical side by the greater thoroughness of its dialectical procedure. The philosophical approach to mathematics, to physical science, to psychology, to economics, to religion, to metaphysics, or to ethics involves in each case an inquiry into (1) the fundamental *terms of discourse* on which the meanings peculiar to each field are based, and (2) the fundamental *presuppositions* of each field. In ordinary types of inquiry into the physical world, for example,[1] *space*, *time*, *event*, and *power* are terms of discourse which must be (and fortunately *are*) understood without definition, and by means of which such terms as *cause* and *velocity* can be defined; *that every event has a cause* is a basic presupposition, on which all specific inquiries into the cause of this or that event must rest. Sometimes, to be sure, there is no settled agreement as to the fundamental terms and presuppositions of a particular field, but the lack does not prevent an effort of dialectical inquiry from being made.

'Good' as a primary indefinable

The most fundamental of the terms employed in ethics seems to be, as argued in Chapter I, the term 'good.' Only if the meaning of 'good' is somehow apprehended without definition can ethical inquiry be carried on. The original ap-prehension may be very rudimentary; a more adequate com-prehension of the meaning of the word is

---

[1]As distinguished from the types of inquiry undertaken by relativity physics, which, being farther removed from concrete aspects of human experience, have less value as illustrations of the dialectical method in ethics.

likely to be developed in the course of the inquiry. Acquaintance, in this as in all other fields, must precede knowledge.

My point is that 'good' is a simple notion, just as 'yellow' is a simple notion; that, just as you cannot, by any manner of means, explain to anyone who does not already know it, what yellow is, so you cannot explain what good is. Definitions of the kind that I was asking for, definitions which describe the real nature of the object or notion denoted by a word, and which do not merely tell us what the word is used to mean, are only possible when the object or notion in question is something complex. You can give a definition of a horse, because a horse has many different properties and qualities, all of which you can enumerate. But when you have enumerated them all, when you have reduced a horse to his simplest terms, then you can no longer define those terms. They are simply something which you think of or perceive, and to anyone who cannot think of or perceive them, you can never, by any definition, make their nature known. . . . We can, for instance, make a man understand what a chimaera is, although he has never heard of one or seen one. You can tell him that it is an animal with a lioness's head and body, with a goat's head growing in the middle of its back, and with a snake in place of a tail. But here the object which you are describing is a complex object; it is entirely composed of parts, with which we are all perfectly familiar—a snake, a goat, a lioness; and we know, too, the manner in which those parts are to be put together, because we know what is meant by the middle of a lioness's back, and where her tail is wont to grow. And so it is with all objects, not previously known, which we are able to define: they are all complex; all composed of parts, which may themselves, in the first instance, be capable of similar definition, but which must in the end be reducible to simplest parts, which can no longer be defined. But yellow and good, we say, are not complex: they are notions of that simple kind, out of which definitions are composed and with which the power of further defining ceases.[1]

---

[1]George Edward Moore, *Principia Ethica*, pp. 7-8. (Reprinted by permission of The Macmillan Company, publishers.)

In spite of this one logical property possessed in common by 'yellow' and 'good' there are two important differences between the terms. The first difference is one of meaning. Yellow is yellow: apart from differences of shade and some rather indefinite differences of emotional tone the meaning of yellow tends to be entirely contained in what is intuited. Good, on the other hand, carries an infinite variety of possible meanings, which it is the task of the student and practitioner of ethics, so far as he can, to realize. This difference is indicated by the fact that there is such a thing as ethics, which purports to be a systematic inquiry into the nature of the good, while a similarly developed inquiry into the nature of yellow[1] would be impossible. The second difference is *epistemological:* a difference of the essential manner in which the terms are known. While both terms are 'intuited'—*i.e.*, known, or an essential part of them known, by direct acquaintance rather than by indirect evidence—the intuition of yellow is entirely perceptual, while the intuition of good seems to be bound up in a most complicated way with various emotional and kinaesthetic responses.

The meaning of good, then, is intuited dynamically as a potential and desirable end of action, and as the actions which it invites are performed or left unperformed, whether actually or in imagination, the meaning which an individual attaches to 'good' undergoes, for better or worse, a development. This development, we must suppose,[2] modifies to some degree the course of future actions and emotions, and thus the interaction of acts and ideals becomes (for those of us who are not entirely creatures of impulse and habit) more and more involved. In its more

---

[1] *I.e.*, the color; not the causally related light-waves, which are objects of inquiry in terms of the science of physics.
[2] See Postulate iii, below.

developed forms the idea of good becomes a matter for deliberate analysis and criticism, such analysis and criticism constituting the form of ethical inquiry. Good is thus on the one hand directly experienced as any object of interest or desire, for whatever appears interesting or desirable to a person appears to him as in some way good, even though conventions of thought and language may not permit a frank avowal. But in another and much more important sense good is taken to mean not what evokes capricious interest and irresponsible desire, but what appears as interesting or desirable after alternatives have been examined, consequences weighed, and implicit values given full conscious recognition.

Five postulates of ethics

The five basic postulates of ethics that are given below are called *postulates* rather than axioms, for it is quite possible to deny any one of them intelligibly. A denial of the mathematical axiom that quantities equal to the same quantity are equal to each other would seem to have no intelligible meaning worth speaking of. But a denial of the presuppositions of ethics could be made logically intelligible. Their truth is established not by internal logical necessity but as implied by certain essential meanings found within the field of ethics. Affirm that ethical inquiry is possible and of some significance, and you necessarily affirm the truth of the ethical postulates; deny these and you deny the possibility of ethics along with them. As the possibility of ethical inquiry (or, more technically stated, the reality of the ethical realm of discourse) is presumably admitted by readers of the present volume, no demonstration of it seems necessary, even if a demonstration were possible.

(1) *Postulate of value.* This postulate has already been

amply discussed.[1] It asserts that *value is a significant category: i.e.,* that some things, whether actual or imaginable, have value. To have value is to be, in the widest sense of the word, good. And since good is a relative term, and has meaning only when applied to what is somehow better than something else, we may assert as a corollary of Postulate *i* that *some things, whether actual or imaginable, are better than others;* which is to say that there are at least sometimes intelligible grounds for preferences.

(*ii*) *Postulate of non-actuality.* This postulate, which asserts that *at least some values are incompletely realized,* is implicit in Nicolai Hartmann's distinction (p. 135) between the ideal Ought-to-be and the positive Ought-to-be. If actual existence were the embodiment for all time of the highest values conceivable, if the Universe were at every point and in every respect perfect, then even if the divinities inhabiting such a universe were by some miracle of insight able to comprehend the nature of good, their comprehension would involve no moral duties, no 'ought'; for since the good and the actual would be *ex hypothesi* eternally identical, any moral effort directed towards making them so would be superfluous.

(*iii*) *Postulate of possibility.* Not only is the good to some extent unachieved; it must also, if there is such a thing as morality, be to some extent achievable. This third postulate affirms the reality of moral choice: *there are some acts which it lies within the power of a moral agent to perform or leave unperformed.* As stated in Chapter I, "neither 'must' nor 'cannot' is in the strict sense compatible with 'ought.'" We say that a person ought to do only what there is reason to believe that he can do: 'ought' therefore implies 'can.'

---

[1]See especially pp. 13–14, and 135–137; *cf.* pp. 49–51.

Although Postulate *iii* is implied by the meaning of 'ought' (*i.e.*, 'ought' in the moral sense, or what Dr. Hartmann has called the Ought-to-do), it does not in turn imply it. That an act is possible does not imply that it ought to be performed. However, when the first three postulates are taken together the validity of the moral 'ought' does follow. When a certain object or state of affairs is recognized by a certain agent as a good (*i.e.*, as better than certain alternatives), when its achievement is not yet actual, and when its achievement lies within the agent's power, then it becomes the agent's duty (so far as not opposed by some superior duty) to achieve it.[1]

(*iv*) *Postulate of permanence.* Moral choice, as declared in Chapter I, is consequential: the alternative values to which it refers are not wholly transitory. The fourth postulate is thus an assertion that moral values persist; that *the same action or situation remains morally good or bad to the same degree, except so far as circumstances relevant to the judgment of it are altered.*

At first glance the fourth postulate seems either false or tautologous. Moral judgments do change, it will be argued, and frequently actions or situations which once seemed to a certain degree good or bad will, even by the wisest and most dispassionate members of a later generation, be judged quite differently. And if, on the other hand, the term 'relevant circumstances' is allowed to cover all the changes of opinions and manners that determine the moral judgments characteristic of a given period and environment, the postulate becomes reduced to a tautology, for it seems now to say merely that actions

---

[1]There is another postulate also involved here: the causal postulate, which asserts that the same causes (means) will in identical circumstances produce the same effects (ends.) The causal postulate is not a postulate of the field of ethics but is presupposed in any application of ethical conclusions to the actual world.

and situations retain the same degree of goodness or badness except to the extent that men's judgments about
them, and the conditions affecting men's judgments,
change.

In reply, let it be said that the circumstances which
are relevant to a reflective moral judgment do not wholly
exclude nor yet wholly include all the changes of opinion,
custom, and sentiment that form the *Weltanschauung* of a
particular age. Relevance never goes by rule; it is a
matter for discrimination. To understand the right relation of the temporal to the eternal is one of the most
crucial tests of human wisdom. At any rate, we do all
of us recognize that some changes in circumstances are
more relevant to a moral decision than others. But judgments of relevance are easily twisted by the forces of
impulse and desire, and trifling mutations of circumstance are made excuses for abandonment of duty. The
fourth postulate, on its practical side, sets limits to the
mutability of moral judgments. It declares the validity
of ideal standards which are relatively independent of
circumstances, and which objectify moral choice by making it *responsible*. "To rate something," writes Ramon
Fernandez, "is precisely to preserve it, in a way of decree,
from the caprices of personal appreciation; it is to give
it a right over oneself, and thereby the cogency of law.
. . . If I judge it proper to act always in such a way
as to respect a certain principle, my judgment can be
analyzed as follows: I have first given consent to the
principle which seems to me to sum up and define my
craving for the good; then, in the same movement, I
have made this principle into a law, in order to guarantee
me against myself."[1] What particular principles are to
be accepted as authoritative is, of course, a further ques-

[1] "A Humanist Theory of Value," *The Criterion*, January, 1930, p. 241.

tion. They may be in agreement with, but they may
equally well be opposed to, the accepted moral conventions of one's time. The essential thing is that they
should be the agent's own; it must be *his* craving for the
good that they sum up and define. They may even,
within limits, change: indeed, it is a generally acknowledged condition of a developed morality that its principles
should be capable of some development. To what degree
moral principles may be made flexible without losing all
their efficacy depends on each moral agent; each makes the
decision at his own risk, and the stakes for each are his
own character and the kind of self he is going to become
—the health, as Socrates was wont to say, of the soul.

  (*v*) *Postulate of social objectivity.* None of the foregoing
postulates refers explicitly to the agent's relation to other
persons. All ethical inquiry seems to involve such a
reference at least implicitly, and in social ethics the reference becomes explicit. The fifth postulate is thus of
significance particularly as a basis for social ethics: an
egoist could consistently ignore it. The postulate affirms that *persons are of equal worth except so far as some
difference other than the bare difference of selfhood is present.*
Of course, some difference other than bare otherness always
is present, so that no situation ever arises in which the
equal worth of two actual persons follows as a simple deduction from this postulate. Instead, the applicability
of the postulate is indirect and contingent: to whatever
extent differences relevant to the moral question at issue
are absent, *to that extent* the rights as well as the duties of
the compared persons approach identity. The same considerations regarding relevance that were made in commenting on Postulate *iv* are applicable here.

  These five postulates establish a framework for ethical
thinking. To deny them is to destroy the theoretical pos-

sibility of ethics. Since they are presupposed in the supposition that ethics is a possible field of inquiry, and since the possibility of significant ethical inquiry is generally admitted, we find in this logical situation a *pragmatic* demonstration of the five postulates. Their acceptance is justified by the importance of the realm of discourse which they make possible. But a pragmatic demonstration, while it is the only kind of demonstration that is possible for certain sets of primary propositions that govern a realm of discourse, is nevertheless valid only if the pragmatically demonstrated propositions are not independently known to be false. The proposition that all men do in all circumstances have as much regard for others' welfare as for their own would no doubt serve as a postulate for a very interesting and important system of social ethics were the proposition by any possibility true. Unfortunately we know that it is not. It expresses a simple judgment of fact, which even a casual knowledge of human nature suffices to discredit. The foregoing postulates of ethics are sometimes challenged on the ground that they too are false statements of fact. Postulate *ii* implies that the actual universe is not in all respects as excellent as can be conceived; a doctrine opposed by that type of theological determinism which postulates a God who is at once completely powerful and completely good. Postulate *iii* asserts man's freedom, or occasional freedom, to choose between still open alternatives; scientific determinism declares this assumption of free choice to be factually false. Postulate *v*, in asserting the *a priori* worth of other persons, seems to imply that other persons exist;[1] the theory known as *solipsism* denies even this. Of

---

[1] It would be more accurate to say not that Postulate *v* but that the possibility of applying it is what implies the existence of other persons. From the standpoint of ethics as distinguished from pure logic, however, the distinction is irrelevant.

these three sceptical challenges the most important in terms of contemporary discussion is the challenge to Postulate *iii*. There are not many who question the existence of imperfections in the universe nor the existence of other persons than themselves, but the possibility of free choice is frequently challenged on grounds supposedly provided by both the methodology and the results of the sciences. We must next examine the status of this question, therefore, which is at bottom nothing less than the question of whether scientific enlightenment has shown all moral problems and decisions to be illusory.

2. THE PROBLEM OF FREE CHOICE

The problem of free choice, or as it is less accurately called 'free will,' is this: Is human behavior, including such private mental aspects as emotions, ideas, and volitions as well as overt physical aspects, wholly predetermined by antecedent events or can a conscious being, at the moment of making a choice, be the real instigator, the ultimate source of his actions? The second of these hypotheses is logically equivalent to the second ethical postulate; for if anyone is unequivocally the author of an action it follows that at the moment of choosing the action he *could* have chosen otherwise; and conversely, if (as the ethical postulate requires) he has power to choose between two alternative actions he can fairly be called the author of the action he does choose. The libertarian doctrine, that we are the authors of such actions as we perform uncoerced and 'with our eyes open,' appears at first sight undeniable, but many an apparently undeniable truth turns out on examination to be false. We must examine, therefore, the arguments on which this dispute between *libertarians* (who affirm the possibility of free choice) and *determinists* (who deny it) rests.

Before considering the arguments for determinism it is necessary to define the word more exactly. Determinism in the strict sense of scientific or 'causal' determinism is sometimes confused with *fatalism*, which may be called 'telic' determinism. Fatalism is not scientific and does not usually involve an absolute denial of free choice. It limits one's freedom of choice to details and means, affirming that certain eventual results are preordained regardless of what particular choices may be made. The argument cited by Cicero, that a sick man has no need of a physician since he is either going to die or not, and in the former case a physician will be futile, in the latter case superfluous—is an expression of telic, not causal determinism. More intelligibly telic is the economic determinism of many Marxists: individual revolutionaries, they grant, have a restricted freedom to give or withhold their best energies in the overthrow of the hostile State, but the State's eventual overthrow is none the less a certainty and the caprices of individuals can affect only minor details of its fulfillment.[1] It is evident that telic determinism if believed in might tend seriously to alter the character of one's moral inquiries and of one's sense of moral obligation, but this type of determinism would not make moral deliberation meaningless. There would still be the question of whether I chose to give or withhold allegiance from a historical process that would go on in spite of me and to some non-essential detail of which my efforts might still make some small contribution. Causal determinism, on the other hand, affirms that every detail of a process is as strictly determined in its causes and effects as the process itself. There is no room for any

---

[1] "The Bolshevik slogans and ideas *in general* are completely confirmed, but *concretely* things have shaped themselves otherwise than anybody (no matter who) could have expected—more originally, uniquely, variously."—Lenin, quoted by Trotsky, *The History of the Russian Revolution*, Vol. I, p. 477.

real choice whatever. Nor does it hold events to be determined by reference to an end (*telos*) but strictly by other temporally prior events. This is the type of determinism that logically contradicts Postulate *iii*.

Arguments for causal determinism

(i) Several types of argument have been brought forward in support of causal determinism. The first of these is the inductive argument, an appeal to the progress of the sciences in discovering causal relations and establishing causal explanations. The appearance of comets and solar eclipses, once thought to depend upon the caprices of malignant divinities, are now reduced to exact astronomical laws. In human affairs no such exactitude has yet been achieved, but is not that an accident of the present state of our ignorance? Does not the fact that science is constantly advancing towards more and more unified explanations of phenomena, each step making possible more intricate and more assured predictions of phenomena, suggest the probability that the goal of a completely integrated set of laws may some day, in however distant a future, be reached? Or, leaving millennial speculations aside, can we not draw the inference that right here and now, *if* there existed a wizard-scientist with an exhaustively complete knowledge of past events, such a one could foretell with unerring accuracy every event still enwombed in the future? If we answer this question affirmatively, holding that there is no inherent impossibility in the existence of a wizard omniscient about every detail of the future, then in that admission we admit that the future is predetermined, fixed, unchangeable. And if we admit the future to be predetermined in every slightest detail we deny that there are ever unpredetermined courses of action between which moral agents can make a genuine choice. Moral deliberations and moral decisions become, on this view, mere *epiphenomena*—that is to say, shadows not creators of events.

That the inductive argument for determinism is not logically coercive is shown by the possibility of challenging the minor premise of the argument. Its minor premise asserts that science is moving steadily towards the goal (however distant) of a complete and exhaustive knowledge of all data. This assumption is false—or at any rate is true only in an abstract and quite irrelevant sense. Science is continually increasing the number and complexity of the data of which it is cognizant, but this fact does not justify the inference that science is moving towards any goal of complete knowledge. Such an inference would be valid only if the data which are potential objects of knowledge were finite in number and in kind. It is no true picture of the universe to suppose that it contains a finite number (however large) of data, of which science is bit by bit discovering the natures and causal interconnections. Data are as numerous and as manifold as anyone's experience or imagination—literally anyone's: scientist's or poet's or religious mystic's or cat's or paramecium's—is capable of making them. Even within the realm of the most exact sciences it is a well-known phenomenon that each new discovery, instead of reducing the remainder of discoverable entities by so much (a situation which would necessarily come about if the static view of knowledge implicit in the inductive argument were justified), actually increases the number of discoverable entities without assignable limit. For every fact or law discovered the possibility is revealed of discovering others hitherto unsuspected. New answers open up new and ever more puzzling questions, and there is no evidence that this recessive process has any end. Plainly then, since the goal of complete knowledge recedes faster at every step we take towards it there is no possibility of inductive evidence that such a goal either can or could under any assignable conditions be reached.   This is equivalent to saying that there is no inductive evidence for strict causal determinism.

(ii).   Secondly, there is the *a priori* argument, which in the last analysis rests on an appeal to self-evidence.   *Ex nihilo nihil fit* is a principle that has a plausible ring. Everything must have what the Greeks called an *archê*, a starting-point, which is at the same time its principle of explanation—its *aition*, by which the Greeks meant its cause, or more literally the thing or principle 'responsible' for it.   How can we conceive of anything beginning without an adequate cause?   A more elaborate form of the appeal to self-evidence is sometimes couched in terms of a syllogism: A thing or event which has had a beginning must have had a cause, otherwise it must have produced itself; but to have produced itself it must have existed (*quâ* cause) prior to its own beginning (*quâ* effect), which is a manifest impossibility; therefore everything which has had a beginning must have been caused by something other than itself.

In whatever way it may be phrased the *a priori* argument is not logically coercive.   The simple appeal to self-evidence may do very well to fortify one's own conviction that a proposition is true but it carries no argumentative force against a disputant who begins by doubting or denying the proposition.   The appeal is really to psychology rather than logic, although if successful it provides a basis upon which further logical and normative (though not ethical) arguments may be built.   The syllogistic form of the argument is a clear case of question-begging.   Instead of demonstrating that everything must have been caused, it *assumes* this as its first premise, expanding it into the form of an alternative proposition. Anything must have had a cause, otherwise it must have produced itself: this is but a disguised way of saying (1) that everything must have had a cause and (2) that this cause must be either identical or non-identical with the effect.   Plainly, the first part of this assumption is an unwarranted 'begging' of the conclusion supposedly to be proved.

(iii) There remains the epistemological argument for determinism.   Epistemology is that branch of philosophy which inquires into the nature of knowledge and the characteristics which necessarily attach to any object whatever purely by virtue of the fact that it is known. Kant, who laid the foundations of modern epistemological inquiry, declared causal connection to be a universal character of this sort.   Our minds are such that we never can know an object in isolation from everything else; the act of perceiving or knowing it includes the act of regarding it as related somehow to other objects.   The causal relation in particular is one in terms of which every object is necessarily known.   Objects are intelligible only in a context of causes and effects which are either known, guessed at, wondered about, or taken for granted.   We may be ignorant of just what caused this hurricane or that explosion, but we never doubt that something did.   It is because we are sure that the hurricane or the explosion had some cause that the question 'Why?' becomes significant.   Whether the hurricane and the explosion 'really' had a cause (if 'really' means as things are apart from anyone's knowledge of them) is an irrelevant and probably meaningless question.   Hurricanes and explosions can be thought about and discussed and inquired into only so far as they are objects of the mind's activity, and so far as they are objects of the mind's activity they are inevitably thought of in terms of their causal relation to other events, known or unknown. It is this universal trait of human knowledge that makes science possible. It is because even a thing whose cause is unknown is invariably and confidently believed to have some kind of cause that we become assiduous in trying to discover just what the cause is.

Kant's argument marks an important step in the development of a critical attitude towards the meaning of cause. It is a modified form of the *a priori* argument, appealing not to the characteristics that things must necessarily have in themselves but the characteristics that anything must necessarily have if it is to be a possible object of knowledge. Hume, in *A Treatise of Human Nature*, had pointed out that in declaring anything to have had a cause we declare it to have followed by necessity from something else; but that a necessary connection between things can never be known, since we can know only what is given in particular experiences, and necessity is not an empirical datum. Hume drew from this situation a sceptical conclusion; Kant agreed that scepticism is the last word regarding things in themselves, but he challenged Hume's assumption that it is things in themselves that we are talking about when we discuss the nature of objects and inquire into their causal relations:

In metaphysical speculations it has always been assumed that all our knowledge must conform to objects; but every attempt from this point of view to extend our knowledge of objects *a priori* by means of conceptions has ended in failure. The time has now come to ask, whether better progress may not be made by supposing that objects must conform to our knowledge. . . . If it were really necessary for our perception to conform to the nature of objects, I do not see how we could know anything of it *a priori;* but if the sensible object must conform to the constitution of our faculty of perception, I see no difficulty in the matter. . . . For, experience is itself a mode of knowledge which implies intelligence, and intelligence has a rule of its own, which must be an *a priori* condition of all knowledge of objects presented to it. To this rule, as expressed in *a priori* conceptions, all objects of experience must necessarily conform, and with it they must agree.[1]

The chief fault of Kant's argument is found in the rigidity of his psychological presuppositions. Kant himself believed that his inquiry was not concerned with the empirical data that belong to the province of psychology, but he is making at least one unwarranted assumption about such data. When he says that "intelligence has a rule of its own" he is assuming (as subsequent pages of the *Critique* make increasingly clear) that all intelligences are equally bound by their natures to observe this 'rule'; that all intelligences are equally unable to be cognizant of any object unless in terms of cause-effect relations. But this psychological assumption is an assumption about fact,[2] and its truth or falsity is therefore a matter to be judged by evidence. What the evidence seems to show is that while everyone thinks to some extent in terms of cause, some individuals have less difficulty than others in conceiving of the possibility that a particular object or event, or a particular aspect of some object or event, may exist or occur without the prior occurrence of anything sufficient to explain it. Aristotle, Epicurus, Hume, Renouvier, Bergson, James, and Whitehead could conceive of this possibility; the Stoics, the Cartesian rationalists,

---

[1] *The Critique of Pure Reason:* Preface. Watson's translation. (By permission of The Macmillan Company, publishers.)

[2] It is important to observe a distinction. *If* the psychological assumption were true, then the proposition, "Every event has a sufficient cause," would be, as Kant asserts, an *a priori* proposition. But the psychological assumption itself—*i.e.*, that no one can think of an object as existing independently of any conceivable cause—is a description of human mentalities and the proposition which it asserts is therefore not *a priori* but 'descriptive,' or 'factual.'

Berkeley, and Kant evidently could not. When this psychological fact of personal differences in the attitude towards causal determinism is recognized the epistemological argument no longer gives an absolute conclusion: we can say only that *if an individual* cannot conceive of anything occurring uncaused or insufficiently caused, *to that individual* causation will be a universal characteristic of everything and causal determinism will accordingly be to him apodictically true.

What appears to be a modified version of the epistemological argument for causal determinism is formulated in the following passage from the writings of a contemporary philosopher:

> Even if uniformity is only partially denied, we can no longer, as it seems to me, proceed in our daily affairs with an intellectually confident attitude, of which we can take advantage for our needs and purposes. For facts, on this new supposition, retain the right to swerve unaccountably and to indulge in fits of waywardness and caprice. To a degree, at least, it remains possible that anything may happen at any moment. . . . Once the logic underlying experience is impugned, we have no right to be surprised at the most fantastic capers in nature: at the cow jumping over the moon, at fish careening through the heavens, at an altogether mad and topsy-turvy world.[1]

The writer of this passage has avoided Kant's error of supposing that all persons are completely incapable of doubting the uniformity of nature. She asserts not that a belief in causal uniformity[2] is intrinsically necessary to

---

[1]Marie Collins Swabey, *Logic and Nature*, pp. 75–76. (New York University Press.)

[2]Causal uniformity means that given the same total cause, the same total effect must follow on every occasion, and given the same total effect, the same total cause must on every occasion have preceded. This is but another formulation of the theory that every occurrence must have been 'adequately' caused, for the only standard of adequacy would be the quantity and quality of cause that had preceded some other effect identical with this one.

all thinking, but that it is necessary *if* predictions about future events are to be guided by any objective standards whatever. Deny at any point the perfect working of causal uniformity, the argument runs, and you have no reason to expect it at any other point. Deny a complete cosmos, and you may expect a complete chaos.

The principal objection to this argument seems to be that it is vitiated by an imperfect disjunction. The assumption is made that either everything and every aspect of everything must be predetermined according to some causal law or else that no significant prediction is possible whatever; in other words, that either no occurrences are fortuitous to the slightest degree or else that there is as much chance of anything happening as of anything else. Causal determinists choose the first horn of this dilemma; no one could seriously choose the second. But obviously one can go between the horns, and a number of distinguished philosophers including Aristotle, Reid, Cournot, and Whitehead have agreed in doing so. Suppose the hypothesis is accepted that there are or may be uncaused events or uncaused aspects of events: *probable* predictions are still just as possible and just as valid as they ever were. A laboratory white rat will often act unpredictably. Accept for the moment the hypothesis that at least some of its unpredicted acts have occurred without the prior occurrence of an exactly sufficient cause: there are still always countless aspects of its behavior for which approximate causal explanations can be found; and the zoölogist and psychologist must and do build their sciences upon generalizations from these. That events should happen in an *approximately* predictable way on a *significant majority* of occasions is sufficient to make a science of probabilities possible; and every empirical science is no more than a science of probabilities.

Indeterminism and the assumptions of science

Causal indeterminism is the logical contradictory of causal determinism; it affirms, therefore, the thesis that there exist some kind of fortuitous occurrences at some points in the universe. Naturally there are limits to the extent to which anyone can seriously accept this thesis. That not all occurrences are fortuitous is proved by the fact that there is such a thing as scientific knowledge, which requires statistical, approximate uniformities—*i.e.*, uniformities which hold good in a significant majority of a certain type of cases. Perhaps we can even say that no occurrence is *completely* fortuitous. Indeterminism need not assert more than that some occurrences are fortuitous *in some aspects*. It is in this sense that Aristotle admits the presence of fortuitous elements in the universe. "It is absurd to suppose," he says, "that there must in every case be a principle which can explain the individual thing: not merely with respect to the time at which it occurs and the fact that it occurs at all but even with respect to *its changes in quality*, a great variety of which may be occurring all at once."[1]   There is a sense, of course, in which science records and explains changes in quality but another sense in which it does not. Honey-water (the illustration is Aristotle's) is usually beneficial in case of fever, but it is not always so. Suppose it should happen to fail in its benefits on a particular day—on the day of the new moon. The fact that it was the day of the new moon would have nothing to do with the inefficacy of the honey-water on this occasion. Science can take account of the fact that honey-water is usually beneficial (a statis-

---

[1] *Physics*, Bk. I, Chap. III (186 a, 13–17). Italics added. 'Principle which can explain' is a translation of ἀρχή. A more literal translation of the last clause would be: "as if the change which occurred were not multitudinous."

tical generalization) and also of the fact that whatever occurs on the day of the new moon can also (by stressing certain of its aspects rather than others) be regarded as an instance of some general connection or other. It is with these approximately uniform aspects of things that science deals: "there can be no science of what is accidental, for all science has to do with what takes place either always or on a significant majority of occasions." But this limitation of science does not deny that the accidental exists: "Since not everything exists or happens by necessity and uniformly, but most things happen simply 'as a general rule,' the accidental evidently exists; as, for instance, a pale man is not always cultured nor is he so as a general rule, but since this sometimes happens it must be set down as accidental." Not all connections can be described as taking place either invariably or as a general rule: "there is besides these two alternatives something else: the fortuitous and accidental."[1]

The refutation in the foregoing paragraphs of logical and scientific 'proofs' of causal determinism has established merely the *a priori* possibility of indeterminism. This is all that an *a priori* demonstration can be expected to do—establish not the actuality of anything but simply its possibility, by the refutation of counter-assertions of its impossibility. To assert absolute necessity or absolute impossibility is a dogmatic attitude susceptible to dialectical refutation, except in the case of certain abstract, *structural* propositions whose truth or falsity is clearly deducible from their meaning alone. To assert possibility, on the other hand, is not dogmatic. Recognition that anything *may* be so is an essential step towards an intelligent attitude. Cows *may* jump over the moon, fish *may* career through the heavens. But it is most unlikely.

---

[1] *Metaphysics*, Bk. VI (E), Chap. II (1027 a, 9–28).

A recognition that anything is possible does not lead to knowledge unless it is supplemented by an examination of relevant evidence to discover what is most *probably* the case.

Does science, then, establish the *probability* of causal determinism? Only in a very much qualified sense. It is a postulate of scientific methodology that every particular is related to some other particular according to some uniform law. This postulate expresses the ideal of the more exact sciences like physics, astronomy, and chemistry, but its employment in these sciences is precisely what makes them so abstract and (however indirectly useful) so remote from vital human affairs. The postulate is not a statement of fact, but a *heuristic* proposition—which is to say, a stimulus and directive to further inquiry. Because of the pragmatic necessity of relating each particular of which it takes cognizance to some other particulars in terms of a uniform law, the exact sciences have stripped the particulars with which they deal of more and more of the concrete familiar meanings, since concrete meanings have always an irreducible element of disorder. The events with which pure physics, the most exact of the empirical sciences, is equipped to deal are not things big with meaning like a snowstorm or a war or a momentous decision, but n-dimensional abstractions unintelligible except to technicians. The exact relation between these n-dimensional abstractions and concrete realities like snowstorms and wars and human efforts—even whether there *is* any exact relation between them—is not known, and is not a problem with which the exact sciences are concerned, for they remain exact only at the cost of restricting themselves to the abstract, quantitative aspects of things.

The affirmation of free choice

The possibility that the universe is not wholly pre-determined removes the *a priori* objections to libertarianism, which is the doctrine that there is in conscious beings such a thing as genuine freedom of choice. The positive evidence for freedom of choice cannot be established dialectically;[1] it is found in the intimate knowledge that each person gets of it as he grapples seriously with a moral situation. Largely it is a matter of one's own *will to believe:* William James once remarked, "My first act of free will shall be to believe in free will."[2] The will to believe in free will (however it may be called) is a new and more practicable form in which the ethical requirement of choosable alternatives may be stated. By willing to believe in freedom it is possible that one is thereby enabled to act in such a way as really to achieve a greater freedom than he would otherwise have had. This at all events is a good working hypothesis for would-be moral agents to accept. The strongest evidence for freedom of choice is that a man can and does affirm his right to believe in it and carries out his affirmation into some of the choices of daily life.

3. IDEALS AND BELIEFS

Distinct from the postulates of ethics, which whether explicitly avowed or not are implicit in all moral reasoning and presupposed by any ethical theory whatever, there are certain beliefs that have a more accidental, though still very important, relation to ethics. The most influential of these have been a belief in God, and within the last two or three centuries a belief in social progress. These be-

[1] See, however, Question 2 of the Appendix to this chapter, for Lequier's ingenious attempt to establish 'free will' dialectically.

[2] *Letters*, Vol. I, p. 147. The remark is quoted from an entry in one of James' notebooks.

liefs are not logically necessary to all theories of ethics. There is no logical contradiction between atheism and the good life. The clash between them, if any, tends rather to be emotive and (in a cosmopolitan society like our own) personal. The same is true of the belief that death is annihilation and of the belief that humanity is irretrievably on the down grade. Men's interest in values and of the ultimate place of values in the universe combines with their intellectual curiosity to make these questions of God and the fate of mankind of high importance.

(i) Belief in God

No demonstrations of God's existence are logically coercive. The ontological, cosmological, teleological, and other historically prominent demonstrations[1] will not convince anyone whose disposition is persistently sceptical. The issue is not between two intellectual theories but between two radically opposed dispositions towards the universe. On the one side there is the attitude expressed in the following passage from von Hügel:

What a happiness, what a joy it is to be *quite* sure that there is a God, not anything built up by mere human reasoning, no clever or subtle hypothesis, nothing particularly French or German or English, but something as infinitely more real than the air around us, and the pollen of the flowers, and the flight of the birds, and the trials and troubles and the needs of our little lives, stimulated and enriched by the lives of creatures so different from ourselves, touching us continually all round; and the fundamental assurance is not simply one of variety or even of richness, it is an assurance accompanying and crowning all such sense of variety, of a reality, of the Reality, one and harmonious, strong and self-sufficing, of God.[2]

---

[1] See Glossary for these three demonstrations.

[2] Quoted by Evelyn Underhill in her essay, " Finite and Infinite," *The Criterion*, January, 1932.

These words express the faith of a man to whom religion is not a mere theory, but a way of life; and conversely, whose moral consciousness is united to a consciousness of the spiritual nature of the universe of which he is a part. Opposed to such an attitude stands the agnosticism expressed in this stanza from the *Rubaiyat* of Omar Khayyam:

> Into this Universe, and *Why* not knowing
> Nor *Whence*, like Water willy-nilly flowing;
> And out of it, as Wind along the Waste,
> I know not *Whither*, willy-nilly blowing.

The principal human motives for believing in God, leaving aside purely traditional and purely intellectual acceptances, are the *mystical* and the *moral*. Mysticism, in its broadest meaning, is the direct awareness and acceptance of God's presence in the various aspects of everyday experience. It represents a tendency to see and feel the universe as alive and endowed with personhood rather than as dead and mechanical. When divine personhood is attributed to all parts of the universe and to all aspects of experience indifferently, the resulting philosophy is called *pantheism;* when it is regarded as individualized, as pertaining to one or more conscious beings in the universe, the resulting philosophy is called *theism—mono-* or *poly-* according as the divinities in question are one or plural. In whichever of these forms the personhood of the universe may be interpreted, they all represent a mode of envisioning things basically opposed to the atheistic[1] philosophy expressed by Bertrand Russell:

That Man is the product of causes which had no prevision of the end they were achieving; that his origin, his growth, his

---

[1] It is unfortunate, though I suppose inevitable, that the words *atheism* and *atheistic* are almost universally employed in a pejorative sense. No such connotation is here intended.

hopes and fears, his loves and his beliefs, are but the outcome of accidental collocations of atoms; that no fire, no heroism, no intensity of thought and feeling, can preserve an individual life beyond the grave; that all the labors of the ages, all the devotion, all the inspiration, all the noonday brightness of human genius, are destined to extinction in the vast death of the solar system, and that the whole temple of Man's achievement must inevitably be buried beneath the debris of a universe in ruins—all these things, if not quite beyond dispute, are yet so nearly certain, that no philosophy which rejects them can hope to stand. Only within the scaffolding of these truths, only on the firm foundation of unyielding despair, can the soul's habitation henceforth be safely built.[1]

The mystical, or cognitive, approach to the problem of God is likely to appear to the practical man as mere moonshine, and to the student of modern psychology as a curious type of hallucination. It is at this point that dialectic comes to the support of mysticism. Dialectic, as previously said, does not work by establishing proofs that reality must be of this or that character, but obversely, by showing the limitations of any positive, dogmatic view as to what reality is. We cannot prove by dialectic that God exists, but we can refute by dialectic any proof of his non-existence. Examining the nature and methods of the sciences we discover that *even if a God or gods did exist the nature of science is such that it could not afford any evidence or knowledge of Him or them.*

A human analogy may be offered by way of making this more clear. No one can consistently doubt that people are sometimes conscious, have conscious feelings, and that therefore conscious feelings exist. To a scientific inquiry, however, they are irrelevant, falling outside of the scope of things with which scientific method can deal, whence it happens that behaviorism, which repre-

---

[1] "A Free Man's Worship," Essay III in *Mysticism and Logic.* (W. W. Norton.)

sents the most extreme and thorough-going attempt to apply scientific method to the subject-matter of psychology, paradoxically denies the existence of conscious feelings.   Both of these denials are inherent in the nature of scientific method.   Science, like every way of knowing, is selective; it selects its data according to its fundamental postulate of *what constitutes a veritable datum*.   The data with which any science deals must be objective, in the sense that they must be observable by any *normal* observer under standard conditions.   Furthermore, science deals with its data rationally, which means that the data are structuralized into a system that is essentially intelligible to reason.   Awareness of God is not a rational experience, and it cannot be completely rationalized without destroying it.   "By love may He be gotten and holden; but by thought never," wrote the anonymous author of *The Cloud of Unknowing*.   Nor is such an experience 'normal.'   Divine illumination of the intense, indubitable kind described by mystical writers comes only, if at all, after prolonged detachment from the world and severe 'mortification' of one's normal instincts.   Even minor religious experiences are not vouchsafed to everyone, nor to anyone at all times.   Does this brand them as illusory?

By dialectical method we are enabled to give an accurate, albeit hypothetical, answer to this question.   The content of all religious experiences must be considered illusory *if* we presuppose the scientific postulate that only those things are real which can be (1) objectively verified by all normal observers and (2) fitted into a logically intelligible relationship with other objectively verified facts and theories.   This postulate may be accepted because it gives 'practical' results or it may be accepted as 'something that any reasonable man would believe' (*i.e.*, as a dogma), but it obviously cannot be proved.   There is no logical contradiction in supposing that truth is revealed to rare, not ordinary, states of consciousness. Such a view of truth, indeed, is incalculably older than the democratic notion prevalent today. The choice between these two theories of truth and of the corresponding methods of inquiry is fundamental, and therefore no demonstration of either as against the other can be logically coercive. It follows that unless one *chooses*, whether from motives of practicality or from prejudice, to accept the scientific interpretation of reality as the true one, there is no *a priori* objection to accepting the testimony of seers and prophets and of one's own non-rational states of consciousness as affording a valuable and, in essential respects, true insight into the nature of things.

We pass now to the moral aspect of the question. Many persons believe that atheism and agnosticism afford no sound basis for a moral way of life. Human intuitions, they argue, are so variable and uncertain that if right and wrong depend on them alone how can moral standards possess objective validity? We may on one occasion be possessed by a strong intuition that a given course of action is right, but what guarantee have we that as circumstances or our own impulses are altered a second intuition, contrary to the first and no less peremptory, may not supplant it? Either (the argument might run) moral laws have no validity and we are left with no better criteria than our own inclinations (however much these may have been refined by the circumstances of our education and by our own will) or else moral laws must have the backing of some principle of goodness actually at work in the world, some 'power not ourselves that makes for righteousness,' to which (or to Whom) we owe supreme allegiance. Or, to put the argument in a more positive form, does not conscience, when we listen reflectively to its dictates, ap-

pear clothed with authority? I desire to gratify this lust
or take that unfair advantage, and it may be that in my
human frailty I shall succumb to the temptation, but
whether my desire overpowers me or I it, the wrongness of
the desire (if it be wrong) is unchanged, and I, if I continue
to be honestly reflective, have in the reproaches of my
conscience a sure witness of my wrong-doing. Can conscience be merely a human product and still speak with
such authority? A feeling of the insufficiency of purely
empirical standards of right and wrong is thus the second
of the main incentives to a religious view of life.

It should be noted in considering the moral argument
that the question of God's existence is logically distinct
from moral questions respecting the allegiance or obedience
that an individual owes Him. One may, like Lucifer,
acknowledge God's existence and power, yet defy Him.
An attitude of religious defiance rings out in these stanzas
from James Thomson's *City of Dreadful Night*:

> Who is most wretched in this dolorous place?
> I think myself; yet I would rather be
> My miserable self than He, than He
> Who formed such creatures to His own disgrace.
>
> The vilest thing must be less vile than Thou
> From whom it had its being, God and Lord!
> Creator of all woe and sin! abhorred,
> Malignant and implacable! I vow
>
> That not for all Thy power furled and unfurled
> For all the temples to Thy glory built,
> Would I assume the ignominious guilt
> Of having made such men in such a world.

While we may not relish the tortured emotionalism of
these verses, they express a certain independence of judgment that may be admired. The existence of a God hav-

ing power to fling sinners into Hell would not prove that His commandments were morally praiseworthy nor that His definition of right and wrong was the true one. Lucifer and Prometheus are personifications of the free spirit of man courageously protesting against the tyranny of the All-Powerful. Facts, as said before, are not logically coercive of values. This principle holds good even when the facts in question are facts of a supernatural order.

From a critical point of view no authority, human or divine, is absolute; for it is dialectically possible to challenge the truth of any significant principle whatever. Of course it may be that there comes a point when the critical point of view ought to be put aside as insufficient, and allegiance given unquestioningly. Whether or not this is so cannot be argued; it is a matter which each individual must decide. The present volume, as its title makes plain, is a *critical* introduction to ethics, and its scope is limited to the exposition of a critical point of view. Whatever one's eventual allegiances may be, it is valuable in early life to develop a critical outlook and a critical method of dealing with all questions; for (paraphrasing an earlier quotation from Epictetus) without criticism one cannot even know whether or not criticism is a good thing. It is by a critical outlook that genuine morality is distinguished from blind obedience, custom, and self-deception. By a critical outlook, therefore, we guarantee the status of ethics as a distinct realm of discourse, and of moral principles as dialectically independent of theological and cosmological beliefs.

(ii) *Belief in progress*

Secular ethics, by which is meant any system of ethical values that stands logically independent of all religious beliefs, has made considerable headway within the last century or two.   It is no longer a universal dogma that a man must be religious to be moral.   This change in popular attitude does not mean, however, that contemporary ethics is becoming independent of all beliefs whatever.   Since the Renaissance, as if to compensate for the diminishing prestige of theological beliefs, a new type of belief has been coming into prominence: the belief in human progress.   It is held that as a result of the moral efforts of past generations the human race has advanced (*i.e.*, changed for the better) from barbarism through the earlier and simpler types of civilization up to the complex and highly differentiated civilization in which we now live, and that as a result of the moral efforts that we make today and hereafter, the race will continue to advance to higher and higher levels in the future.   This belief is very widespread.   Persons holding the most diverse views as to what constitutes the ultimate human goods often agree in believing in progress—which is to say, in the gradual realization of that particular kind of good that each of them has in mind.   Capitalist reactionaries are found predicting an unlimited future development of national resources and increase in national wealth; H. G. Wells, representing a liberal middle-of-the-road attitude, foresees (after the hurdles of several more catastrophic wars have been taken) an evolutionary improvement of the social intelligence and of social institutions through more scientific methods of education; and it is by appealing to a hope of future progress that many radical philosophers undertake to justify a communist millennium.[1]

Concerning the distant future it would seem as if one man's guess were about as good as another's, since there can obviously be no direct evidence for such prognosti-

[1] *Cf.* the quotation from Trotsky in the footnote on p. 323.

cations. There is one type of indirect evidence that is
commonly offered, the progress that the race has allegedly
made since the earliest known period of its existence.
Such progress, however, can only be asserted, not proved.
Any attempted demonstration is by the nature of the case
a begging of the question. How the question is begged
can be illustrated by an imaginary but typical example of
such a demonstration.

"Is not our civilization an obvious improvement over
the civilizations of the ancient Egyptians and Greeks?"
one might ask.

"In what way?" is the reply.

"Why, look at our superbly efficient means of production, exchange, transportation, domestic comfort, disease
prevention, etc."

"Well, I grant you that to us these innovations seem to
be great steps forward, for we have become used to and
dependent on them, but consider the ancient Egyptians'
and Greeks' point of view: Would either of those peoples
willingly have exchanged their civilization as a whole for
ours as a whole? Is there any evidence in their literature
that they wanted the kind of thing we could give them?
Do they not seem, on the contrary, to have rejoiced
enormously in that way of living and of carrying on their
affairs to which they were accustomed?"

"Ah, but that is because living when and as they did
they had not yet evolved any higher ideals than the ideal
of continuing in and realizing their own type of culture
and way of life. It is just in that complacency of theirs
that their moral inferiority to us is shown."

The fallacy in such an argument as this is evident. The
apologist for progress begins by asserting that contemporary life and civilization is an improvement over earlier
forms; when forced to admit that it is only by contempo-

rary standards that this is so he rejoins that contemporary standards are justified because they are superior to standards held in earlier ages. But since the standards of an age are a part and expression of its life and civilization this superiority claimed for our own standards, appealed to now as a premise for the argument, cannot validly be used to support the conclusion that contemporary life and civilization (including contemporary standards) are better than the life and civilization (and standards) of the past. The argument is circular and therefore invalid. As any demonstration that the human race has progressed must be founded at bottom on a similar begging of the question there can be no logical justification for asserting progress as a universal trait of humanity.

When the relativity of the idea of progress has been recognized we are in a position to ask whether according to the most enlightened standards that our own reflective judgments can set up there has been, for us, progress in this or that particular direction. There has, for instance, been progress in the development of large-scale production, but no comparable progress in regulating the distribution of buying power so that the articles produced can be satisfactorily consumed. There has been progress in the prevention and cure of diseases, but owing to such phenomena as the congestion of life in big cities, increasingly sedentary habits, and the deleterious effects of canned and 'prepared' foods there has been no proportionate increase in the improvement of people's health. There has been progress in making instruments of war but none in securing the conditions of peace, progress in the broadcasting of mechanical noises but a loss of the art of making fine toned organs and violins, progress in electrotype printing and the manufacturing of books but no progress in the discovery of things worth writing about. It is of distinctions like these that a critical morality must take cognizance; for it is only by distinguishing specific bads from specific goods in the world and evidences of progress from evidences of retrogression that moral ideals can be intelligently formulated and effectively applied.

APPENDIX

READINGS AND
QUESTIONS FOR DISCUSSION

APPENDIX

READINGS AND QUESTIONS FOR DISCUSSION

CHAPTER I

Recommended:

Warner Fite, *Moral Philosophy:* Chapters I–IV; VII; XIV.

George Herbert Palmer, *The Nature of Goodness.*

William James, *Principles of Psychology* (2-vol. edition): Chapters IV ("Habit"), IX ("The Stream of Thought"), X ("The Consciousness of Self"), XXII ("Reasoning"), XXIV ("Instinct"), XXV ("Emotion"), XXVI ("Will"). These chapters, while not directly concerned with ethical problems, furnish some valuable background for ethics.

Suggested:

Dewey and Tufts, *Ethics:* Chapter I.

Nicolai Hartmann, *Ethics:* Introduction and Section I.

Friedrich Paulsen, *A System of Ethics:* Chapter I.

Henry Sidgwick, *Methods of Ethics:* Chapter I.

Wilbur M. Urban, *Fundamentals of Ethics:* Chapter I.

Horace G. Wyatt, *The Art of Feeling.*

QUESTIONS

1. Compare each of the following statements about ethics with the definition given in the text. Where they differ, decide which you think to be the more adequate statement, and why. Are (d) and (e) mutually consistent?

(a) "[Ethics is] the science or study of what ought to be, so far as this depends upon the voluntary action of individuals." (Sidgwick, *op. cit.*)

(b) "Morality is the self-conscious living of life." (Fite, *op. cit.*)

(c) "Ethics is then, in the last analysis, just the science of systematized valuing; or, otherwise expressed, the valuing activity of man made systematic." (Urban, *op. cit.*)

(d) "Ethics does not teach directly what ought here and now to happen in any given case, but in general how that is constituted which ought to happen universally. . . . It does not teach finished judgments, but how to judge. In this sense it takes the question: 'What ought we to do?' It does not determine, describe, or define the proper 'What' of the Ought; but it gives rather the criteria by which the What is to be recognized." (Hartmann, *op. cit.*)

(e) "Since we are moved to action not by reason alone but also by desires and inclinations that operate independently of reason, the answer which we really want to the question 'why' is one which does not merely prove a certain action to be right, but also arouses in us a predominant inclination to do it." (Sidgwick, *op. cit.*)

2. How might the seven steps of a deliberative act be applied to each of the three *dilemmatic* situations described on pp. 3–6? How might they be applied to the following *trilemmatic* situation?

> *Duke Theseus:*
>   Upon that day either prepare to die
>   For disobedience to your father's will,
>   Or else to wed Demetrius, as he would,
>   Or on Diana's altar to protest
>   For aye austerity and single life.
>   Shakespeare, *A Midsummer-Night's Dream:* I, i.

3. May all conduct be interpreted also as behavior? May all behavior be interpreted also as conduct?—What use would ethics make of psychology in considering a jealous husband's murder of his unfaithful wife? At what point would ethics pass beyond psychology and become independent of it?

4. What type of 'ought' is found in each of the following sentences—ethical, logical, or prudential? Of those 'oughts' that have not strictly an ethical character do you find some to contain more ethical significance than others?

(a) You're on the wrong road: you ought to have turned left.
(b) We ought to speak the truth.
(c) From what I have heard the party ought to be a gay one.

(d) Your tie ought to be darker, to match your socks.

(e) You ought not to wear such hideous clothes.

(f) "And the day Jasper came home, a cold day it was, too—let's see, that ought to be back last March some time . . ."

(g) There ought to be a law against it.

5. "To live a life on the principle, 'Only my interests count,' is not only immoral, it is illogical. It says, My interests are better simply because they are mine. But 'better' raises the question, Better for whom? For me? Then you are saying, 'My interests are better for me because they are my interests,' which is a tautology. Better for other individuals? You could not say that without assuming an unhoped for altruism on their part. One alternative remains: Better objectively? If my interests are objectively better than someone else's it must be that they possess some distinction besides the purely subjective one of being mine, for this in itself is of no significance except to me." (From a student's paper.) Analyze this *trilemma,* and estimate its validity.

6. Examine the seven proposed tests of right and wrong in Section 4. Which of them do you regard as having the greatest ethical significance, and why?

7. (a) "Ethics is useless because people do not need theories to tell them the difference between right and wrong." (b) "Ethics is futile; it tries to set up standards of right and wrong, whereas these are only matters of opinion." How would you answer each of these objections to the study of ethics?

CHAPTER II

Recommended:

R. H. Thouless, *Straight and Crooked Thinking.*
George Herbert Palmer, *The Field of Ethics.*
Plato, *Euthyphro; Republic,* Book I.
Descartes, *Discourse on Method.*

Suggested:

Plato, *Protagoras.*
Aristotle, *Nicomachean Ethics,* Book I.

Spinoza, *Treatise on the Improvement of the Understanding.*
Schopenhauer, *The Art of Controversy.*
John Dewey, *How We Think.*
Graham Wallas, *The Art of Thought.*
Wilbur M. Urban, *Fundamentals of Ethics*, Chapter II.
Nicolai Hartmann, *Ethics*, Volume I, Section II.
Columbia Associates in Philosophy, *An Introduction to Reflective Thinking*, Chapters XI–XII.

For further study of logic:

B. F. Bode, *An Outline of Logic.* Avoids unnecessary technical terms and offers many illustrations of the application of logic to ethics.

R. W. Sellars, *Essentials of Logic.* An elementary survey of traditional logic.

Morris R. Cohen and Ernest Nagel, *An Introduction to Logic and Scientific Method.* More advanced.

QUESTIONS

1. What fallacies do you find in the following arguments? Do not merely give each fallacy a name but explain as precisely as possible just wherein it consists:

(a) If their theories were sound, ethical philosophers would agree among themselves.

(b) "Thus moral laws exist. They are natural laws. That they, just like physical laws, are best for us and for the world we live in is revealed to us by the wail of the victims which arises when these laws are violated." (Jacques Rueff, *From the Physical to the Social Sciences.*)

(c) By virtue of the Law of Survival of the Fittest, the Japanese are entitled to seize Manchuria provided they are strong enough to get away with it.

(d) The evils of life are transitory, so why regard them as important?

(e) Everyone desires happiness; virtue is happiness; therefore everyone desires virtue. (Hint: What do you take the word 'is' to mean?)

(f) Suicide is irrational if one does not believe in a future life.

For in that case, one pretends to choose non-existence. Non-existence, however, is not something but nothing, and it is impossible to choose rationally when the object to be chosen is nothing.

(g) Your proposal may be all right in theory, but in practice it is utterly absurd and unworkable.

2. *Ad hominem* arguments are invalid only so far as the appeal to the individual's character is irrelevant to the matter in hand. Estimate the degree of validity of each of the following *ad hominem* arguments:

(a) "Well Sir, if you want to believe that your own ancestor was an ape or a gorilla you may do so, but don't ask me to trace my lineage in that direction."

(b) Dr. Johnson said of a man who had cleverly maintained that the difference between virtue and vice is illusory: "When he leaves our house, let us count our spoons."

(c) "One of the reactionary and therefore fashionable historians of contemporary France, L. Madelin, slandering in his drawing-room fashion the great revolution—that is, the birth of his own nation—asserts that 'the historian ought to stand upon the wall of a threatened city and behold at the same time the besiegers and the besieged': only in this way, it seems, can we achieve a 'conciliatory justice.' However, the words of Madelin himself testify that if he climbs out on the wall dividing the two camps, it is only in the character of a reconnoiterer for the reaction. It is well that he is concerned only with war camps of the past: in a time of revolution standing on the wall involves great danger. Moreover, in times of alarm the priests of 'conciliatory justice' are usually found sitting on the inside of four walls waiting to see which side will win." (Trotsky, *The History of the Russian Revolution.*)

(d) The behaviorist denies that consciousness exists. What, then, is the use of my retorting to him, since by his own admission he would not be conscious of what I say?

(e) The determinist declares that there is no freedom of choice. Let him acquiesce in the decrees of fate if he believes he must, but for my part I shall go on choosing my courses of action.

3. "The egoism which enters into our theories does not affect their sincerity; rather, the more our egoism is satisfied, the more robust is our belief." (George Eliot, *Middlemarch*.) To what type of *ad hominem* argument might this be an effective reply?

4. "Whenever you are perfectly clear about anything you may be pretty sure of having left out some important factor." (A. N. Whitehead, quoted in Eaton, *General Logic*.) Discuss this statement, and give examples.

5. Against what contrary pair of fallacies is the writer of the following passage admonishing?

"We do not at all pretend to deny the significance of the personal in the mechanics of the historic process, nor the significance in the personal of the accidental. We only demand that a historic personality, with all its peculiarities, should not be taken as a bare list of psychological traits, but as a living reality grown out of definite social conditions and reacting upon them. As a rose does not lose its fragrance because the natural scientist points out upon what ingredients of soil and atmosphere it is nourished, so an exposure of the social roots of a personality does not remove from it either its aroma or its foul smell." (Trotsky, *op. cit.*)

6. Estimate step by step the validity of Socrates' discussion with Euthyphro.

CHAPTER III

Recommended:

Plato, *Gorgias.*

Epicurus, *Letter to Menoeceus.* Contained in Diogenes Laertius, *Lives of Eminent Philosophers.* Reprinted in: Epicurus, *The Extant Remains*, translated and edited by Cyril Bailey.

Lucretius, *On the Nature of Things* (*De Rerum Natura*): Books III, IV.

John Stuart Mill, *Utilitarianism.*

Fite, *Moral Philosophy:* Chapter XIII, "The Enjoyment of Life."

Suggested:

Plato, *Philebus.*

Aristotle, *The Nicomachean Ethics:* Book X, Chapters I–V.

Bernard Mandeville, *The Fable of the Bees; or, Private Vices, Publick Benefits.* Particularly the essay in Volume II of the recent Clarendon Press edition, entitled "An Enquiry into the Origin of Moral Virtue."

Jeremy Bentham, *An Introduction to the Principles of Morals and Legislation.*

Henry Sidgwick, *The Methods of Ethics.*

John Watson, *Hedonistic Theories from Aristippus to Spencer.*

Recent Criticisms of Hedonism:

F. H. Bradley, *Ethical Studies:* Essay III, "Pleasure for Pleasure's Sake." Somewhat difficult.

John Dewey and James H. Tufts, *Ethics.* In the revised edition (1932): Chapter XI, "Ends, the Good and Wisdom." In the original edition (1908): Chapter XIV, "Happiness and Conduct: the Good and Desire."

Thomas Hill Green, *Prolegomena to Ethics:* Book III, Chapter I.

Nicolai Hartmann, *Ethics:* Volume I, Section III.

G. E. Moore, *Principia Ethica:* Chapters III, IV.

Horace G. Wyatt, *The Art of Feeling:* Part III, "Feeling and Happiness." A more sympathetic treatment.

Novels:

George Eliot, *Romola.*

Walter Pater, *Marius the Epicurean.*

J. K. Huysmans, *Against the Grain,* together with the introductory remarks by Havelock Ellis in the Modern Library edition.

Anatole France, *Thaïs.*

Dostoyevsky, *The Brothers Karamazov.*

Tolstoy, *Anna Karenina.*

Drama:

Shakespeare, *Antony and Cleopatra.*

QUESTIONS

1. Study several of the hedonists with whom you may have become acquainted in works of literature, such as Romola in George Eliot's novel of that name, Gwendolyn in the same author's *Daniel Deronda*, Emma Bovary in Flaubert's *Madame Bovary*, Marius in Pater's *Marius the Epicurean*, Jean des Esseintes in Huysmans' *Against the Grain*, Thaïs and Nicias in Anatole France's *Thaïs*. What important differences among their several characters do you find?

2. Consider whether hedonism, in both of its principal forms, is consistent with Kant's second principle of moral conduct: "Act so as to treat humanity, whether in your own person or in that of any other, in every case as an end and never as only a means."

3. "*De gustibus non est disputandum*—there's no use arguing about tastes. Hedonism, however, reduces moral value to a question of individual taste." Complete this argument, and examine it.

4. What logical objection could be made to the following argument by J. S. Mill? "No reason can be given why the general happiness is desirable, except that each person, so far as he believes it to be attainable, desires his own happiness. This, however, being a fact, we have not only all the proof which the case admits of, but all which it is possible to require, that happiness is a good: that each person's happiness is a good to that person, and the general happiness, therefore, a good to the aggregate of all persons." (*Utilitarianism.*)

5. Summarize the logical steps and estimate the validity of each of the following criticisms of hedonism. Are there any other criticisms which you consider more valid than these?

(a) *Socrates.* Don't you perceive the conclusion, then—that if you say a man drinks when he is thirsty, you are saying that he enjoys himself while suffering discomfort. . . . Is this so or isn't it?

Callicles. It is.

Soc. But then you say that it is impossible to be well off and badly off at the same time.

Call. Yes, I do.

Soc. But you have admitted it is possible to enjoy oneself while feeling pain.

Call. It seems that way.

Soc. Enjoying oneself, then, is not being well off, and feeling pain is not being badly off, whence it follows that the pleasant is something other than the good.

Call. I don't understand all this hair-splitting of yours, Socrates.

(Plato, *Gorgias*, 496E–497A.)

(b) "What, then, is meant by 'my own good'? In what sense can a thing be good *for me?* It is obvious, if we reflect, that the only thing which can belong to me, which can be *mine*, is something which is good, and not the fact that it is good. When, therefore, I talk of anything I get as 'my own good,' I must mean either that the thing I get is good, or that my possessing it is good. In both cases it is only the thing or the possession of it which is *mine*, and not *the goodness* of that thing or that possession. There is no longer any meaning in attaching the 'my' to our predicate, and saying: The possession of this *by me* is *my* good. . . . In short, when I talk of a thing as 'my own good' all that I can mean is that something which will be exclusively mine, as my own pleasure is mine (whatever be the various senses of this relation denoted by 'possession'), is also *good absolutely;* or rather that my possession of it is *good absolutely*. The *good* of it can in no possible sense be 'private' or belong to me; any more than a thing can *exist* privately or *for* one person only. The only reason I can have for aiming at 'my own good,' is that it is *good absolutely* that what I so call should belong to me—*good absolutely* that I should *have* something, which, if I have it, others cannot have. But if it is *good absolutely* that I should have it, then everyone else has as much reason for aiming at *my* having it, as I have myself. If, therefore, it is true of *any* single man's 'interest' or 'happiness' that it ought to be his sole ultimate end, this can only mean that *that* man's 'interest' or 'happiness' is *the sole good, the* Universal Good, and the only thing that anybody ought to aim at. What Egoism holds, therefore, is that *each* happiness is the sole good —that a number of different things are *each* of them the only good thing there is—an absolute contradiction! No more complete and thorough refutation of any theory could be desired."

(G. E. Moore, *Principia Ethica*, pp. 98–99.   Courtesy of Cambridge University Press, London, and The Macmillan Co., New York.)

(c) "If hedonism is true, then one pleasure or sum of pleasures ought never to attract me more than another except when it is greater in amount.   But it is a matter of common experience that a near pleasure tends to exert a stronger pull than a remote pleasure, even when the remote pleasure is foreseen to be just as great and practically as certain.   What I often desire, then, is apparently not the *most* pleasure but an *immediate* pleasure.   In other words, the fact that an imagined pleasure is foreseen to possess greater intensity does not mean that it therefore has a greater constraining power over the will.   Does not this admission break down the main psychological premise of hedonism? It shows that we are often led by impulse to choose consciously and knowingly a course of action other than that which promises most pleasure in the long run."   (From a student's paper, based on an argument by Hastings Rashdall, in *The Theory of Good and Evil*.)

(d) "Hedonism breaks down as soon as we have forced the hedonist to differentiate *kinds* of pleasure.   For the only real difference between kinds is in terms of the species—the special qualities of the different sorts of ends.   'Choosing the better pleasure' then becomes 'choosing the better end'—naming the end: books or religion or athletics or bodily lusts.   'Preferring one pleasure to another' becomes logically interchangeable with 'preferring one pleasurable end rather than another pleasurable end.'   The common term, 'pleasurable,' may now be canceled out from both sides of the comparison, just as in the proposition, 'Blue color is darker than pink color,' the word 'color' may be canceled out."   (From a student's paper.)

CHAPTER IV

Recommended:

Plato, *Republic:* Book I.
Herbert Spencer, *Data of Ethics.*
Friedrich Nietzsche, *The Genealogy of Morals.*
George Bernard Shaw, *Back to Methuselah.* Preface.

Suggested:

Machiavelli, *Discourses on the First Ten Books of Livy.*
Nietzsche, *Thus Spake Zarathustra; The Will to Power.*
W. M. Salter, *Nietzsche the Thinker.*
Darwin, *The Descent of Man:* Chapter XXVII. Also his *Expression of the Emotions in Man and Animals.*
Thomas H. Huxley, *Evolution and Ethics.*
M. C. Otto, *Things and Ideals:* Chapter IV, "Might Makes Right."
Urban, *Fundamentals of Ethics:* Chapter V.
For an acquaintance with the theory of evolution at its source: Darwin, *The Origin of Species.*
On the philosophy of evolution: Bergson, *Creative Evolution.*

Drama:
Shakespeare, *Richard III.*

QUESTIONS

1. "Man exists as a natural and necessary product of universal forces and, like other organic beings, obeys the law of self-expression. . . . In pursuing its own interests, every organism constantly finds itself in the presence of other organisms whose interests and welfare cannot but conflict with its own; whence results a struggle wherein the inferior organism must succumb and the superior organism survive and propagate. Whether this condition of affairs be repulsive or shocking, and whether it 'ought' to be different from what it is, are questions no longer to be asked, once we have discarded the old idea of an arbitrary will governing the phenomena of nature." (Antonio Llano, "Morality the last of the Dogmas," from *The Philosophical Review.*)

(i) Is the first statement of this passage a scientifically established fact, or is it vague and more or less empty rhetoric? Could you formulate the so-called law in concrete and non-question-begging terms that would adequately account for such facts as symbiosis and herd instinct in animals, and generosity and self-sacrifice in men?

(ii) Is the disjunction in the third sentence logically sound? Are we really obliged either to believe in an arbitrary will governing nature or to discard all notions of value? Or is a middle ground possible? *I.e.*, can you go 'between the horns' of the dilemma?

(iii) Examine the phrase 'cannot but conflict.' Granted that some conflict is inevitable, is it not often possible to have different interests without their necessarily clashing? And if this is possible may not it be accepted as a value—as an ideal to be striven for?

(iv) Do you find any curious logical inconsistency in the statement that whether things 'ought' to be different from what they are is a question 'no longer to be' asked?

2. Analyze and discuss the two passages that follow:

(a) "Deep-seated preferences are not to be argued about—you cannot argue a man into liking a glass of beer—and, therefore, when differences are sufficiently far-reaching, we try to kill the other man rather than let him have his way. But that is perfectly consistent with admitting that, so far as appears, his grounds are just as good as ours." (Former Supreme Court Justice O. W. Holmes, in *The Harvard Law Review.*)

(b) "Colonel A. C. Yate M. P., for instance, wrote not long ago, from the Athenaeum Club, to the *Times*, to complain that Mr. Carnegie had called War a degrading evil. 'Does Mr. Carnegie,' he asked, 'really understand human nature and the immutable laws which govern and guide it? Is the grand law of the 'selection of the fittest' to give way to the miserable mediocrity of compromise fostered by charity?' Colonel Yate might perhaps find it more difficult than he would expect to put his 'immutable laws' into explicit language." (Graham Wallas, *The Great Society*. Harcourt, Brace.)

3. Do you agree with the following statement? "What is ethically best involves conduct that is in all respects opposed to that which leads to success in the cosmic struggle for existence." (Huxley, *op. cit.*)

4. "In his excellent little book, *First Steps in Philosophy* . . . Mr. W. M. Salter says: 'It might be better that there should be no animal or human life than that it should maintain itself by violating ethical requirements.' Unless for those ethical requirements to be determined by arbitrary and irrational

volitions of Deity, I can see no meaning in Mr. Salter's proposition." (Ritchie, *Natural Rights*.)   Discuss.

5. Do you think that Nietzsche's philosophy should be classified under naturalism?

CHAPTER V

Recommended:

The Bible: The Book of Job; the four Gospels.   The Gospel according to Luke is recommended as offering on the whole the most satisfactory version.

Plato, *Apology; Crito*.

The Discourses of Epictetus.

St. Augustine, *Confessions*.

Thomas à Kempis, *Imitation of Christ*.

Pascal, *Thoughts*.

Suggested:

Selby-Bigge, *British Moralists:* Selections from Wollaston and Shaftesbury.

David Hume, *A Treatise of Human Nature:* Book III, "Of Morals."

Fite, *Moral Philosophy:* Chapter XVI.

Hartmann, *Ethics:* Volume I, Section VI.

Paulsen, *A System of Ethics:* Book II, Chapters I, V, VIII.

On the nature of religious belief: Cardinal Newman, *An Essay in Aid of a Grammar of Assent*.

On the nature of religious experience: Evelyn Underhill, *Mysticism*.

Rudolf Otto, *The Idea of the Holy*.

Novel:

George Eliot, *The Mill on the Floss*.

QUESTIONS

1. What relation does the following passage bear to the doctrines discussed in this chapter?

"For the phenomenological method the most complex psychological data may be '*simple*' if included in one act of awareness

—a friendship, the outlook of a phase of childhood, etc.—these are 'phenomena,' forming unities of experience, and therefore determining actions or attitudes. While analyzable into component elements—a look on the face of a friend, etc.—such elements have their meaning only as factors in the wholes, and do not themselves constitute significant experiences. Accordingly, what is simple and what is complex in the two methods are entirely different, and their analyses can never wholly coincide." (Max Scheler, *Ethics.*)

2.   Do you consider that a naturalistic interpretation of conscience destroys the authority of its dictates? Consider what light is thrown on this question by the following passage: "In the study of the moral sense we contemplate the last and noblest product of evolution which we can ever know,—the attribute latest to be unfolded in the development of psychical life, and by the possession of which we have indeed become as gods, knowing the good and the evil." (John Fiske, *Outlines of Cosmic Philosophy.* Houghton Mifflin.)

3.   How far do you think the following criticism of Shaftesbury by Mandeville justified? "He imagines that men without any trouble or violence upon themselves may be naturally virtuous. He seems to expect and require goodness in his species as we do a sweet taste in grapes and China oranges." Would the criticism be equally justified against Wollaston? Against Newman?

4.   Consider what light is thrown on the problem of moral duty by any of the following works of literature that you have read: Sophocles, *Antigone;* Plato, *The Apology of Socrates;* Shakespeare, *Hamlet;* Ibsen, *The Master Builder;* Tolstoy, *Anna Karenina;* Conrad, *Lord Jim;* Thomas Mann, *Tonio Kröger* (contained in the volume entitled *Death in Venice.*)

5.   Discuss the attitude towards duty implied in the following lines from Wordsworth's *Ode to Duty.* Do you think Wordsworth's reasons for accepting duties a valid one?

> "Me this unchartered freedom tires;
> I feel the weight of chance-desires:
> My hopes no more must change their name,
> I long for a repose that ever is the same."

CHAPTER VI

Recommended:

For early Stoicism: Epictetus, *Discourses;* Marcus Aurelius, *Meditations;* Edwin Bevan, *Stoics and Sceptics.*
Spinoza, *Ethics:* Book V.
Kant, *Fundamental Principles of the Metaphysics of Ethics.*
Warner Fite, *An Introductory Study of Ethics:* Chapter IX.

Suggested:

Selby-Bigge, *British Moralists:* selections from Cudworth, Cumberland, and Henry More.
F. H. Bradley, *Ethical Studies:* Essay IV, "Duty for Duty's Sake."
Dewey and Tufts, *Ethics* (1932 edition): Chapter XII.
G. C. Field, *Moral Theory:* chapters on Kant.
N. Hartmann, *Ethics:* Volume I, Section IV.
J. W. Scott, *Kant on the Moral Life.*
Sidgwick, *Methods of Ethics:* Book III.

QUESTIONS

1. How valid do you consider each of the following criticisms of Stoicism?

(a) "The Stoics pretend to infer their rational ideal from the nature of the universe. But really it is the other way round. Their ideal is rational and so they suppose that the universe must be rational too, in order to have something by which to justify their rational ideal. This is circular reasoning." (From a student's paper.)

(b) "In lazy apathy let Stoics boast
Their virtue fix'd; 'tis fixed as in a frost;
Contracted all, retiring to the breast;
But strength of mind is Exercise, not Rest:
The rising tempest puts in act the soul,
Parts it may ravage, but preserves the whole."
(Alexander Pope, *An Essay on Man.*)

2. How much do you think the following passage contributes to the establishment of an *a priori* basis for ethics?

"In disquisitions of every kind, there are certain primary truths, or first principles, upon which all subsequent reasonings must depend. These contain an internal evidence which, antecedent to all reflection or combination, commands the assent of the mind. Where it produces not this effect, it must proceed either from some defect or disorder in the organs of perception, or from the influence of some strong interest, or passion, or prejudice. Of this nature are the maxims in geometry, that the whole is greater than its part; things equal to the same are equal to one another; two straight lines cannot enclose a space; and all right angles are equal to each other. Of the same nature are these other maxims in ethics and politics, that there cannot be an effect without a cause; that the means ought to be proportioned to the end; that every power ought to be commensurate with its object; that there ought to be no limitation of a power destined to effect a purpose which is itself incapable of limitation." (Alexander Hamilton, in *The Federalist*, No. 31.)

3. G. C. Field in his book *Moral Theory* gives the following as the most fundamental of Kant's ethical assumptions. Do you think, from your knowledge of Kant, that the list is adequate? How many of the individual assumptions can you accept as true?

(a) If there is a moral law it must be absolute and universal: it cannot (i) admit of favored persons, (ii) be suspended or altered in special circumstances.

(b) If a thing is really good, it must be good in and for itself, not as a means to something else.

(c) The goodness or rightness of an action is independent of what we want.

(d) The goodness or rightness of an action does not depend on its actual results; for actual results depend partly on accident.

(e) The goodness of an action presupposes a free agent.

4. Suppose a hedonist to argue: "I believe that everyone should strive to achieve the greatest possible amount of pleasure. That is to say, whenever I seek pleasure I am entirely willing that the motive from which I act (the greatest pleasure principle) should be a universal moral law governing the actions of everyone. I am therefore a good Kantian at the same time that I

am a good hedonist."—What do you think of this argument?
How would Kant have been likely to reply?

CHAPTER VII

Recommended:

Plato, *Protagoras; Symposium.*
Aristotle, *Nicomachean Ethics.*
Montaigne, *Essays* (Trechman's translation preferred).
Fite, *Moral Philosophy.*

Suggested:

Confucius, *Analects.*
Irving Babbitt, *Rousseau and Romanticism.*
G. C. Field, *Moral Theory:* chapters on Aristotle.
Joseph Wood Krutch, *The Modern Temper.*
Ramon Fernandez, *De la personnalité.*

Drama:

Shakespeare, *The Tempest.*
Goethe, *Faust:* Part I. John Anster's paraphrase translation
makes the best reading.

Novel:

Thomas Mann, *The Magic Mountain.*

QUESTIONS

1. In what respects would each of the following doctrines
fall short of the humanist ideal: epicureanism, utilitarianism,
Spencer's evolutionary naturalism, Nietzsche's ideal of the
superman, Shaftesbury's intuitionism, stoicism, Kantian rationalism?

2. Both Aristotle and Spencer base their ethics upon their
respective conceptions of biology. In what important way do
their conceptions of biology differ?

3. In the light of the ethical theories that you have so far
studied, discuss the meaning and adequacy of the following
expressed or implied moral attitudes:

(a) "Never have I trusted Fortune, even when she seemed to be offering peace; the blessings she most fondly bestowed upon me—money, office, and influence—I stored all of them in a place from which she could take them back without disturbing me. Between them and me I have kept a wide space; and so she has merely taken them, not torn them, from me. No man is crushed by hostile Fortune who is not first deceived by her smiles." (Seneca, *To Helvia on Consolation*. Translated by John W. Basore, in the Loeb Classical Library.)

(b) "Eat, drink, and play: for nothing else would I give a snap of the fingers. . . . The dinners I have eaten, the wanton acts I have exulted in, the delights of love I have enjoyed —all these things still belong to me, although my blessings have now disappeared." (Sardanapalus, an ancient Assyrian king.)

(c) "I perceive now why there is no real moral life. Wise men suppose moral law to be something too lofty, and fools have no acquaintance with it at all. I perceive now why the moral law is not understood. Men of noble natures strive for too high and unattainable a goal, while the ignoble do not strive for one that is high enough." (Confucius.)

(d) On a marooned ship described in one of W. S. Gilbert's ballads the starving sailors have turned cannibal, drawing lots to determine which of their number are to be, one by one, the victims. Finally only two survive, one of whom is the ship's cook. Which of them shall devour the other? The cook offers the argument that he could prepare a more savory dish of the sailor than the sailor could prepare of him.

(e) The Second Murderer, discussing his conscience: "I'll not meddle with it; it makes a man a coward; a man cannot steal, but it accuseth him; a man cannot swear, but it checks him; a man cannot lie with his neighbor's wife, but it detects him: 'tis a blushing shamefac'd spirit, that mutinies in a man's bosom; it fills a man full of obstacles; it made me once restore a purse of gold that, by chance, I found; it beggars any man that keeps it; it is turned out of towns and cities for a dangerous thing; and every man that means to live well endeavors to trust to himself and live without it." (Shakespeare, *Richard III*: Act I, Scene iv.)

CHAPTER VIII

Recommended:

Plato, *Republic:* Book IV (on virtues); Books VIII–IX (on vices).

Aristotle, *The Nicomachean Ethics:* Books III (latter half) and IV on virtues; Book VII on vices.

Fite, *Moral Philosophy:* Chapters IX, "The Wisdom of the Serpent"; XII, "Justification by Knowledge."

Suggested:

Plato, *Hippias Minor, Laches, Charmides.*
Dante, *The Divine Comedy:* "Inferno."
Spinoza, *Ethics:* Book IV.
Paulsen, *A System of Ethics:* Book III.
N. Hartmann, *Ethics:* Volume II, Sections IV–VII.

Novel:

Dostoyevsky: *Crime and Punishment.*

QUESTIONS

1. "'To understand all is to forgive all' is a dangerous principle. From there it is just a step to: 'To him of superior understanding all may be forgiven.' There seems to be a close connection between a religion of sympathy and outrageous moral scepticism." (From a student's paper.)—Do you agree?

2. Can the following code of morality, on which Tolstoy pours bitter irony, be rationally justified?

"Vronsky's life was particularly happy in that he had a code of principles, which defined what he ought and what he ought not to do. This code of principles covered only a very small circle of contingencies, but then the principles were never doubtful, and Vronsky, as he never went outside that circle, had never had a moment's hesitation about doing what he ought to do. These principles he laid down as invariable rules: that one must pay a card sharper, but need not pay a tailor; that one must never tell a lie to a man, but one may to a woman; that one must never cheat anyone, but one may a husband; that one must never pardon an insult, but one may give one, and so on.

These principles were possibly not reasonable and not good, but they were of unfailing certainty, and so long as he adhered to them, Vronsky felt that his heart was at peace and he could hold his head up." (Tolstoy, *Anna Karenina.* Translated by Catherine Garnett. Reprinted by permission of The Modern Library, New York.)

3. Are there any *purely* individual virtues? How far would one's virtuous habits be likely to be undermined if one possessed Gyges' ring of invisibility? (See Plato, *Republic*, Book II.)

4. "Whosoever will save his life shall lose it, and whosoever will lose his life shall find it." A. E. Housman, quoting this from the Douay translation of the Bible, calls it "the most important truth which has ever been uttered, and the greatest discovery ever made in the moral world." What justification can you offer for this estimate?

CHAPTER IX

Recommended:

Plato, *Republic:* Books I–IV.
John Stuart Mill, *Utilitarianism:* Chapter V.   *On Liberty.*
Henry George, *Social Problems.*
Reinhold Niebuhr, *Moral Man and Immoral Society.*

Suggested:

Aristotle, *The Nicomachean Ethics:* Book V.
T. N. Carver, *Essays in Social Justice.*
Warner Fite, *Individualism.*
William Godwin, *An Enquiry Concerning Political Justice.*
Henry Sidgwick, *Methods of Ethics:* Book III, Chapter V.
T. V. Smith, *The American Philosophy of Equality.*

Novel:

Anthony Trollope, *The Warden.*

QUESTIONS

1. "Men may one day feel that they are partakers of a common nature, and that true freedom and perfect equity, like food and air, are pregnant with benefit to every constitution. If

there be the faintest hope that this shall be the final result, then certainly no subject can inspire to a sound mind such generous enthusiasm, such enlightened ardor, and such invincible perseverance." (Godwin, *An Enquiry Concerning Political Justice.*) What logical objection might be raised against hoping for both 'true freedom' and 'perfect equity' as a final combined result? Can you outline a social program in which they might be combined with perfect consistency? If not, how far do you think such a goal might be approximated, and by what means?

2. "Americans are so enamored of equality that they would rather be equal in slavery than unequal in freedom." (De Tocqueville.) Do you think this observation accurate?

3. Ladislaus, King of Naples, having besieged the city of Florence until the Florentines were on the point of surrendering, agreed to leave them in possession of their city on condition that they deliver up to him a certain young girl of good family and of great beauty, for whom he had conceived a lust. Suppose it could have been foreseen by the Florentines that this exchange would mean the moral ruination of the girl; would their delivery of her have been morally justified? How would a utilitarian have answered? Can you provide any theoretical interpretation for a contrary point of view?

4. It has been objected against demands for the greater equalization of wealth, that this would merely take away from the rich, while adding to the incomes of the poor an amount so small as to be negligible. Analyze this objection, to show how it is based upon an assumption of the *static* character of wealth. Is such an assumption valid?

5. Godwin objected to punishment by the State on three grounds: (i) the evidence of guilt is never absolutely conclusive; (ii) the same external action will admit of every possible shade of virtue or vice; (iii) punishment is not the appropriate mode of correcting the errors of mankind—for it does not convey to the understanding a truth of which the malefactor is ignorant, but merely excites resentment in him. Estimate the validity of each of these objections.

6. "Neither intellectual nor spiritual superiority seems to constitute an intelligible ground for assigning to a man a larger share of carnal delights than his neighbor." (Rashdall, *The*

Theory of Good and Evil.) Formulate and discuss the point of view on which Rashdall's statement is an attack.

CHAPTER X

Recommended:

Plato, *Republic:* Books IV–V.
Dante, *De Monarchia* (translated by Aurelia Henry).
Hobbes, *Leviathan:* Chapters XIII–XV; XVII–XVIII.

Suggested:

Aristotle, *Politics.*
Machiavelli, *The Prince.*
John Milton, *Areopagitica.*
Rousseau, *The Social Contract.*
Bentham, *An Introduction to the Principles of Morals and Legislation.*
Hegel, *The Philosophy of Right* (translated by S. W. Dyde).
William Godwin, *An Introduction to the Principles of Political Justice.*
Westel W. Willoughby, *The Nature of the State; The Ethical Basis of Political Authority.*
Norman Wilde, *The Ethical Basis of the State.*
Bernard Bosanquet, *The Philosophical Theory of the State.* This is a development of Hegel's State-idealism. The doctrine is subjected to thorough criticism in L. T. Hobhouse, *The Metaphysical Theory of the State.*
D. G. Ritchie, *Natural Rights.*
Harold J. Laski, *The Problem of Sovereignty.*
W. Y. Elliott, *The Pragmatic Revolt in Politics.*
The Federalist: A collection of papers by Alexander Hamilton, James Madison, and John Jay, explaining and defending the Constitution, prior to its adoption.
J. S. Barnes, *Fascism.*
On Marxism: See readings for Chapter XI.

QUESTIONS

1. "The whole developed apparatus of constitution and government would have absolutely no end or meaning if their

activities did not ultimately result in the good of individuals."
(Sidgwick, *op. cit.*)   —Can you formulate any plausible theory
of social value, by means of which this statement might be challenged?

2. "Bosanquet's mistake seems to me to lie in treating error
as pure negation. When the individual's will diverges from
the will of the State it is considered to be, to that extent, unreal.
I challenge this. My will, whatever its imperfections, is the
real thing to me, and its dissatisfactions do not stop being real
because they are based on a partial view of things. When I
examine this will of mine without prejudice I am forced to
agree that my mean and bad traits may be (in some cases) every
bit as enduring and every bit as much *the real me* as my good
ones. So if we are realists, why not admit that our real wills
often work at cross-purposes to one another and at cross-
purposes to the interests of the State?" (From a student's
paper.) Do you consider this a valid objection to Hegel s
State-idealism?

3. Estimate the merits of these two contending views of the
rôle of the State:

(a) "We then give to this particular group [the State] no
peculiar merit. We refuse it the title of creator of all else.
We make it justify itself by its consequences. We stimulate
its activities by making it compete with the work of other groups
coextensive with or complementary to itself. As it may not
extinguish, so it may not claim preëminence. Like any other
group, what it is and what it will be, it can be only by virtue
of its achievement. So only can it hope to hand down un-
dimmed the torch of its conscious life." (Harold J. Laski,
quoted by Elliot, *op. cit.*)

(b) "The propositions that the State may not extinguish, as
well as that it may not claim preëminence, are equally incompatible with the rule of law. . . . The rule of law can not
exist side by side with, say, the Ku Klux Klan. The 'torch of
conscious life' gutters or is trampled out if the State permits the
law of the land to be thrown into the arena of social strife, for
the law is the very breath of its flame. Law represents a certain
area of agreement for the settlement of disputes, for the protection of generally recognized rights and the enforcement of duties

corresponding to them." (W. Y. Elliott, *op. cit.* Quoted by permission of The Macmillan Co. In the originals of both of these passages the word 'State' is not capitalized.) Do you agree with Professor Elliott's further statement, that "a man may with good conscience obey laws which do not command his approval separate from their context in the larger purpose [served by the State]"? What could be said on both sides of this question?

4. Estimate the validity of Dante's several arguments for monarchy. In addition to the two arguments given in the text of this chapter, consider the following (from *De Monarchia*):

(a) "When it is possible to do a thing through one agent, it is better done than through more. We prove it in this way: Let A be one agent able to accomplish a given end, and let A and B be two through whom the same thing can be accomplished. If the end accomplished through A and B can be accomplished through A alone, B is added uselessly, as nothing results from the addition of B which would not have resulted from A alone. Now inasmuch as every addition is idle and superfluous, and every superfluity is displeasing to God and Nature, and everything displeasing to God and Nature is evil, as is self-evident; it follows not only that whatever can be done through one agent is better done through one than through more, but that whatever done through one is good, done through more becomes manifestly evil."

(b) "In whomever right love can be present to the highest degree, in him can justice find the most effective place. . . .

"Everything loved is the more loved the nearer it is to him who loves; men are nearer to the Monarch than to other princes; therefore they are or ought to be most loved by him. The first statement is obvious if we call to mind the nature of agents and patients; the second if we perceive that men approach other princes in their partial aspect, but a Monarch in their totality."

5. "Under bad government the good man is a bad citizen; but under upright government 'good man' and 'good citizen' are one and the same." (Dante, *op. cit.*) Can you offer examples in support or refutation of this?

6. What can be said in favor of each side of the following controversy?

(a) "Vicious conduct is soon discovered to involve injurious consequences. Injustice, therefore, by its own nature is little fitted for a durable existence. But Government lays its hand upon the spring there is in society and puts a stop to its motion. It gives substance and permanence to our errors." (Godwin, *op. cit.*)

(b) "Government implies the power of making laws. It is essential to the idea of a law, that it be attended with a sanction; or, in other words, a penalty or punishment for disobedience. If there be no penalty annexed to disobedience, the resolutions or commands which pretend to be laws will, in fact, amount to nothing more than advice or recommendation." (Hamilton, in *The Federalist*, No. 15.)

7. The following argument, contributed by James Madison to the series of newspaper articles known collectively as *The Federalist*, for which he was responsible conjointly with Alexander Hamilton and John Jay, is a classical statement of the reasons for preferring representative over direct democratic government. Distinguish the logical steps of the argument and offer a critical estimate of its validity.

"By a faction, I understand a number of citizens, whether amounting to a majority or minority of the whole, who are united and actuated by some common impulse of passion, or of interest, adverse to the rights of other citizens, or to the permanent and aggregate interests of the community.

"There are two methods of curing the mischiefs of faction: the one, by removing its causes; the other, by controlling its effects.

"There are again two methods of removing the causes of faction: the one, by destroying the liberty which is essential to its existence; the other, by giving to every citizen the same opinions, the same passions, and the same interests.

"It could never be more truly said than of the first remedy, that it was worse than the disease. Liberty is to faction what air is to fire, an aliment without which it instantly expires. But it could not be less folly to abolish liberty, which is essential to political life, because it nourishes faction, than it would be to wish the annihilation of air, which is essential to animal life, because it imparts to fire its destructive agency.

"The second expedient is as impracticable as the first would be unwise. As long as the reason of man continues fallible, and he is at liberty to exercise it, different opinions will be formed. As long as the connection subsists between his reason and his self-love, his opinions and his passions will have a reciprocal influence on each other; and the former will be objects to which the latter will attach themselves. The diversity in the faculties of men, from which the rights of property originate, is not less an insuperable obstacle to a uniformity of interests. The protection of these faculties is the first object of government. From the protection of different and unequal faculties of acquiring property, the possession of different degrees and kinds of property immediately results; and from the influence of these on the sentiments and views of the respective proprietors, ensues a division of the society into different interests and parties.

"The latent causes of faction are thus sown in the nature of man; and we see them everywhere brought into different degrees of activity, according to the different circumstances of civil society. . . .

"The most common and durable source of factions has been the various and unequal distribution of property. Those who hold and those who are without property have ever formed distinct interests in society. Those who are creditors, and those who are debtors, fall under a like discrimination. A landed interest, a manufacturing interest, a mercantile interest, a moneyed interest, with many lesser interests, grow up of necessity in civilized nations, and divide them into different classes, actuated by different sentiments and views. The regulation of these various and interfering interests forms the principal task of modern legislation, and involves the spirit of party and faction in the necessary and ordinary operations of the government. . . .

"The inference to which we are brought is, that the *causes* of faction cannot be removed, and that relief is only to be sought in the means of controlling its *effects*.

"If a faction consists of less than a majority, relief is supplied by the republican principle, which enables the majority to defeat its sinister views by regular vote. . . . It may clog the administration, it may convulse the society; but it will be unable to execute and mask its violence under the forms of the Constitution. When a majority is included in a faction, the form of popular government, on the other hand, enables it to sacrifice to its ruling passion or interest both the public good and the rights of other citizens. To secure the public good and private rights against the danger of such a faction, and at the same time to preserve the spirit and the form of popular government, is then the great object to which our inquiries are directed. . . .

"By what means is this object attainable? Evidently by one of two only. Either the existence of the same passion or interest in a majority at the same time must be prevented, or the majority, having such coexistent passion or interest, must be rendered, by their number and local situation, unable to concert and carry into effect schemes of oppression. . . .

"From this view of the subject it may be concluded that a pure democracy, by which I mean a society consisting of a small number of citizens, who assemble and administer the government in person, can admit of no cure for the mischiefs of faction. . . .

"A republic, by which I mean a government in which the scheme of representation takes place, opens a different prospect, and promises the cure for which we are seeking. . . .

"The two great points of difference between a democracy and a republic are: first, the delegation of the government, in the latter, to a small number of citizens elected by the rest; secondly, the greater number of citizens, and greater sphere of country, over which the latter may be extended.

"The effect of the first difference is, on the one hand, to refine and enlarge the public views, by passing them through the medium of a chosen body of citizens, whose wisdom may best discern the true interest of their country, and whose patriotism and love of justice will be least likely to sacrifice it to temporary or partial considerations. . . .

"The other point of difference is, the greater number of citizens and extent of territory which may be brought within the compass of republican than of democratic government; and it is this circumstance principally which renders factious combinations less to be dreaded in the former than in the latter. The smaller the society, the fewer probably will be the distinct parties and interests composing it; the fewer the distinct parties and interests, the more frequently will a majority be found of the same party; and the smaller the number of individuals composing a majority, and the smaller the compass within which they are placed, the more easily will they concert and execute their plans of oppression.   Extend the sphere, and you take in a greater variety of parties and interests; you make it less probable that a majority of the whole will have a common motive to invade the rights of other citizens; or if such a common motive exists, it will be more difficult for all who feel it to discover their own strength, and to act in unison with each other. . . .

"Hence, it clearly appears, that the same advantage which a republic has over a democracy, in controlling the effects of faction, is enjoyed by a large over a small republic,—is enjoyed by the Union over the States composing it. . . .

"A rage for paper money, for an abolition of debts, for an equal division of property, or for any other improper or wicked project, will be less apt to pervade the whole body of the Union than a particular member of it. . . .

"In the extent and proper structure of the Union, therefore, we behold a republican remedy for the diseases most incident to republican government."

James Madison, in *The Federalist*, No. 10.

CHAPTER XI

Recommended:

Charles and Mary Beard, *The Rise of American Civilization.*
Berle and Means, *The Modern Corporation and Private Property.*
Sidney and Beatrice Webb, *The Decay of Capitalist Civilization.*
Stuart Chase, *The Tragedy of Waste.*
Editors of *Fortune*, "Arms and the Men." A brief account of the munitions scandal.

Suggested:

Willard E. Atkins and others, *Economic Behavior.*
John Bakeless, *The Economic Causes of Modern War.*

Engelbrecht and Honighan, *Merchants of Death*.
Henry George, *Progress and Poverty*.
Karl Marx, *Capital*. A convenient selection of important passages from this work has been published by The Modern Library. Two good explanations and commentaries on Marx are: Sidney Hook, *Towards an Understanding of Karl Marx*, and A. D. Lindsay, *Karl Marx's "Capital."*
Bertrand Russell, *Proposed Roads to Freedom*.
John Strachey, *The Coming Struggle for Power*.
Bulletins of Consumers' Research, Inc.

Novels:

Robert Cantwell, *The Land of Plenty*.
Elizabeth C. Gaskell, *North and South*.
Grace Lumpkin, *To Make My Bread*.
Charles G. Norris, *The Octopus*.
Upton Sinclair, *The Jungle*.

QUESTIONS

1. "Thus a government, entirely occupied with wealth and commerce, looks upon society as a workshop, regards men only as productive machines, and cares little how much it torments them, provided it makes them rich. . . . It wishes only for a great production of the means of enjoyment, while it is constantly putting new obstacles in the way of enjoying." (Bentham, *Principles of Morals and Legislation*.) How truly do you think that this describes modern capitalist society? How serious an indictment do you consider it?

2. "The happiness of the community depends on its wealth; the wealth of the nation depends on maintaining and increasing its annual product; the best way of doing this is by letting each citizen make himself as rich as he can in his own way; the quickest way to personal riches is profit-making in a free market; hence unrestricted profit-making by individual capitalists is the best way of securing the welfare and happiness of the nation." (Quoted, without approval, by Sidney and Beatrice Webb, *op. cit.*) Which of the steps in this sorites can be most successfully attacked?

3. Stanley, the famed explorer, told the Chamber of Com-

merce of Manchester, England: "There are forty millions of people beyond the gateway of the Congo, and the cotton spinners of Manchester are waiting to clothe them. Birmingham foundries are glowing with the red metal that will presently be made into ironwork for them and the trinkets that shall adorn those dusky bosoms, and the ministers of Christ are zealous to bring them, the poor benighted heathen, into the Christian fold." (Quoted by P. T. Moon, *Imperialism and World Politics*.) When the economic and the religious motive are thus combined in the promotion of an enterprise, which do you think plays the more important rôle? Why?

4. Do you agree with the comparative valuation made in the last paragraph of the following passage?

"May the atrocities on both sides during the war be forgotten; but I do not hesitate today to repeat the bitter words which I used in February, 1919, at a time when our enemies were still killing 800 German non-combatants daily with perfect deliberation:

"'The Entente is no longer in a position to say that it is being misled regarding the effect of the blockade by colored war statistics. The whole of Germany lies open to an impartial investigation of the full situation; trouble has also been taken to place irrefutable scientific evidence in the hands of the Entente, which shows:

"'(1) that about 800 human beings in Germany are dying every day from the effects of the blockade;

"'(2) that in many centers the mortality among young children has almost doubled;

"'(3) that the harvest of tuberculosis among children and growing youths in big cities is twice as large as before the war, while the death-rate of mothers from puerperal fever has increased by two-thirds for the whole of Germany;

"'(4) that doctors are helpless in face of many curable cases of illness, because they lack the necessary medicines and foods;

"'(5) that as a result of underfeeding the whole population is suffering from a nervous exhaustion, which paralyzes initiative and weakens moral restraint;

"'(6) that hundreds of thousands of mothers are not in a

position to nurse their convalescent children back to health, because they cannot feed them up; that the result in many cases is life-long infirmity; and that, in a word, the vitality of the growing generation has been sapped at the root. . . .

"'I would point out the fundamental distinction which must be drawn in the moral judgment between war atrocities and armistice atrocities. War necessity, real or imagined, is no excuse, but it creates extenuating circumstances; the summoning of all a nation's energies to battle and victory naturally drives humanity and international equity from the place which rightly belongs to them in the hierarchy of motive; but they must necessarily be restored to their rights, as soon as the guns cease fire. The wrong of war is heavier in the scales, if it lasts after war and the war necessity are at an end. The victims of the Armistice bring a more awful indictment before God and mankind than the victims of the war.'" (*Memoirs* of Prince Maximilien of Baden.)

5. The two passages that follow are from the encyclical of Pope Pius XI, *Reconstructing the Social Order*. The first passage describes the contemporary situation, the second prescribes a remedy. How adequate do you think the remedy to the described situation?

(a) "Free competition is dead; economic dictatorship has taken its place. Unbridled ambition for domination has succeeded the desire for gain; the whole economic life has become hard, cruel, and relentless in a ghastly measure. Furthermore, the intermingling and scandalous confusing of the duties and offices of civil authority and of economics have produced crying evils and have gone so far as to degrade the majesty of the State. The State, which should be the supreme arbiter, ruling in kingly fashion far above all party contention, intent only upon justice and the common good, has become instead a slave, bound over to the service of human passion and greed. As regards the relations of peoples among themselves, a double stream has issued forth from this one fountain head: on the one hand, economic nationalism or even economic imperialism; on the other, a not less noxious and detestable internationalism or international imperialism in financial affairs, which holds that where a man's fortune is, there is his country."

(b) "Economic life must be inspired by Christian principles. For this pitable ruin of souls, which, if it continue, will frustrate all efforts to reform society, there can be no other remedy than a frank and sincere return to the teaching of the Gospel. . . .

"All those versed in social matters demand a rationalization of economic life which will introduce sound and true order. But this order, which We ourselves desire and make every effort to promote, will necessarily be quite faulty and imperfect, unless all man's activities harmoniously unite to imitate and, as far as is humanly possible, attain the marvellous unity of the divine plan. This is the perfect order which the Church preaches, with intense earnestness, and which right reason demands: which places God as the first and supreme end of all created activity, and regards all created goods as mere instruments under God, to be used only in so far as they help towards the attainment of our supreme end.

". . . . Those who engage in production are not forbidden to increase their fortunes in a lawful and just manner: indeed it is just that he who renders service to society and develops its wealth should himself have his proportionate share of the increased public riches, provided always that he respects the laws of God and the rights of his neighbor, and uses his property in accord with faith and right reason. If these principles be observed by all, everywhere and at all times, not merely the production and acquisition of goods, but also the use of wealth, now so often uncontrolled, will within a short time be brought back again to the standards of equity and just distribution.

"Mere sordid selfishness, which is the disgrace and the great crime of the present age, will be opposed in every deed by the kindly and forcible law of Christian moderation, whereby man is commanded to seek first the Kingdom of God and His Justice, confiding in God's liberality and definite promise that temporal goods also, so far as he has need of them, will be added unto him."

CHAPTER XII

Recommended:

William James, *The Will to Believe* and *The Dilemma of Determinism.* Both essays are contained in the volume entitled *The Will to Believe.*

Henri Bergson, *Time and Free-Will.*

Suggested:

Plato, *Protagoras, Meno, Phaedrus,* and *Philebus.*

Kant, *Critique of Practical Reason.*

Lawrence Buermeyer, *The Aesthetic Experience.*

Bernard Bosanquet, *The Principle of Individuality and Value.*

Mary Evelyn Clarke, *A Study of the Logic of Values.*

John Dewey, *The Quest for Certainty.*

Warner Fite, *Moral Philosophy:* Chapters XIV–XVII.

Nicolai Hartmann, *Ethics:* Volume I, Sections I, V, VI, VII.

John Laird, *A Study in Moral Theory; The Idea of Value.*

G. E. Moore, *Principia Ethica:* Chapters I, IV, VI.

John Henry Newman, *An Essay in Aid of a Grammar o, Assent.*

Ralph Barton Perry, *General Theory of Value.*

Annette T. Rubinstein, *Realistic Ethics.*

J. B. Bury, *The Idea of Progress.*

For the study of philosophy:

Berkeley, *Principles of Human Knowledge.*

Bergson, *Introduction to Metaphysics.*

Burnham and Wheelwright, *Introduction to Philosophical Analysis.*

Morris R. Cohen, *Reason and Nature.*

Descartes, *Meditations.*

Hume, *A Treatise of Human Knowledge.*

Hoernle, *Matter, Life, Mind, God.*

C. I. Lewis, *Mind and the World-Order.*

David R. Major, *An Introduction to Philosophy.*

M. C. Otto, *Things and Ideals.*

G. W. T. Patrick, *Introduction to Philosophy.*

Ralph Barton Perry, *Present Philosophical Tendencies.*

Bertrand Russell, *Philosophy; Scientific Method in Philosophy.*
George Santayana, *Scepticism and Animal Faith.*
Edward G. Spaulding, *The New Rationalism.*
Marie Collins Swabey, *Logic and Nature.*
Alfred North Whitehead, *Adventures in Ideas; Science and the Modern World.*

QUESTIONS

1.   "The country is going to the dogs, and there's nothing any of us can do about it." Is this determinism or fatalism? What distinguishes it as the one rather than the other?

2.   "Shall I believe in absolute determinism or in the possibility of free choice? The dilemma may be further expanded; for (A) if I believe in determinism it may be (1) that I am causally predetermined to do so, or (2) that I freely choose to do so. Likewise (B) if I believe in the possibility of free choice it may be (1) that I have been causally predetermined to do so or (2) that I freely choose to do so. Now let us examine each of these four alternatives. (A, 1) and (B, 1) both make the supposition that my belief has been predetermined by past causes; if either of these alternatives is true, therefore, there is no room for choice on my part as to what I shall believe, and consequently there is for me no genuine problem. The only alternatives constituting a genuine problem are the two remaining ones: (A, 2) and (B, 2). The former of these (A, 2) represents the possibility that I freely choose to believe that there is no such thing as freedom of choice. To do this is no doubt possible but it is hardly rational. No one would seriously accept so paradoxical an alternative if he were clearly aware of what he was doing. Only one alternative, therefore, is left: freely to choose to believe in the possibility of free choice."

The foregoing argument is a paraphrase and abridgment of 'Lequier's dilemma'—so named after its author, Jules Lequier, a French Catholic philosopher of the last century. Discuss its validity.

3.   "Thus, because we discover in our minds the idea of God, or of an all-perfect Being, we have a right to inquire into the source whence we derive it; and we shall discover that the perfections it represents are so immense as to render it quite

certain that we could only derive it from an all-perfect Being; that is, from a God really existing. For it is manifest by the natural light of reason not only that nothing cannot be the cause of anything whatever, and that the more perfect cannot arise from the less perfect so as to be thereby produced as by its efficient and total cause, but also that it is impossible we can have the idea or representation of anything whatever, unless there be somewhere, either in us or out of us, an original which comprises, in reality, all the perfections that are thus represented to us; but, as we do not in any way find in ourselves those absolute perfections of which we have the idea, we must conclude that they exist in some nature different from ours, that is, in God, or at least that they were once in him; and it most manifestly follows, from their infinity, that they are still there." (Descartes, *Principles of Philosophy*.) Do you consider this argument valid? Do you consider that the God herein demonstrated would be a fitting object of worship?

4. Which of the following attitudes towards the Universe seems to you to furnish the better philosophical foundation for ethics? Is there some third attitude that you find preferable to either of these?

a)   "For us the winds do blow,
   The earth doth rest, heaven move, and fountains flow.
      Nothing we see but means our good,
      As our delight, or as our treasure;
   The whole is either our cupboard of food
         Or cabinet of pleasure."

(George Herbert, *Man.*)

b)

   "Life's but a walking shadow, a poor player
      That struts and frets his hour upon the stage
      And then is heard no more. It is a tale
      Told by an idiot, full of sound and fury,
      Signifying nothing."

(Shakespeare, *Macbeth.*)

5. "But the prerequisites for the determination of physical progress are (1) an object to move, (2) a goal, (3) a measure of proximity to that goal, and (4) an ability to compare the object's proximity to it at various times. If there is not a reason-

able identity between an arrow as it leaves the bow and as it hits the target, there is no common antecedent for 'it.' If there is no target, the arrow to all intents and purposes is wandering about—it may even be going in a straight line—but it is not 'progressing.' If we cannot tell whether it is near or far from its target, it may be progressing in some transcendental sense but certainly not in any experiential sense, nor is a progress which is pragmatically non-existent of any interest. Finally, if we cannot compare its proximity to the target or to its terminus *a quo* at different times, we shall never know but that it is standing still." (George Boas, "The Measure of Progress," in *The Symposium*, July, 1930.) Professor Boas asserts that all four of these prerequisites are lacking to society, and that therefore social progress does not exist. Attempt to apply the prerequisites one by one, and see whether you reach the same conclusion.

6. "Now the end of life puts the longest life on a par with the shortest. For of two things which have alike ceased to be, the one is not better, the other worse—the one greater, the other less." (St. Augustine, *The City of God*.) Do you accept this argument? How valid do you think the following criticism? "One might as well argue that because each of two things perish it cannot be said that one is lighter or darker or bigger than the other." (From a student's paper.)

GLOSSARY

[NOTE.—This glossary contains most of the unfamiliar and technical words and phrases that occur in the text, with the exception of such words and phrases as have already been adequately explained or whose meaning has been made clear by the context in which they were employed. For such words, consult the Index.

The letters p, q, r, s, designate propositions; other letters have a more general reference.]

A fortiori argument. A special type of argument by analogy (*q.v.*). Formula: A, having the character k, possesses or is judged to possess the attribute m; therefore B, having even more markedly the character k, is inferred to possess all the more markedly, or with a higher degree of probability, the attribute m. Example: "Since a democratic theory of government is based on the assumption that individual voters can be trusted to hold competent opinions on public affairs, surely this assumption ought to apply even more forcibly to voters who are college graduates, for their education has been superior to that of the average voter."

Analogy, argument by. Formula: A, having the character k, possesses or is judged to possess the attribute m; therefore B, also having the character k, is inferred also to possess the attribute m. This type of reasoning is very apt to be fallacious, especially (1) when little is known of the connections between k and m outside of the context of A, or (2) when relevant known differences between k and m are ignored. Example: "Having a national defence is like having an efficient fire department. We don't want a fire, but when it does break out we want to be ready for it." (National Commander Hayes, of the American Legion.)

Analytic proposition. See *proposition.*

Antilogism. Three propositions so related that all three cannot be true: *i.e.*, the assertion of any two of them implies a denial of the third. Example: "Democracy involves equal opportunities for everyone; there are not equal opportunities for everyone in America today; America today, however, is a democracy."

Apodictic.   Self-evident; logically coercive.

As such.   In so far as meant without qualification.

Asymmetrical relation.   See *symmetrical relation.*

Autonomous.   Having the right or power of making its own laws, or of determining its own nature.

Categorical.   Unconditional.   See *proposition.*

Category.   One of the highest classes to which the objects of knowledge or thought or experience can be reduced.   Thus, *value* is a fundamental category of ethics; *space, quantity,* and *law* are among the fundamental categories of experimental science; *thing, quality,* and *cause* are those of ordinary experience.

Contradiction, logical.   Two propositions are said to stand in logical contradiction to each other, and are called logical contradictories, when they are so related that the truth of either one implies the falsity of the other, and the falsity of either one implies the truth of the other.   That is to say, they are mutually exclusive and together they exhaust the possibilities of the situation to which they refer.   Logical *contraries,* on the other hand, are mutually exclusive without exhausting the possibilities of the situation; *i.e.,* they cannot both be true but it is possible that both may be false; *i.e.,* the truth of either one implies the falsity of the other, but the falsity of one does not imply the truth of the other.   Example. —"To yield to natural impulse is always wrong" and "To yield to natural impulse is always right" are contrary propositions: there are intermediate possibilities in the situation to which both refer.   The contradictory of the former of these propositions would be: "To yield to natural impulse is at least sometimes not wrong"; or, in a more positive form, "To yield to natural impulse is sometimes either right or morally indifferent."

Terms also may stand in relations of mutual contradiction and mutual contrariety.   'Noble' and 'base' are contraries, because there are intermediate possibilities in the series of moral values to which 'noble' and 'base' as opposed terms belong: a man can be something other than either noble or

base. 'Moral situation' and 'non-moral (amoral) situation'
are contradictories; for, as they have been defined in Chapter
I, if a situation is not one of them it must be the other.

Contraposition. An implicative relation is contraposed by substituting for its two terms (or component propositions) their
respective contradictories in reversed order.   Examples.—
(1) Seeing is believing; therefore (contrapositive) not to believe is not to have seen."   (2) "If men cannot ever freely
choose their actions then punishment cannot rightly be in-
flicted."   Contrapositive: "If punishment can rightly be in-
flicted men must sometimes be free to choose their actions."

Conversion.   Interchanging the subject and predicate of a categorical proposition.   This is always permissible when the
relation between the original subject and predicate is one of
mutual exclusion.   Thus, from the proposition, "Hedonists
are never truly religious," we may legitimately infer the
converse, "Truly religious people are never hedonists."
Affirmative propositions, however, are convertible only by
setting an indefinite limitation upon the new subject.   "All
acts of holiness are virtuous" does not imply "All virtuous
acts are acts of holiness."   To make such an inference would
be a case of *illicit conversion.*   We could legitimately infer
only the *partial converse,* "Some virtuous acts are acts of
holiness"—and even this inference would be legitimate only
on the assumption that 'acts of holiness,' the subject of the
original proposition, referred to something that existed.

Cosmological argument for God's existence.   There are two principal forms.   (1) "Whatever exists must have had an antecedent cause, which in turn must have had an antecedent
cause, and so on.   Either this series extends back into the
past without limit or it has had a beginning.   It could not
have extended back into the past without limit; for in that
case an infinite series of causes and effects would have actually
taken place in time, but an actually existing infinite series is
inconceivable, because actually existing things form a totality,
while that which is infinite can never be a totality.   Since,
therefore, the series of causes cannot be conceived as extending
into the past without limit, it must have had a beginning.
Whatever has had a beginning must have had a cause of its
beginning.   The whole series of causes and effects, therefore,

since it had a beginning had also a cause, and this first cause of all things we call God." (2) "Whatever exists has been caused by some other existing thing. A cause must be endowed with at least as much perfection as the effect; otherwise the effect could not be fully explained in terms of the cause— *i.e.*, would not be entirely its effect. The cause of the universe must therefore be at least as perfect as the highest degree of perfection manifested in the universe. The degree of perfection that can be discovered in the universe depends upon the degree of insight with which the universe is studied, for as our insight is developed we perceive intelligible relations that persons of more blunted sensibilities fail to perceive. We may suppose, then, that if we possessed perfect intelligence we would perceive the universe to be perfectly intelligible and perfectly good, each part being interpreted in its relation to the whole. This perfect universe must have a cause as perfect as itself; and to that cause we give the name God."

Cosmology. That branch of philosophy which treats of the structure, relations, and tendencies of the existent universe.

Deduction. See *inference.*

Definition. A logical statement of the meaning of a word, phrase, or idea. The term to be defined is called the *definiendum;* the part of the definition that explicates the definiendum is called the *definiens.* For general purposes the most valid and most useful type of definition is the definition *per genus et differentiam,* also called the Aristotelian type of definition. The *genus* is the more inclusive class under which the definiendum is subsumed; the *differentia* (plur. *differentiae*) is the characteristic or set of characteristics that distinguishes the definiendum from other species belonging to the same genus. Example: "Virtue is—a disposition of the soul (*genus*) to choose that course of action which is intermediate between excess and deficiency (*differentia*)." Or, following Bentham rather than Aristotle: "Virtue is—that mode of conduct (*genus*) which tends to produce a greater amount of social happiness than would be produced by any alternative mode of conduct (*differentia*)."

There are four requirements to be observed in defining a term: (1) the definition must be intelligible and unambiguous; (2) the definiens must be logically coextensive with—*i.e.*, neither (a) broader nor (b) narrower than—the definiendum; (3) it must specify a meaning that is essential to the definiendum rather than (a) one that is trifling or accidental or (b) that represents a particular theory about the definiendum; (4) it must not merely repeat the definiendum either (a) directly or (b) by obversion. Examples of fallacious definitions, which violate one or another of these requirements.— (2a) "Capitalism is a form of society in which profits are made by the purchase and sale of commodities." (3b) "Justice is expediency." (4a) "The soul is that spiritual principle which animates the body." (4b) "Courage is the avoidance of cowardice." Logicians sometimes add a fifth requirement, that a definition should not be expressed in figurative language. But this depends on whether the figurative language clarifies or obscures the logical meaning which it is the purpose of the definition to explicate. Plato's statement that "Time is the moving image of eternity," however pleasing as an imaginative collocation of ideas, is worthless as a definition; whereas Samuel Butler's language is at once picturesque and logically accurate when he defines a definition as "the enclosing the wilderness of an idea in a wall of words."

Dialectic. Critical analysis of conceptions in order to determine their meaning, implications, and presuppositions.

Dichotomy. Logical division of a class into two contradictory sub-classes; as, animal into vertebrate and invertebrate; situations into morally significant and morally indifferent.

Dictum de Omni et Nullo. Whatever is asserted or denied universally of any term may be asserted or denied of any term subsumed under it.

Differentia. (Plur., *differentiae*.) See *definition*.

Dilemma. The typical dilemma has the form: If p then q, and if r then s (major premise); either p or r (minor premise); therefore either q or s (conclusion). Example: "The ministers . . . wasted hours in those days discussing such problems as whether to remove or not to remove the bones of the saints from Kiev. The tsar submitted that it was not necessary, since 'the Germans would not risk touching them, and if they did touch them, so much the worse for the Germans'." (Trotsky, *The History of the Russian Revolution*.) In this example, as frequently, not all parts of the dilemma are made explicit. Fully expressed the dilemma would read as follows. Minor premise: "Either the Germans will risk touching the saints' bones or they will not." Major premise: "If they do risk touching them, so much the worse for the Germans (presumably because Heaven would avenge the sacrilege); if they do not risk touching them, so much the better for the Russians (whose dead saints would thus be spared an affront)." Conclusion: "There will result either an injury to the Germans or a benefit to the Russians"— either of which, it is implied, could be regarded as a comparative advantage from the Russian war-time point of view.

The alternative premises (*p*, *r*) are called the *horns* of the dilemma. To challenge the minor premise—*i.e.*, to question whether *p* and *r* exhaust the possibilities of the situation or whether there is not some third alternative possibility—is called 'going between the horns.' To challenge the major premise—*i.e.*, to question whether *q* necessarily follows as a consequence of *p*, or whether *s* necessarily follows as a consequence of *r*—is called 'taking the dilemma by the horns.'

Every moral deliberation is a practical exemplification of a dilemma—*p* and *r* being alternative courses of action between which we must make a choice as a means of attaining one of the respective ends, *q* and *s*.

Disjunction, imperfect. A disjunctive proposition (see under *proposition*) in which the alternatives are not mutually exhaustive—*i. e.*, in which there is a third possible alternative.

Eidolon. An image supposed by certain ancient philosophers, notably Democritus and Epicurus, to emanate from an object and impinge on the sense-organs, thus producing perceptions.

Enthymeme. A syllogism in which one of the premises or the conclusion is not expressed. Example: "Law is an abridgment of liberty and consequently of happiness." The unexpressed premise is, "Whatever abridges liberty abridges also happiness."

Epistemology. That branch of philosophy which treats of the grounds, the methods, and the limitations of valid knowledge, as such.

Ex hypothesi. To reason *ex hypothesi* is to deduce the consequences of some proposition or theory whose truth has not been adequately established. In logical demonstrations this method is sometimes employed as a means of demonstrating the falsity of the original proposition. (Cf. *reductio ad absurdum*.) In experimental science the method is employed in order to work out the specific factual implications of an abstract theory so that these implications and thus indirectly the theory itself may be empirically tested.

Ex nihilo nihil fit. (Lat.) 'From nothing, nothing comes.' An older form of the popular metaphysical principle that everything must have a cause. Especially influential in the development of early Greek philosophy.

Heuristic. (From the Greek εὑρίσκειν, to discover.) Applied to theories and beliefs that are accepted not because there is adequate direct evidence that they are true but because an acceptance of them aids in the interpretation of experience or in the discovery of other truths.

Horns of a dilemma. See *dilemma.*

Hypostatize. To treat an abstract quality as if it were a thing or substance.

Ideology. As used in social ethics: a set of moral principles and ethical beliefs so far as these have been determined by the social situation and social habits of the moral agent.

Illicit conversion. See *conversion.*

Implication. One proposition is said to imply another when their relation is such that if the first is true the second must also be true. One concept implies another if in any proposition in which the first is asserted of anything (*i.e.*, used as the predicate of the proposition) the second can logically be substituted for it. The implicative relation is non-symmetrical. (See *symmetrical.*) That an action ought to be performed implies that it would promote some good or other; but the converse relation does not hold—*i.e.*, because an action would promote some good or other it does not follow that it ought to be performed. Implication should be distinguished from inference (*q.v.*).

Induction. See *inference.*

Inference. To derive a conclusion either from general premises (*deduction*) or from factual evidence (*induction*). Not to be confused with implication. Implication is a strictly logical relation; inference is a mental operation. Example: The three propositions—(*p*) "Many people eat apple skins."

(*q*) "Apple skins contain a residue of lead arsenate from spraying," and (*r*) "Lead arsenate is a cumulative poison"—*imply* the proposition (*s*), "Many people are taking a cumulative poison into their systems"; but it may be the case that no one has ever known the propositions *p*, *q*, *r* simultaneously and has therefore never *inferred s* from them.

Ipso facto. (Lat.) By virtue of that very fact; for that very reason.

Laissez-faire. (Fr.) An idomatic paraphrase would be, 'Let nature take its course,' or 'Let well enough alone.' Its economic application is explained in Chapter XI.

Metaphysics. That branch or aspect of philosophy which investigates the relations subsisting between the various realms of discourse (*q.v.*) and between the categories and first principles essential to each realm. Sometimes identified with ontology; sometimes regarded as including ontology and cosmology together (*q.v.*).

Millennium. Literally, a thousand years. Hence (see the Bible: Revelation, Chap. 20, Verses 2–6) a time or period of fulfilment.

Monism. The doctrine which refers all phenomena, of whatever type, to a single constituent or agent, or to a single principle of explanation or to a logically interrelated set of such principles.

Obversion. To obvert a categorical proposition is to change its logical 'quality' (*i.e.*, from affirmative to negative or from negative to affirmative) without changing the proposition's meaning. This is done by changing at the same time the quality of the predicate term (never the subject term). Example.—"Solipsism is a self-refuting philosophy." Obverse: "Solipsism is not a self-consistent philosophy."

Ontological argument for God's existence. By 'God' is meant a Being absolutely perfect. A non-existent God would lack one of the attributes essential to perfection—namely, existence. Since, therefore, perfection is a part of the very meaning of God, it follows from the very meaning of God that He exists: *i.e.*, if we understand what we are talking about when we refer to God we shall know *a priori* that He exists.

Ontology. That branch of philosophy which investigates the nature, essential properties, and relations of being, as such.

Paradox.   A statement seemingly self-contradictory or opposed to common sense but which is nevertheless possibly true.

Phenomenology.   The philosophical method employed and developed by the contemporary German philosopher Edmund Husserl and his school.   It consists in 'bracketing off' the abstract concepts employed by science, common sense, and traditional metaphysics—concepts such as 'matter,' 'physical cause,' 'objective fact'—and in attempting to describe and classify the various aspects and types of experience as they actually appear rather than as they have been interpreted by preconceived theories.

Pluralism.   The doctrine which *denies* that all phenomena are completely reducible to a single logically interrelated set of explanatory principles.   Cf. *monism.*

Postulate.   See *proposition.*

Pragmatism.   The doctrine that the meaning of an idea or theory is to be found in the practical conduct to which, in the long run, it gives rise.   There is some difference among pragmatists in their interpretation of 'practical conduct.'   To the instrumentalists, headed by John Dewey, it has primarily a social reference; to humanists, such as William James, it includes the activity of one's inner emotional life as well.   In general, it may be said that pragmatism interprets truth *heuristically (q.v.).*

Premise.   See *syllogism.*

Proposition.   A meaning that can be significantly affirmed or denied; *i.e.,* be significantly judged to be true or false. Normally but not always expressed in a declarative sentence. "We eat bread every day" is a proposition; "Give us this day our daily bread" is not.

Propositions may be classified (1) according to form, (2) according to meaning.   They differ in form according as they are *categorical* ("Justice is a virtue") or *conditional.* Conditional propositions may be either *hypothetical* ("If justice is a virtue we ought to make greater sacrifices to attain it") or *disjunctive* ("Either men have power to choose or else every moral situation is illusory").   Propositions differ in meaning according as they are *normative, factual* (descriptive), or *a priori.*   A normative proposition affirms a value: *e.g.,* "Cowardice is less vicious than perfidy."   A factual proposition affirms what purports to be an actual state of affairs: e.g., "Cowardice is less strongly condemned by most people than perfidy." A factual proposition is entirely a matter of evidence and can only be more or less probable, never certain. An *a priori* proposition is a proposition whose truth or falsity is demonstrable either (i) from its meaning alone, or (ii) from the meaning of the realm of discourse to which it bears reference. *A priori* propositions of the former sort, when true, are called *axioms; a priori* propositions of the latter sort are called *postulates*. Example of an axiom: "A proposition which implies a second proposition implies also all that the second proposition implies." Ethical postulates have been discussed in Chapter XII, Section 1.

An independent classification of propositions according to meaning is into *synthetic* and *analytic* propositions: in the former the meaning of the predicate is distinct from the meaning of the subject and the proposition therefore makes a real assertion; in the latter the predicate merely explicates the meaning already implicit in the subject. That drunkenness and fornication are morally bad is a synthetic proposition; that vice is morally bad is (in the ordinary manner of speaking) an analytic proposition.

Pudenda origo. (Lat.) Shameful origin.

Quâ. (Shortened form of the Latin *quatenus*.) 'In so far as'; 'to just the extent of being.' Example: biology studies men *quâ* living organisms, ethics studies them *quâ* moral agents. Again, conduct may be defined as 'behavior *quâ* ethically evaluated.'

Q.v. (Latin, *quod vidê.*) 'Which see.' *I.e.*, Look up the word just given or the matter just referred to. Used extensively in the present glossary.

Realm of discourse. A major branch of inquiry, distinguished by the categories which it employs and the first principles (axioms or postulates) on which it rests.

Reductio ad absurdum. Formula.—Assume p to be true, in a case where p implies q and p also implies r. If it is found that q and r cannot both be true, it may be concluded (by contraposition) that p must be false. Example.—Suppose a Being endowed with absolute omnipotence. An absolutely omnipotent Being could issue decrees which would never be broken. An absolutely omnipotent Being would have the power to break decrees that He had already made. The issuing of unbreakable decrees and the breaking of the same decrees once issued are mutually incompatible. Absolute omnipotence, therefore, is logically impossible.

Redundancy. Needless repetition of the same words or of the same idea expressed in synonymous language. More generally, the use of more words than useful to express an idea. To be distinguished from 'tautology' (*q.v.*). The distinction may be illustrated by Kant's definition of dogmatism: "Dogmatism, in a word, is the dogmatic procedure of reason without any previous criticism of its own powers." This definition is redundant because of the superfluity of the adjective 'dogmatic,' but it is not tautologous (*i.e.*, as a definition it is not purely circular), because the superfluous word is afterwards explained by the final phrase, 'without any previous criticism of its own powers.'

Solipsism. The theory that only I (*i.e.*, the solipsist) exist; that other persons have no independent existence of their own but exist solely as objects of my consciousness, when and so far as I am conscious of them.

Sorites. A chain of three or more premises so related that given the truth of the first, the truth of each of the others down to the last follows. Example: "We are all human; to be human is to err; and to err is to deserve punishment. There is not one of us, then, who is not deserving of punishment." A sorites can be restated as a series of complete syllogisms, of which the conclusion of the first becomes a premise of the next and so on.

Subsumption. One term is logically subsumed under another when the particulars to which the first refers are wholly included within the class of particulars to which the second refers. Thus Eskimo is subsumed under man, man under vertebrate, and vertebrate under organism.

Summum bonum. (Lat.) Highest good.

Syllogism. Two propositions (*premises*) so related that they logically imply a third proposition (*conclusion*). The proposition containing the predicate term of the conclusion is called the major premise; the proposition containing the subject term of the conclusion is called the minor premise. Consult the Index for examples of syllogisms occurring in the text.

Symmetrical relation. A relation such that if *a* bears it to *b*, *b* must also bear it to *a*. An *asymmetrical* relation is one such that if *a* bears it to *b*, *b* cannot bear it to *a*. A *non-symmetrical* relation is one such that if *a* bears it to *b*, *b* may or may not bear it to *a*. 'Equal to,' 'unequal to,' 'fellow-citizen of,' and 'rival of' are examples of the symmetrical relation; 'ruler of' and 'better than' are asymmetrical; 'friendly towards' and 'implies' are non-symmetrical.

Synthetic proposition. A proposition in which the predicate expresses a meaning not already implicit in the subject. In this book normative and descriptive propositions (*q.v.*) are treated as synthetic; *a priori* propositions as non-synthetic, or *analytic*.

Tautology. In a categorical proposition: the predicate simply restates a meaning already implicit in the subject. Example: "Every effect must have had a cause." ('Having a cause' is connoted by the word 'effect': if there were an event that had not had a cause it would not be called an effect.) In a hypothetical proposition: the consequent (main clause) simply repeats a meaning implicit in the antecedent ('if'-clause).

Teleological argument for God's existence. The universe as a whole shows evidences of adaptation to ends. Adaptation of means to ends is a mark of conscious intelligence. There must, therefore, be Something endowed with conscious intelligence at work in the universe as a whole, and this Being is called God.

Teleology. The interpretation of phenomena in terms of tendencies, aims, or implicit purposes.

Transitive relation. A relation such that if *a* bears it to *b*, and *b* to *c*, *a* must bear it to *c*. An *intransitive* relation is one such that if *a* bears it to *b*, and *b* to *c*, *a* cannot bear it to *c*. A non-transitive relation is one such that if *a* bears it to *b*, and *b* to *c*, *a* may or may not bear it to *c*. 'Equal to,' 'better than,' and 'implies' are examples of the transitive relation; 'one degree higher than' is intransitive; 'unequal to' and 'friendly towards' are non-transitive. The transitive relation is what gives logical validity to the syllogism and is thus the basis of all ordinary logical reasoning.

Trilemma. Similar to a dilemma (*q.v.*) except that the minor premise specifies three alternatives ('has three horns') instead of two.

Validity. An argument is called valid when its conclusion is strictly implied by its premises. Validity should be distinguished from truth. The following, for example, is a valid argument, although its premises and conclusion are probably false: "All men strive after sensual pleasures; to strive after sensual pleasures is a sure path to wisdom; therefore all men follow a sure path to wisdom."

Volenti non fit iniuria. (Lat.) No injury is done to one who is willing.

Weltanschauung. (Germ.) Outlook on the world; world-philosophy.

INDEX

[Figures in bold-faced type indicate the most important or most direct references under a given heading.]